PENGUIN BOOKS

GORBACHEV

Dusko Doder, author of *Shadows and Whispers: Power Politics Inside the Kremlin from Brezhnev to Gorbachev*, and winner of the Overseas Press Club Citation for his Moscow dispatches, was the East European bureau chief for *The Washington Post*, then the Moscow bureau chief.

Louise Branson reported from Geneva and Eastern Europe before becoming the Moscow bureau chief for *The Sunday Times* (London). Doder and Branson now live in Yugoslavia.

DUSKO DODER
and LOUISE BRANSON

GORBACHEV

Heretic in the Kremlin

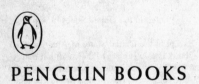

PENGUIN BOOKS

PENGUIN BOOKS
Published by the Penguin Group
Viking Penguin, a division of Penguin Books USA Inc.,
375 Hudson Street, New York, New York 10014, U.S.A.
Penguin Books Ltd, 27 Wrights Lane,
London W8 5TZ, England
Penguin Books Australia Ltd, Ringwood,
Victoria, Australia
Penguin Books Canada Ltd, 2801 John Street,
Markham, Ontario, Canada L3R 1B4
Penguin Books (N.Z.) Ltd, 182–190 Wairau Road,
Auckland 10, New Zealand

Penguin Books Ltd, Registered Offices:
Harmondsworth, Middlesex, England

First published in the United States of America by Viking Penguin,
a division of Penguin Books USA Inc., 1990
This edition with a new epilogue published in Penguin Books 1991

1 2 3 4 5 6 7 8 9 10

THE LIBRARY OF CONGRESS HAS CATALOGUED THE HARDCOVER AS FOLLOWS:
Doder, Dusko.
Gorbachev: heretic in the Kremlin / Dusko Doder and Louise
Branson.
p. cm.
ISBN 0-670-82472-0
ISBN 0 14 01.1535 8
1. Gorbachev, Mikhail Sergeevich, 1931– . 2. Heads of state—
Soviet Union—Biography. 3. Soviet Union—Politics and
government—1985– I. Branson, Louise. II. Title.
DK290.3.G67D63 1990
947.085'4'092—dc20
89-40665

Printed in the United States of America

For our parents,
Tom and Joyce Branson
and Marija Doder

Acknowledgments

We never expected to collaborate on a book about Mikhail Sergeyevich Gorbachev. We held different views of the man when he came to power in March of 1985. Dusko viewed the Kremlin power transition with more hope than Louise, who was skeptical that much could change in Russia. It took five years of debates and often-heated arguments for our views to mesh. We hope that the result will help readers understand the complexities of far-reaching changes now under way in Russia through the actions of Gorbachev. "History," as Aristotle put it, "is what Alcibiades did and suffered." Present Soviet history, we feel, is what Gorbachev is doing and suffering.

We are grateful to a number of Soviet friends and acquaintances for their help and guidance in putting together this account. We talked to hundreds of people. Some of the senior officials we interviewed spoke on the condition that they not be identified as sources of the information necessary to assemble a narrative about their leader's private views and attitudes. Others, in keeping with the spirit of glasnost, spoke on the record and we are grateful for their time and their candor. Among them were Politburo member Alexander Yakovlev; Georgi Smirnov, former special assistant to Gorbachev and currently director of the Institute of Marxism-Leninism in Moscow; Valentin Falin, head of the Central Committee's International Department; former Soviet ambassador in Washington Anatoly Dobrynin; Gennady Kolbin, first secretary of Kazakhstan; Colonel General Nikolai Chervov; economists Abel Aganbegian, Gennady Lizichkin, Nikolai Fedorenko, and Leonid Abalkin;

political scientist Fyodor Burlatsky; historians Roy Medvedev and Yuri Afanasiev; Georgi Arbatov, director of the Institute of the U.S.A. and Canada, and a number of his associates, including Radomir Bogdanov, Nikolai Shmelyov, Andrei Kokoshin, Nikolai Popov, Andrei Zamoshkin, and Andrei Melvile; alternate Politburo member Yevgeny Primakov; Sergei Losev, the late director general of Tass; the ophthalmologist and member of the Supreme Soviet Dr. Slava Fyodorov; legal expert Vladimir Kudravtsev; Professor Leonid Ilyin, head of the State Radiation Control Board; sociologist Boris Grushin; writers Anatoly Rybakov, Sergei Zalygin, Grigori Baklanov, and Vitali Korotich; and journalists Ivan Laptiev, Igor Sedykh, Alexander Bovin, Yegor Yakovlev, and Sergei Grigoryants.

We also thank several colleagues and diplomatic friends who read portions of the manuscript or discussed in detail some of its aspects. In particular we want to mention C. V. Ranganathan, Kemal Siddique, McKinney Russell, M. M. Sathiah, Shaun Byrnes, Michael Dobbs, Milan Veres, Dusan Lazic, Jeff Trimble, Mihailo Saranovic, Xan Smiley, Antero Pietila, Patrick Cockburn, Abdel Malek and Tanya Khalil, Arkady Lvov, Fernando Mezzetti, Masashi Egawa, Mark Hopkins, Melissa Roberts, James and Kathy McGregor, Per Egil Hegge, and Alexander Novacic. Louise's mother, Joyce Branson, read the whole manuscript when it was finished and proved one of our best critics. However, we alone bear responsibility for the facts and judgments in this book.

The Soviet Union being the country it is, we would never have had the chance to get to know it and assemble the material for this book had it not been for our assignments. Dusko, who covered Moscow for the Washington *Post* from 1981 to 1986, was subsequently sent by *U.S. News & World Report* on a number of different assignments to the Soviet Union. The magazine's editor-in-chief, Mortimer B. Zuckerman, deserves our gratitude.

The Sunday Times (London) asked Louise to open its Moscow bureau. Andrew Neil, the editor, deserves a debt of gratitude for his unfailing help and support, as does the former foreign editor, Stephen Milligan.

Finally we wish to acknowledge special gratitude to our superb editor, Nan Graham of Viking Penguin, without whom this book would not have been possible. Theodora Rosenbaum's sharp eye made the final manuscript more concise and readable.

—Louise Branson and Dusko Doder

Contents

GORBACHEV
Heretic in the Kremlin

Chapter 1

EDUCATION
OF A COUNTRY BOY

Mikhail Sergeyevich Gorbachev was born on March 2, 1931, in Privolnoe, a village in the gently rolling steppe lands of southern Russia's Stavropol territory. His father, Sergei, was a peasant farmer, following in the tradition of his ancestors. Sergei must have expected his three sons to follow him. But by the time Mikhail, the second, was born, the certainties of country life were already crumbling. The first months and years of Gorbachev's life coincided with the onset of famine.

For the Gorbachev family and for everyone else in the region, 1931 was a turbulent year. Stalin was in the midst of his drive to force farmers like the Gorbachevs off their private land and into collective farms. But the peasants were resisting in every way they knew how. They slaughtered their livestock and gorged themselves on the meat rather than surrender it to the anonymous kolkhoz. They attempted to withhold grain but the state seized it by force and introduced the death penalty for anyone found guilty of hoarding. Parts of the Ukraine and the North Caucasus, which includes Gorbachev's native Stavropol territory, erupted into open rebellion.[1] Arson, killings, and riots throughout the countryside marked the beginning of a nightmarish period in Soviet history. Soviet agricultural output collapsed. Human casualties numbered in the millions. In his authoritative book *The Great Terror*, Robert Conquest puts the number at some 14.5 million. He also estimates that rebellious peasants slaughtered half the country's farm horses and cattle between 1928 and 1935.

Stalin's cruel retribution was staggering in its scope, and it affected the Gorbachev family directly. Millions of farmers who actively resisted being herded into the collective farms were shipped off to Stalin's notorious gulag of prison camps flung across Siberia. Among them was Mikhail's grandfather Andrei, a fact that has never been made public but which was to have a great impact on the young boy.

Exactly why Andrei Gorbachev was sent to the gulag is unclear. He was charged with stashing away about forty pounds of grain for his family.[2] A senior Soviet official who told us about it privately said a jealous neighbor in Privolnoe had informed on Andrei to the authorities, who then sentenced him to nine years in the forbidding Siberian camps. But this may well have been a pretext. In the days of Stalin's collectivization, people could disappear for many reasons or for none at all, and witnesses were always found to bring charges against them. Possibly, Andrei questioned Stalin's policy. Anyone who publicly voiced doubts about the wisdom of collective farms was automatically regarded as an "enemy of the people." Or Andrei may have been one of countless peasants whose only crime was to be well off, a crime for which they joined millions of innocent victims in the gulag, from which many never returned. Andrei did survive, however, and returned to Privolnoe just before the outbreak of World War Two.

On only a few occasions has Gorbachev ever alluded to his grandfather's arrest. In 1953, shortly after Stalin's death, he talked to university colleagues about a close relative who was repressed in the thirties, describing his grandfather as a "middle peasant," a class of farmers who owned the land they farmed though their holdings were not big enough to require hiring outside help. Much later, while addressing, as general secretary, a commemorative session on the seventieth anniversary of the Bolshevik revolution, he spoke with a lingering sense of grievance at the "injustice" and "excesses" committed against the middle peasants in the thirties. They were, he said, a "staunch and dependable ally of the working class, an ally on a new basis."

Then, in the fall of 1986, after viewing the anti-Stalinist movie *Repentance,* Gorbachev confided in unpublicized remarks to three Italian Communist visitors that he had choked back tears during several of the scenes. One episode in the film—when secret police knocked on the door of an innocent musician to imprison him without any valid reason—had brought back, he said, his grandmother's stories of the night when his grandfather was arrested.[3] Afterward Gorbachev remarked to his aides, "Make sure enough copies are made so that everyone in the country can see it." It was the first movie to reveal, with brutal frankness, the terror of Stalin.

The arrest of Andrei Gorbachev acquired intrinsic importance after Mikhail embarked on a career in politics. As a rare opening into his private world, it is central to our conception of Gorbachev's character and our interpretation of many of his later actions. For although he was reared as a good communist, Gorbachev must have grasped early on the difference between what he knew to be the truth about his country and the Stalinist "truth" that pervaded Soviet life, a "truth" dispensed by the party, which so often engaged in the falsification of the past and the alteration of reality.

Once Mikhail moved into the tsar's office, the automatic impulse of Soviet propaganda was to refurbish his image by turning his ancestors into model communists. While Gorbachev never made false claims, the story of Andrei Gorbachev was kept a secret and instead the emphasis was placed on his maternal grandfather, Panteley, whose family name has never been disclosed but who was the first chairman of a collective farm in the area, though its precise location remains something of a mystery. He did not want his own affairs pried into, not because he wanted to cover his tracks but, rather, because of the unwritten imperial code of Russia. The Russian people have traditionally regarded it as inappropriate to examine the private life of the ruler in detail because, as a tsar, he is supposed to loom high above human affairs.

Stalin's campaign of repression, coupled with the poor harvest in the fall of 1931, led to the famine of 1932–33, which eventually helped break the will of the peasantry. More than fifty thousand people are said to have died from hunger in Stavropol alone.

These troubled times, with his grandfather in the gulag, provided the backdrop for Mikhail's early years. He was secretly baptized, but, as often happened during the years of strident antireligious agitation by the Bolsheviks, his baptism was not registered. The ritual itself presumably did not leave a lasting imprint on his mind. Another event did, though: the arrival of his younger brother, Alexander, who became the apple of his mother's eye. She doted on him more than on the rest of the family, Alexander being her last child, sixteen years younger than Mikhail. Probably there was rivalry between the two brothers after their oldest brother died on the front in World War Two. There was little evidence of affection in later life. Alexander turned out to be an average man of no particular talents or virtues. The prominent Moscow ophthalmologist Slava Fyodorov, who has treated all members of Gorbachev's family, noted that Mikhail Gorbachev's relationship with his younger brother was correct but somewhat distant and that Alexander, when he occasionally visited the Soviet president, was allotted time like any other visitor.[4]

Mikhail, however, got more than his share of affection from his grandparents. Grandfather Andrei, released from the gulag, brought him up after his father, Sergei, joined the Red Army and went to the war. His grandmother taught him the words of old Cossack songs, which would remain with him for the rest of his life. From her he inherited a love of language and storytelling, which led him into the kingdom of the imagination. As Soviet leader, he would frequently resort to images from old Russian folktales to make a point.

She also taught him survival. Years later he would remember her whispered stories about his grandfather, and he knew even then that the stories caused her pain. Who could inflict so much anguish on his grandmother? How could his grandfather be an "enemy of the people"?

Only much later was he to understand the full meaning of the answers.

Neither his grandmother nor any other member of the Gorbachev household could have entertained any notions that young Misha, as he was affectionately known, would one day make the long journey from their village in the northern foothills of the Caucasus Mountains to the Moscow Kremlin, that fifty years later he would be sitting in Stalin's chair as the seventh supreme leader of the Soviet Union. The story of his rise is itself like a page from a Russian folktale.

After the man-induced famine of 1932–33, which caused an estimated 14.5 million deaths from hunger and privation, the countryside began a slow process of recovery.[5]

The first benefits of collectivization appeared in the form of new agricultural machinery. Gorbachev's father, Sergei, became an operator of tractors and combines. An official Soviet account described him as "a modest man, deeply respected for his skills and knowledge of economic matters and his wisdom and even-handedness in party affairs." The phrasing suggests that Sergei Gorbachev was a Communist Party supporter; he was not a party member, however. Nor was anyone else in the Gorbachev clan.

World War Two severely disrupted the pattern of life in much of the Soviet Union. Gorbachev was ten when Hitler's armies launched their invasion, but the people of Stavropol felt too far away from the front to be acutely concerned. Older Stavropol residents remembered four decades later that, at least initially, there was no panic. They thought it was impossible for the Germans to reach Stavropol.[6] Instead, they recalled, there was a patriotic fervor that appeared almost overnight, to cause the memory of the social wounds of the thirties to fade. Gorbachev's older brother and father were drafted and sent to the front. His brother died in 1943 during the battle of Kursk, while his father fought all the way to Poland, where he was wounded.[7] He returned to Privolnoe, where he lived until 1976. "He went out in the morning to feed the animals and he just fell down and died," Georgi Gorlov, a family friend and former local official told David Remnick of the Washington *Post* in the fall of 1989. Gorbachev and Gorlov were in Moscow at the time as delegates to the twenty-fifth Congress of the Soviet Communist Party. "The Defense Ministry flew him down for the funeral," Gorlov continued, and Gorbachev returned to Moscow the next morning on time to attend the opening session.

But the impossible happened. By the time Gorbachev was eleven, Nazi troops occupied his native province in their push toward the Caucasus and Caspian Sea oil wells.

The Nazi occupation of the Stavropol territory lasted only eight months and does not seem to have left a deep impression on Gorbachev's mind. The reason may be that the Germans concentrated their forces in the cities and along the communication lines and left the countryside more or less alone. The occupation did disrupt his education, though, so that by the time he started college he was slightly older than many other freshmen.

Gorbachev was much more profoundly affected some years later when he saw the scope of devastation wrought by the Germans in other parts of Russia. In this respect he was typical of his generation, which only dimly remembers the war itself. When he traveled from Stavropol to Moscow in the fall of 1950 to start his university education, he recalled later, he passed "through Stalingrad, which had been destroyed, through Voronezh, which had been destroyed. Rostov was destroyed. Kharkov was destroyed, nothing but ruins everywhere. The whole country was in ruins."[8] By comparison, Stavropol had escaped major destruction.

The immediate postwar reconstruction years were the last years of revolutionary enthusiasm that the country was to experience. Given the acute shortage of male labor, children were taken from classrooms at sowing and harvest time to help the women and the old. The young Gorbachev, according to his official biography, started immediately after the war, at age fourteen, as an assistant to a combine harvest operator. Four years later he was awarded the Order of the Red Banner of Labor, which marked his emergence as a public figure; it was a distinction that opened for him a most important door—the next year he was recommended by local authorities for study at Moscow State University. It is this incident that became the starting point of official Gorbachev biographies, as if to suggest that already as a teenager he was marked for greatness. His

unexceptional antecedents and the years of his boyhood in the Stavropol backcountry have been ignored.

Only when his fortunes and authority began to decline did his
Stavropol contemporaries begin to reveal nuggets of information
about the local boy who made the long journey from a two-room
mud hut in Privolnoe to the Kremlin's St. George's Hall. They told
how as a boy he used to work under the blazing sun in dusty corn-
fields, afterward cooling off with other youngsters by sitting in barrels
of water from the muddy Yegorlik River. These friends and acquaintances of his youth, only naturally, told the best things of him.
They spoke of his tenacity—how, though he walked ten miles a day
to High School Number 1 in nearby Krasnogvardeyskoe, his grades
were all excellent except for one "very good" in German. They
emphasized his curiosity; as his chemistry teacher Yekatarina Chaika
put it, he was "interested in everything." And they spoke about his
"certain presence," some suggesting that they always knew he was
someone destined for high things. The most revealing information,
however, came from his high-school girlfriend, a schoolteacher's
daughter, who is now a researcher at a local institute and who talked
to David Remnick on the condition that he use only her maiden
name, Karagodina. She had been attracted to Gorbachev, she recalled, because he was "magnetic." He was fearless for someone his
age, she said. "I remember him correcting teachers in history class,
and once he was so angry at one teacher he asked, 'Do you want to
keep your teaching certificate?' He was the sort of man who felt he
was right and could prove it to anyone, be it in the principal's office
or at a Komsomol meeting."

It was perhaps his high-school drama club that prepared him for
the world stage. "The truth is, he was a very good actor," said
Karagodina, who was his costar though she was a class ahead of him.
Some of his roles were as mighty as the real-life role he was destined
for—Grand Prince Zvezdich in Lermontov's *Masquerade* and the
tsar in Ostrovsky's *The Snowgirl*. At one point he even talked about
"trying for a theatrical institute," but he rarely discussed the future
with her except "that we would go to study to Moscow and study
there together."

Karagodina revealed a side of Gorbachev that was to reemerge at times when he dealt with officials in public. She said he could be cool and abrasive and recalled that once he publicly humiliated her for failing to finish a school newspaper on time. "Despite our friendship, he reprimanded me in front of everyone," only to suggest when they were alone together after the meeting that they go to the movies together. "My dear, one thing has nothing to do with another," she remembered his saying. Years later, after they had drifted apart and Gorbachev was first secretary of the Stavropol region, she wrote to him asking his help in obtaining an apartment in the city. "I got a letter soon afterwards, and on it he had written simply that it wasn't his area . . . I should apply to city authorities, not him. Just like that, so businesslike. Not one warm word."

Karagodina finished school in 1949, a year before her sweetheart, and went to Moscow alone. But she soon returned because of lack of funds. "I've always thought that Gorbachev somehow thought I was weak for having come home." Gorbachev was nineteen when he went to the capital the next year. Inevitably, Karagodina recalls, their "young love" began to fade. He was forging ahead, and "I suppose I didn't want to acknowledge that he was getting further than me in life," Karagodina said with a tinge of bitterness. Soon she married another man.

One of the rare photographs of Gorbachev at age nineteen shows him, on the eve of his departure for Moscow, sporting a Cossack fur hat at a rakish angle, but his facial expression is that of a purposeful young man. He was curious about many things, and before he reached the capital he could not make up his mind what to pursue in his studies. "I have always shown interest in many things in different fields," he recalled later. "I cannot say which discipline in school attracted my special interest. For instance, I joined the law department at the university, but at first I wanted to enroll in the physics department. I liked mathematics very much, but I also liked history and literature."[9]

His choice of a legal education is unusual. In the Soviet Union, law is neither a stepping-stone to a political career nor the prime choice of upwardly mobile youths, as it is in the West. In fact, the absence of law was the underlying feature of Stalinism—despotism recognized only one law, and that was whatever the despot proclaimed the law to be. Perhaps young Gorbachev modeled himself on Lenin, who was a lawyer. Or his interest in juridical matters may have come, as we once heard a senior Soviet official speculate, from the traumatic experiences of his grandfather.

Stavropol taught Mikhail some lessons that he never forgot, and which equipped him with an almost blind faith in himself. He had grasped that any hardship could be endured if one had resources of one's own; he was stubborn to a fault, once he had made up his mind. He had learned too that family affection was one of the greatest treasures in life. And, curiously enough, he had understood the stoic lesson that one had to make one's own happiness. The latter was a matter of the mind, of inner psychological strength.

Moscow State University offered a world that was very different from anything he had ever known.

His student days in Moscow, Gorbachev said later, were the period when he was pondering his "moral values, the meaning of life, happiness and justice and mankind's future."[10] Stalin's Moscow was not the place for such contemplation, though, and he was probably referring to normal adolescent philosophizing. Certainly he betrayed no hints of any revulsion toward the lawlessness of Stalinism during the dictator's lifetime. His interest in politics was evident and led him to the Komsomol, or Young Communist League. He immediately became a Komsomol activist, and in 1951 a candidate for membership in the Communist Party, serving the mandatory one-year probation period during which prospective communists attended party meetings without taking part in the decisionmaking process.

Since he had opted for a political career, his publicly expressed views almost certainly reflected a politician's understanding of what should be said, rather than his personal philosophy. Otherwise he could not have survived politically. At the very minimum, he must have extolled Stalin and his policies and argued forcefully against "bourgeois liberalism," "cosmopolitanism," and other imagined enemies of the state. The idolatry of Stalin was at its apogee.

The Komsomol was the only path to political authority; only active Komsomol members were eligible to apply for party membership. Like all Soviet youngsters, Gorbachev was required to join the Komsomol at age fourteen. But unlike most young people, he was not a passive member. Once he arrived in Moscow, Gorbachev plunged into Komsomol activism. He became *komsorg,* the Komsomol leader of his class, or the party's monitor and organizer. The job included propagandizing current Kremlin policies and watching over and reporting on the political mood of his classmates. In Stalin's time, *komsorg*s frequently got their hands dirty as they carried out their jobs; yet Soviet émigrés who attended the Law School at approximately the same time, while remembering Gorbachev as unusually officious and even strident in the performance of his duties, could not cite a single instance of his misbehavior.

The only specific charge against him was made by Fridrikh Neznansky, who emigrated from the Soviet Union in 1978 and who graduated one year before Gorbachev. He claims that Gorbachev's elevation to the initial *komsorg* job was accomplished in an unscrupulous way—he was said to have got his main competitor for the job drunk the night before the *komsorg* elections and then denounced his behavior at the meeting the next day.[11] But nobody else recalled this, nor does it seem to be in his character.

Gorbachev's political career was advanced in 1952, when he became *komsorg* for the entire Law School. At the same time, he was admitted to the Communist Party as a full member. The recollections of Soviet émigrés about his being a zealous promoter of the Kremlin line at the time are undoubtedly accurate. He must have embraced the anti-intellectualism and paranoid anti-Semitism of Stalin's last years with conviction. When the dictator, a few months before his death, "uncovered" a fictitious scheme by Kremlin doctors (most of whom happened to be Jewish) allegedly plotting to poison the Soviet leadership, the campaign against "Zionism" and "cosmopolitanism" reached horrifying proportions. Only Stalin's death in March 1953 prevented the execution of his plans for mass arrests of Jewish citizens and their deportation to the "autonomous Jewish territory of Birobidzhan" in the eastern reaches of Siberia. Yet, in those turbulent months that preceded Stalin's death, many Soviet Jewish intellectuals were publicly denounced and forced out of their positions. Moscow State University was no exception. And university *komsorg*s played a key role in organizing anti-Semitic meetings and haranguing the crowds.

These were the things to be considered at this turning point in Mikhail's life. His personal decency stood in contrast to his rhetoric, which was that of Stalinist propaganda. His critics would later see this as indicative of his personal ambition and love of power, speculating that a young and ambitious man from the provinces had no reason to suppose that Stalinism would soon come under attack from Nikita Khrushchev, who succeeded the dictator.

But even before that, according to his Czech friend Zdenek Mlynar,* who lived in the same dormitory as him at Moscow University, Gorbachev had privately begun to question the harsh Stalinist dogma they were forced to study. He knew that Stalin's agricultural policy was wrong. As Mlynar remembers, "Gorbachev explained to me how insignificant farm legislation was in everyday life and how important, on the other hand, was brute force which alone secured working discipline on the collective farms."[12] It was an unusual thing to confide to a foreigner in a xenophobic country that had been drilled in Stalin-worship. Gorbachev felt, early on, that it was unwise to keep the country completely isolated from the rest of the world.

His inchoate sentiments aside, Gorbachev believed in Stalin. Gorbachev's closest political associate, Alexander Yakovlev, confirmed this indirectly by saying, "We all deeply believed in Stalin. We deeply believed we were building a new society," for the "New Soviet Man."[13] Mlynar made the same point by saying, "Gorbachev, like everyone else at the time, was a Stalinist. In order to be a true reforming communist, you have to have been a true Stalinist."[14]

Mlynar was right. Indeed, Stalinism came to embody two of Gorbachev's deep and enduring preoccupations—with the injustice and inefficiency of the system, and with his dream of correcting them. He rose within that system to its greatest heights, most likely justifying ethical compromises along the way as the unavoidable price he had to pay. But once he reached the top, he began to fight the system

---

*After graduation, Mlynar rose in the ranks of the Czechoslovak Communist Party to become one of its leaders during the 1968 Prague Spring. After the Soviet intervention, Mlynar was expelled from the party and eventually went into exile in the West.

with a zeal and obduracy that surprised everyone, as a rebel from an orthodox faith seeking to atone for his past excesses, a betrayed believer bent on the destruction of his god.

The spring of 1953 after Stalin's death was a time of reappraisal.

Young Gorbachev, at that stage, seemed a man in search of a wider life. His optimism and an insatiable appetite for life were accompanied by the apparent conviction that everything, sooner or later, can be turned to positive advantage. His youth belonged to a generation that, like a great frozen mass, had been insulated from the external world by the rigid orthodoxy of Stalinism. But now, after the dictator's death, that mass began to melt, and the agony and trauma of his rule started to surface in the national consciousness. Khrushchev's shift produced first a shock, then a sense of relief.

The impact of Khrushchev's thaw was tremendous. Gorbachev had arrived in Moscow at the height of the Cold War, when Soviet hostility toward the West had reached fever pitch with the outbreak of the Korean War. The competition between socialism and imperialism had been presented by the authorities as so stark and everlasting that it precluded all debate. The anti-intellectualism of the time had stifled all cultural expression.

Stalin's death changed the atmosphere dramatically.

Within a year, Moscow was talking about "peaceful coexistence" with the West. By 1955, Khrushchev had gone to Yugoslavia to apologize to Marshal Tito, the archvillain of communism and alleged U.S. agent, and to acknowledge formally his right to his own brand of socialism. Gorbachev had not only to absorb these changes, but to absorb them thoroughly enough to inject conviction into his job as *komsorg*.

Such ideological somersaults speeded his intellectual awakening. They reinforced the pragmatic side of Gorbachev and may explain the fact that he seemed more comfortable with empirical decisions based on common sense than with ideological prevarications about distant communist goals. His ideology would never be doctrinal again. His detachment from traditional Bolshevik communism, which began at the time, would eventually give his perceptions their peculiar freshness and freedom. This became apparent after he became general secretary in 1985; and this accounts for a vision of his country so peculiarly pragmatic and modern that it took his orthodox party a long time to understand him.

Temperamentally, he was a doer. Such men, as a rule, are less doctrinaire and more capable of adapting ideas to their needs. Mlynar, writing about Gorbachev in *L'Unità,* the Italian Communist Party daily, a month after he took power in 1985, recalled how Gorbachev the student was struck by Hegel's aphorism "Truth is always concrete." Mlynar said: "Unlike us, he [Gorbachev] did not use this in the precise sense of Hegel's philosophy. He liked to repeat it whenever a teacher or student waffled on about general principles, ignoring the issue of how much they had in common with real life. Unlike most Soviet students, he did not see Marxist theory as a collection of axioms to be committed to memory."

For Gorbachev, theory provided a framework for understanding the world. He also believed in long-term strategy and mistrusted improvisation. For his supporters (and Mlynar seems to be among them) there was nothing crass about his ambition, then or later. Even during the darkest days of Stalinism, he was impatient with the outright falsifications of Soviet propaganda. Once, after they had watched together the Stalin-era film *Cossacks of the Kuban,* about collective farm life, Gorbachev dismissed the theme of happy peasants amid an abundance of food by remarking to Mlynar, "It's not like that at all."

Mlynar says he was "loyal and personally honest, [and] he earned an informal, spontaneous authority." He made friends with other activists. Among them was Anatoly Lukyanov, one of the most brilliant law students of his generation, who was two years ahead of Gorbachev. Gorbachev would eventually appoint Lukyanov a secretary of the Central Committee and head of its General Department, the post that makes him in effect Gorbachev's chief of staff, the man who directly supervises the most sensitive areas—personnel, the armed forces, and the KGB.

Scholastically, Mikhail was initially somewhat behind his city-reared classmates, but moved to the top of the class during his second year, winning the Kalinin Prize, which was usually accorded to the second-best student (Mikhail Kalinin was the titular head of state under Stalin; the Stalin fellowship was given to the top-ranking student). A member of the class of '55 recalled thirty years later, after Gorbachev had reached the pinnacle of Kremlin power, that he had struck her during their student days as someone who wanted to be a man of power. "He worked extremely hard but despite his high grades it was clear to us that he was more interested in public affairs than in law."[15]

Another Law School classmate said, "He reminded me of a good provincial actor who arrives in the capital and is doing well, but who constantly feels an inner need to prove himself on and off the stage." This classmate found him to be "romantic and somewhat naïve— no, the right word is 'innocent,' I think."[16] He read the right books, attended lectures and art exhibitions, read essays and then discussed them because he liked to improve himself; he believed in the force of ideas, and accepted almost literally the official image of Lenin the scholar and philosopher; he took seminars more seriously than other students did, always doing his homework, always asking a weighty question.

Apart from having a disciplined intellect, Gorbachev was a puritan. He displayed a proclivity for order in his personal life. During the first year, he and his roommates were accorded the "neatness award"; it was given annually at the university's dormitory at Sokolniki for personal neatness and the tidiest room. Gorbachev was at the time sharing Room 324 of the Stromynka dormitory with five other students. It was the first occasion on which his name appeared in the student newspapers.

Mlynar, who lived in a room across the hall, remembers him as bright and confident. Gorbachev was "an open man whose intelligence never carried over into arrogance, who knew how to listen and wanted to listen to his interlocutors." He had doubts about the Stalinist approach to the world, which divided people into regime supporters and criminals. Gorbachev knew, Mlynar said, that "there can exist [among communists] opponents, critics, reformers, who are not criminals for that reason."

As a law student, Gorbachev read authors as diverse as Rousseau, Hegel, Thomas Aquinas, Hobbes, Machiavelli, and Mill. He studied different political cultures and the history of ideas about the state. The professors were mostly intellectuals from pre-Bolshevik days who survived political turmoils by pursuing scholarly studies. The setting was an eighteenth-century colonnaded building across from the old tsarist stables in the heart of Moscow, where the Law School was located before it was moved to the twenty-four-story skyscraper atop the Lenin Hills in 1953.

Gorbachev, according to Mlynar, was particularly impressed by an old professor, Stepan F. Kechekyan, who conducted a two-year course on the history of political ideas. Gorbachev would later recall phrases he had memorized at the time, such as Lord Palmerston's assertion that "Britain has no eternal enemies or eternal friends, only eternal interests," which he later used in discussions with British leaders.

But it was Raisa who extended Mikhail's interests and sensitivities. Gorbachev met his future wife, Raisa Maximovna Titorenko, at the university. Raisa was born on January 5, 1932, in the Siberian city of Rubtsovsk, and as a child moved with her family to Sterlitamak, a town near Ufa, in Bashkiria, where her father, a railway engineer, was posted. She was a strong and purposeful girl of great and unusual beauty, and also of acute intelligence and exacting intellectual ambition. She graduated from high school with the gold medal as the top student in her class. (Mikhail came away with the silver.) A philosophy student and a voracious reader, she was hungry for the cultural experiences offered by the capital. Misha and Raya became known as avid theatergoers, the couple who discussed books. The wide range of her interests, her literary tastes, influenced him greatly. She had learned to read English, and she summarized books she was reading to him. Later, when some foreign authors presented their book in English to him, he said, "Raisa will help me read it."[17]

During their last year at the university, the Gorbachevs had a Komsomol wedding but did not live together until a few months before graduation, when married-student housing became available. The wedding night was spent in Gorbachev's room, after all his roommates agreed to disappear for one night. The next night, Raisa was back in her room (which she shared with Mlynar's wife). Their wedding photograph was typical of the time: Mikhail, his scalp covered by thinning hair, sporting a thin mustache and a short beard, in a black suit, white shirt, and tie, looming over Raisa, in a black dress, looking into the distance. A few months later, after graduation in June 1955, they went to his native province, where he took a job as a Komsomol organizer.

In the long run, the Law School equipped him for political leadership far better than engineering or physics would have done. It was a risk-free environment for an aspiring politician to practice courtroom rhetoric, to learn the art of oral persuasion. He probably never intended to work as a lawyer. In fact, his successful Komsomol activism at the university made it natural for him to opt for politics.

Gorbachev's thirst for knowledge was authentic; but his approach, even in his twenties, was more that of an enlightened Western business tycoon than of a Russian intellectual. His intellectualism was slightly self-conscious. He read largely for information, partly for comparison and insight, but apparently less for sheer pleasure in the veracity and beauty of ideas. He continued to do the same later in life. When he quoted Voltaire and Saint-Exupéry at a Palais de l'Elysée dinner in 1985, his remarks seemed to be intended to impress his French hosts. He evidently wanted to cut the image of an intellectual, and he offered his own ideas, while at the same time inducing people in his entourage to think about various issues confronting their country. (This in itself was a significant change after the years of anti-intellectualism in the Kremlin.) He would frequently mention that he was interested in philosophy, but never mentioned any particular philosopher he had read, leaving the impression that it was not so much that he was philosophical as that he liked to be thought of as philosophical.

Without question, he was a self-improvement man. In 1986, after a confrontational meeting in Moscow with Senator Edward M. Kennedy, he was told by an adviser that he could profit by reading Dale Carnegie's book *How to Win Friends and Influence People*. Several of the best Soviet translators were promptly engaged to turn out a Russian version of the volume. Arthur Hartman, then U.S. ambassador to Moscow, found Gorbachev a different man when he attended a Council on Foreign Relations meeting with Gorbachev some weeks later. "He didn't begin with a long lecture, as he used to. Instead, in a very flattering way, he asked them questions, got them to pose their own questions, and then in a very nice sort of way answered them. He was able to make all the points he wanted to make, but they were flattered and charmed by the idea that he wanted them to ask questions and express views."[18] It was textbook Dale Carnegie.

He had trained his mind to retain more and more information, and his personal associates said that in private conversations he frequently recalled verses of Pushkin, Mayakovsky, and the old Cossack rhymes of his youth, and quoted spontaneously from nineteenth-century Russian classics. He said the first modern English novel he had read was C. P. Snow's *Corridors of Power,* and the American author he liked best was Arthur Miller. Georgi Smirnov, who served as his personal assistant during his first two years in power, said Gorbachev liked Dostoyevsky but occasionally read detective novels for recreation. His favorite contemporary Soviet author is Chingiz Aitmatov, an ethnic Kirghiz who has become one of the masters of Soviet prose. The choice may provide an insight into Gorbachev's preoccupation with recent history. Aitmatov's novel *And the Day Lasted Longer Than an Age* makes heavy allusions to the destruction of the past by the Soviet regime; his heroes are "*mankurts,*" who according to a Central Asian legend were prisoners who had been turned into slaves by having their heads wrapped in camel skin, which under the hot sun dried tight as a steel band. A *mankurt* did not remember his tribe or family, nor could he recall his name; he "did not recognise himself as a human being."

Gorbachev's deepest beliefs, however, did not come from books he read but, rather, from his experiences and upbringing, both linked to Stavropol and its common stock of ideas, from the very air that he had breathed most of his life. He said later that, although education and books are important, "they are not what ultimately molds the individual."[19] His mind was analytical but evidently not burdened with interest in speculative truth. One of his key supporters in the

Central Committee said in private that Gorbachev "is not a reflective person, but he has a restless and doubting mind. His memory is prodigious and so is his energy. He is a quick study."[20]

An American who met Gorbachev in 1986 described him in private as "a brilliant tactician and a masterful PR guy, but not a strategist"; he described Gorbachev as lacking "a profound sense of history."[21] When a senior Gorbachev aide was confronted with this characterization, he laughed it off as the judgment of someone who was only vaguely familiar with Russian history.

Gorbachev's journey home to Stavropol in 1955 must have been a cultural shock. After the bustle of Moscow and its active cultural and social life, being back among his own people meant a return to an almost pastoral existence. The city of Stavropol, the capital of the territory, had a population of 130,000 and almost nothing to offer in the way of entertainment and culture.

The Gorbachevs did not succumb to the boredom of provincial life. During that period, Mikhail established relationships with a number of young Komsomol officials in Stavropol and men in neighboring republics who shared his ideas. He would eventually bring several of them with him to the seat of power in Moscow. Among his early companions was a Komsomol activist from neighboring Georgia, Eduard Shevardnadze, who later became leader of that republic. The two men gradually became close friends and visited each other's homes; once in power, Gorbachev would appoint Shevardnadze to be his foreign minister.

Despite their backgrounds, the Gorbachevs were not outdoor people. They preferred the world of books. Gorbachev conceded he had no idea how to mount a horse, an odd thing for the descendant of Stavropol Cossacks to say. During his final meeting with President Reagan and President-elect Bush in December 1988, Gorbachev remarked on Reagan's love for horses, saying he did not even know on which side to mount a horse. This gave Reagan the opportunity to crack a joke. "The left, the left," he quipped, to the laughter of American and Soviet officials.

Instead, both Mikhail and especially Raisa were intellectual buccaneers, in the context of the Stavropol and provincial party elite. Both read widely. Raisa's interests were broader, her aesthetic feelings stronger. She would later startle foreigners with her knowledge of literature—as she did during their visit to Britain in 1984 with questions about the plot structure of C. P. Snow and Iris Murdoch novels.

The Gorbachevs also showed a surprising degree of intellectual ambition. He, already an up-and-coming party apparatchik, enrolled in the Stavropol Agricultural Institute's evening school in 1964, at the age of thirty-three. Raisa worked on her doctoral dissertation and took care of their only daughter, Irina, who was born in 1956.

There was a pragmatic purpose to Gorbachev's agricultural schooling. Having two academic degrees seemed designed to meet the needs not only of his interior life but also of his thirst for power. Even if he had failed earlier to understand the crucial importance of food in Russian politics, he could not have missed the fact that his boss, Fyodor Kulakov, first party secretary of Stavropol, had parlayed the agricultural successes of his fiefdom into a major job in Moscow in 1964. Kulakov became a secretary of the Central Committee in charge of agriculture, then joined the Politburo.

Three years later, in 1967, Mikhail completed his agricultural degree, and Raisa, then thirty-five, finished her dissertation and submitted it to Moscow's Lenin Pedagogical Institute. Entitled "The Emergence of New Characteristics in the Daily Life of Collective Farm Peasantry (Based on Sociological Investigation in the Stavropol Territory)," her work is available at the Lenin Library in Moscow. It shows an above-average quality of work and, for the Soviet Union at the time, a surprisingly unorthodox methodology; besides using official statistics, state archives, and governmental analysis, she had conducted personal interviews based on carefully devised questionnaires. Her husband—whose job was to deal with the "difficulties and contradictions" of new patterns in rural life, the principal focus of Raisa's interest—probably not only helped with the research but also discussed it with her.

Talking about the Gorbachevs in 1987, Yakovlev noted their strong attachment to each other, adding almost wistfully, "One could only envy them as a family." In dealing with those close to him, Mikhail is said to be firm but tactful, avoiding reproaches. "Even in family relations reproaches are harmful," he once noted.[22] Gorbachev always tried to take his wife along on trips. While still an official in Stavropol, he was part of a group of Soviets invited to France in 1966 by Jean-Baptiste Doumeng, a leftist French businessman, who paid their expenses. He took Raisa with him and made a five-thousand-kilometer automobile trip through the country. They also vacationed in Italy a year later—first in Sicily, where they lived in the town of Terrasini ("We made a bus tour of virtually the entire island," he recalled later), then in Rome, Turin, Florence, and San Gimignano.

These visits gave the Gorbachevs a chance to take a personal look at the West, not as members of an official delegation, but as tourists exploring whatever their fancy dictated. The trips left a lasting impression on both. (Years later, while walking through Dubrovnik, Yugoslavia, Gorbachev turned to the diplomat Milan Vereš and said, "What a lovely place! It reminds me of San Gimignano.")

He used Raisa the way some American presidents use intelligent first ladies, sending her to events that he as leader could not attend without incurring political costs, as when she sat among bearded bishops in the front row at the Bolshoi Theater on June 10, 1988, at the ceremonies commemorating the one thousandth year of Christianity in Russia. In order to help him, in 1985 Raisa gave up her job as philosophy professor at Moscow State University, and Gorbachev placed her on his staff as an unpaid worker.

But although she left a favorable impression abroad, Raisa became something of a political liability at home. She was too intellectual and assertively self-confident for tradition-bound Russian women; they resented her sharing her husband's limelight. As time passed, Raisa's very presence in his entourage provoked more derisive and envious comments, particularly about her tasteful wardrobe and her proud mien, which many assailed as being "imperious."

Her unpopularity escalated with the growth of opposition to his policies and was already pronounced by 1986. Gorbachev opponents could indirectly attack him by publicly criticizing his wife. He was aware of this problem; he never referred to her in public meetings at home, something he would do abroad—as, for example, at a press conference following his summit meeting with President Reagan in Reykjavík.

He valued her advice. Raisa's intuitive grasp of situations and understanding of human character made her an indispensable and trusted adviser. They discussed "everything," including Soviet affairs at the highest levels, he said in a televised interview with Tom Brokaw.[23] She had shaped his intellectual tastes at the university, and Mlynar, who knew them both well (he and Gorbachev married women who were themselves close friends), believes that "a certain share of the credit" for his successes in Stavropol belonged to Raisa. He drew her to his work, and they grew together intellectually. Once he became leader, Gorbachev took her along wherever he went. She provided a reassuring presence. In the fall of 1985, as he was about to address the French National Assembly, his gaze scanned the audience restlessly until he spotted Raisa in the front row; then he smiled and gave her a tender look before beginning his delivery. "I am very lucky with Mikhail," Raisa told a dinner host the next day. "We are really friends, or if you prefer, we have great complicity."[24]

Occasionally she would prompt him to correct a misimpression or an oversight. During his 1987 visit to Prague, while he was talking to a street crowd, he failed to notice a young boy who had come close to stare at him with fascination. "Misha, the child!" Raisa whispered. Obviously she saw a significant and, above all, spontaneous opportunity in a country still recoiling from anything Russian since the day of the 1968 Soviet invasion. His attention was elsewhere. "Mikhail Sergeyevich," she said loudly in her high-pitched voice, pointing at the boy. And Gorbachev picked the boy up in his arms, to the delight of an already friendly Czech crowd.

On at least one occasion during his first year in power, he used Raisa to deliver a confidential message. Monique Raimond, wife of the French ambassador to Moscow, was taken aside by Raisa during a Lenin Hills annual Women's Day reception for the wives of foreign envoys, and when she rejoined other guests she said, "For the first time I'm carrying a message to my government."[25]

He confided privately that he was enormously proud of his wife, who, he told the editors of *L'Unità,* was "one-quarter Jewish." It was a surprising thing for a Soviet leader to volunteer such information, given the deeply rooted anti-Semitism of the Russians. But Gorbachev is a self-confident man. Political scientist Fyodor Burlatsky, who knows him well, ascribed this to his Stavropol background. The fact that Gorbachev's ancestors were not serfs but free peasants, he said, likely accounts for his spontaneity and self-confidence. He remains a Russian to the core, intensely patriotic as only people living in the border regions can be. This is a vital element in his constitution and a source of inner strength.[26]

But this also had led Gorbachev to commit a public slip of the tongue in Kiev, the capital of the Ukraine, when he twice referred to the country he led as "Russia" before correcting himself to say "the Soviet Union as we call it now, and as it in fact is." Like most Russians, he thinks of the Soviet Union as Russia; but unlike most of them, Gorbachev has a nature that seems less dominated by that streak of bigoted nationalism which breeds belief in the righteousness of any Russian enterprise. "There is no reason," he would write later, "why anyone should assume the role of an omniscient, implacable oracle. There is no state that has nothing to learn from others. We are all teachers and pupils in one way or another." He added, acerbically, that people beset by internal difficulties frequently vent their anger on others, learning to "drape even the most blatant, vulgar greediness in national colors, wrapping it in high-flown rhetoric."[27]

It is puzzling to some in the Soviet Union and to many foreign Gorbachev-watchers that a promising young party member who had completed law studies at the top of his class should decide to forgo lucrative opportunities in the capital and settle down in remote and provincial Stavropol. But all who knew him in Moscow believed that Gorbachev harbored great ambitions even then, and that he was fully aware that the path to power led through regional party organizations rather than through the Moscow bureaucracy.

The twenty-three years he spent as a party official in Stavropol shaped his political vision more than any other experience.

Gorbachev's first year there coincided with enormous political turmoil, precipitated by Khrushchev's denunciation of Stalin. All party members were called to meetings in late March 1956 where Khrushchev's "secret speech" to the Twentieth Communist Party Congress was read aloud. It was an exposé of Stalin's crimes that had never been made public in the Soviet Union. Khrushchev blamed Stalin's incompetence for the early defeats in World War Two; he denounced the gross violations of law and decency during the mass purges of the thirties and the show trials of Lenin's leading associates.

For Gorbachev, who had witnessed the German occupation of Stavropol, whose grandfather had been taken away under Stalin, the revelations themselves were hardly shocking. But Khrushchev's denunciation of Stalin was shocking. It is easy to imagine Gorbachev never having wanted to think through these personal experiences before, for fear that he could come to heretical conclusions. Heretical thoughts in Stalin's Russia, where suspicion was pervasive, were dangerous. But it was probably at this time that he began to sense the bankruptcy of the system.

He had had a strange experience a few years earlier. His college friend Mlynar sent him a postcard from Prague, where he was spending the summer. Its arrival aroused grave suspicions, even though it came from a communist friend in an allied communist country. The act seemed so subversive to the local police that the police chief felt it necessary to deliver the mail to Gorbachev personally while he was helping with the harvest in the fields of the Privolnoe collective farm.

Gorbachev chose to tell Mlynar about it in a joking way. But his remarks were more damning than he ever realized or admitted. They revealed that Gorbachev privately agonized over the paranoia and arbitrariness of the system he was a part of. But it was not until after Khrushchev's 1956 "secret speech" detailing Stalin's crimes that Gorbachev consciously rejected the Stalinist system. Later, after he became Soviet leader and spoke about his ideological convictions, he would say that individuals "come to a philosophy of their own, agonizing over it and accepting it with mind and heart."[28]

Associates who have known Gorbachev since his student days see his reaction to Khrushchev's speech as the opening round in the definition of Gorbachev's political identity. That identity was to gel five years later at the Twenty-second Party Congress. Indeed, one of his aides described him as a "child of the Twenty-second Party Congress," the most anti-Stalinist gathering ever convened by Khrushchev.[29]

The 1961 congress in Moscow was the first young Gorbachev attended as a delegate from Stavropol; he voted for the resolution to remove Stalin's body from the honorable place next to Lenin in the Red Square mausoleum for his "abuses of power, mass repressions of honest Soviet people, and other actions."

Moscow's international prestige was at its apogee in 1961 as the old colonial empires were dying and new countries sympathetic to socialism emerging. The Russians were beating the Americans in space. Yuri Gagarin, who attended the gathering inside the gleaming new Kremlin Palace of Congresses, had become, a few months earlier, the first man to orbit the earth in space and the living symbol of socialist superiority. Economic indicators showed Soviet growth on all fronts. Socialism, it seemed in the heady atmosphere of the time, had already been achieved; the updated Communist Party Program, the party's bible, containing the first revisions of goals and policies since Lenin's time, pledged that Marx's dream of communism was within reach, proclaiming without qualification that "the present generation of Soviet people shall live in communism." By 1980, it said, the population would be assured an abundance of everything; all workers would be fed free lunches; schoolchildren and students would get free clothing and books; all people would enjoy free housing, water, gas, heating, electricity, and all means of transport. And so on.

It seemed as if total good was pitted against total evil: Khrushchev versus Stalin, socialism versus capitalism. Mikhail identified strongly with the good, as represented by Khrushchev and his vision of socialism. But he was to discover that the outcome of this struggle was neither total victory nor total defeat. In retrospect, it must have served as a useful history lesson for Gorbachev about the endurance of institutions and the frailty of men who challenge them. Had he read Russian history—which his generation did not do—he might have taken note of Count Mikhail Speransky's warning that "in no other state do political words stand in such contrast to reality as in Russia." History also would have instructed him about the invariably unhappy fate of Russian reformers. Speransky, one of the most gifted statesmen of imperial Russia and the architect of Alexander I's reforms, himself became the victim of a sudden volte-face; he was arrested and shipped off to Siberia after the sovereign changed his mind about reform. He was subsequently rehabilitated by Alexander's grandson Nicholas I. (Ironically, the writings of Speransky, who died in 1839, saw the light of day for the first time in 1961 in Moscow.)

It is tempting to imagine young Gorbachev's state of mind in this moment of boundless euphoria, and to sympathize with it. His mind was finally in step with his heart. He had fretted over past injustices. How was it possible that the glorious goals of socialism could be advanced, at least in part, by murderous figures such as Stalin and his henchmen? Khrushchev's soothing answer was that the goals of socialism were noble, that the system itself was superior to other systems, but that both were perverted by man. The congress confirmed this judgment by casting Stalin's body out of the mausoleum. It outlined a magnificently bountiful future to come in less than twenty years.

Belief in the system served as the foundation of Gorbachev's career, and eventually of his reformist program. He was a true believer, and remained one even after he became leader, a trait bound to become a political drawback; others who had reached the peak of Kremlin authority were cynical and pragmatic men who easily resorted to political expediency without needing to justify their actions to themselves. Gorbachev, however, was imbued with the righteousness of the socialist cause; if things went wrong, the reason was ignorance and human frailty, but not the system itself. Steingrimur Hermannson, the foreign minister of Iceland who met with Gorbachev in 1987, quoted him as saying that the hardest decision he ever had to make was "to expose the faults of previous Soviet leaders." He had to do so, Gorbachev said, because the failings of the past were the fruit of the leaders, not of the system.[30]

Khrushchev's de-Stalinization also revealed the dark side of Soviet politics, its troublesome continuum between means and ends. Khrushchev's report had shown Kremlin politics as a jungle. Despite his professed belief in the system as the best of all possible systems,

Khrushchev tried at the congress to make serious reforms. One of the attempted institutional changes—changes that ultimately resulted in Khrushchev's ouster three years later—limited the tenure of Communist Party officials to no more than three five-year terms of office. This meant that any official would have a maximum of fifteen years to enjoy privileges and power before turning both over to someone else. Another seemingly innocuous institutional change pushed by Khrushchev required that at least one-third of the members of every regional party committee, the real seat of power, be changed at each election. The party worthies had approved these reforms with a show of enthusiasm at the congress, but when they returned home they grumbled and tried to ignore them. What Khrushchev asked posed too disturbing a challenge to the party bureaucracy and its way of life. They were now lying in wait for Khrushchev to make mistakes and allow disgruntlement to coalesce into active opposition.

From his Stavropol vantage point, Gorbachev observed the power process develop in the early sixties. Khrushchev seemed firmly at the wheel, yet the ship of state was not responding to his wishes. His problem was that, although assailing Stalin, Khrushchev failed to rid himself of Stalin's heirs. One Gorbachev aide said much later that the scope of the problem was symbolized by Khrushchev's inability to acquire establishment approval to publish his "secret speech." The aide added, "There are the roots of glasnost."

Gorbachev also seems to have grasped the essential weakness of Kremlin politics. Whereas all meaningful changes in Russia had to be initiated from the top, their success depended on support from all levels of the bureaucracy. The problem was that the *nomenklatura,* the Communist Party elite, had become a privileged and self-contained world that could frustrate even the best men; only by reforming the system could a leader hope to modernize it.

Gorbachev had sympathized with Khrushchev and, after his ouster in a 1964 palace coup, had tried to understand where Khrushchev went wrong. He could see that Khrushchev had vacillated too much; the struggle against Stalin's ghosts and the remaining Stalinists exhausted his energies and allowed the bureaucracy to move against him. Speaking to a Writers' Union meeting in June 1986, Gorbachev recalled how the bureaucracy had managed to "break Khrushchev's neck" and said it would like to do the same to his.

As early as the sixties, Gorbachev thought of democratization as the prerequisite for effective reforms in economic and political life. Mlynar, whose rise through the ranks was faster than Gorbachev's, reports meeting his old friend in Stavropol in 1967. Gorbachev was then a senior provincial official, while Mlynar was a secretary of the Czechoslovak Central Committee, touring Russia as a member of an official Prague delegation. The two men met privately, and Mlynar's recollection shows Gorbachev as having moved toward a more liberal political position. This was not the result of any ideological change; rather, Gorbachev's mind was more practical than doctrinal. They talked about the prospects of reforming the socialist system. Gorbachev had sympathized with Khrushchev's desire to liberalize and reform the system, but, he argued, the moment was inopportune and the people were unprepared for major changes. Also, he thought of Khrushchev's methods as having been more in the nature of authoritarian intervention than a genuine devolution of power and responsibility to local governments. Assessing Gorbachev on the basis of his friendship with him and their meeting in 1967, Mlynar said, "I do not believe that he would be a man for whom politics and power might have become ends in themselves. He has never been a cynic; he was by character a reformer who considered politics to be the means and the people's needs to be the objective."

When Italy's Prime Minister Bettino Craxi visited Moscow in May 1985, he told Gorbachev that he had read Mlynar's article in *L'Unità*. "Was it a positive article?" Gorbachev asked. "Very much so," Craxi replied. "A Prague Spring intellectual issuing a positive verdict on me could cause some tongues to wag," Gorbachev said.

Chapter 2

THE FOOTHILLS OF POWER

It was one thing to reject Stalin's terror; most people in the establishment, including those at the very top, had been personally afraid of Stalin and his power. But it was quite another thing to dismantle Stalin's system. Gorbachev saw Khrushchev's attack on the system as being far too erratic. His impetuousness was part of the problem. Khrushchev was engaged in perpetual and frequently chaotic efforts to change the economy. He sought to strengthen state farms and curtail the cultivation of private plots. He also introduced the policy (though not the term) of glasnost to fight the party bureaucracy. His opening up of the mass media in the service of his policy was similar to Gorbachev's later approach.

Moreover, Khrushchev had surrounded himself with second-rate figures who lacked the will and imagination to carry out his program and who eventually turned against him. They represented systemic interests. Gorbachev must have witnessed their resistance to Khrushchev's reforms—Khrushchev's fatal mistake was to act wholly independently of the bureaucratic elites that had brought him to power, and especially the party, confident of the solidity of his personal power base.

Gorbachev must have seen how Khrushchev's base was shrinking in Stavropol. Although Gorbachev most certainly was not in on the plot to overthrow Khrushchev—he was too junior at the time—he must have heard the intimations of trouble. His Stavropol patron, Kulakov, moved into the top leadership in Moscow shortly after Khrushchev's fall in a way suggesting that he was with the plotters. Historian Roy Medvedev, in his biography of Khrushchev, suggests that detailed discussions of the coup took place while the plotters were on a hunting-and-fishing trip near the Manych lakes in the Stavropol territory as guests of Kulakov.[1]

Perhaps the most significant lesson of the Khrushchev ouster and the rise of Brezhnev was that anyone aspiring to the highest Kremlin office who did not share the prevailing view imposed by the leader had to bide his time. Gorbachev saw Khrushchev do that. When he was a member of Stalin's inner leadership, nobody ever suspected Khrushchev of harboring reformist zeal; yet he turned out to be an entirely different man from what he had seemed. Brezhnev had also awaited his moment. The lesson Gorbachev may have drawn from this is that one had to be a nimble operator of great patience and self-control, and a faithful soldier of the party, if one entertained hopes of reaching the top. High-profile exposure against the monochrome political landscape spelled trouble. Above all, it was mandatory to observe the forms and rituals of the party.

Gorbachev apparently learned this lesson well. Like everybody else, he drifted with the current. While in Stavropol, he paid extravagant public homage to Brezhnev that fitted neatly into the general chorus of adulation. When the first volume of Brezhnev's memoirs came out, Gorbachev manfully pronounced that the volume was "not very large, but in the depth of its ideological content, in the breadth of the author's generalizations and opinions, it has become a great event in public life. It has evoked a warm echo in the hearts of Soviet people, the delighted response of frontline soldiers."[2]

Later, after Gorbachev moved to the capital in November 1978 and when he began to appear at the edges of the photographs of official leadership lineups, he cut the nondescript figure of a young man deferring to his seniors. His speeches began to gain media attention, but they were boring and repetitious; there was never a hint that behind the façade was an extraordinarily skillful politician and spellbinding orator, let alone someone who wanted to carry out a national reconstruction.

•   •   •

That discussions of the Brezhnev coup took place in the Stavropol territory was not unusual. The northern slopes of the Caucasus Mountains, which divide Europe from Asia Minor, are an area of exotic and stunningly beautiful landscape whose subtropical river valleys are set off by jagged peaks and inaccessible mountain ranges with everlasting snow. For Russian colonizers of the eighteenth and nineteenth centuries, the new and distant outpost of the empire was also a world of unusual freedom—far away from the old Russia of dark autocracy, serfdom, venal clerks, and oppressive gentry. The settlers paid for their freedom by rendering military service to the empire, warding off Turkish and Tatar armies as well as rebellious Moslem tribes and hot-blooded highland warriors who frequently threatened the line of communications to Azerbaijan and Georgia. This southern world of danger and beauty and its frontiersmen's freedom had captivated the imagination of many Russian writers— including Pushkin, Lermontov, and Tolstoy—and inspired some of the finest literature. To this day, the Caucasus retains a grip on the imagination of Russians, and they flock to Stavropol each year for their holidays. Kislovodsk and the nearby Mineralnie Vody have been favorite summer resorts of Russia's rulers for more than a century. It would have been above suspicion, for example, for Kulakov, as first secretary, to host Brezhnev, Mikhail Suslov, and other senior members of Khrushchev's Politburo for their coup-plotting session. Most of them came regularly to Stavropol at that time of the year. Moreover, it was a duty of top regional party barons to welcome visiting Politburo figures personally.

The frequency of their visits to Stavropol permitted the local chief to establish more than a perfunctory relationship with them and gain powerful protectors in the highest council of the land. Once he became the boss of Stavropol in 1970, Gorbachev began to have regular contacts with top Kremlin officials in leisurely Caucasus settings. Some of them were taken by his engaging personality and intelligence. He was a great charmer; his extrovert personality and humor, bold ideas expressed in moderate language, and perpetual references to specific material achievements disarmed the old men of the Kremlin. His official biography makes an unusual reference to this aspect of his personality. "Gorbachev," it says, "was able to captivate people with his brilliance, and to interest them. He was not embarrassed to learn from friends, to adopt better ideas, and to support new ones. His originality of thought and his charm attracted people to him." By then he was a totally political creature. His detractors saw him as a young man with the talent of pleasing the right people at the right time—first Kulakov, then Suslov, and eventually his most important mentor, Yuri Andropov.

Gorbachev quickly moved through a progression of jobs, starting in 1955 as an official of the Propaganda Department of the Komsomol and quickly being promoted to the post of first secretary of the Komsomol. He was quite good at inspiring the young with a lofty sense of their mission.

He could pass easily from the rural banter into the realm of ideas, confronting both with confidence in his ability to hold his own. He possessed an almost uncanny talent for improvising. He could master the details of any issue. His tone of voice, his accent, the broad range of his humor, his love of language, his turn of phrase, all rooted in the Stavropol territory, made him brilliantly persuasive. He could reduce the jumble of recommendations coming from Moscow into practical policies. Among Stavropol residents who remember him then, nobody has suggested that he had been ambitious in any vulgar way, or that he had acted as a pompous provincial governor. They recall him as a forceful administrator who telegraphed his own viewpoint, often unconsciously, by his body language or the way he summarized a problem.

One thing that was apparent at the time was Gorbachev's dislike of violence and his reliance on words as his main political weapon. In difficult situations he was given to hectoring and lecturing; he believed that, if his conclusion was logical and based on good evidence, others should accept it automatically. For those who ignored or discounted his views, he was ready to explain them one more time, but his tone would suddenly acquire an authoritarian edge ("Come on, come on, you are quoting only one sentence from my speech," he would later interrupt a Central Committee member who was giving a speech Gorbachev didn't like). Among his most beguiling qualities were a self-deprecating humor and a sense of proportion, both of which he used to win people over. But he also showed himself unrelenting and profane when necessary, which, in the setting of his native province, was often. Classmates remembered him during his student days as being an extrovert southerner who relished the *ruski mat* (Russian mother), as the rich compendium of Russian obscenities is known generically. Later, as leader, he would show his love of language, as when he told his opponents in 1985 that they "fear reconstruction as the devil fears the incense."[3]

He was not a bureaucrat by nature. Smirnov, his former special assistant, ascribed this to his Stavropol experience. Gorbachev did not spend much time sitting in his office while in Stavropol, Smirnov said. "He was out talking to people, always on the move, always active." Smirnov accompanied him in 1985 on a visit to Kuibyshev, an industrial city on the Volga, and was surprised both by his prodigious energy and by his sheer delight in long discussions with groups of people. Gorbachev said such meetings had always given him pleasure and sustenance. "I was, for a while in 1963, the *partorg* [party organizer] in a small area of Stavropol. Two other fellows and I, that was the whole office. But I never stayed in the office. I was on the road most of the time."[4] In his mind, his Stavropol years were ones of political education. He would later comment, "There is no such school that could replace a person's independent work of self-education."[5]

Even Gorbachev, though, would acknowledge the value of a mentor and patron. For him, that figure was Kulakov, who in 1960, the year Gorbachev became the top Komsomol official in Stavropol, was appointed first secretary of the Stavropol territory. Kulakov was instrumental in including Gorbachev among the selected Stavropol delegates who attended the Twenty-second Congress in 1961. And the next year, Kulakov moved his young protégé into the party headquarters of Stavropol, making him the key person in charge of personnel in administration, farms, and industry.

After Kulakov's promotion to the Secretariat in Moscow, the post of first secretary of Stavropol was given to an alternate Politburo member, Leonid Yefremov, whose career was tainted by his support of Khrushchev and who, after Khrushchev's fall, was ousted and sent to a lesser job to await his retirement.

With his patron now at court in Moscow, Gorbachev's continued upward progression was assured. By 1968, he had risen to become the second-ranking official in the province, and when Yefremov retired in 1970, he was appointed to replace him. He was only thirty-nine, though he looked older than his years because of his premature baldness.

First secretaries in the Soviet system—and there are roughly one hundred of them—exercise immense power and considerable autonomy in their regions. Some run the region almost like a personal fiefdom. Given the vastness of the country, first secretaries must be among the most trusted persons in the Soviet regime. Most of them automatically become members of the Central Committee, the key policymaking body.

The appointment of Gorbachev to run the Stavropol territory was due to Kulakov's lobbying in Moscow. But it could not have been made without the endorsement of Mikhail Suslov, the party's chief ideologist, who had a special interest in Stavropol. He served as first secretary of the territory during the early years of World War Two, before he moved to Moscow to join the leadership in 1947. Gorbachev detractors have speculated that the young man had used his charm to ingratiate himself with the Stalinist high priest of dogma. But little is known about the relationship between the two men, and Gorbachev allies have vehemently denied reports that they were close. The only indication of closeness—something we saw at the time of Suslov's funeral in 1982—was Gorbachev's apparently easy familiarity with the members of Suslov's family.

It could have occurred to Gorbachev in the early seventies—if not before—that a high Kremlin office was not outside his reach. The precedent was there. Suslov and Kulakov had moved from Stavropol to the Kremlin management team. Yefremov, his immediate predecessor, had been among its members. Moreover, the mighty Krem-

lin figures whom he entertained in Stavropol did not seem conspicuously better qualified than he. Quite the contrary. A vast majority
of them were poorly educated and ill equipped for the tasks of running a modern superpower. A Gorbachev adviser who also saw the
principal figures at close range and in unguarded moments privately
described Old Guard politicians as well-meaning but fundamentally
weak figures who grew up in Stalin's shadow. Their ideas of socialism,
he said, were primitive at best. For them, the victory in the war
confirmed the value of the system. That was socialism. Men like
Brezhnev, Konstantin Chernenko, and others lacked the imagination
and the talent to move the country to a higher plane of economic
and spiritual growth. Nor did they deeply feel the urgency of the
moment in the late seventies. The advancement of technology to
them meant the nuclear bomb and modern means of delivering it.
They were the true heirs of a military empire; their minds had been
formed in the years of "war communism," and that was the only
guidepost they knew.

Their rhetoric was, of course, admirable. They wanted to improve
things. But Alexander Yakovlev would say later and in private that
the official rhetoric of the Brezhnev years comprised "a lot of won-
derful words that turned out to be fiction." ("We call that 'sputnik
rhetoric,' " Yakovlev said, "flying very high but burning into ashes
when it approaches the earth.") Gorbachev himself would make the
same point by saying his unnamed predecessors had thought "how
to improve the economy without changing anything"—paraphrasing
the nineteenth-century satirical writer Saltykov-Shchedrin, who
viewed Russian officials of his day as people incapable of taking
timely and decisive action.

Once in power, Gorbachev spoke almost with contempt about the
incomprehensible inertia of the Brezhnev era. "You know," he told
a group of Soviet writers, "Brezhnev once said we need to hold a
plenum on scientific-technological problems. I was shown sacks of
documents prepared in this connection, all sorts of information and
so forth. When they began to sort this out, they suddenly saw that
nobody knew where to take it, what to do with it. So they abandoned
it; everything remained in sacks."[6]

• • •

Yuri Andropov was an exception among Brezhnev's entourage. It is not clear when Gorbachev first established personal contact with him. Since Andropov regularly vacationed in the Caucasus, they certainly met during Gorbachev's first year as Stavropol leader in 1971, though their first encounter may have been earlier. Gradually Andropov took a liking to the young man, and they began spending a lot of time together, walking in the woods, discussing politics. He liked Gorbachev's wit and intelligence and the fact that he and his family were untouched by any whiff of corruption. For an official in his position, Gorbachev lived an almost spartan life. His mother, Maria Panteleyevna, and their numerous relatives continued to live as they always had in Privolnoe and to work on the local collective farm. His younger brother, Alexander, who had chosen a military career, was merely a captain at the time. Only one Gorbachev relative, his cousin Ivan Vasilyevich Gorbachev, was active in local politics in the district.

But what attracted Andropov most was Gorbachev's cast of mind, his capacity for teamwork, his curiosity, and above all the strength of his character. The younger man combined an acute and somewhat ironical awareness of the flaws and absurdities of the Soviet system with a devoted attachment to it. Their conversations became progressively more searching and candid, and they found themselves in agreement on the key issues of policy.

As chairman of the KGB, Andropov was becoming more and more preoccupied with the signs of economic and social decay in the late seventies. He used to tell his associates that, unless checked and reversed, this stagnation threatened to push the Soviet state onto a dangerous path—a path that had led other great nations, trapped by bureaucracies and habits too rigid to accommodate new problems, to lose their empires. Later he found the same ideas in Lenin's work and used them, once he became Soviet leader, to press for openness and change. "All revolutionary parties that have perished up till now have perished because they became too pleased with themselves and could not see in what their strength consisted, and were frightened to speak of their weaknesses," said Andropov, quoting Lenin. And

Gorbachev would use the same quotation when he needed support for his radical Kremlin policies.

It was Andropov who propelled Gorbachev into a far higher political orbit than he would have ever been able to reach on his own, and who mapped the strategic path that Gorbachev took as his own once he became leader. But this long and close relationship, which was so important to Gorbachev's career as well as his country's future, is not intelligible unless we realize that Andropov found in his young friend the attributes he valued and admired.

Andropov was not the kind of man easily duped by flattery or charm. He had early on assessed Gorbachev's potential and sought an opportunity to bring him to Moscow. A private and reserved person, Andropov was harboring great political ambition of his own, and he wanted to have capable allies in key positions. His natural curiosity and lifelong passion for learning had made him a shrewd judge of people. He translated these qualities into a gift for attracting and using the best and the brightest young men around. Even before he became KGB chairman in 1967, he had gathered as his "consultants" some of the ablest and most intelligent people in the party: Lev Tolkunov, who later became parliament chairman; Georgi Arbatov, director of the U.S.A. and Canada Institute; Fyodor Burlatsky, political scientist and commentator; Georgi Shakhnazarov, futurologist, a senior Central Committee official, and eventually a personal assistant to Gorbachev; journalist Alexander Bovin; sinologist Lev Delusin; economist Oleg Bogomolov. Andropov tried to do the same during his short tenure as Soviet leader, promoting from obscurity to high office virtually all major officials of the early Gorbachev era, including Prime Minister Nikolai Ryzhkov and Politburo members Yegor Ligachev, Alexander Yakovlev, Vitali Vorotnikov, Viktor Chebrikov, and Lev Zaikov.

To those who knew Gorbachev in Stavropol, his later populist approach did not come as a surprise.

The Gorbachevs lived from 1970 until they left for Moscow in a nineteenth-century house that had once belonged to a tsarist officer but had since been equipped to house the first secretary of the territory. The green one-story building on Dzerzhinsky Street was located directly opposite the local KGB headquarters. Their life in Stavropol was in slow motion. Mikhail usually walked to work—his office being a few hundred feet away, inside a gleaming white five-story building that faces a large square with a statue of Lenin. Because Gorbachev spent most of his career in daily contact with people, everyone in Stavropol knew him. Later on, as Soviet leader, he would frequently illustrate his arguments by referring to real people and situations from his Stavropol days. At a Politburo meeting in April 1986 to discuss the pension system, he stunned his colleagues by saying that his own mother was supposed to live off a wretched monthly pension of 29 rubles (about $38). "Who can live on that sort of pension?" he said. "Nobody, comrades, nobody!"

Gorbachev started his career as first secretary of Stavropol by implementing pragmatic economic measures that appeared to undermine the basic justifications for collective farms. He had seen the efficiency of private-plot production in his own village, and he was aware of the effects of excessive centralization and the absence of financial incentives. In 1971, he introduced a bonus system based on production results. This system in selected areas of Stavropol allowed groups of farmers to sign a contract with their collective making them responsible for a piece of land. They sowed, fertilized, and harvested their land and were paid according to what they produced. He would argue later that these contract workers harvested on average 20–30 percent more produce, with lower outlays of labor and resources, than did collective farmers. According to press reports at the time, the approach boosted harvest yields by almost 50 percent on irrigated lands. By 1976, Gorbachev was pushing for a trend to adopt this approach throughout the Stavropol territory.

A year later, however, he initiated another type of experiment at the Ipatovo state farm that was a complete reversal of his first approach. Ipatovo became the symbol of a centralized "agro-industrial" approach involving vast areas of land and mobile fleets of tractors, harvesters, and transport vehicles. It was a scheme close to the hearts of the conservative Old Guard, and Gorbachev's unexpected about-face in policy was a sign that he was ready to make sudden reversals, if not to advance his political career then at the very least to avoid steps putting himself on a direct collision course with the Brezhnev conservatives.

He pursued the new experiment with vigor. Indeed, in its first year, Ipatovo was a resounding success, making Gorbachev an agricultural miracle worker in the eyes of the diehard conservatives. But the agro-industrial approach only worked so well for one year at this one farm because of Gorbachev's personal involvement. The conservatives, citing Gorbachev's success, began touting the method as the way to solve the country's food problems. But elsewhere it was a failure. Harvest yields declined sharply and by the second half of the decade, the Ipatovo experiment was not mentioned anymore.

But by 1978 Gorbachev had moved to join the leadership in Moscow. In retrospect, apart from political expediency, the incident revealed a potential flaw in Gorbachev's makeup. He liked to quote Hegel's "Truth is always concrete"; but the truth he knew from his own experience was that the huge agro-industrial complexes were not likely to be successful. Yet he mounted the experiment with the conviction that, if he set an irreproachable example, if his policy was well thought out and rational, other party members would work equally hard to ensure successful implementation. This positive, optimistic, and constructive energy was the source of his strength but later led him to ignore human weaknesses—prejudice, vanity, fear, acts of spite and treachery, in particular the obstructive tactics of ill-disposed officials, which cumulatively could block any policy.

In the summer of 1978, Gorbachev's first patron and former boss, Fyodor Kulakov, died in Moscow under mysterious circumstances, leaving an opening in the leadership. Kulakov was a Politburo member and a secretary of the Central Committee responsible for agriculture. Rumors at the time said that Kulakov, who was under attack for failures in agriculture, had committed suicide. Although he was given a state funeral, at which Gorbachev was one of the main speakers, the key figures in the regime—Brezhnev, Chernenko, Premier Alexei Kosygin, and Mikhail Suslov—were absent from the ceremonies, lending credibility to the rumor.

It was the kind of opening that Andropov, a master of behind-the-scenes maneuvers, had been waiting for. Gorbachev, as an agricultural expert and the successful administrator of a major grain-producing territory, was a natural choice to succeed Kulakov.

Andropov, as usual, had gone to Stavropol at the end of August for his annual vacation. Before leaving Moscow, he must have broached Gorbachev's candidacy with Suslov, the widely feared ideological chief and kingmaker, and secured his endorsement. Nothing could be done without Brezhnev, however, and Andropov seized an unexpected opportunity to have the Soviet leader meet and assess the young man from Stavropol. Brezhnev, accompanied by Chernenko, was traveling by train from Moscow to Baku, the capital of Azerbaijan, on the Caspian Sea, where he was always received with accolades, excessive flattery, and gifts, which are a part of the area's Moslem tradition. The train was passing through the Stavropol territory, and when it stopped at the Mineralnie Vody station on the evening of September 19, 1978, Andropov and Gorbachev were there to greet the travelers. The train's departure was delayed for two hours as the four men who would rule the country in succession— Brezhnev, Andropov, Chernenko, and Gorbachev—met and talked on the narrow platform of the old tsarist railway station.

Two days later *Pravda* reported that Brezhnev and Chernenko had made a brief stopover at Mineralnie Vody, where they talked with Andropov and Gorbachev. This was, in effect, Gorbachev's job interview, and it went well.

Two months later he was summoned to Moscow and appointed a secretary of the Central Committee, in charge of agriculture. He was now among the twenty or so Politburo members and secretaries of the Central Committee, who constitute the highest ranks of the country's leadership. The promotion, announced in the briefest possible way, was the last in a set of changes noted on the front page of *Pravda*'s November 28, 1978, edition: "The Central Committee plenum elected Comrade M. S. Gorbachev as a secretary of the Communist Party of the Soviet Union." The position of secretary of the Central Committee was the first step toward becoming a Politburo member. The nine secretaries supervise the main areas of economic and political life under the guidance of the Politburo.

He was forty-seven, by far the youngest member of the leadership.

Here was a man with no public recognition who literally would thrust himself on the national political scene and, in the short span of six years, come to dominate it. But there was nothing grand to say about him at the time. Brezhnev was at the zenith of his power and prestige. Despite signs of a gathering economic and social storm, his government projected an image of stability and order. Brezhnev's propaganda machine hummed so smoothly it suggested that his reign would last forever.

Gorbachev's first year in his new position could hardly have gone better. The harvest of 1978 produced 237 million tons of grain, an all-time record. Though largely due to the good weather, this raised hopes that the food problem was being dealt with effectively. But the agricultural crisis had in reality become more acute throughout the seventies, even though the problems were obscured by the euphoria over the 1978 harvest. Gorbachev continued to prosper, although the years of his tenure as the top agricultural official of the land were disastrous. In 1979, the grain harvest was under 180 million tons; in 1981, the figure dropped to 158.2 million tons; total average grain output in the years 1981–85 was only 180.3 million tons, 25 percent below the planned annual production of 239 million tons. The figures represented the worst performance of Soviet agriculture since 1966–70 and were much lower than the average 205 million tons of the previous five-year plan. They were not released by the Soviet Central Statistics Board until November 1986.

Grain imports, which had been increasing by leaps and bounds despite huge capital investments in domestic agriculture, had become a serious drain on the Soviet treasury by the late seventies. Where did all the money go? Gorbachev was later to be haunted by this question, since, no matter how much money was invested in agriculture, it somehow disappeared without a trace. Moscow's food imports had increased tenfold, from $700 million in 1970 to $7.2 billion in 1980. An official Soviet survey showed a disastrous deterioration of Soviet agriculture. According to the survey, direct losses attributed to negligence and lack of storage facilities were enormous—one-fifth of the grain harvest and one-third of the potato crop were left to rot. The primitive state of road transport did not help. Only two out of every five villages were served by paved roads. Trucks broke down so frequently that four times as many men were engaged in repairing them as in making them. The monumental mishandling of agricultural equipment was illustrated by the fact that the number of tractors available to collective farms had remained constant although the country produced 550,000 tractors every year and added most of them to its pool of agricultural machinery.

Most of the agricultural imports came from the United States. But after the December 1979 invasion of Afghanistan, the situation was complicated by the Carter administration's partial embargo on food exports to the Soviet Union. The Russians had to scurry around trying to develop alternate sources of grain, using their stockpiles in 1980 and then importing forty-six million tons in 1981, mostly from Argentina, Canada, Australia, and some from the United States. There were severe food shortages in Russia in the fall of 1981, in part because of Soviet food shipments to Poland, where the confrontation between the independent trade union Solidarity and the government had degenerated into a grave crisis. Agriculture was showing up the Kremlin as vulnerable and weak.

It is difficult to explain why Gorbachev's career did not start to go wrong at this point. One plausible explanation is that he was too junior at that stage to be included in Kremlin power politics; he confided to his colleagues much later that, although a nonvoting Politburo member, he had not been consulted about the invasion of Afghanistan and learned about it from the newspapers.[7] Another possible explanation is that agriculture was only one aspect of a generally gloomy picture. All indicators showed that the economy was slowing down, that it was riddled with corruption and inefficiency, that alcoholism had reached epidemic proportions, that crime was soaring, and that the cost of energy and mineral extraction was rising sharply. The gathering economic crisis only underscored the dismal state of society in general. Although the establishment was throbbing with pessimism, Brezhnev and his colleagues simply ignored the ominous portents. The illusion of cohesion and sense of purpose would begin to unravel if they were to start housecleaning at the top, apportioning the blame for one misfortune or another.

It seems more likely that the ruling bureaucracy, finding itself in a transitional limbo, focused much of its time and energy on its own internal upheavals and power struggles. The absence of strong leadership and cohesion, an assortment of other misfortunes, and a strong challenge by a new and confrontational American president made it seem like the wrong time for changes at the top.

By mid-1982, the rivalry between Andropov and Chernenko was so intense that a major shakeup in the Politburo affecting the balance of forces was either impossible or would have required profuse blood-letting. The political world was by then becoming polarized.

The party bureaucracy and most of the established institutional interests saw Chernenko as the true heir of Brezhnev. Chernenko's control of the party machinery made him a strong player. Younger generations, alarmed by the decay, saw the country at a crossroads. Technocrats, experts in institutes and research centers, younger establishment members, the new generation in general, looked to Andropov for leadership. Perhaps the crucial factor that made Andropov an even stronger contender, apart from his formidable political skills, was the support of the KGB and the military chiefs. The competing forces were stalemated. However, one victim of this state of affairs was Andrei Kirilenko, seventy-six, second only to Brezhnev in Politburo seniority, and as such an obstacle in the path of both rivals. Both camps found it advantageous to ease him out of the Politburo shortly before Brezhnev's death.

Gorbachev kept a low profile, behaving cautiously and avoiding actions that could lead his colleagues to see him as a potential threat. In his speeches, he focused on agriculture and its problems. He appeared to be already aware of the limits of power. As a trained agronomist with considerable practical experience, he did publicly raise the troublesome issues of private enterprise and supplemental earnings shortly after he came to Moscow and later. In his first speech as Central Committee secretary—addressing a collective-farm conference on December 20, 1978—he voiced strong support for increasing the number of existing private plots; the private plots, he subsequently argued, constituted about 3 percent of the country's total arable land, but produced about one-quarter of all fruit, vegetables, and other produce. He wanted—but failed—to implement the extension to other parts of the country of experiments he had initially tried in Stavropol, moving away from collective farming toward individual and group contracts.

As the youngest man in the leadership, he was outside the inner circle of power brokers fighting over the shape of the post-Brezhnev leadership. The intricate backroom power play involved men like Chernenko, Andropov, Kirilenko, Defense Minister Marshal Dmitri Ustinov, Andrei Gromyko, Viktor Grishin, and Grigori Romanov. Given the absence of a free press, rumors became a key weapon. Yet, throughout the protracted struggle, Gorbachev's name never came up in the rumor mill.

The widespread public discontent over the severe food shortages during the winter of 1981–82 forced Brezhnev to act. In May 1982, Brezhnev's Food Program was launched with considerable fanfare, but Gorbachev managed to distance himself from the jumble of halfway measures and public-relations schemes that made up the Program. Although he was the man in charge of food, Gorbachev did not present the Program to the Central Committee plenum, and subsequently, in a *Kommunist* article, he went out of his way to praise Brezhnev's personal role in devising it. Predictably enough, Andropov also ignored the Food Program, simply by never mentioning it in his speeches. Neither man wanted to be associated with a policy he knew would not work.

The May 1982 plenum, however, was a significant event for both of them. As long as he remained KGB chairman, Andropov's room for political maneuvering in the succession struggle was limited. He had indicated earlier that he wanted to move back into the Central Committee. The vacancy left by Suslov, who died in January, was not yet filled, although Chernenko had assumed most of Suslov's functions on an informal basis. The May plenum named Andropov a secretary of the Central Committee, clearing the way for him to assume supreme power after Brezhnev's death on November 10, 1982. Once in power, Andropov would vault his young friend from Stavropol to the center of the national consciousness.

·   ·   ·

After Andropov's death in February 1984, his brief tenure in the Kremlin gradually came to be regarded as a crucial turning point in recent Soviet history. Although a member of the Old Guard, at age sixty-eight Andropov sided with the new generation preparing to claim national recognition. He forcefully initiated economic and social changes, and pushed forward Gorbachev and other younger men. Most important, he gave the country an extraordinarily candid appraisal of its ailments. He had, he said in his first speech as Kremlin leader, "no ready recipe for their solutions." The country and the party had to find the solutions by assessing "our own and world experience" and the "accumulated knowledge of the best practical workers and scholars." Slogans, he added, "won't get us anywhere." Some cherished party policies were simply wrong—"they have failed the test of time," as Andropov put it—while other objectives were so utopian as to contain "elements of separation from reality." The party, which claimed to base its ideas and actions on scientific principles of Marxism-Leninism, had failed to study "the society in which we live and work." The Soviet economy was being run in "a quite irrational manner of trial and error."

These were staggering admissions, and they introduced new themes. Apart from inheriting the support of Andropov's coalition and the intellectual groundwork for many of his own changes, Gorbachev was to benefit mightily from Andropov's critical analysis of the system. Andropov was a household name in Russia, a man who had grown up in Stalin's Soviet Union, a man above ideological suspicion. He rose to high office in the early sixties and subsequently served for fifteen years as chairman of the KGB, the ultimate watchdog of the system.

A man with lesser credentials could hardly afford to speak the truth so bluntly, at least in 1982. By doing so, even Andropov created a hostile backlash among substantial sections of the party bureaucracy; but with the KGB behind him, nobody dared oppose him openly.

Andropov quickly moved to provide a clear sense of direction, though he was vague about what exact measures were to be taken regarding the economy and society. A master tactician, he was careful to add protective coloration to reformist ideas, which might provoke conservative resistance. Yet nothing could obscure the initial impression that he was a man of power, prepared to exploit it thoroughly to fulfill his purposes, and that his overriding goal was to carry out a national reconstruction. That his brief tenure should prove so crucial to Gorbachev's rule was all the more remarkable since Andropov was seriously ill for most of it. After his fourth month his kidneys collapsed, and he had to use a dialysis machine for the remaining year of his life.

In retrospect, Andropov's political accomplishments may appear less important than they are. Though all of Gorbachev's major themes were developed during the Andropov period, they were advanced far more forcefully and further by Gorbachev than the ailing Andropov could have thought possible. More forcefully and further than Andropov would have wanted, Gorbachev's critics later said.

In 1982, Andropov's close personal relationship with Gorbachev was not known, except in high party circles. The relationship grew stronger after Andropov's accession, although he was sufficiently skilled in political tactics to advance the younger man gradually, making the upward progression look more natural.

They complemented each other. Andropov was more intellectual, and his grasp of both strategy and tactics in Soviet politics was far deeper. He was looking toward a new future while going back to Lenin, seeking theoretical justifications not from the firebrand revolutionary Lenin trying to seize power, but from the more thoughtful and pragmatic Lenin in power and confronting its limitations. Lenin had urged the party to confront the truth—"however bitter"—and to attack problems head on; besieged by economic difficulties, he had denounced the bureaucratic apparat for its failure to accept his changing policy and called for dismissal of "well-meaning" but inefficient officials and the shutdown of "enterprises that have gone to sleep."[8] Almost immediately, Andropov broadened Gorbachev's domestic responsibilities to include more than the agricultural sector. They were enlarged even further after Andropov fell ill in February 1983. Andropov also began to draw him into foreign affairs, a field in which Gorbachev had little experience. More and more, Gorbachev was brought into meetings with foreign visitors, and brief

Tass accounts of such events usually included his name near the end of the list of dignitaries. He was selected for the singular honor of being the keynote speaker at the April 22 Lenin Birthday celebration, where he delivered a broad outline of the policies and reforms of the Andropov administration. In the eyes of his colleagues, the party, and the establishment, he was being groomed for leadership.

Gorbachev started in early 1983 to make contacts with think tanks and specialists on foreign affairs. He frequently asked Georgi Arbatov, director of the U.S.A. and Canada Institute, to brief him. Arbatov and other specialists whom Gorbachev consulted saw nothing unusual in it, particularly since he was preparing to visit Canada in May. Moreover, since all Politburo members were voting on foreign-affairs issues, his interest in foreign affairs and particularly in the United States was natural. Gorbachev grasped points quickly. Arbatov was impressed by his insights into the great Soviet-American propaganda struggle over the deployment of new U.S. medium-range nuclear missiles in Europe, being debated that spring.

Gorbachev's long trip to Canada was his first sustained exposure to the West since he had joined the leadership, but it was barely noticed elsewhere. Western specialists at that point had not identified him as a potential successor to Andropov, and the Western media ignored him. For ten days he pottered around farms and factories as someone interested in learning the secret of Canada's economic efficiency. He was not given to proselytizing, and when his host, Agriculture Minister Eugene Whelan, at one point began talking enthusiastically about the advantage of free enterprise in producing an abundance of cheap food for everyone, Gorbachev quipped, "Gene, you don't try to convert me to capitalism and I won't try to convert you to communism."

His hosts were impressed by his poise and wit. But his political arguments were standard Soviet arguments—he vigorously defended the invasion of Afghanistan (although he told Whelan privately that the Afghan invasion "was a mistake"), the deployment of SS-20 missiles, and other controversial Soviet policies. There was nothing in his debate with Canadian parliamentarians to suggest that Gorbachev would eventually reverse much of Brezhnev's foreign policy or that he was concerned about the bankruptcy of Soviet-style socialism. The transcript of his remarks provides interesting pointers to the evolution of Gorbachev's thinking on foreign affairs, even though he may have privately entertained serious doubts about Brezhnev's policy.[9]

On this trip, Gorbachev established a close personal relationship with the Soviet ambassador to Canada, Alexander Yakovlev. They spent eight full days together and found themselves on the same wavelength. In discussions with Andropov, Gorbachev had already reached basic conclusions: the system had failed, it had to be reformed. Whelan's proselytizing, buttressed by the expansive wealth of Canadian farms and their efficiency, reinforced this view. Canada's economy appeared like a miracle to him. Yakovlev, as he was explaining the way things worked in Canada, seemed to point out the path to salvation.

Gorbachev was so taken by the clarity of Yakovlev's views, the solidity of his strategic judgment, and the quiet competence of his analysis that he decided to engage him as his personal adviser. Less than a month later he had Yakovlev recalled home and appointed director of a major institute; once in power, he made him a Politburo member and a secretary of the Central Committee, a combination of posts that made Yakovlev one of the top four officials in the country and, because of his closeness to the leader, the *de facto* number two.

Yakovlev, who earned a doctorate in history and subsequently worked as a propagandist in the Central Committee, had been sent into diplomatic exile ten years earlier because of his outspokenness. His mind was sharp and incisive, and he seemed prepared to question and probe matters that his colleagues preferred to avoid. One such critical essay, documenting the revival of Russian nationalism under Brezhnev, resulted in Yakovlev's exile. He had taken up his post in Ottawa with great seriousness, learning the ins and outs of Canadian politics and its major players.

Years later Yakovlev could remember the names and sketch character profiles of key aides of the then prime minister, Pierre Trudeau. But it was Trudeau himself who had the greatest impact on Yakovlev's mind—the fiercely independent and proud Trudeau who was occasionally given to scathing criticism of American policies and attitudes, and who secretly viewed with contempt some of his partners in Washington; and the Trudeau who saw the virtues of the U.S. political system and was a friend of America.

Yakovlev remained fascinated by Trudeau, his Cartesian intellect and burning interest in speculative truth. Trudeau seemed to have been equally intrigued by a Soviet diplomat who, as an exchange student, had attended Columbia University in the late fifties, and whose outlook seemed so unlike that of the stereotyped Soviet apparatchik. The two met frequently. "We sometimes had long private sessions without ever talking politics," Yakovlev would recall later. "We discussed philosophical issues, Dostoyevsky, and Pushkin."[10]

The long Canadian sojourn had changed Yakovlev, smoothing the sharp edges of his intellectual abrasiveness. He was enthralled by the vast expanses of Canada and fascinated by its politics. He became more a man of the world, and he taught himself to lubricate the wheels of diplomacy. More important, however, he could talk to Gorbachev at great length and in private about what he had seen from his Ottawa perch as the emergence of a multipolar world with new centers of power—Europe, Japan, the Pacific rim, China.

They also analyzed their country's severe limitations in a changing strategic landscape; nobody in Moscow seemed to pay much attention to a new and threatening equation in the global balance of power as the bipolar world was crumbling. Nor were the Russians making *real* efforts to join the age of high technology. The traditional Soviet concept of the contest between capitalism and communism had become irrelevant and harmful. Yakovlev saw defeat as inevitable— Soviet communism· simply could not keep up, since it had trouble motivating people and promoting innovation. Instead of accepting defeat, they had to come up with a plan, change the rules of the game, set up new goals.

Yakovlev knew that the Soviet Union's power, its military might, rested upon adequate wealth. Countries derived wealth from their productive base, from healthy finances, and from superior technology. Other factors having a direct bearing on power included geography, national morale, and leadership. What the Soviet Union needed, according to both Yakovlev and his new patron, was a renaissance, a national revival.

Chapter 3

THE OLD GUARD'S LAST HURRAH

Gorbachev came back from Canada in the spring of 1983 with a new ally and aide in Yakovlev and with a more developed understanding of foreign affairs. But Andropov needed him on the domestic front. Of all the problems he faced as leader, Andropov felt least at home with the economy. His practical experience had been negligible compared with that of other leaders. He had never run a major province or supervised a major industry. At the start, he acted as though he were still the KGB chairman, seeking to restore social and labor discipline through administrative measures. But Andropov also turned to the experts, and he entrusted his young protégé with sifting through their advice and planning economic strategy.

The experts argued that action had to be taken to reinvigorate the economy. But there were disagreements among them as to what kind of action. Andropov managed to map out the general shape of the needed changes. He assailed the principle of *uravnilovka,* or leveling off of wages, insisting that each person should earn according to the "quality and quantity of work" he or she performed. Andropov never used the word "perestroika"; he even shunned the word "reform," to say nothing of the term "radical reforms," which was to become Gorbachev's rallying cry. Yet he spelled out plans for changes of the entire economic machinery, the use of economic levers such as prices and credits, a new management structure, and redefinition of the lines of authority. In order to galvanize the bureaucracy into action, he set January 1, 1985, as the target date for the establishment of these reforms. He also raised the question of glasnost, or openness, which was to become another major Gorbachev theme. Glasnost, he said at the June 1983 plenum, would bring government and party activities "closer to the interests and needs of the people" and make officials accountable to the population. Andropov himself had first introduced weekly communiqués on the Politburo deliberations, which had been secret before, and he had published, for the first time since the days of Khrushchev, a verbatim account of plenum speeches.

By the summer of 1983, Gorbachev seemed to be the man directing the thrust of Andropov's policies. Next to Andropov, he was the most visible figure on the scene, though he provided a physical contrast to his frail, elderly boss.

Gorbachev was five foot nine, bald, stocky but not fat, and wore steel-rimmed glasses. His only distinguishing features were a red birthmark clearly visible on the front part of his dome and a soft voice with a distinct southern intonation. As far as Russian sophisticates were concerned, he placed the accent on the wrong syllable, the first rather than the second, in words such as *nosil* or *otkril*. This underscored his Stavropol roots. But his age—he was fifty-two at the time and the youngest figure in the leadership—made him, almost by default, the representative of the new generation.

Knowing that he had only a short time to live, Andropov deliberately pushed his protégé to the forefront. He was clearly preoccupied by two things: the fate of his program, and his place in history. In Gorbachev and other men he had advanced to the top ranks, Andropov saw faithful disciples who would continue his work. While still able, Andropov wanted to tell a country accustomed to the rule of a gerontocracy that new and younger men were better equipped to deal with the existing challenges. So he selected Gorbachev to preside over an August 1983 meeting in Moscow with the Old Bolsheviks, who are revered as the founding fathers of the Soviet Union. This was an unusual distinction. Andropov, who on this occasion made his last nationally televised speech, gave a ringing endorsement of the new generation and its representative Gorbachev. The younger, better-educated people were "different and new," he said, but their generation "is in no way worse than ours." Andropov added: "Comrades, we have to admit, though that is not easy for everyone, that each new generation is in some way stronger than the one before. It knows more. It sees further."

This calculated move to make Gorbachev his heir apparent came at the last possible moment.

At the end of August, Andropov went to the Caucasus for a vacation and was never seen in public again. Shortly after Andropov began his "vacation," the sound and fury of the Soviet-American political struggle over the Euromissiles reached unprecedented levels of propaganda and vitriol because of the disastrous shooting down of a Korean jetliner on September 1, and the deaths of all 269 on board. The impact of the disaster on Andropov can only be guessed. His health took a sharp turn for the worse at the end of September, and doctors removed one kidney in early October. He never left his hospital apartment again, becoming an invisible ruler running the country by remote control. Were it not for the loyalty of the KGB, he probably would not have retained his personal authority after October. Only his personal assistants and Gorbachev had regular access to the leader, but they lacked the authority to impose decisions on the senior Old Guard members who still held a majority of Politburo seats.

As executor of Andropov's policies, Gorbachev confronted an extraordinary power struggle at home and one of the major East-West propaganda battles abroad. As the news of Andropov's kidney operation filtered to the upper ranks of the elite, his opponents sensed that the end was near. Their spirits were lifted with each passing day. Andropov's spell over the party bureaucracy was almost shattered by his physical vulnerability, so graphically conveyed by his absence. The prospects for his economic reforms were bleak. So were the chances that Andropov loyalists might secure Gorbachev's immediate succession. The Brezhnevites began quietly but firmly to oppose the leader. Chernenko, the Brezhnevite standard-bearer who had vanished from public view after his defeat in the succession struggle with Andropov, suddenly became visible and active. Government ministries began to manipulate regulations to slow down the movement for change. In November 1983, Georgian leader Eduard Shevardnadze, one of Gorbachev's closest personal friends in the leadership, publicly complained that he had to obtain Andropov's personal intervention to save two "experiments" in his republic from being choked by the bureaucracy.

But Andropov was not in a position to intervene everywhere. By the end of the year, his "economic experiments" and the widespread debate on economic reforms had foundered. The Andropov loyalists still held the levers of power, but they formed a much looser, less powerful coalition than the more numerous and tightly knit Brezhnevites.

Despite the re-entrenchment of the Brezhnevites, it was during this period of transitional politicking and plotting that Gorbachev managed to consolidate the loyalist ranks and expand them through the advancement of younger people in local and regional hierarchies. Initially, Andropov had been slow to purge the party of his opponents. But his illness apparently convinced him that the best thing he could do in the short time left to him was to accelerate the purge. The pretext was provided by elections scheduled for March 1984. As chairman of the election campaign machinery, Gorbachev could select candidates for new party committees in the country's 140 regions and districts. This gave him a chance to strengthen his position within the party machinery and carry out the biggest purge of the regional committees since Khrushchev's day. More important, however, he and Andropov were able to bring new people to the Politburo and Secretariat and to weaken the Old Guard stranglehold on these two key executive bodies.

The new men promoted to the Politburo in December were Vitali Vorotnikov and Mikhail Solomentsev as full members, and KGB Chairman Viktor Chebrikov as alternate member. Yegor Ligachev, whom Andropov had brought from Siberia, joined the Secretariat. Earlier, Andropov had advanced to top posts a number of other figures, including Nikolai Ryzhkov, Lev Zaikov, and Geidar Aliev. It was with the help of these Andropov men that Gorbachev eventually came to power, but not before the Old Guard made their last stand: they succeeded in electing Chernenko general secretary.

∙　　∙　　∙

Chernenko's rule began with incomparable gloom.

Andropov's death on February 9, 1984, came as a surprise. His illness had been a state secret, astonishingly well kept. The choice of another old and sick man to succeed him was a shock. Public reaction, to the extent that it had any importance in Soviet politics at the time, was devastatingly negative.

Along with the sense of vulnerability in the individual leadership was a deepening perception of the degeneration of the system. During Chernenko's short rule, a very telling joke gained widespread currency. "How old is the socialist system in Russia?" the joke began. "Sixty-seven years?" answered the historically minded listener who knew that the Bolshevik revolution occurred in '17. "No, only seven years," said the trickster, "six years under Lenin and one under Andropov." The joke reflected the popular view of the perversion of the system under Stalin, Khrushchev, Brezhnev, and Chernenko. There was something inhuman about the system they created and perpetuated; it had demonstrated only its ability to defend itself by creating a powerful military machine. It had yet to prove—first of all to its own people—that it was capable of delivering enough bread and butter, let alone a better quality of life and opportunity for all. Gorbachev would later address this issue by questioning publicly how it was possible that the Soviet Union could produce sophisticated missiles and nuclear-powered ships but could make only "defective household appliances, shoes, and clothes."[1]

Chernenko had no program of his own. For three decades he had served as Brezhnev's most intimate aide, and he shared his mentor's ideas on domestic and foreign issues. He could not reverse the thrust of Andropov's policies, but he slowed things down so effectively as to render them meaningless. As one senior official later said, "It was like having the driver take his foot off the accelerator." Chernenko's conservative style reassured the bureaucracy and restored the comfortable illusion of order and control. The conservative restoration was the order of the day.

Typical of this world of make-believe was the formal opening of the Baikal–Amur (BAM) railway line on September 27, 1984. Millions of Soviet television viewers saw two crews of jubilant workers lay the "golden link" of this two-thousand-mile railroad, which was designed to complement the famous Trans-Siberian line and move railway traffic farther north, away from the sensitive Chinese border. Amid elaborate ceremonies and self-congratulatory speeches, the "project of the century," a key factor in the future development of Siberia's mineral deposits, was declared completed ahead of schedule. That the Soviets did not allow foreign journalists to ride on the first train—from Irkutsk, near Lake Baikal, in the heart of the country, to the shores of the Pacific Ocean—was suspicious, but not unprecedented. Not until Gorbachev came to power did Soviet newspapers suddenly discover that miles of track were rusting from disuse because the railway had not in fact been finished. It would be completed only by 1989. The 1984 ceremonial opening, it turned out, was an exercise in what the Russians call *pokazukha*—"for show."

Pokazukha is an old Russia standby that has acquired aspects of an art. *Pokazukha* was rampant at the 1980 Moscow Olympics, when entire streets were repaved and planted with trees, and hundreds of city blocks freshly painted almost overnight, to impress foreign guests. *Pokazukha,* which is instinctively practiced on foreigners, far outstrips most nations' efforts to make a favorable impression. Yet only the rare outsider appreciates the extent of deception Russians have traditionally practiced on one another in order to sustain official optimism about their future. From the day the Baikal–Amur Railway project was started in 1974, there had been nothing but good news from the site. It produced official heroes as well as books, films, and songs praising the endurance of workers who braved the inclement Siberian cold and operated in the delicate permafrost conditions. The goal to complete the project by 1983 was never questioned under Brezhnev. Gorbachev, who was in charge of the economy during Andropov's rule, knew that the deadline could not be met and pushed the projected completion date to 1984. When 1984 rolled around with still no end in sight, Chernenko opted for the *pokazukha* opening, rather than acknowledge reality. It was a predictable decision.

The official psyche seemed to be modeled on Oblomov, the antihero of Ivan Goncharov's classic 1859 novel, which Gorbachev was to cite both publicly and privately. A man of pure heart, good intentions, and fanciful ideas, Oblomov is incapable of sustained action. He wallows in inertia, unable to come to terms with life. Shying away from reality, he compensates with his fantasy.

Gorbachev dissociated himself from two other grandiose projects under the Chernenko leadership. One involved the diversion of Russian rivers to irrigate the dry areas of southern Russia and Soviet Central Asia, which was opposed by Russian nationalists in and out of the government because it risked changing the climate and would destroy many old Russian churches and other monuments. The other was the revival of a land-reclamation scheme, something that Gorbachev had publicly criticized before it was introduced in 1984[2] but which Chernenko's ally, Prime Minister Nikolai Tikhonov, announced as government policy at the October 1984 meeting of the Central Committee. The fact that Gorbachev did not speak in support of the project was an eloquent statement of his opposition. Tikhonov presented the policy as a new way of dealing with agricultural problems, although his speech writers lifted large sections of his address from a 1979 article in the journal *Tekhnika Molodyozhi*. The notion of increasing yields by placing more land under inefficient cultivation, instead of extracting greater yields from the already available acreage through more efficient farming, was at the heart of Moscow's developmental problems.

These projects underscored the poverty of ideas of the Chernenko administration. Only in foreign affairs did he leave a mark, by forcing a shift in policy toward the United States. Andropov had broken off the Soviet-American arms talks in Geneva; within a year, Chernenko had resumed the dialogue.

In retrospect, it is clear that Gorbachev never had a chance to challenge Chernenko, nor did he mount an open fight for the job. Gorbachev had grasped the realities of Kremlin politics. He had a fine instinct for maneuvering, but reality provided little space for it. Part of the problem was that the Old Guard still controlled the Politburo, and one of its younger members, Grigori Romanov, fifty-nine, who himself aspired to the top post, was a rival. The majority included Chernenko (seventy-two), Prime Minister Nikolai Tikhonov (seventy-nine), Dinmukhamed Kunaev (sixty-six), Vladimir

Shcherbitsky (sixty-four), Viktor Grishin (sixty-five), and Romanov. Gorbachev had the support of Geidar Aliev, Vitali Vorotnikov, and Mikhail Solomentsev.

The other problem was the prevailing perception that Gorbachev lacked sufficient experience. At fifty-three, he still was regarded as too young and untested; he had been in Moscow for only five years. Two key Politburo figures who denied Gorbachev their support were Defense Minister Dmitri Ustinov (seventy-five) and Foreign Minister Andrei Gromyko (seventy-four). Both owed their high standing to personal talents and accomplishments rather than allegiance to any particular clique. They had supported Andropov, but now they voted against his real heir.

That the Old Guard recognized Gorbachev's strength was demonstrated by the fact that he was presiding officer at the Central Committee plenum that elected Chernenko general secretary of the party. But the new leader did not begin his reign by reassuring the losers; instead he chose to put the younger man in his place by withholding from the public information about Gorbachev's role at the plenum: Gorbachev's brief closing speech to the Central Committee was not published until a week after the event. Chernenko also conspicuously disclosed figures for the 1983 harvest saying that the 190-million-ton yield was not as high as Andropov's men had indicated. The harvest figures for the previous three years, equally poor in production, had been kept secret under Brezhnev. What Chernenko was telling the party, in the oblique way of Soviet politics, was that Gorbachev had not yet earned his spurs. It was an act of malice that made personal relations between the two men chilly, although both tried to obscure that in public.

Chernenko moved against a number of Andropov loyalists, but the most significant victim of the purge was Marshal Nikolai Ogarkov, chief of staff under Andropov, who was dismissed from his job and reassigned to an obscure theater command. A brilliant and forceful figure, Ogarkov was one of the main Andropov supporters in the armed forces. During the last year of Brezhnev's rule, Ogarkov openly criticized the leadership in his book *Always on Guard in Defense of the Fatherland.* In the conditions of American technological challenge, he said, "the failure to change views in time, and stagnation in the development and deployment of new kinds of military construction, are fraught with serious danger."

With the death of Andropov, Gorbachev's position in the establishment changed dramatically. He was no longer a loyal aide and assistant, but the leader of a coalition put together by his mentor. He had matured politically, and he was on his own. It was during the Chernenko interlude, his aides said later, that Gorbachev gained a clear view of the country's problems and of the kind of leader he meant to be. His true personality, which would be revealed fully only once he was in power, began to show through during the Chernenko interlude. He began to say unpopular things, addressing himself invariably to reason rather than to the passions. He became more assertive. Gromyko, when he nominated Gorbachev to the post of general secretary, admired his independent style. Gorbachev, Gromyko told the Central Committee, was a man of strong convictions who said what was on his mind, regardless of whether it pleased the person he was talking to.

Gorbachev's situation, however, was difficult, and could be compared to that of an American vice-president running for election. Power was within his reach, yet he had to moderate his thirst for it. He could not criticize Chernenko, whom he privately despised, yet he had to uphold the banner of the Andropov loyalists and cultivate an image of a forceful politician with his own leadership style.

It was during this period, particularly after the perpetually ailing Chernenko began to spend more time in the Kremlin hospital, that Gorbachev displayed his political skills. In Chernenko's absence, he chaired the weekly meetings of the Politburo, and did so "brilliantly," as Gromyko would say later, "without any exaggeration." He was also involved in building alliances and making deals. While acting as a loyal deputy, he asked experts within the establishment to prepare position papers along the lines of Andropov's program, with the result that he was able to present his own program five weeks after he assumed power. He hailed Chernenko as "the soul of the

Politburo" but kept a cautious distance from his master, complaining about the "inertia of thinking" that "as a rule generates inertia in practical matters."

In a December 1984 speech in Moscow, Gorbachev also indirectly contradicted his chief's benign and optimistic pronouncements. The country, he said, must be prepared for a new industrial revolution, which would require the same sacrifices and the same demonstration of political will that made possible Stalin's industrialization of the thirties. "Without the hard work and complete dedication of each and every one," he said, "it is not even possible to preserve what has been achieved." In short, the Soviet Union had entered a period of decline, which if not arrested and reversed, would become irreversible. He talked about the need to have confidence in people who do not accept "simplistic answers" and who perceive "acutely the hypocrisy that stems from inability or reluctance to see the real contradiction of social development." Gorbachev revealed that he was moving in the direction of market socialism. He asserted that "commodity-money relations do exist under socialism" and that he was looking for ways to apply "such economic levers as prices, realistic cost, profit, credit, and some others." It was, he added, "essential to learn how to make better use of these levers without forgetting of course that under socialism their character and purpose are different from those under capitalism." It was a strong speech that could not have been published in the press without creating a sensation. Only a hundred thousand copies of the full text were distributed to party organizations in pamphlet form, and not until a week later.[3]

In one other arena, Gorbachev expressed his own, rather than his leader's, views. Andropov had initiated a revision of the Communist Party program with the admonition that parts of it were "divorced from reality." Chernenko, who did not share this view, undertook to supervise its revisions, assuring the party bureaucracy that he intended to "retain everything that has been earlier accomplished," adding the conservative cry "This is how it was in the past; this will always remain so in the future." Gorbachev distanced himself from this view. In a February 1985 speech in Stavropol, Gorbachev addressed the issue less than obliquely, arguing for the need to "consolidate and to develop positive trends, and to bolster and augment everything new and progressive that has become part of our social life recently"—defining the word "recently" as coinciding with the fifteen months of Andropov's rule.

But although such rhetorical high-wire acts were scrutinized by the establishment and by foreign Kremlinologists, they were generally ignored by ordinary people. What the country at large knew about Gorbachev was next to nothing.

The population got its first real glimpse of Gorbachev during his visit to Britain in December 1984, a visit that decisively turned a substantial section of the establishment in his favor.

Gorbachev took a considerable risk by exposing himself to the focus of the Western media, which guaranteed that any mistake he made would be published and magnified. His enemies may have remembered another ambitious Soviet politician, Politburo member and former KGB Chairman Alexander Shelepin, whose visit to London in 1966 turned into a public-relations disaster and led to Shelepin's disgrace. Shelepin had been involved in the plot against Khrushchev and was vaulted to full Politburo membership on the day of Khrushchev's ouster. He was later appointed KGB chairman, but then moved back into the Central Committee in a bid for supreme power. Brezhnev, who viewed him as a dangerous rival, engineered his removal from the leadership following the British visit, which produced mass demonstrations against Shelepin as KGB chairman and proved his ineptness in operating in the Western environment.

If Chernenko's supporters hoped that England would be as inhospitable to Gorbachev as it had been to Shelepin, they were disappointed. Gorbachev's visit turned into a public-relations triumph. His intelligence, poise, and composure commanded the attention of television viewers everywhere—in England, in Europe, in the United States, and, every night, at home. After a series of old leaders who read monotonous speeches from sheets of paper held in their trembling hands, the sight of a vigorous young Soviet leader displaying showmanship, smooth public relations, charm, and grace delighted the Soviet public. He was a natural television personality, conveying a casual tone, a self-deprecating wit, a quick repartee, and a sense of personal warmth. Here was someone who could compete with President Reagan in the public-relations game that he had invented.

The Soviet public also saw Raisa for the first time; and the reaction was positive. Although a grandmother, she was trim and elegant, defying the embarrassing stereotype of the good-natured, fat *babushka* with gold teeth, felt boots, and a bright scarf tied under her chin. She had more than a touch of her husband's Luciferian pride. In London, the Gorbachevs stood together as a couple who represented the new Soviet generation.

Prime Minister Margaret Thatcher summed up the Western view by describing Gorbachev as "a man I could do business with." Though Yakovlev was at Gorbachev's elbow throughout the visit, and provided excellent briefings, they could not have given a less secure visitor the poise and confidence Gorbachev displayed. His manner was so striking at the time (he was being compared with his predecessors) that it obscured his inexperience.

There was one incident that showed this up but it went unnoticed during his London visit. Acting in terms of his Stavropol experiences, he unexpectedly stopped his cavalcade in Whitehall, walked along Downing Street, and rang the bell of Number 10, telling startled officials that he had already met Mrs. Thatcher at Chequers and now just wanted to see her London home.

Defense Minister Ustinov's death while Gorbachev was traveling in Britain underscored the feebleness of the Old Guard. Gorbachev announced the fact to his hosts, and then rushed back home. Ustinov's death and Chernenko's hospitalization in January 1985 ushered in a period of backstage political struggles that left the Kremlin adrift. Rumors began to circulate in Moscow that Chernenko was dying and that either Romanov or Grishin was his designated successor.

Romanov, a forceful figure of unquestionable administrative ability, was for many years the communist boss of Leningrad, the second most important industrial area of the country, and had developed close links with the military-industrial complex. His mind was conventional, and his manners were crude. In Leningrad, he ruled like a medieval potentate and behaved like one too. For his daughter's wedding he requisitioned Catherine the Great's china from the Hermitage Museum, a fact that became known when some priceless pieces were broken in the revelry. Romanov's strategy to stop Gorbachev involved advancing the candidacy of Grishin, the party boss of Moscow since 1967, who was known for his corruption. In February and early March, Grishin was the most visible figure of all the Politburo members, and Gorbachev supporters were worried. If he was not elected after Chernenko's death, they feared, Gorbachev's political future looked bleak.

At the end of February, Chernenko failed to appear at a Kremlin pre-election rally, and his speech was read for him. The elections themselves were meaningless—a preordained ritual to give a democratic gloss to political life. But the leaders were required to play their scripted roles. Grishin, who presided on this occasion, told the nation that the leader had stayed home "on the doctor's recommendation" but that he had asked Grishin to convey his greetings to the voters in his district. For Soviet audiences, this meant that the leader was seriously ill and that yet another transition was under way. Two days later, escorted by Grishin, a visibly weak Chernenko appeared on television as he cast his vote. He looked pathetically frail, his face blank, his eyes unfocused, and he seemed to be in pain, not fully aware of what was going on. Journalists were not invited to watch the leader cast his ballot, which raised suspicions that the television footage might have come from a makeshift polling station inside the Kremlin hospital compound at Kuntsevo. These suspicions were compounded by an unusual Foreign Ministry invitation to observe Gorbachev cast his ballot.

Casting his vote, Gorbachev looked tense and worried, although he sought to appear relaxed. His granddaughter Oksana helped him cast his ballot, acting as a diversion for foreign television crews. But national television that evening showed only Chernenko and Grishin at the polling station, a macabre exercise that seemed to have been staged to show Grishin as Chernenko's anointed heir apparent.

The dying Chernenko, accompanied by Grishin, appeared once again on television, on March 2, this time receiving a group of electoral officials. That was his last public function. With Chernenko out of sight, other actors continued to follow the implacable Kremlin protocol as if nothing unusual was happening. It was difficult to sort out the confusing signals. The Soviet Union seemed at that point an empire without an emperor. Its day-to-day business was conducted by Chernenko's personal aides, acting in his name. In an atmosphere of Byzantine intrigue, key players were positioning themselves for the power transfer. Romanov and Gorbachev vanished from public view. Gorbachev, who had earlier been scheduled to lead a Soviet parliamentary delegation on a visit to the United States in early March, decided to remain in Moscow; Shcherbitsky, the Ukrainian leader, took his place.

On March 5, Chernenko's wife, Anna, hosted an annual reception for the women of Moscow's diplomatic community at the Kremlin guest house in the Lenin Hills. The sumptuous banquet was followed by a dance, despite the absence of men. Brezhnev's widow, Viktoria, was there, and so was Raisa Gorbachev. Guests noticed, however, that Raisa remained on the sidelines and seemed careful not to up-stage the more senior Kremlin wives. A few months earlier she had captivated Britain's gossip columnists with her chic wardrobe, appearing in a cream satin two-piece dress, gold lamé sandals with chain straps, and pearl-drop earrings; on this occasion she wore a dark suit and no jewelry.

A week later, on March 12, 1985, Chernenko's death was announced, after about twelve hours of funeral dirges broadcast by radio and television. Four hours later Moscow Radio and Tass announced Gorbachev's election as general secretary of the Soviet Communist Party.

How had it all come about? Predictably, the official version reported harmony and the enthusiastic support of the old barons for the young tsar.

It is difficult to know what exactly transpired during the twenty-four-hour period following Chernenko's death. The Kremlin chooses its leaders in total secrecy. But from public pronouncements and private disclosures it is clear that Gorbachev's election was no straightforward matter. It was, in fact, a close call.

The tactic chosen by Gorbachev and his supporters was one of quick action. The plenum of the Central Committee was convened within twenty-four hours as the top officials in Moscow debated candidates. As expected, Romanov advanced the candidacy of Grishin, who had the support of Tikhonov, Kunaev, and Shcherbitsky. Gromyko proposed Gorbachev, who was supported by Solomentsev, Aliev, and Vorotnikov. The stalemate among full Politburo members began to turn in Gorbachev's favor when other members of the leadership, nonvoting Politburo members and secretaries of the Central Committee, were taken into account. As luck would have it, Shcherbitsky was in the United States, and returned to Moscow only after the succession issue was settled. Gorbachev supporter Vorotnikov had broken off his visit to Yugoslavia and returned home on the night of March 10 in time to cast his vote for Gorbachev. Gorbachev's personal friend Shevardnadze, a nonvoting Politburo member, turned out to be his most articulate supporter during the leadership session in the evening hours of March 10. Other key supporters at this level included Chebrikov, the KGB chairman and a nonvoting Politburo member, and Yegor Ligachev and Nikolai Ryzhkov, both secretaries of the Central Committee. The leadership in general—the twenty-odd men at the top—was leaning toward Gorbachev.

All credible accounts from knowledgeable sources, including Central Committee members present at the meeting, agree that the candidacies of both pretenders were advanced at the March 11 plenum, and that Gorbachev was victorious by a slim margin. More than three years later, during a riveting and unusually personal defense of party conservatives at the Nineteenth Party Conference, Yegor Ligachev told a nationwide TV audience that he, Gromyko, Chebrikov, and Solomentsev had helped tip the balance in Gorbachev's favor. "A completely different decision could have been made," Ligachev said. "Quite different people could be sitting on this podium, and this conference might not be taking place at all."[4] Ligachev delivered his speech in response to sharp criticism from the reformists, and after public calls for the removal from power of Gromyko, Solomentsev, *Pravda* editor-in-chief Viktor Afanasiev, Georgi Arbatov, and other figures perceived as opponents of perestroika.

The crucial role at the plenum was played by Gromyko, the senior Politburo member who had come to symbolize in the eyes of the party the continuity of more than four decades of Soviet history. Gromyko's vote of confidence carried great weight with the three-hundred-member Central Committee, whose average age was sixty-six and who were temperamentally more favorably disposed toward the familiar Grishin. Gromyko spoke without notes, an indication of the haste and uncertainties surrounding the proceedings. He was both eloquent and unusually emotional, trying to reassure the Old Guard that Gorbachev was tough and shrewd and that they should not be deceived by his youth.

"Comrades," one Central Committee member later quoted Gromyko as saying, "this man has a nice smile but he's got iron teeth." The remark, which was excised from the published text, was more than revealing about the kind of doubts the Soviet elite had about Gorbachev. They did not know much about him; nor had he spent sufficient time in Moscow to establish firm links with the main institutions of power, especially the military-industrial complex. What did he know about foreign and security issues? The twenty-three years in provincial Stavropol, and the subsequent four years dealing with agriculture in Moscow, did not seem like the proper training for a leader of Russia. In practical terms, he had fewer ties with the main branches of party and state administration than any other top leader in Soviet history.

Gromyko repeatedly praised Gorbachev's "sharp and deep" mind and his "brilliant" analytical skill. Gromyko extolled Gorbachev's political gifts, his ability to relate to the people, adding that "this is not given to everyone." During Chernenko's illness, he said, Gorbachev provided "brilliant" leadership. Gromyko reassured the Old Guard, as only he could, that Gorbachev had an excellent grasp of foreign affairs. This, he said, is "perhaps somewhat clearer to me because of my long service than to some other comrades."

What were Gromyko's motives in making a breach within the Old Guard? Did he know that quite soon he was to be promoted to a weak presidency? Most likely he did. What he probably could not anticipate at the time was that he would be nudged out even from this ceremonial position once Gorbachev decided to turn it into the executive presidency and assume the title himself. Colleagues close to Gromyko said later that at seventy-six he was truly concerned that the country appeared to be drifting dangerously and that his siding with Gorbachev was an act of patriotism.[5]

Finally, in what was perhaps the clearest indication of a strong opposition to the man from Stavropol, Gromyko warned the Politburo that foreign enemies of Moscow, "hungry for a glimpse of disagreements," were looking for "some cracks in the Soviet leadership."

The news of Gorbachev's election was greeted with joy by a nation weary of the shadow of death that had been hanging over the Kremlin for the preceding three years. Gorbachev was now fifty-four, still the youngest member of the leadership. He was strong and healthy. Finally the Russian people could count on a leader who would be around for years to come. Brezhnev had died in 1982 after holding power as a dying man during his last year. His successor, Andropov, lasted only fifteen months before he was succeeded by another dying man, Chernenko, whose tenure was two months shorter. The frequency of state funerals fueled a joke about the authorities' issuing season passes for the best viewing places in Red Square. It was not so much Gorbachev's personality and program that made people rejoice: he was an uncertain and dim figure unknown even within the establishment. What was important was that Gorbachev's accession symbolized an end to troubled transitions and the anxieties they bred.

Chapter 4

BOLD BEGINNINGS

The new reign did not begin with a blaze of hope.

On March 14, 1985, as Mikhail Gorbachev appeared before the country for the first time as its new leader, he looked very much like the dour men in black coats and fur hats who stood with him atop the Lenin Mausoleum. His voice was firm and clear, but his message was conventional.

Few people watching Gorbachev on that balmy and sunny March morning in Red Square had any idea that they were witnessing the inauguration of a powerful reformist leader. The iron Kremlin protocol was followed to the letter. To the strains of Chopin's "Funeral March" echoing through the cavernous square, Chernenko's open coffin was rolled out on an olive-green gun carriage in a resplendent procession led by army officers in full dress uniform: Persian-lamb hats, light-gray overcoats, white gloves, gold belts and lanyards.

At noon sharp, the country came to a standstill as the body was lowered into the ground behind the mausoleum. The leaders and family members lined up by the grave; Gorbachev threw in the first shovelful of earth, and the others followed. The Politburo members then climbed back onto the deep-red granite structure that glistened in the sun. The fifteen-hundred-man band struck up a martial tune, and the troops staged a colorful and spirited parade. The tsar was dead; long live the tsar.

And yet, even in this first public function, there were subtle intimations of changes to come—hints caught by diplomats and observers but not by the country at large. The most striking was the absence of senior military men—only three of them were present—in the leadership lineup atop the mausoleum (and even they were carefully cropped out of the photographs that appeared in the next day's newspapers).

Other changes simply involved concessions to modernity and common sense in the somewhat macabre, Byzantine ritual of state funerals. For the first time soldiers, not the Politburo members, carried the dead leader's open coffin to its resting place. The leaders followed at some distance behind the coffin. They also dispensed with the tradition of kissing the dead man's lips shortly before the coffin was closed.

After the military parade, Gorbachev went to the Kremlin for a two o'clock reception at which he presented himself to presidents, prime ministers, princes, and potentates from more than 120 countries. He subsequently held separate, private conversations with foreign dignitaries, including Prime Minister Margaret Thatcher of Britain, Chancellor Helmut Kohl of West Germany, President François Mitterrand of France, Vice-President George Bush and Secretary of State George Shultz of the United States, President Zia ul-Haq of Pakistan, and Deputy Premier Li Peng of China. The Western impression was of a smart and decisive man.

"Kuda driftuyet Federalnaya Respublika?"—"Which way is the Federal Republic drifting?"—was the way he greeted Kohl.[1] Andreas Meyer Landruth, the West German deputy foreign minister at the time, perhaps the West's most knowledgeable analyst of Soviet affairs, accompanied Kohl and was struck by Gorbachev's use of the English word "drift" rather than a Russian word, suggesting that he either was studying English or had accepted the jargon of Moscow think-tank experts. Kohl later publicly likened Gorbachev's skills to those of Nazi propaganda chief Joseph Goebbels, an invidious comparison which angered Gorbachev and delayed their next meeting by several years.

Only Mrs. Thatcher saw him as an entirely new phenomenon, having seen him at some length in London four months earlier.

George Bush, upon his return to Washington, described Gorbachev as an "impressive idea salesman," an assessment that stuck for a long time in official Washington, even after it became clear that Gorbachev was a doer with a strong sense of mission rather than merely a huckster trying to con the West.

Few Russians who watched Gorbachev perform his initiation rites that day expected much from the new man. All too frequently they had seen their hopes dashed. They had just begun to believe in Andropov when he died, leaving Chernenko to throw a wet blanket over popular aspirations. They knew next to nothing about Gorbachev's past. Except for his youth, there was very little to distinguish him from his colleagues. Like them, he wore conservative business suits. Like them, he had been seen sitting stony-faced through interminable Kremlin rituals and speeches whose purpose was incantational rather than informative. Like them, he praised Chernenko as "an outstanding party leader and statesman." How were they to know that it was the last time Gorbachev would say anything positive about Chernenko, and then only because it was the man's funeral? Gorbachev's career seemed conventional, a sure sign that he would become a replica of his predecessors.

Most people simply did not care. The crises of the eighties—such as the war in Afghanistan and the rapidly declining economy—had made the Soviets weary. At the popular level, few paid much attention to the speeches and promises of Kremlin leaders. In Russia, one of our acquaintances said at the time, paraphrasing the nineteenth-century literary critic Alexander Nikitenko, "all our enterprises begin with words and evaporate in words." And the propaganda had made them cynical. "Where are we going to have the next crucial military event in history?" intellectuals jested, alluding to the fact that military history had been rewritten in order to glorify the careers of his precedessors, and that Gorbachev was too young to have taken part in World War Two and therefore would tax severely the inventiveness of the regime's public-relations department. Stalin, of course, won the war and was described as a military genius. Khrushchev was also depicted as a great military leader who had engineered the victory at Stalingrad. The propaganda machine turned a World War Two battle at Malaya Zemlya, in which Brezhnev took part as a colonel, into the most decisive point of the war. Everyone knew that Andropov ran partisan units on the Soviet-Finnish front, but once he became leader the propaganda machinery extolled the importance of partisan warfare. Partisans, operating behind Nazi lines, suddenly seemed to have done far more to ensure victory than was previously known. Chernenko's service as a private with the border troops in Central Asia in the early thirties produced literature about his fearless exploits as a cavalryman fighting Moslem insurgents. No military service could be as important as securing the frontiers of the motherland.

Virtually all initial assessments of Gorbachev turned out to be wrong. The heavily conservative ruling establishment, however reluctantly, had entrusted him with supreme power following the advice of men such as Andropov and Gromyko. But few of its members had any inkling at the time that Gorbachev would turn out to be a forceful figure whose relentless quest for change would so severely upset the traditional pattern of life. Even one of his closest advisers and strongest supporters in the Politburo, Alexander Yakovlev, conceded that much. "I knew that there would be changes," he said a few years after Gorbachev's leadership began, "but if in 1985 you had said that all these things that are now happening would happen, I'd have given my arm that that was not possible."[2]

Only in Stavropol did people know that he was a man of much tougher fiber than was generally perceived in the initial months of his stewardship. Gorbachev had been three months in power when we traveled to Stavropol to hear people who knew him in the past say with knowing smiles that the country was in for a surprise, that Gorbachev was an activist with an unconventional mind and a man who meant business, a brilliantly persuasive human bulldozer determined to get his own way. "The Muscovites had better wait a bit—they have yet to see the real Mikhail Sergeyevich."

With the accession of Gorbachev, the Soviet Union entered a new phase in its history. After a long interregnum and two temporary tsars, a real transfer of power had been accomplished. The spring was an exciting time for people around him; they felt they were ushering in a new period of action and forward movement. It did not seem to matter that the surge of optimism in the reformist camp was based more on possibilities than on accomplishments. What mattered was the prospect of a new beginning.

Gorbachev plunged into his job with zest. As was his style when he was preparing major decisions, he spent long hours in brainstorming sessions with his top aides, either in the Kremlin or, more frequently, at a dacha outside Moscow. He rarely appeared tired and always seemed ready to accept responsibility. Later he would talk of his eagerness to do things well and to "work an *extra bit harder*. For me it is not just a slogan, but a habitual state of mind, a disposition. Any job one takes on must be grasped and felt with one's soul, mind and heart; only then will one work an extra bit harder."[3] From the first, there was a revealing stylistic difference between him and his predecessors when talking about policies. They suggested that they were speaking for the whole Soviet people; Gorbachev kept saying, "*I* think."

His aides said later that his general course was set from the very beginning and he wanted to make it public as soon as possible. But a formulation of practical policies had yet to come. Gorbachev was caught in a dilemma. He felt strongly that "timid, creeping reforms" could not take the country out of "the quagmire of conservatism and [break] the inertia of stagnation." But at the same time, he felt, "acting in a revolutionary way does not imply a headlong dash. Cavalry attacks are far from being always appropriate."[4]

Gorbachev's overall strategy involved modernizing the country, which, as he was already aware, would necessitate modernizing its political system. The pressures for a political reform came from an accumulation of social strains and problems, rather than from any particular power base.

Initially Gorbachev talked in general terms about the need for contested elections, at least at lower levels of authority, for the rule of law, and even for mandatory rotation of political positions and public accountability. These checks and balances, he felt, should be a standard part of the socialist system.

He was painfully aware that the country's despotic past was weighing heavily on its present, and that the resulting lack of political and social culture would make his quest to take the Soviet Union into the high-tech age very difficult. "Today," he told a meeting of young communists, "we clearly see that many of the problems in the reconstruction and renewal of society are brought about by the lack of culture in the broad sense. Research-intensive high technology cannot exist and develop without a corresponding cultural infrastructure, without further development of our way of life as a whole. Any gap between these spheres poses the threat of social tensions."[5] His "historic task" was to improve living standards and "create conditions for the all-round realization" of each individual's abilities.

The Stalinist system of coercion and deception was hindering social and economic development, producing a chaos Gorbachev wanted to tame. He had an abiding faith in man as a rational being committing rational acts. Having reached the conclusion that the system was no longer rational, he wanted to improve it and make it rational. If he explained things, he believed, his compatriots would share his conclusions.

The Soviet system had been perpetuating the worst features of imperial Russia, enforcing a uniformity and obedience that spawned passivity and a lack of social and civic responsibility. The system, in effect, had turned Russia into a country of "political illiterates," as one Gorbachev aide put it. Gorbachev wanted to restructure the system (perestroika), and he wanted to do so in his own way. He was not prepared to use violence as Stalin did when he carried out the country's industrialization with the utmost brutality while hiding the facts from the people. Nor did he want to succumb to the practice of deception, which even the reformist-minded Khrushchev used with relish, attempting to galvanize the country with the promises of a nebulous future bliss which could be shaped to anyone's fantasy. In private, Gorbachev had frequently quoted Goncharov's hero Oblomov, who dreamed of a land where people did nothing but enjoy themselves and had no cares and sorrows.[6]

Oblomov had captured a quintessential part of the Russian character, the tendency to escape from reality into make-believe. Gorbachev felt that the system was feeding on this negative streak, that it survived by playing on the theme of future happiness and bliss, and that it therefore shied away from the present. This had been

Gorbachev's main quarrel with Khrushchev's boundless optimism. Even after Khrushchev's ouster, pretense had remained at the heart of the system, something that would prompt Gorbachev to decry publicly the situation of the late seventies and early eighties, when, as he put it, "the world of day-to-day realities and that of make-believe well-being were increasingly parting ways."[7] *"S narodom nelzya zaigrivat!"* he told the country early in his leadership. "One mustn't toy with the people"—boldly suggesting that his predecessors had done just that.

Gorbachev would not recognize publicly the magnitude of the contradiction between his quest for democratization and a Marxist-Leninist party's rule. It seems he did not do it privately either, accustomed to the coexistence of all the contradictions within his own soul. Although he was brought up in a communist society, and although Leninist jargon had become his native tongue, his mind was not conventional; he lacked the doctrinaire belief in the sanctity of Bolshevik traditions. Encouraged by the teaching of his mother and grandmother and the events of his Stavropol youth, including his grandfather's arrest, he absorbed many traditional religious and nationalist values. He instinctively took the communist side in a historical argument, but he rejected the pompous rhetoric, the anti-intellectualism, the anticlericalism, and the fear of the West that had characterized the Bolshevik era. He sought to rescue communist doctrine from fundamentalism and revive its relevance to the modern world.

Only when the political facts of life began pounding away at his program—woefully early in his tenure—did Gorbachev come down from the stratosphere of his initial euphoria to feel the full impact facing those who challenge the deeply embedded interests of the elite or ruling *nomenklatura*.

Nor did he seem in his first year to appreciate fully just how intractable the problems were—the old traditions, the poverty, the scope of economic mismanagement, the overextension of the empire under Brezhnev, the insoluble issues of the arms race, and especially the party bureaucracy's insidious grip on power. The Gorbachev

team was optimistic, and perestroika was its rallying cry during the first year.

Gorbachev's populist approach was partly rooted in his makeup. In Stavropol he had relied on personal contact, on seeing for himself. Now he went to the people, because he wanted to "see, hear, learn, and understand as much as possible [about their problems] and form my own judgment on the basis of my impressions."[8] Then, convinced that his motives were pure and his judgment flawless, he would decide what was good for them, like a good tsar.

As an empiricist, who treated ideas primarily as tools of practical judgment, he thought that by opening up society he would not only draw people into the political process but also subdue the crusty party bureaucracy. The paradox of the leaden age of Brezhnev, who disliked changes, was that it did not prevent a natural change in Soviet society. The Brezhnev era produced a large professional middle class—younger, better educated, and more highly skilled. But it gave that new class no share of power. Andropov had identified the growing tensions between a new society and the old system; Gorbachev had to appeal directly to the new society. Andropov had started, however cautiously, to move toward market socialism; Gorbachev wanted to move forcefully and quickly break down the inertia. It was a daunting course, but it was "the only way that made sense," his close adviser Yakovlev said privately.[9]

But optimism, as Raymond Aron once said, and as the Gorbachev camp was soon to discover, usually involves an intellectual error. The error among Gorbachev advisers was that they miscalculated the scope of resistance to change, within both the party and society. And also the capacity of the system to be changed. These misjudgments were due to a large extent to the narrow political background of the leader and most of his men. They were from the provinces. Men like Brezhnev, Andropov, and Chernenko, whatever their shortcomings of intellect and background, had long association with the central and regional party organizations and were able to create a wide personal network of alliances long before they conquered the central machinery of power in Moscow. Brezhnev was for a while in charge of the military-industrial complex; Andropov spent fifteen years as KGB chairman. Chernenko ran the country for several years in the name of the ailing Brezhnev. Gorbachev, however, had spent most of his career in Stavropol and, when first in Moscow, dealt with agricultural problems.

Gorbachev had seized the levers of power in Moscow in the belief that once he controlled the machinery of party and state he would be able to bend both to his wishes. But his approach was something like Jimmy Carter's, and it soon would lead him into the same fundamental clash that sabotaged Carter's presidency. Like Carter, he was a provincial politician, well educated, dedicated, and imbued with a sense of mission. Like Carter, he had limited links to his establishment and surrounded himself with people of similar background. And, like the former peanut farmer, who ran against Washington only to learn later that he badly needed the establishment if he were to be an effective president, Gorbachev too would discover that control of the machinery of government is not enough to secure effective power.

Gradually Gorbachev's increasing frustrations with the party, which he needed as a tool of change, would harden his view that the party bureaucracy could not cleanse itself of corruption, inertia, and self-preoccupation, and that instead he would have to turn to the people to bring the party into line with his program. Early on he began forging ties to the intellectual and professional classes and easing pressure on the Russian Orthodox Church, which was preparing to celebrate in 1988 the millennium of Christianity in Russia. There was speculation that he held out an olive branch to the church because his religious mother and other relatives had made him aware of the strength of religious sentiment in the country, despite seven decades of antireligious policies.[10] More likely, however, he was rallying public support, particularly in rural areas, by subtly appealing to Russian nationalism. According to official Soviet estimates, forty million of the country's 280 million people consider themselves believers; the real number, however, is probably more than twice that figure, and Gorbachev seemed to be inviting them to celebrate their faith: "Believers are Soviet people, workers, patriots, and they have full right to express their conviction with dignity," he said to church leaders he invited to the Kremlin in April 1988.[11]

In retrospect, his generous stance toward the church anticipated his steps toward a far broader public openness: an openness that would be known as glasnost. In his second year, as his frustrations grew, Gorbachev would add glasnost to perestroika as a second rallying cry. The idea was that the mass media would expose the procedures and corruption of the government machinery to the critical gaze of the people, who would be enlisted as watchdogs against bureaucratic abuse.[12] Glasnost would also allow Gorbachev to keep his finger on the pulse of the nation. (Gorbachev and many of his colleagues were aware that the term "glasnost" also had been used by Andropov. But it was when researchers discovered that Lenin had used the word twenty-three times that "glasnost" was assured a patina of historical and ideological respectability.)

In his first months as leader, Gorbachev revealed his strong mistrust of verbosity and sloganeering by cutting off or criticizing senior figures who resorted to the banality of official rhetoric when presenting their briefs. He himself was garrulous as he preached perestroika, but he would not listen to a windbag. Georgi Arbatov, his adviser on American affairs, described Gorbachev in this way: "He likes to call in experts and grill them in detail on topics he feels uncertain about. He keeps you on your toes. He will forgive you once, or even twice, if you are unable to brief him well. But after that he will be ruthless and just cut you off. He does not like to waste time."[13]

When Health Minister Sergei Buryenkov was summoned to give an analysis of the state of alcoholism in the country, Gorbachev practically expelled him from his office. "We did not ask you to come here and tell us that alcoholism is bad; we know that," Gorbachev said. "You'd better come back and tell us what we can do about it." He wanted facts and dispassionate analysis of them. And he did not forget what he heard. He confounded experts by having more facts and figures at his fingertips than they did, publicly humiliating those who disagreed with him.

He was a consummate politician, and as such he was prepared to use calculated stratagems to meet the needed ends; he was prepared to hide facts, to maneuver in the dark and act in secret, to plot against opponents and use people and situations to his advantage. In foreign affairs, he was ready to deploy the tools of diplomatic deception to advance his country's interests. From the start he had focused on efforts to crimp the advance of America's Strategic Defense Initiative (SDI), Reagan's plan for a Star Wars–type space shield against incoming missiles, and his skillful and subtle maneuvering was potentially more effective than the heavy-handed approach of his predecessors.

But he also wanted to level with his people. Even while Chernenko was in power, Gorbachev was critical of the absence of "honesty and frankness" in dealing with the population. He felt that any policy built on lies and deception could not be sustained over a long term. He broadened his criticism to an even more sensitive issue when he directly assailed the Kremlin's preoccupation with security policies at the expense of living standards. "Any decision, any step in practical matters should be appraised above all from the point of view of what they would bring to the people," he said. "Disregard for the people's needs cannot be justified by any reference to circumstances outside individual control."[14]

Once in power, he would emphasize the first point by saying that the country was at a historical turning point and that at such time "moments of truth are as necessary as the breath of life."[15] And he stated that the challenge of raising the living standards of the Soviet people while maintaining adequate defenses—he put it in that order—would determine "the fate of socialism in the world."[16]

That was his central approach—an approach that made him seem, in the West, a moderate and less threatening figure. It also alarmed Western skeptics into suspecting that the Gorbachev image was packaged and merchandised solely to lull the West while the Kremlin continued stealthily to pursue its dream of world hegemony.[17] This view reduced every change Gorbachev was making to another, this time devilishly more clever, plot by the Bolsheviks to deceive the West and the world.

Arthur Hartman, the U.S. ambassador to Moscow from 1981 to

1987, saw Gorbachev as different—but only in style. "I think he is a very orthodox man who wants to see the Marxist-Leninist system work, but he talks in a very different manner. He is less hidebound by the ideological terminology and so he sounds like a modern man." When Gorbachev talks about democracy, Hartman said, he means "more involvement by the mass of people; it does not mean that the mass is going to direct anything."[18]

The skeptics in the United States and Europe had a powerful argument, at least initially. As Gorbachev's reforms unfolded, it was clear that they involved attempts to change the nature of the Communist Party without endangering its primacy. When he talked about democracy, he talked about achieving it as a long-term process. But within a year his language was tougher. On one occasion, when addressing Soviet writers in a June 1986 closed meeting, he bemoaned the absence of a "loyal opposition"—doing so to underscore the lack of a correction mechanism within the party. "How can we control ourselves?" he added. More and more he seemed to move away from the traditional Kremlin attitudes. It was no longer possible to dismiss what was happening in Russia as illusion or to debunk his policy as sham.

A year later, in July 1987, he told a group of editors that glasnost had engaged Soviet society in a learning process. "We do not have a cultural tradition of discussions and polemics, where one respects the views of an opponent. We are an emotional people and possibly we shall grow out of that. I do not pretend to know the absolute truth; we have to search for truth together."

The remark revealed the historical grain of Gorbachev's intelligence. State power in Russia had always been intimidating, crushing. This was a legacy most evident during the quarter-century of Stalin's supreme power when an all-pervasive system of patronage developed. Lower officials were indebted to higher officials, and all higher officials were indebted to the leader. Stalin's wanton liquidation of his generals and high party officials in the purges of the 1930s were a logical consequence of the totalitarian machinery of the state. The legacy prevented the people from developing a sense of civic responsibility and precluded the evolution of the concept of freedom under the law. Early on Yakovlev talked about his boss's preoccupation with the idea of legality, with the development of laws and practices that would ensure that each individual would "know his rights and obligations. These notions may sound banal," he said, "but people's rights should be a natural thing. The problem is, our people tend to forget their obligations."

In the brainstorming sessions of that spring of 1985, the main preoccupation was to prepare society for changes. As Yakovlev put it, "The first thing was to eliminate the stupidities and injustices in life and to establish a firm ground for economic development. But the main task was to establish civilized relations in society and to teach people to think. We have to make them think on their own. Man has to have the freedom of choice, and make his choices by himself."[19]

But at that stage the freedom of choice Yakovlev and others talked about was limited. There were echoes of the Russian past in this contradiction. Gorbachev was like a benevolent tsar whose motives were beyond reproach and who knew what was best for his people. His call for a transformation of national values and purposes, his desire to enlighten the people and bring them into the modern age in the full sense of that term, his entire perestroika, were almost exclusively inspired and justified by economic necessity and constituted "a revolution from above." In *Perestroika,* the book he wrote in the summer of 1987, he insisted that his was a revolution "from above and from below." But what would happen if the workers rejected it? Gorbachev had no answer to the question he himself raised except to say that his government "will listen to and take into consideration everything that strengthens socialism" and do so "within the framework of the democratic process." First the situation required "drastic changes in thinking and psychology" to galvanize the people behind perestroika.

The system designed by Stalin to encourage blind obedience was largely responsible for turning the majority of the population into a passive and unthinking mass. It worked because the state provided welfare services to meet the elementary needs of each citizen. But by the early eighties, all key components of the welfare state—a nationwide free health service, old-age pensions, child-care and massive food and housing subsidies—were cracking under financial and sociological strains.

"We are responsible for this, we [the Communist Party] are guilty," Yakovlev explained privately. "We told the people, 'Don't sell flowers and cherries! Don't be a capitalist!' We told the farmers not to grow and sell produce—the state and collective farm would do everything. We taught people that everything was *bezplatno* [free of charge], that all benefits were guaranteed. This was harmful. The concept of the value of work was distorted. So after many years you want to change things but nobody is responding. Why the hell work, they say. What for?"[20]

The new leadership's insistence on legality—the codification of extant laws as well as the passage of new laws to prod people out of inertia—had as a precedent the "Rechtstaat" of Prussia. Anatoly Lukyanov subsequently defined it by saying that "everything that is not prohibited by law is permitted"—a proposition that ran precisely against centuries-old Russian behavior. Lukyanov, one of Gorbachev's closest advisers, saw socialist legality as a balance of legal protection of society's interests and the interests of the individual and cooperative. The Soviet state had provided its citizens with the right to work, education, social security, and health protection, but "for all the importance of these socio-economic rights they naturally do not embrace every aspect of the individual's constitutional status." In short, Gorbachev was distancing the new leadership from the concept of the welfare state.[21] Sounding like Margaret Thatcher, Gorbachev described the welfare state as "on the one hand" a "major achievement" of socialism; "on the other," he said, "it makes some people spongers."[22]

Gorbachev had promptly assembled a team of economists to advise him about what he described as the "high degree of social protection in our society," and their conclusion was that before any major economic reforms could be initiated, the regime would have to confront the pillar of Bolshevik egalitarianism, known as *uravnilovka,* or the leveling off of incomes. In theory, at least, *uravnilovka* was supposed to be an expression of social justice, but in practice it had inflicted enormous psychological distortions on Soviet society. The idea that all people should make more or less the same salary had created a climate in which envy had a social force strong enough to quash any manifestation of individual initiative, talent, or entrepreneurial vigor. Everybody should be brought down to the same level, seemed to be the motto.

The attitude generated by *uravnilovka* was captured by an old Russian joke that a reformist economist cited to illustrate the difficulties inherent in perestroika. Peasant Ivan is plowing his field and unearths a bottle, which he uncorks. A genie rushes out and, grateful for being freed, tells Ivan that he may have one wish. Ivan's eyes light up. "See that cow over there?" he says, pointing toward his neighbor Vasya's field. "That cow belongs to Vasya, and Vasya has become prosperous ever since he got it. He milks it, makes cheese and butter, and then sells them at the market for a fat profit. It's just not fair." The genie asks Ivan if it is his wish to be given a cow like Vasya's. "No, no, no," says Ivan. "I want you to kill Vasya's cow."

The leveling off of income was a key ingredient of the Stalinist system. The revolution was against money, the symbol of capitalism, which meant profit for a few, therefore inequalities, and therefore was bad. So was trade. Not only wealth but any sort of unusual distinction was frowned upon. The New Soviet Man was not encouraged to advance himself and instead saw to it that his neighbor did not get ahead of him. Each year millions of anonymous denunciations were reported to the KGB, the Central Committee, or local police. Individual inventors usually were dismissed as charlatans; students were rewarded for good discipline and high grades, but anyone possessing exceptional talent or drive was actively discouraged from breaking the monochrome social ranks. The legal system explicitly prohibited private initiative in a Criminal Code that defined the "sale and resale of goods for profit" as speculation, a crime carrying a mandatory two-year sentence. And the political system made individual enterprise and initiative seem unnecessary, given the extravagant promises about an inevitable communist paradise in the future when everyone would get everything he or she needed.

Though few of these promises were kept, most Soviets had grown up regarding the system as the natural order of things. And the system was, in some ways, soothingly protective. People did not have to worry about mortgages, overdrafts, credit cards, and balanced checkbooks. *Uravnilovka,* psychologically speaking, made this state of affairs more palatable; everyone was in the same boat.

Gorbachev's economic advisers pointed out to him that the Stalinist system, while in the past ensuring the growth of industrial capacities, had failed to develop human resources. "Man," Tatyana Zaslavskaya wrote in a 1983 critique of the Soviet system, "is the weakest link in the technological chain." To correct that weakness, Gorbachev proposed that the people be rewarded according to "the quality and quantity of their work." This, he said, would eventually "bring out the humane nature of our system."

Gorbachev and his advisers moved quickly to try to re-educate the nation, to carry out, as he was to put it later, "a major transformation of the mind." He also wanted to re-educate the party, to open it up and make it into an effective tool of progress.

But re-education wasn't going to solve the economic crisis. Its scope had become clearer to Gorbachev as he was preparing economic reforms during Andropov's rule. He had held long discussions in 1983 and 1984 with reformist economists such as Abel Aganbegyan and Tatyana Zaslavskaya, and their arguments substantiated his personal observations. They were alarmed not so much by the declining economic indicators and inefficient management—although those were alarming enough—as by new and seemingly intractable obstacles to any reversal of the trend. Among these were rampant cynicism, alcoholism, and, in general, the catastrophic degeneration of the work ethic. He was on the same wavelength. Their talks, Zaslavskaya said later, were "discussions of professionals. He understands everything."[23]

Nothing seemed to work properly. Gorbachev complained that Soviet rockets could find Halley's Comet and reach the planet Venus, but Soviet refrigerators were shoddy. Liberal economist Abel Aganbegyan, who had just been summoned to Moscow to join the Gorbachev clique of advisers, discovered to his amazement that even the Kremlin elite was starting to suffer from the collapse of quality work and productivity. He had been given an apartment in a newly constructed building set aside for high party officials, ministers, and their deputies. But the building had been so badly constructed that it was almost uninhabitable.[24]

Much of what the specialists told Gorbachev he already knew, especially that the downward trend could eventually make the Soviet Union a second-rate economic as well as political power. He asked Aganbegyan to gather all the best economists to work out a specific set of remedies that addressed both the political and the economic causes of decline. Gorbachev was already convinced that the huge and highly centralized bureaucratic edifice had become a brake to development, and that political changes were imperative.[25] And he knew he had to curb the rapacious appetite of the military. But his first task was to consolidate his power, to build a solid political foundation based on new and younger people who owed their advancement to him and who shared his ideas about change.

Conscious that his election had been seriously contested and his opponents still retained their power, Gorbachev moved cautiously. When he outlined his program at the April 25, 1985, meeting of the Central Committee, his tone was still somewhat liturgical, in the style of the Old Guard. To avoid alarming the party, the terms "perestroika" and "glasnost" were not used, although the ideas were advanced. Seeming to speak with Andropov's voice, Gorbachev told the committee that the entire economy would have to be "retooled," its management streamlined, the notion of "cost accounting" introduced, and the price system made "flexible." Local authorities, accustomed to the "armchair method of work," should be made responsible for dealing with their situations and "quickly rid themselves of dependent attitudes." Increased production should be encouraged at collective farms, as well as private smallholdings and subsidiary farms. The party, he said, was working ineffectively and was enmeshed in "formalism, exhortation, and idle talk." Local party officials should not be economic managers. Economic losses often come "from the inability to tell the people the truth." Gorbachev advanced the idea of a limited term in office as "food for thought," adding that some senior officials who occupy "one and the same post for a long time quite often stop realizing what is new and get used to the shortcomings." Gorbachev also said he wanted a more open and aggressive press, heralding more specific references to glasnost. "Radical changes" in the economy, he said, were mandated by the "historic destiny of our country. The position of socialism in the modern world will largely depend on the direction we take now."[26]

The party leaders listened respectfully, seemingly unimpressed by the expressed determination of the leader, at the outset of his rule, to change things. Successive leaders, one after another, had said much the same—and nothing drastic had happened.

Journalists and Kremlin watchers focused their attention, not on the speech, but on the shifts in Politburo membership. Gorbachev was able to add three of his allies—KGB Chairman Viktor Chebrikov, Nikolai Ryzhkov, and Yegor Ligachev—to the Politburo. He also named agricultural expert Viktor Nikonov a secretary of the Central Committee. Ligachev, Ryzhkov, and Chebrikov were all Andropov men—allies, though not clients, of Gorbachev. Only Nikonov was a Gorbachev protégé, a distinction that we did not pay attention to at the time.

Marshal Sergei Sokolov, seventy-three, a World War Two tank commander who was appointed by Chernenko to replace Ustinov as defense minister, was made a nonvoting member of the ruling council This was a significant omen in view of the Politburo's political importance. For the first time since 1973, the armed forces were not represented by a full member of the Politburo. As if to compensate, Gorbachev did make a rhetorical bow to the military, pledging, as his predecessors had routinely done, that the military would get "everything necessary" to ensure "that no one will take us by surprise."

Two weeks after the Central Committee meeting, the country was due to celebrate the fortieth anniversary of the victory in World War Two, presenting Gorbachev with another tactical challenge: how to deal with the Stalin question.

The dictator's name was associated with the war to the extent that Gorbachev could not ignore it. More significantly, Chernenko had fully rehabilitated Stalin as a military leader and a diplomat. The dictator's picture, for the first time in decades, had appeared on the cover of a national magazine that winter.[27] His former deputy Vyacheslav Molotov, ninety-three, was readmitted to the Communist

Party, from which he had been expelled by Khrushchev. Many influential conservatives had urged Chernenko to restore the name of
Stalingrad to the city that was the site of a major World War Two
battle and that was renamed Volgograd by Khrushchev. The change
of name seemed almost a sure thing, and when we visited Volgograd
that April, we were told by city officials that they had been encouraged to formally request the change, which was to coincide with the
May 9 Victory Day. But Gorbachev ruled against it.

When, on the eve of the celebrations, he addressed some five
thousand party faithful assembled in the Kremlin Palace of Congresses, he carefully avoided any shocks. Instead he struck the themes
dear to their hearts—discipline, patriotism, hard-line foreign policy,
and only partial economic reforms. Although his anti-Stalinism was
authentic, Gorbachev's politics at this stage reflected his instinct as
to how much his audience could take. Later he would sharply change
his views about his own ultimate political obligations, but not yet.
When he made a standard reference to Stalin as the country's wartime
leader, the thunderous standing ovation it evoked seemed to cast
Gorbachev in the mold of a more intelligent and better-educated
Stalinist. Gorbachev himself must have seen the ovation as a symbol
of his future difficulties—many people, particularly in the establishment, still had Stalin in their hearts.

Chapter 5

GATHERING FORCES

Few people anticipated that the fortieth anniversary celebration of the end of World War Two would be the last alcoholic hurrah, the last time much of the nation would be able to obtain vodka, to get roaring drunk.

Throughout April and May, the bureaucracy was engaged in discussions about a new campaign against alcoholism amid signs that the new leader was dead serious about it. But the country had also gone through repeated halfhearted campaigns against alcohol before, and nothing effective had been done to arrest the growing problem. Quite the contrary. Alcohol consumption in the period 1964–82 had almost quadrupled, reaching mammoth proportions; Soviet experts claimed that alcoholism had a major negative impact on productivity, demographic trends, and crime. According to official reports, two-thirds of the increase in the divorce rate was caused by alcohol abuse, while 70 percent of all crimes were alcohol-related. One study showed that the average age of chronic alcoholics had gone down by five to seven years during the 1970s. The average life expectancy for Soviet men declined from sixty-seven in 1964 to under sixty-two in 1980. Infant mortality rates showed an alarming rise, a unique experience for an advanced industrialized country. One study (*Selskaya Zhizn,* November 12, 1983) showed that "90 percent of all alcoholics were drawn to drinking before reaching the age of fifteen, and two-thirds before reaching the age of ten."

Ironically, the more liberal strain in Russian communism was always associated with antialcoholism. Lenin himself had vowed that the socialist state would never produce and sell alcohol. Nikolai Bukharin, the member of Lenin's Politburo whom Stalin had executed in 1938, made the first Soviet study of the problem of alcoholism in 1931, when he unsuccessfully sought to stop Stalin from introducing a state monopoly on alcohol; Stalin needed alcohol to raise money for industrialization. Khrushchev also tried to curb alcohol consumption. But under Brezhnev alcohol was one of the major sources of federal revenue.

Gorbachev waited until after the Victory Day festivities to announce his campaign against alcoholism. And he made his first real impression on the country not only with his conviction, but with his method of relaying it. He went directly to the people, using walkabouts and television to convey his message.

The move was one of the most unpopular campaigns in Soviet history. The new antialcoholism regulations were sweeping and had a sharp impact on Soviet life. Gorbachev introduced strong coercive and punitive measures against drunkenness, particularly against drinking on the job. Alcohol became much more difficult to obtain, because there was a steep increase in prices and a reduction both in the number of alcohol sales outlets and in their business hours: liquor stores were forbidden to open before 2:00 P.M. (they had opened at 11:00 A.M. formerly). Within days we saw lines forming two hours before opening time. Restaurants were barred from selling alcohol except with evening meals. Perhaps the greatest shock was that alcoholic beverages were eliminated from official receptions and banquets, a move that swiftly ended the bacchanalian character of these events. Communist Party members were deeply displeased by the regulations, and by the additional Central Committee edict declaring "absolutely impermissible" any drinking in any party organization. Those in the party who continued to show a weakness for alcohol could be dismissed.

The campaign gave rise to scores of anti-Gorbachev anecdotes. One of the most acerbic jokes circulating three years after the crackdown has Gorbachev arriving in a village that is completely deserted, apart from a solitary muzhik (peasant) guarding the liquor store with a rifle. "Where are the people?" Gorbachev asks him. "I want to make a speech." The muzhik fires a shot in the air. Shutters slowly creak open and voices call, "Did they bring the vodka?" "No," says the muzhik. "It's Gorbachev and he wants to make a speech." The shutters bang closed. "Well," Gorbachev asks, "where are the people?" The muzhik fires a second shot in the air, and the shutters again creak open. Again: "Did they bring the vodka?" "No," repeats the muzhik. "It's Gorbachev and he wants to talk to you." After a moment of silence comes the incredulous question: "You mean you didn't get him the first time?"

Gorbachev was aware of the jokes and later told a crowd that he knew his nickname was the "Mineral Water Secretary" (Mineralny Sekretar) instead of General Secretary (Generalny Sekretar) and that many people were unhappy with the measures. But he would press on with the campaign, a Rational Man who wanted to instruct his compatriots about (impose on them, if necessary) what was good for them. It was rationalism bordering on authoritarianism; it also indicated a fair streak of conservatism that had been masked by his push for changes. To fight the vice, he was prepared to sacrifice one of the country's principal sources of revenue. Taxes on liquor amounted to 12 percent of the Kremlin's annual receipts. (By contrast, China's Zhao Ziyang gave a practical twist to his campaign against alcoholism and smoking: he simply lifted price controls. Prices rose by up to 500 percent, ensuring more revenue for the state treasury and decreasing consumption.)

An equally potent but more encouraging surprise for the nation was Gorbachev's visit to Leningrad in mid-May. One of the perennial characteristics of Soviet politics had been the absence of any meaningful interplay between the leadership and the population. Except for the tentative populism of the Khrushchev period, the tensions of public life had been reflected in bureaucratic struggles between established institutional interests and their competition for the Politburo's attention. Occasionally Khrushchev, and later Brezhnev, would mouth phrases about the significance of the people's input, but they really did not believe them. Nor did anyone else.

Gorbachev's Leningrad speech foreshadowed a change.

Until mid-May, Gorbachev had shunned publicity, hiding behind the dull, liturgical style of leadership. But when he and Raisa landed in Leningrad on that late-spring day, Gorbachev began showing his true colors, both his charm and his convictions. He started out by saying that the customary flowers he received at the airport should be distributed to the women present. Then he took the Leningrad party chief, Lev Zaikov, aside and on the spot rearranged the program of the visit. He did not want to be caught up in *pokazukha* again, as he had been a month earlier, when he made a supposedly surprise tour of a Moscow suburb. Officials had urged him to drop in on a "typical young family" for tea. The "impromptu" visit went fine until he noticed Central Committee markings on a saucer and realized that the exquisite china had been brought from the Kremlin especially for the occasion. He was furious. He had been "Potemkinized" by his rival Grishin, then Moscow party boss, who presumably wanted to impress the new leader with the quality of life in Moscow. The word "Potemkinize" in Russian refers back to the time when Catherine the Great decided to sail down the Dnieper River to tour her domains. Count Potemkin, an influential magnate in her court, set up mock village fronts along the banks to create a comforting illusion that the wilderness around them was a prosperous, densely populated province of the realm. Hence the term "Potemkinized." And Gorbachev wanted none of it.

In Leningrad, Gorbachev ignored the prearranged schedule. He frequently broke away to look at ordinary shops that had not been spruced up for the visit; this was where he displayed for the first time his capacity for exploiting television cameras to his advantage. Television footage revealed a new kind of leader. He looked comfortable with ordinary people. When he talked, he seemed to be talking to individuals in the audience, not to the *narod* or masses. His face was expressive, his body language informal and spontaneous. His images and his turn of phrase confirmed his vivid awareness of reality—a quality greatly admired by Russians. He seemed to speak his mind, so much so that he bewildered television executives and propaganda chiefs in Moscow. In their confusion, they delayed broadcasting his main address for several days, not knowing whether such an unprecedented performance should go on the air.

No leader had ever talked to the people so openly. Though Khrushchev was a compulsive talker and loved exchanges with ordinary people, Soviet television in his day was in its infancy and of no great use to him. Brezhnev, Andropov, and Chernenko had been uncomfortable in front of the cameras, and either never made attempts to learn modern television techniques or failed in their efforts. Gorbachev seemed naturally prepared to use television's vast power to shape public opinion. He spoke mostly without notes, a self-confident and assertive man outlining with emotion and frankness the country's problems. A woman in the crowd shouted, "Just get close to the people and we won't let you down." Hemmed in by the crowd, he shot back, grinning, amid laughter, "Can I be any closer?"

It was during the Leningrad visit that Gorbachev launched his perestroika program, a program of "revolutionary changes." He chose to speak to the party at the Smolny Institute, which served as Lenin's headquarters during the 1917 Bolshevik revolution, perhaps to underscore his links to Lenin. The day was May 17, the end of his visit. The most important party officials were assembled at Smolny, all in a mood of anticipation and excitement. But they weren't prepared for the surprise of Gorbachev's main theme. The management of a modern society involved problems, he said—not of ideology but of efficient and rational administration. He wanted to induce people to think in terms of a challenge coming from within rather than from without: the challenge of tackling apathy, alcoholism, shoddy workmanship, inefficiency, and vast man-induced losses. Underlying Gorbachev's speech was the idea that the state of the Soviet economy was the fundamental reason American technological advances threatened strategic parity. Talking about outside dangers, he sought to cast them in terms of domestic economics.

Perestroika, he said, had been imposed on the country. Why not enjoy life, resting and lying at anchor? No, comrades, he said, his face turning grave. "This is not the choice. We do not have such a choice." Just to maintain the existing standard of living and defense needs, the country needed a minimal growth of 4 percent a year, instead of the current 3 percent. Everyone, "from workers to ministers to the party Central Committee secretaries and government leaders, all of us must learn new approaches and understand that for us there is no other way."

Adjustments, he continued, would have to be made. "Those who do not intend to adjust and who are an obstacle to solving these new tasks must simply get out of the way." He paused and added for emphasis, "Get out of the way. Don't be a hindrance!"

Some of the statistics and economic figures he cited revealed inefficiency and waste the scope of which we had only suspected before. Nearly one-fourth of the country's drinking water, for instance, was wasted because of faulty faucets; and the electric power used to pump this irrationally wasted water equaled the total output of Dnieproges, one of the largest hydroelectric power plants. The people, he said, "simply don't care." He also talked openly about the illegal economy. What happens when you try to fix your apartment? he asked as he criticized the notoriously inefficient and corrupt state firms. "You will have to go to the *shabashnik* [a private contractor operating semilegally]. And he is going to steal materials from a state company."

When a sanitized version of the address was broadcast by national television a few days later, we found people for the first time listening with great interest to a leader's speech, virtually hanging on his every word. People who had missed the broadcast wrote letters and made phone calls to ask for a repeat, prompting Moscow Television to air it again.

That his dramatic approach had a real impact could also be seen in the considerable resentment within the party bureaucracy. He was immediately accused of merely wooing people, and some party members said he could get "oxygen poisoning" during street encounters with ordinary people, who might tell him "something unwelcome, something the men in the Kremlin should not know." But, he said later in his book, he felt the need to go to the people, because "there are no hints, recommendations, and warnings that are more valuable than those you get straight from [them]."

Gorbachev seemed to draw sustenance from such encounters. He started to regard his own rise as a personification of Soviet possibilities, and he began to see in his own story a moral for other people. Privolnoe, his native village, he would point out privately, was a backward area of Stavropol; but it had all changed and become modernized. "I saw this happening in my own lifetime, and I dismiss the views that claim it can't be done. I've seen it with my own eyes." As a young boy, he had dreams that took him beyond the village of Privolnoe and the Krasnogvardeyski district. His brother Alexander later recalled privately that Mikhail's teachers had urged him to persevere. They saw him as a promising young man of truly uncommon industry and discipline, perhaps the brightest boy in the school, who spoke so well on his feet—why shouldn't he go far? And it was typical of Gorbachev, serious and single-minded, to have high-minded goals. They were similar to the dreams of others, except that his intelligence and his enormous industry, energy, and ambition would open up the great center of power for him and then carry him to the very top. He wanted to change things, to make the system as responsive to every man and woman as it had been to him. People simply had to know what was available to them.

He began seeking support for his policies while believing that he was re-educating the people. On a trip to the Tyumen oil field in Siberia a few months after the Leningrad visit, he told a group of workers that, without popular support, "no policy is worth anything. . . . Policy is policy when it expresses these pressing requirements and finds support among the people."

For his ardent supporters in the establishment, these direct encounters, however limited, posed problems. One was the prospect of assassination, although who might do the deed was something nobody could specify. The other concern was that, as the summer of 1985 wore on and Gorbachev continued to tour the country—he also visited the Ukraine, Kazakhstan, and Byelorussia—it was apparent that the glow of Leningrad could not be sustained, and that Gorbachev risked looking more and more like the garrulous Khrushchev. He must have understood that too, for in the autumn he stopped his solo travels and performances, to concentrate instead on party politics. Not until the following spring did he take to the road again.

•   •   •

Gorbachev had a clear view of the kind of leader he wanted to be. Early in his reign, in a meeting with Leningrad party leaders in May 1985, he offered an insight into his determination to be a strong ruler. "People expect their leaders to be strict, well organized, exacting, considerate, [and] a model of conscientiousness in their work." He added that such a leader also had to be "close to the people." His resolution would reveal itself more fully and publicly in his later pronouncements and speeches, but it was clear here too: he believed that genuine modernization required popular participation in politics. He also had to seize control of a machinery of government that was filled with strong men who seemed to prefer conducting affairs as if they were running their own fiefdoms.

Unlike in the West, where a new leader appoints new Cabinet ministers and a multitude of administrators to run the country, a new Soviet leader is constrained by inheriting his predecessor's administration. This is a grave flaw in a one-party state, and it circumscribed the power of even such strong figures as Andropov. Andropov, the feared former KGB chairman, did manage to bring new blood into the leadership, although not nearly enough to push through so ambitious an experiment as Gorbachev was mounting. Nonetheless, the timing of Gorbachev's accession was on his side. The next Communist Party congress, which would elect a new Central Committee, was scheduled for February 1986. The ten-month interval gave Gorbachev a multitude of opportunities to man the ship with his people. Moreover, the congress, which is something akin in form to an American political-party convention, was scheduled to replace the 1961 Party Program, a document setting out a utopian vision of the country's future, with a new, more realistic blueprint. Now in charge of developing the new program, Gorbachev could shape it to fit his own vision for the country's future.

During his first month in power, Gorbachev assembled a group of men of ability and integrity, delegating to them defined areas of responsibility. Most visible were those who, like Gorbachev himself, had come to the fore during Andropov's reign. But the next echelon included men little known in Moscow, men "made" by Gorbachev. The new leader had a temperamental preference for people outside the bureaucratic establishment, who shared his sense that they were writing on a clean slate.

These new figures were not newly converted reformists; they had previously entertained ideas of a national reconstruction, and some had deliberately chosen to live far from Moscow, because their strong views were unpopular with the Kremlin. Aganbegyan the economist, who spent twenty-three years at an Academy of Sciences think tank in Novosibirsk before moving to Moscow in 1985, had an established reputation as a reformer. But, he joked, "it was easy to be an economic reformer in Siberia—nobody paid much attention to you."

Editors and writers brought forward by Gorbachev had also been in self-imposed exile because of their views. Sergei Zalygin, who took over the monthly *Novy Mir,* the intellectual flagship of Gorbachev's reforms, had lived in Siberia since 1955, writing novels and short stories, refusing any administrative position, and declining Communist Party membership. Why, at age seventy-two, did he accept the editorship of *Novy Mir*? "Because I feel that now I could do something the way I want to."[1] Zalygin began to publish formerly forbidden authors, brought out Boris Pasternak's *Doctor Zhivago* for the first time, and enabled the public to read the works of anti-Soviet exiles such as Vladimir Nabokov and Joseph Brodsky.

Another key media figure, Yegor Yakovlev, who became editor-in-chief of the weekly *Moscow News,* had fallen from grace at the time of the 1968 invasion of Czechoslovakia and had spent more than a decade in self-imposed exile, making a living as a free-lance film scriptwriter. When Andropov took power, the tall, burly journalist was brought back from the wilderness and sent to Prague as *Izvestia* correspondent. The advent of Chernenko was a new blow to him. When Gorbachev took power, Yegor Yakovlev was in the middle of his own personal journey, unsure whether to remain in Prague or return to Moscow to take over a weekly newspaper and join the fight. Valentin Falin, the new chairman of Novosti Press Agency, the publisher of *Moscow News,* promised to give Yakovlev full control over the paper. He took it, soon becoming a major player, serving as a ramrod, pushing through a newer and freer tone and publishing articles no one had ever expected to see in the Soviet press.

Perhaps the most controversial of Gorbachev's new intellectuals was historian Yuri Afanasiev, a plain-speaking man with bright-blue eyes and a shy smile, who confronted the way the regime used deliberate lies and falsifications to eliminate events and contentious political figures from the country's history. Under pressure from the reformers, he was appointed dean of the State Historical-Archival Faculty, an administrative post from which he could press for the opening up of secret archives and urge the establishment to take a new and honest look at such prominent Bolshevik figures as Leon Trotsky, Nikolai Bukharin, Lev Kamenev, and a host of others who had been turned into "nonpersons" by Stalin. As a society, Afanasiev said in 1986, long before Bukharin and others were formally rehabilitated, "we should be ashamed of ourselves every single day of our lives until we tell the truth about Bukharin."[2]

Along with Aganbegyan and a team of other economists, Gorbachev appointed a cultured and highly educated man to take over Gosplan, the State Planning Commission, a stronghold of the Stalinists that had been in the hands of Nikolai Baibakov for a quarter of a century. Baibakov's replacement was Nikolai Talyzin, a professor of electrical engineering at Moscow University who had served four years as minister of telecommunications before being shunted aside in 1980 and assigned to be Moscow's representative to Comecon, the Soviet-bloc economic alliance. Another former professor, Vadim Medvedev, whom Gorbachev met while Medvedev was rector of the Social Sciences Academy, became a key adviser on scientific and educational issues.

Most of the new appointees belonged to a new generation of well-educated but frustrated officials who had stood by too long watching a complacent Brezhnev government ignore the signs of economic slowdown and the collapse of the welfare system. In general, they were suspicious of incantational rhetoric and dogmatic moralizing. They wanted to do something rational. Some had worked with Gorbachev in Stavropol—men such as Vsevolod Murakhovsky and Georgi Razumovsky, both promoted rapidly and assigned the most important jobs in Moscow. Murakhovsky was put in charge of food supplies and Razumovsky handled personnel. Some, such as Alexander Vlasov, he knew from the regional North Caucasus area meetings. Vlasov was an efficient and incorruptible administrator of the Rostov region and the Checheno-Ingush autonomous area. Boris Yeltsin of Sverdlovsk and Lev Zaikov of Leningrad had made reputations as efficient administrators of their regions.

For the most sensitive jobs on his personal staff, Gorbachev turned to trusted friends and intimates: his longtime secretary, Anatoly Lushchikov; Viktor Sharapov, a former Andropov aide; and Valery Boldin, an ex–*Pravda* news editor. He named Anatoly Chernyaev, the veteran deputy chief of the International Department of the Central Committee, as his national security adviser (until 1987). But the appointment that stunned the Soviet establishment, in July 1985, was Gorbachev's designation of his old friend Eduard Shevardnadze as foreign minister and full Politburo member. The decision to move a Georgian, a non-Russian, into the job held for a quarter of a century by Gromyko, was extraordinarily bold. The new foreign minister spoke Russian with an accent and had no experience in foreign affairs. Gorbachev made it clear that he wanted control over foreign policy. He made Gromyko titular head of state—president of the Presidium of the Supreme Soviet, thus placing in the innermost circle of power a man who reflected his own opinions and vision, who reinforced his political position.

Gorbachev and Shevardnadze had become close friends when they were both Komsomol activists in the late fifties. In the interim twenty-five years, Shevardnadze had proved to be the most original and most reformist regional politician in the country. Shortly after he was appointed Georgia's police minister in the mid-sixties, he was reported to have remarked to the communist elite of the notoriously corrupt southern republic, "Is there anything here that is not for sale? If there is, I cannot think of it!" He conducted massive anti-corruption campaigns in the province. After 1972, as Georgia's leader, he quietly moved his republic away from highly centralized and inefficient agricultural practices. His introduction of material and financial incentives in agriculture coincided with Gorbachev's experiments in Stavropol in the early 1970s. Shevardnadze was more successful. As leader of Georgia, he made remarkable steps toward democratization of his society within the bounds permitted by the Soviet system, also promoting sociological experiments and a renaissance of Georgian cultural traditions. It was a Georgian film director, Tengiz Abuladze, who made the movie *Pokayanie (Repentance)*, about the horrors of Stalinism; he began making the film as early as 1983, shortly after Brezhnev's death, and it was released three years later. While Shevardnadze invariably paid extravagant tribute to Moscow—at a party gathering in 1976 he asserted that "for us Georgians, the sun does not rise in the east, but in the north, in Russia"—he quietly put the interests of Georgia first. In 1978, when Georgians were angered by the draft of a new Georgian constitution that made Russian, together with Georgian, an official language in the republic, Shevardnadze went to Moscow and successfully halted the move to impose Russian on his people.

It was Shevardnadze's pragmatism, the can-do attitude, that Gorbachev wanted in his innermost circle in Moscow. He was frustrated by the Russian penchant for reflection "on man's destiny and on the right path to take in life," which seemed to breed inactivity and which "may be the reason that pragmatism is not typical of our people's national character." Shevardnadze possessed a sense of proportion and compromise and a keen appreciation of the chasm between the desirable and the possible. He was known for his personal modesty, integrity, and the readiness to speak his mind. Under the appearance of bland composure, he was capable of great charm and a southern satiric humor. His flow of jokes enlivened intimate dinners after long working sessions. Gorbachev knew him as a superb organizer and an imaginative administrator. Later, as foreign minister, he quietly but firmly exorcised Gromyko's spirit from the Foreign Ministry, so long dominated by Gromyko men and Gromyko's overwhelming combative preoccupation with the United States. In a revealing remark about the conduct of Soviet foreign policy, Gorbachev said, "It is very bad for us when a Soviet representative is called Mr. Nyet [Mr. No]." Gromyko, who came to personify Soviet foreign policy, had earned the nickname Mr. Nyet with the repeated "no" votes he cast in the United Nations.[3]

Shevardnadze did what Gorbachev wanted him to do. He had no rigid agenda of his own.

Two other key men wholly dependent on Gorbachev for their

spectacular careers were Alexander Yakovlev and Anatoly Luky-anov.

Yakovlev, who had come to Gorbachev's notice during his Canadian visit and who in no time at all won so much favor and trust that he became the leader's right-hand man, was his principal adviser on the policies of perestroika and glasnost. Although he was naturally courteous, his wit was acerbic, and his independence of mind, experience, and reading endowed him with qualities that put him in a class by himself.

Like Gorbachev, Yakovlev came from peasant stock, but his family was rooted in ancient Russia; he was born outside the city of Yaroslavl, in 1924. Yakovlev's father was a wholehearted supporter of collectivization, a policy his son now describes as "not justified." Because his father became the first collective-farm chairman in his village, the family suffered at the hands of rebellious peasants. Alexander was seven when the family had to flee their house, which was set ablaze by opponents of the policy. They moved to a house vacated by the local priest, only to have to flee again, in the middle of the night, when the rebels set their new home on fire. Even the chairman of a collective farm so wretchedly poor had difficulty feeding his family, and Yakovlev has recalled his father's making ends meet by selling firewood to the railroad. His schooling was interrupted by the war; young Yakovlev was wounded on the front—he has an artificial leg—and returned to Yaroslavl to continue his studies. He joined the party in 1944 and held a variety of jobs in his hometown while continuing his education at night. In 1953, he advanced to the Central Committee bureaucracy in Moscow, but he left in 1956 to pursue graduate studies at Moscow University. In 1959, he attended Columbia University in New York as an exchange student, and later got a doctorate in history. After rejoining the Central Committee bureaucracy in 1960, he spent thirteen years in the Propaganda Department, ultimately serving as its acting chief. In a series of books about American foreign policy, he forecast a decline in U.S. power, and the world's growing fragmentation into different centers of power. In particular, he foresaw that Europe, Japan, and eventually Brazil and other developing nations would become more serious economic competitors of the United States, something that, he said, should heighten "contradictions" within the Western alliance and diminish America's political and economic dominance. An outspoken and polemical man, he angered Russian nationalists and Kremlin cultural chiefs when, in 1973, he publicly denounced Russophile writers who idealized the "stagnation" of the Russian village. In a ten-thousand-word literary review specifically attacking the nationalist line in the journal *Molodaya Gvardia,* Yakovlev criticized Solzhenitsyn, not for his political dissidence, but for his almost mystical Russian chauvinism. The attack on the cult of Russian nationalism, an unpopular step in the Russian-dominated apparat, provided Yakovlev's enemies with new ammunition. Whoever his enemies were, it was Chernenko who ordered that Yakovlev be sent into diplomatic exile as ambassador to Canada. He was discovered there by Gorbachev in 1983 and promptly reassigned to Moscow as director of IMEMO, the government think tank on international economic and political affairs.

Gorbachev was captivated by the play of Yakovlev's civilized mind, the bite of his language, and the apparent clarity of his thinking about foreign and domestic affairs. There is also a pugnacious and irreverent streak in Yakovlev's makeup, and his sense of humor appealed to Gorbachev. He was almost like a man from North Caucasus.

Yakovlev became Gorbachev's closest adviser, acquiring the two highest party positions (Politburo member and Central Committee secretary). No other person reflected so vividly the embryonic change in the Kremlin and Soviet foreign and domestic policies, the change from tough orthodoxy toward a more enlightened authoritarianism.

Anatoly Lukyanov was tall, austere, impressive, selective with his words, rarely entering into petty fights. Underneath the appearance of bluntness and taciturnity, he was capable of a frivolous if biting humor. He possessed a dazzling clarity and speed of mind—something that attracted Gorbachev to him while they were attending the Law School. They had both been Komsomol activists at Moscow University, and Lukyanov subsequently made a career as a legal consultant for the government and legislature, rising to be the top administrative official in the Presidium of the Supreme Soviet. The two men re-established close contacts after Gorbachev moved to Moscow in 1978.

During Andropov's rule, when he was searching for energetic men to carry out the new program, Gorbachev recommended Lukyanov for a sensitive position in the Central Committee's General Department, which runs the party leader's day-to-day affairs. Lukyanov was appointed deputy chief in 1983, and after Gorbachev's accession he became chief. It is a crucial appointment for a leader, roughly equivalent to the White House chief of staff. Chernenko held the same post for many years under Brezhnev.

Gorbachev later elevated his university friend to the leadership by making him first a secretary of the Central Committee and subsequently a candidate Politburo member and first vice-president. But Lukyanov's most important job during the first years of the Gorbachev administration was to handle all the most confidential paperwork and other matters for the leader. He was also given charge of key projects, including the special commission to prepare the overhaul of the legal system. It was the sort of work that excited Lukyanov. He worked fourteen-hour days, he said later, but he was "living through a happy period and we spare neither our time, nor our energy for Perestroika."[4]

These key personnel changes were less immediately noticeable than the change in style, manifested most vividly by Gennady Gerasimov, the new Foreign Ministry spokesman. Although he was outside the sphere of power brokers, the urbane and witty former journalist set a new tone in public discourse by holding regular press briefings twice a week—answering questions on such formerly taboo matters as political prisoners, giving a running commentary on Moscow's preoccupations and agenda, and doing so while frequently bantering with correspondents. He appeared to pattern his style on that of Jody Powell, President Carter's press secretary, whose briefings Gerasimov attended while serving as Novosti correspondent in Washington in the late seventies. As far as both form and substance were concerned, this was revolutionary. During Brezhnev's rule, briefings were pompous nonevents that happened a dozen times a year.

While the conservative opposition was coming to terms with the new regime, Gorbachev moved forcefully against the Brezhnevites. At the beginning of July 1985, Grigori Romanov, his main and most serious rival, was ousted from the Politburo. The move seemed swift and painless. He was a vain and snobbish man who hid his drinking and philandering behind a stony-faced façade of businesslike efficiency. Six years older than Gorbachev, he was given to wearing high heels to add to his five-foot-six-inch frame. His weaknesses, known to those in the establishment, were offset by his political credentials. He was a dogmatic communist and an able administrator with links to the military-industrial complex. What made ousting him easier was the fact that Romanov had been promoted from Leningrad to Moscow—a move that cut him off from his power base. His dismissal was preceded by rumors that began to circulate that spring of 1985—apparently emanating from the KGB and sanctioned by Gorbachev's ally Chebrikov—about two recent indiscretions by Romanov. On an official visit to Finland the previous winter, he had got roaring drunk at a Helsinki reception; his drinking habits were out of sync with the new antialcoholism drive. The second charge revived an old transgression, also involving Finland. Having been the party boss of Leningrad for a long time, Romanov had frequently gone yachting in the Bay of Finland. On one such occasion, accompanied by a pop-singer girlfriend thirty years his junior, he accidentally strayed into Finnish territorial waters and was stopped by a Finnish patrol boat, which ordered the Russian yacht into a Finnish port for inspection. When the Finns realized that they had detained a member of the Soviet Politburo, they immediately released him.[5] These indiscretions, suddenly given widespread currency, undermined Romanov's position, and Gorbachev managed to engineer his ouster at a Politburo meeting.

In October, the old prime minister, Nikolai Tikhonov, submitted his resignation. Tikhonov, eighty, a member of Brezhnev's inner circle, yielded to the inevitable without a struggle, and Gorbachev appointed his ally Nikolai Ryzhkov in Tikhonov's place. In December, Viktor Grishin, the other candidate in the succession struggle, put up a fierce fight before he was dislodged from his post as communist leader of Moscow and replaced by Boris Yeltsin.

Gorbachev decided to confront some of the signs of opposition to perestroika and concern about the quick pace of changes. In the early summer of 1985, he traveled to the Ukraine, the stronghold of Brezhnev and Chernenko, where he was greeted politely but without much enthusiasm. He chose to raise troublesome issues on the spot, saying that some critics were wondering: "Aren't things being done too abruptly?" Then he put the question to party cadres at Dnepropetrovsk, Brezhnev's and Chernenko's political base: "What do you think about it, comrades?" Only several voices from a visibly skeptical audience responded by shouting he was "doing everything right!" Gorbachev seemed disappointed. "Are those just voices, or is it everybody's opinion?" he asked the audience. The voices shouted back, "It's everybody's opinion."

Gorbachev's advisers thought the lukewarm responses amounted to a standard quota of friction and discontent. Gorbachev decided to put the provinces on the back burner and focus his attention on gaining control of the central institutions of power in Moscow, apparently believing that once that was accomplished other levels of authority would fall in line. That might have been true under normal circumstances, with a leader who was not hell-bent on changing the entire mechanism of economic and social management. But the struggle in Moscow itself should have served as a warning that control of the central apparat does not necessarily translate into control of the political base.

The long and difficult maneuvering to dislodge Grishin from his Moscow base seemed to foreshadow the nature of conservative resistance to a reformist leader as well as the resilience of the party bureaucracy in Soviet life. Even with the KGB behind him, and the mass media publicly attacking Grishin, it took Gorbachev's personal intervention to force the hand of the Moscow party organization.

In terms of tenure, Grishin was the Politburo's most senior figure. Appointed by Brezhnev as Moscow party boss in 1967, Grishin over the years built an organization that in its strength and the web of its links and alliances in the capital made Mayor Richard J. Daley's Chicago machine look like a symbol of clean and uncorrupt big-city government. Apart from outright graft and plunder, particularly in the areas of housing construction and consumer goods, the local bureaucracy became firmly entrenched through patronage involving virtually anything worth obtaining, from jobs to health services to educational opportunities. This was not the ordinary *nalevo* (under-the-table) type of corruption average citizens are exposed to whenever they want to obtain scarce goods and services. Rather, it was an organized distribution of state property, funds, or services by the Moscow apparat, which comprised thousands of party bureaucrats. At the apex of this pyramid stood Grishin. That such a situation could exist in the capital for years underscored the institutional weakness of the system—the degeneration of the party and the vulnerability of the civil service.

The assault on Grishin started in the early fall, with rumors reviving old stories about his personal corruption. Meanwhile, major newspapers began to print articles calling attention to instances of mismanagement and power abuse in the administration of the capital. In the clamor and confusion—direct public attacks on a Politburo member were a new experience—the government kept issuing heavy hints through the media urging district party committees to elect new people, on the assumption that they would in turn elect a new Moscow party committee, which, at its scheduled elections in December, would dump Grishin and elect a new man as its leader. The Grishin network simply ignored these hints and re-elected most members of its city committees. Despite pressure from the Central Committee, the city committee, dominated by Grishin loyalists, seemed determined to re-elect Grishin. Gorbachev himself decided to attend the session, in an effort to influence the outcome, but the committee ignored the message of his presence and re-elected Grishin. In the dramatic hour that followed, Gorbachev asked for the floor to urge the committee members to reconsider their choice. He was armed for the occasion with documents from the district attorney's office implicating Grishin in a criminal investigation of the city's housing authority. Some sources said that Grishin himself bowed out, in order to be allowed to retire without facing possible criminal charges. The committee voted to elect Boris Yeltsin in his place.

·   ·   ·

Boris Yeltsin in many ways typified the new "perestroika gang" Gorbachev assembled.

Although they were the same age, he looked younger than Gorbachev, with clean-cut features, straightforward manners, and flowing hair. He seemed to speak for a new generation, and quickly became a symbol; he was optimistic, honest, firm; a man of force, moving, nudging, getting things done. His look was part of his drive; a fat Yeltsin was as hard to imagine as a vacillating one. He possessed a very Russian certitude and conviction.

It was amazing that a man like Yeltsin had come from the communist establishment. The underlying theme of his extemporaneous public remarks was that totalitarianism was bad and "democracy" good. This helped explain the strength of his popular appeal. So did the fact that, after he was appointed the Communist Party chief of Moscow, he tended almost invariably to side with the common citizen. He began taking the bus to work and resorted to guerrilla tactics of his own to fight corruption. No wonder his reputation grew: many were in awe.

Even to some of those in his immediate entourage Yeltsin sometimes seemed so idealistic as to be naïve. He never talked of power and did not seem to covet it. When a sense of disillusionment with perestroika became noticeable, he was stricken with a profound feeling of failure and did not want to spare anyone from the responsibility.

For some he seemed to embody the virtues of Gorbachev's era; for others he personified the contradictions. Yeltsin portrayed himself as an idealistic bystander, yet he was conniving and dissembling enough to gain the upper hand over his critics. He loved power and sought it intensely, ultimately becoming a ferocious infighter. He quickly learned the importance of public relations and played the game with surprising skill and wit.

One of the more celebrated manifestations of his showmanship in 1986 involved a shipment of forty tons of West German veal, a large portion of which was delivered to the city's premier grocery, the ornately decorated Gastronom Number One on Gorky Street, known by its tsarist-era name of Yeliseyevsky Store. Aware that the shipment had been delivered to the shop that morning, Yeltsin joined the line as an ordinary customer and, when his turn came, asked for veal. "Sorry," the shop assistant said, "no veal today." Yeltsin insisted that there must be some veal in the store. "If you don't stop pestering me, I'll call the police," the shop assistant shouted. Yeltsin turned the tables on her and brought in the police himself. Investigation revealed that the veal had been sent to the farmers' private market, where it fetched four times the price set at state shops—the difference was pocketed by Yeliseyevsky's managers. The performance was vintage Yeltsin, and people loved it.

Yeltsin was a model of glasnost. He would not only respond to questions he liked but also take those that were "complicated, quarrelsome, angry, and prickly," as *Pravda* reported later. Few party leaders at the time were so open. In his February 1986 televised address to the party congress, after making a blistering attack on the party bureaucracy and its abuse of power, Yeltsin suddenly posed a question to himself. "Delegates may well ask why I did not say all this in my speech at [the previous congress, in 1981]. Well, I can answer, and answer frankly—I obviously did not have enough courage or political experience at the time." (From the same rostrum, exactly thirty years earlier, Nikita Khrushchev had denounced Stalin's murderous rule in the "secret speech." Khrushchev had raised a similar question: "Some comrades may ask why I and my colleagues did not stand up against Stalin's policies, and why we are doing so now." But Khrushchev did not have a straight answer and dwelled instead on Stalin's enormous power and paranoid suspiciousness, which "choked a person morally and physically and created a situation "where one could not express one's own will.")

Yeltsin turned to television to dramatize the dismal conditions in some sections of Moscow and to generate pressure from below. He seemed to solicit popular discontent with communal services and sanitary conditions. Television cameras accompanied him as he toured the poorer neighborhoods, and television viewers saw people hanging out of windows and yelling complaints. "You haven't seen anything," a woman shouted from her third-floor window as Yeltsin was emerging from a neighboring building in the spring of 1987. "Our basement is completely flooded. Nothing works!" In one Moscow district, where the deeply rooted Brezhnevite party bureaucracy vehemently resisted change, Yeltsin dismissed the entire local administration and called in the KGB to run all offices while new men were found to take over. A few months later he reported to a party meeting that he had received two anonymous death threats, and read out a letter claiming that he held the job of Moscow party leader only because he was "Gorbachev's own man." "Go back to Sverdlovsk before it is too late," the letter warned.

Chapter 6

FOREIGN AFFAIRS, DOMESTIC BLISS

Although his primary interest was in internal regeneration, Gorbachev was thrown into foreign affairs literally from the moment he was elected general secretary. Chernenko, who had worked hard to re-establish arms-control talks with the United States, died two days before their resumption in Geneva, sparking questions and doubts in Washington about his successor's position. Gorbachev felt it necessary to reassure the Americans immediately, in his inauguration speech, that the talks would begin on schedule.

A few hours after Chernenko was buried behind the Lenin Mausoleum, Gorbachev was faced with a new challenge as President Reagan publicly proposed a meeting with him. Despite all his preparations during the previous two years, Gorbachev had little experience in foreign affairs. British officials had noticed his insecurity during his visit to England four months earlier, when Gorbachev sat back and let Alexander Yakovlev and Leonid Zamyatin advance many of the Soviet positions.[1] "When he came to power," Georgi Arbatov said later, "he was very green on foreign affairs. But he has learned fast."[2]

In the minds of Gorbachev's advisers, the Americans seized the initiative because they were curious about the new Soviet leader and eager to take his measure. His advisers suspected that Reagan was trying to have a Kennedy-Khrushchev summit in reverse, with Gorbachev in the role of the untested young adversary; they promptly ruled out a visit to Washington, seeing in that a ploy to impress Gorbachev with the achievements of American technology and industry and thus put him on the defensive.

By making his invitation public, Reagan placed Gorbachev in a position where he could not turn it down without appearing unnecessarily unyielding and hostile. Since the hope of arms limitations meant a great deal to the rest of the world, a Gorbachev rejection would have damaged the Soviets' self-advertised image as humankind's party of hope and nuclear responsibility. Temperamentally, Gorbachev preferred face-to-face meetings; he wanted to find out things for himself. He was curious about Reagan and felt that it was impossible to get at second hand a complete impression of what he was up against in the American leader.[3]

As a result of Reagan's move, Gorbachev was forced to show resolution and capacity for drastic action immediately, by seizing hold of the nuclear-decisionmaking machinery. The passing of the Kremlin's authority into the hands of a largely unknown and possibly inexperienced man who might lack the toughness of his Old Guard predecessors raised concerns within the Soviet military establishment. Tensions between the military and political leaders had become all too apparent during Brezhnev's last year. As Reagan dramatically boosted U.S. defense expenditures, the Soviet military began clamoring for more money to counter the threat. Even while serving as Andropov's deputy, Gorbachev became involved in maneuverings to rein in the military and weaken its iron grip both on Soviet resources and on policy at the arms talks. Gorbachev's advisers felt that the conservative predecessors and the military-industrial complex were prisoners of their own narrow-minded and dogmatic background and illusory conception of Soviet-American rivalry.

The problem of Soviet nuclear strategy was not a very complicated matter from the time of Stalin to that of Brezhnev. It was in the hands of the military, who re-examined it occasionally, but always within its military context. Brezhnev had succeeded in curbing the almost total military domination of nuclear issues by bringing into the process top experts from the Foreign Ministry and KGB. But the nuclear strategy remained the work of military minds, for whom

Gorbachev had no admiration. With the exception of Marshal Nikolai Ogarkov, Gorbachev once remarked to an aide, none of the
ranking military figures were sufficiently impressive.[4]

Gorbachev belongs to a new generation of Russians, without vivid
memories of the war or of the postwar years of American nuclear
monopoly. In the context of nuclear parity, which the Russians
achieved in the seventies, Gorbachev saw these weapons less as the
means of direct aggression by either side—in fact, both superpowers
maintained that such aggression would be suicidal—than as an
expression of political competition between the two systems. This
called for new concepts, new assessments, a new strategy that, in his
view, would have to be developed by civilian leaders. "Too long
have we fixed our eyes on traditional military needs," one aide
quoted him as saying on this issue.

He knew the supreme importance of first impressions, and he acted
forcefully, as if the civilians had always been in charge of strategic
issues. The military chiefs were stunned; they were consulted on
technical problems but were not asked their views on political-
military issues. Moreover, in April 1985, the new defense minister,
Marshal Sokolov, was kept from full membership in the Politburo.
In May, wasting little time on preliminaries, Gorbachev in one fell
swoop forced the retirement of more than a dozen top officers, including Marshal Vladimir Tolubko, commander of the strategic
forces; Admiral Sergei Gorshkov, chief of naval operations; and
General of the Army Alexei Yepishev, chief of the political directorate of the armed forces.

The retirement of these senior military men was of great symbolic
importance, particularly that of Gorshkov, the father of the new
Soviet navy, which grew dramatically during his tenure and was the
instrument of the Kremlin's worldwide ambitions. Gradually Gorbachev would reduce the role of military might as a component of
his foreign policy, insisting instead on the revival of the economy.
The forced retirements also gave Gorbachev some freedom to maneuver. He began "to pave the way toward" the summit by sus-
pending all nuclear testing (to begin on the day of the fortieth
anniversary of Hiroshima, an obvious propaganda touch), reaffirming Andropov's moratorium on antisatellite weapons tests and ad-

vancing the proposal for a 50-percent cut in strategic weapons. He had some fears, he said, that the Soviet-American confrontation had gone "too far to count on any accords at all," but he felt that the situation was "too dangerous to neglect even the slightest chance of rectifying things."[5] By July, an agreement was reached to hold the summit in Geneva on November 19–21.

There were two practical incentives for Gorbachev to go to the November summit. One was that it would help strengthen his position at home. Gorbachev had to establish his authority, had to convince the establishment that his policy approaches were sound and that he was supremely competent. By dealing with Reagan directly, he was bound to enhance his standing. The second incentive was that the summit gave him an opportunity to assess Reagan's intentions personally, particularly with respect to SDI. Moscow was preparing its economic plans for the rest of the decade, and the military budget would be severely strained if Reagan got the funding he wanted for SDI.

For Gorbachev, SDI had become more and more exasperating. Since March 23, 1983, when Reagan unveiled his "Star Wars" program, Moscow had become obsessed by its implication of a high-tech breakthrough that would leave Russia behind. For Gorbachev, SDI was a threat to his perestroika program; here was an issue of foreign and security policy that would siphon off energy and resources needed for domestic programs. More than that, the SDI competition interfered with the very essence of Gorbachev's economic modernization; he wanted to build an integrated modern economy to replace Russia's two economies—military and civilian—which had existed side by side since Stalin's day. He wanted to escape the disastrous status quo that allowed the military to claim all the resources and talent for its nefarious enterprises while the civilian economy suffered like a retarded stepchild of the government and fell further and further behind the economies of other countries.

The secrecy and isolation in the military economy promoted waste—the military-industrial complex did not worry about the costs involved; in the name of national security, no cost was too high when it came to keeping up with the Americans. It also prevented any exchange of innovations between the military and consumer sectors.

Rapid development in the high-technology age underscored the perils of the segregated Soviet economies. The Soviet high command had not come to grips with the changing pace of technological innovation and its impact on the armed forces, although Marshal Ogarkov, the brilliant and forceful chief of staff ousted by Chernenko, had publicly warned both political and military leaders that Soviet technology was failing to provide the country with up-to-date weaponry, and that the country's military power was gravely threatened. Moscow, Ogarkov argued, had more than enough nuclear weapons and must concentrate its future efforts on high-technology conventional arms. Four months before his dismissal, Ogarkov said in a May 9, 1984, interview with the armed-forces daily *Krasnaya Zvezda* that "nothing is as dependent on economic conditions" as the military. He added, "The rapid development of science and technology in recent years is creating realistic prerequisites for the appearance in the near future of even more destructive and heretofore unknown types of weapons based on new physical principles . . . and it would be a serious mistake not to take this into account right now."

Gorbachev consulted Yevgeny Velikhov, forty-nine, a nuclear physicist and vice-president of the Soviet Academy of Sciences, and commissioned several studies of SDI. Their conclusions revealed great concern about Moscow's capacity to join the high-tech age, something Gorbachev's predecessors had never conceded. In Gorbachev's mind, continued economic vulnerabilities would create future military and political consequences.[6] As far as he was concerned, the high-technology issue made it clear how weak Moscow's foreign-policy position had become and how few alternatives were open to him. The acceptance of Reagan's "get-acquainted summit," something Moscow had derided in the past, was an effort at damage control, something that would at least provide a chance for him to influence the framework for future Soviet-American relations.

The collapse of Soviet-American détente in the late seventies had produced a new situation that, after the December 27, 1979, Soviet invasion of Afghanistan, set relations on a downward slide. A series of U.S. punitive measures against Moscow—a grain embargo, a ban on the sales of high technology, restrictions on Soviet fishing in U.S. waters, and withdrawal from the 1980 Moscow Olympics, among others—opened the way for Soviet-bashing rhetoric in an American presidential election year. As Gorbachev put it, "Virtually every thread of bilateral cooperation was snapped."[7]

The situation under Reagan had first become envenomed by neglect, then inflamed alike by the "evil-empire" rhetoric and poisonous Tass retorts comparing Reagan to Hitler. Moscow's hope of salvaging the established arms-control process was badly shaken following Reagan's Star Wars speech in 1983. From that point on, the tone of propaganda salvos in the Soviet Union became gradually more fierce over the scheduled deployment of new American nuclear missiles in Europe.

The shooting down of a civilian Korean airliner on September 1, 1983, sealed the confrontational mode. The Soviet walkout from the Geneva arms talks in late 1983 signified an overall breakdown in relations. Diplomacy, for both sides, became an exercise in public relations. That the situation was unacceptably dangerous became clear when Reagan signaled interest in the resumption of a serious dialogue by sharply moderating his rhetoric in January 1984, underscoring the need for "peaceful competition" between the two superpowers and their "common interest" in avoiding war. A dying Andropov, however, made it clear that the resumption would have to be on Soviet terms, which included a removal of Pershing Two and cruise missiles from Western Europe. Gorbachev, as executor of Andropov's policies, must have been involved in all the key decisions during his reign. But Gorbachev's personal attitude on these issues at the time is not known; Andropov was his own foreign minister, and he probably sought support—not advice—from his protégé.

Andropov's death, in February 1984, offered an opportunity to arrest the downward slide in relations, an opportunity that Chernenko eagerly seized. Restoring the Brezhnev-era attitude, he quickly moderated Moscow's rhetoric and shifted the government toward accommodation. In the summer of 1984, Chernenko reached two critical conclusions that opened the way for the resumption of the Geneva talks. First was his assessment that Reagan would be reelected in November; second was his decision to abandon Andropov's insistence on the removal of Pershings and cruise missiles as a precondition for talks. That led to a Geneva meeting between Gromyko and Shultz in January 1985 and the formal agreement to restart the arms talks in March.

It is unclear to what extent Gorbachev had been involved in these major decisions. Prior to 1985, he had made only one speech on foreign affairs, in which he offered what appeared to be a slightly different angle of vision on relations with the United States. In December 1984, speaking on ideological matters at a party conference, he obliquely criticized the bipolar view of international politics to which Chernenko and Brezhnev had subscribed and talked about the emergence of new centers of power that offered fresh opportunities to Soviet diplomacy. He saw "a gradual but ever clearer loss of America's earlier economic and political hegemony." Perhaps the only clear conclusion one could draw from his remarks was the growing influence on his thinking of Alexander Yakovlev. The basis of Gorbachev's thinking about Soviet influence abroad was formulated by his mentor, Andropov, who maintained that this would rest on domestic achievements. Yakovlev shared Andropov's views about the relationship between domestic improvements and foreign reputation, and he was an even more forceful critic of the tendency to believe that all problems have military solutions.

In the months before the Geneva summit, there were several attempts to reach agreements on arms control; but despite four meetings between Shevardnadze and Secretary of State George Shultz, the gulf between them was so wide that it was impossible to set a meaningful agenda. Nor could they agree on a communiqué, even when Shultz made the last trip to Moscow, in early November. "They had a communiqué and we had a communiqué," Shultz said after the meeting, "and it was clear that there was nothing in between."[8] The failure of Geneva was thus guaranteed.

Also that fall, Gorbachev signaled a new and tough approach on matters of diplomatic reciprocity. In September, the British government ousted twenty-five Soviet diplomats and journalists on spying charges; the Kremlin promptly ousted the same number of Britons from Moscow, a move that surprised the British, whose diplomats in Moscow had hoped for a "milder" Soviet response. In the past, the Russians had responded in such circumstances by expelling fewer foreigners or not retaliating at all. Still under the illusion that Gorbachev might behave more moderately, Britain the next week expelled six additional Russians from London, only to have six more British staff ousted from Moscow. If the British had followed with more expulsions, Gorbachev was prepared to match them, as long as the battle continued. Privately aides described him as annoyed by what he called "Western hypocrisy," saying that diplomatic missions on both sides were engaged in the same type of work but the West saw it as convenient to keep raising the specter of Soviet spies.

Though a novice in foreign affairs, Gorbachev displayed both his toughness and his understanding of the international press, the importance of becoming a media personality. In late August, he gave an interview to the editors of *Time* magazine. A month later he met a group of French reporters before his official visit to France. In a world where impressions are formed by television images, he was able to show that he was quite as elegant and open-minded as the leaders of the West. When a chic and self-assured Raisa Gorbachev arrived at Versailles for a state dinner, she seemed to carry with her some of the glamour of a movie star, projecting the image of a new and different Kremlin first lady. At the Geneva summit, both managed to hold their own against the more skilled Reagans.

The summit itself was extraordinary in the sense that both leaders tossed aside the agenda and pursued personal diplomacy. The only negotiations involved the contents of the joint "statement" issued at the end. Gorbachev, in his press conference, professed to be satisfied. "We spoke the language of politics, open and straightforward," he said. It was important for him to understand "the starting point for the shaping" of Reagan policy and appraise things "without bias." He said that at the start both leaders had agreed "not to tell each other banalities," that the exchanges were productive but that "at the moment" Reagan was not prepared to make major decisions. Both men, he said, left the summit with a better understanding of the differences between them. SDI remained the major issue; Gorbachev wanted to ban all space weapons, quoting Lyndon B. Johnson as saying that the nation that dominates space would also dominate the earth. Later, when talking about the nuclear age, he would quote the Buddha that "the only real victory is one in which nobody is defeated and all are equally victorious."[9]

On his way home, he stopped in Prague, where he met with the leaders of the Warsaw Pact countries and briefed them on his summit talks—the first such prompt briefing of allies by a Kremlin leader. He reported to the Politburo a few days later that economic and political ties between Moscow and Eastern Europe were intensified and their unified "foreign policy is becoming more closely coordinated."[10]

During the summit, Gorbachev managed to score a number of propaganda points. With intuitive dexterity he seized opportunities when they presented themselves, showing the agile mind that both the Soviets and the rest of the world would come to know. He welcomed Jesse Jackson and a group of antiwar activists at the Soviet consulate in Geneva, but did not make too much out of it. His voice was the voice of a new generation. He did not rant and rave about American "imperial" foreign-policy ambitions; he likened them to "perpetual motion machines which are born out of the lack of knowledge of elementary laws of nature."

When a reporter asked him about Gromyko's assertion earlier that year that Gorbachev had "a nice smile but iron teeth," the Soviet leader fielded the question with a breezy "It hasn't yet been confirmed. As of now, I'm still using my own teeth." On another occasion, as the two leaders met the press, Gorbachev outshone Reagan in public relations. A question was directed at Reagan about his chief of staff, Donald Regan, who had angered women in the United States in a presummit interview by suggesting that women would not understand such serious issues as "throw weights, or what happens in Afghanistan, or what is happening in human rights." Asked to comment on Regan's statement, the American president looked pained, saying he was certain that Regan had not meant the comment in the way it was taken. Reagan failed to recognize an opportunity to state eloquently his own, enlightened views. The reporter turned to Gorbachev for a comment on the level of female interest in summits. Not knowing the background to the question, Gorbachev looked puzzled. He asked Reagan's Russian interpreter, William Krimer, for an explanation, then seized the opportunity to present his view that women all over the world were interested in peace and in arms reduction, as Reagan squirmed.[11]

The reaction in Russia was positive. Gorbachev looked good on television, showing himself an adroit and purposeful leader. People in the establishment were proud of his performance in Geneva. "The world could see that we are not Martians," a political journalist commented privately, echoing the opinions of many at the time. The shrill rhetoric of the previous years began to fade away. On January 1, 1986, Reagan and Gorbachev exchanged simultaneous televised New Year's messages and talked to each other's citizens with a degree of optimism about safeguarding peace. A relative air of civility was restored.

Gorbachev's performance during his first year in office was a triumph of politics.

Throughout the winter, Gorbachev and his aides worked on the perestroika program and kept revising the draft of a new Communist Party program. But by the time the Twenty-seventh Communist Party Congress convened on February 25, 1986, only the party program was completed. A specific blueprint for economic reforms, the heart of perestroika, required another year before Gorbachev could introduce it as he wanted. In his book *Perestroika* he said that he had contemplated putting off the congress, given that there was such a short time to prepare for it. But, wanting to forge ahead as quickly as possible, he had rejected that option. In retrospect, his political triumph may have been due to this hasty preparation, which resulted in an absence of specific reform measures, which would have threatened major vested interests of privilege and power. Instead the general secretary was philosophical, presenting only the direction of change, when he addressed some five thousand party officials in the Kremlin Palace of Congresses.

The congress gave him a formal mandate for the rest of the eighties. It endorsed his program and his vision of the future and confirmed most of the people he wanted in the top leadership. The biggest surprise was the appointment of Anatoly Dobrynin, the veteran Soviet ambassador to Washington, as secretary of the Central Committee, although other promotions would be more significant in the long run. Lev Zaikov was made a full Politburo member, with responsibility for the military-industrial complex; Yuri Solovyov and Nikolai Slyunkov were made nonvoting Politburo members. In addition to Dobrynin, the new Central Committee secretaries included four Gorbachev protégés—Alexander Yakovlev, Georgi Razumovsky, Vadim Medvedev, and Alexandra Biryukova, the first woman in the leadership since Yekaterina Furtseva, who had served in Khrushchev's Politburo. A suave and sophisticated diplomat, thoroughly at home in the West, Dobrynin was suddenly put in a position from which he could create policy, pretty much the way Henry Kissinger did during the first Nixon administration—a comparison that incidentally set off joking banter and denials so weak as to suggest that it was very much on Dobrynin's mind. Zaikov, former mayor of Leningrad, would eventually become one of the most important players, rising to the post of deputy chairman of the Defense Council.

So far Gorbachev had been lucky—everything had broken right for him. He projected control and competence, reinforced by his growing mastery of political and diplomatic skills. His reforms, presented in a long report to the congress, were almost exclusively inspired and justified by economic necessity rather than ideology.

His personal imprint was clearly seen in the newly adopted course. He was a communist, a true believer, and a Russian patriot who foresaw continued struggle with the United States and the West. However, he did not see it as a sort of final battle between good and evil but, rather, as a complicated conflict of national interests in which men and institutions should eschew the traditional self-righteousness lest they rush humanity toward self-destruction. He wanted to free his party from mysticism and stereotypes. Marxism-Leninism, he said, was not "an assortment of rigid schemes and formulas which would be valid everywhere and in all contingencies." The party was responding to a "fundamentally new situation in the country and in the world." He quoted Lenin to support his modernization of the ideology. Lenin, he said, saw the precepts of Marx and Engels as setting out general tasks "which are necessarily modified by the concrete economic and political conditions of each particular period of history." That is why, Gorbachev said, the party had to show its creativity, capacity for innovation, and "ability to transcend the limits of accepted but already outdated notions." To justify his revisions of the party's policy and program, Gorbachev used the existence of nuclear weapons, which "endowed man for the first time in history with the physical capacity for destroying all life on earth." It was perhaps the only acceptable explanation for tinkering with the dogma. While retaining the liturgical attacks on imperialism, and particularly on the United States, Gorbachev had changed at least the rhetorical objectives of communism. His party program did not see the current period in history as one of "struggle" between imperialism and communism but, rather, as one of "historic competition." He had dropped the Bolshevik expectation of the "downfall of imperialism" and the "triumph of communism and socialism on a worldwide scale." Gorbachev's program was holding out hopes that "mankind's movement toward socialism and communism" could not be reversed. Gorbachev justified his retreat from Lenin's dream of revolutionizing and reordering the world, from his declaration of war against bourgeois societies everywhere, on the grounds that such policy was suicidal in the world of nuclear weapons. Moscow, he said, was no longer in the business of "stimulating revolutions" in other countries. Nor would it any longer insist that the Soviet model of socialism was the only true one. There are, he said, "endless variations of socialism but they have one general objective: socialism and peace."

Gorbachev talked about "radical reforms," and advanced the concepts of supply and demand, devolution of managerial authority, realistic prices, modernization of the banking and financial systems, and workers' participation in the decisionmaking process at the workplace. Because the package of reforms would not be ready until 1987, he confined himself to generalities, but his overall thrust foreshadowed the introduction of market instruments, something bound to confront a vast reservoir of resistance at all levels.

Only in retrospect did it become clear that Gorbachev's generalities were designed to camouflage his real intentions, that he had sought to avoid alarming the opposition unnecessarily, especially since the drafting of reform would take another year. His men were engaged in a careful analysis of reforms in Yugoslavia, China, Hungary, and other socialist countries, and their preliminary conclusion was that economic reforms were bound to fail if they were not accompanied by political reforms. Those who listened attentively to the congress speeches of Gorbachev's lieutenants knew to anticipate a major overhaul of the system. Vsevolod Murakhovsky, Gorbachev's confidant and the new superminister of agriculture, declared that the party was "not afraid of a market" economy. Premier Nikolai Ryzhkov became the first Soviet leader to talk at a congress about the "theory of value" and the principle of "self-financing," which meant that firms not making a profit would have to go bankrupt.

Although there was never any question about Gorbachev's preeminence at the Twenty-seventh Party Congress, there were some jarring notes, a few dark clouds, to make it clear that doubts existed within the party establishment, even at that early stage, about the scope and pace of his modernization.

The guerrilla warfare between reformers and conservatives was, of course, inevitable. Gorbachev tried to work around his opponents, but, despite his impressive political skills, some of his proposals were not translated into policy. The party balked at his proposal for multiple candidates in elections for local party leaderships; the central apparat normally appoints the candidate who runs unopposed. The suggestion to limit the tenure for any party official to three terms—in order to prevent the leading organs of power from becoming too old—was also quietly set aside. People aged seventy or over constituted a solid 10 percent of the new Central Committee members, a result of unexpected re-elections of veterans who had earlier been pensioned off: Tikhonov (eighty), Boris Ponomarev (eighty-two), and even Nikolai Baibakov (seventy-eight), the former chief of Gosplan. The French Kremlinologist Michel Tatu interpreted this as "the result of the will of the majority to emphasize continuity, to give to some old conservative spokesmen a right to express their position in the party's parliament and at the same time to reduce Gorbachev's majority, if any, in that body."

Gorbachev had argued the need for fresh blood in the highest levels of the party as a means of "assuring continuity in the leadership and its renewal." In the past, he said, "the violation of this natural process resulted at a certain stage in the weakening of the capacity for work of the Politburo and the Secretariat and the Central Committee as a whole, its apparatus and also the government." He noted that, as a result of brief and formal plenums under Brezhnev and Chernenko, "many crucial problems remained outside plenum agendas for several years. Many Central Committee members had no opportunity throughout their membership to participate in debates or even to put forward proposals."[12] Nikita Khrushchev had sought similar changes and had met equally strong resistance. The bureaucracy was comfortable with the Brezhnev-style stability, the security of tenure, the absence of upheavals, and the soothing rhetoric, which—unlike Gorbachev's—did not demand exertions and sacrifices. The party chieftains paid excessive homage to the leader, turning him into an emperor, cut off from the substance of daily politics by Kremlin rituals—endless presentations of honors, the incessant quotation of the general secretary's remarks by every conceivable speech-giver and editorial writer, the larger-than-life portraits throughout the land, in every office and bureau and shop. Brezhnev and Chernenko relished that attention, which appealed to their vanity. But Gorbachev—like his models, Lenin and Andropov—was interested in effective use of political power rather than the rituals of leadership. "Why should one keep quoting Mikhail Sergeyevich!" Gorbachev exclaimed irritably during the congress, interrupting a speaker who had repeatedly quoted him to buttress his own position.

From the outset, he had asked the Soviet media not to refer each day to his old speeches or mark his birthdays, and made it clear that he disliked empty phrases and patriotic exhortations. Later, in the course of fierce political struggles, the establishment continued to try to entice him into abandoning his activism in favor of a Brezhnev-style role. They wanted to deify him in order that he stop pressing them. "They are trying to make me into a god, but I'm not one," he told Athos Fava, the Argentine communist leader. He summarized the weaknesses of the system; "Dogmatism, bureaucracy, suppression of criticism, and the elevation of the leader—the number one."[13]

The week of the congress was too tense and confusing to give anyone a clear idea of disagreements at the top. With the exception of a handful of Brezhnev holdovers, the majority of Kremlin leaders had been advanced either by Andropov or by Gorbachev. But it was noted at the time that Yegor Ligachev, who held the second spot in the party hierarchy, had taken a slight distance from the leader. Ligachev's speech included all the proper words about perestroika and reforms, but there was a distinctly conservative tinge to it. Some liberal intellectuals began to portray him as the Darth Vader of reforms, a sinister and scheming conservative; others ascribed the tone to the fact that he was an old war-horse who spoke the language of the provincial bosses and World War Two veterans and was thus able to captivate the ideologically faithful.

Ligachev was the only speaker to use the word "collegial" to describe the work of the leadership, conspicuously suggesting his self-image as one of equality with the leader. He also sharply criticized an article that appeared in *Pravda* on the eve of the congress that had set off shock waves throughout the party elite, and which for the first time publicly listed some of the *nomenklatura* benefits. On this and other key issues, he stood in direct opposition to Yeltsin, who told the congress that the time had come for the elimination of positions and people "beyond criticism." We speculated at the time that Ligachev, who was ten years older than Gorbachev, may have been deliberately assigned his conservative role to calm that important constituency and bring it into the fold. Between him and the radical firebrand Yeltsin, Gorbachev held together the centrifugal forces of the party by his political skills and the strength of his personality. Although far closer to Yeltsin, Gorbachev conspicuously held the middle ground, as if to reassure the elite that future reforms would be prudent, that nothing would be done precipitously, and that he would loosen the system but not go so far as to provoke a political cataclysm.

But after the congress was over, Ligachev gradually emerged as the man whom conservatives began to regard as their soulmate in the leadership. That he should eventually become a rival of Gorbachev speaks more about the radical nature of the challenge Gorbachev had placed before the party and country than about Ligachev's personal ambition.

Yegor Ligachev never had a consuming interest in ideological matters. An engineer by profession, he spent only one year working in an aircraft factory during World War Two before becoming a Komsomol activist and then a party worker. A serious, energetic, and incorruptible man, he spent most of his political career in Siberia. Intelligent but not brilliant, hardworking, a decent apparatchik in the communist context—he would not fire a man for incompetence but would ruin careers of people for the suggestion of promiscuity or drunkenness—he worked from 1944 to 1961 in Novosibirsk. But his career got its first real boost when he caught Khrushchev's attention in 1957. In May of that year, as the government decided to establish the scientific-research city of Akademgorodok, outside the city of Novosibirsk, Ligachev was named party leader of the new community being hacked out of the taiga.

Since Khrushchev had made Akademgorodok a top-priority project, Ligachev frequently traveled to Moscow for high-level consultations. In 1959, he was promoted to a higher regional position, and two years later was summoned to Moscow and made deputy chief of the Central Committee Propaganda Department for the Russian Republic. His appointment required the personal approval of Khrushchev, and Khrushchev's personal patronage was confirmed in 1963, when Ligachev was promoted to the sensitive post of deputy chief of the party personnel department for Russia. Promptly after Khrushchev's ouster, Ligachev was removed to the Siberian city of Tomsk, where he spent the next eighteen years.

But when Andropov was looking for people not associated with the Brezhnevite machine to take over sensitive jobs, Ligachev's name came up near the top of the former KGB chief's list. At Tomsk, Ligachev had managed to enlarge his reputation as an efficient administrator who insisted on discipline but was also sensitive to popular moods. When asked what he had done during the Tomsk years, he said, "I answer proudly, I was building socialism."[14] His image was that of a no-nonsense headmaster, strict but caring. He was a puritan and an almost obsessive opponent of alcoholism; as an old-fashioned, humorless communist, he was given to saying that "daily life is also party work." He distrusted sloganeering and was not vain or narrow-minded. He praised caution, and his favorite piece of folk wisdom, which he often quoted, was "Before going into the room, make sure you can get out again."[15]

Andropov knew that, while Ligachev possessed a conservative cast of mind, he was not a Stalinist. Ligachev was uneasy about the Brezhnevite drift in the national course and disturbed by the decline in the country's vitality and prestige. As Tomsk leader, he showed an impatience with the inefficiencies of the system, and he tried to streamline the bureaucratic establishment and force accountability for its performance. (Among other things, he cut the number of party and trade-union meetings to raise productivity and established antialcoholism clinics.) But although such things may have been featured in KGB files, few people in Moscow knew about them.

Even within the establishment, Ligachev was a largely unknown figure when he arrived in Moscow in April 1983. A powerfully built man with thick strands of white hair flowing above his horn-rimmed glasses, he seemed, at least in appearance, to belong to the Brezhnev era. His face was strong and sharp. He was an organization man, superb at managing but a mediocre public speaker, reading his texts in a liturgical rhythm, and repeating the banalities that had become a part of the official Soviet lingo. But these very banalities, the interminable references to patriotic duty, discipline, and optimism, struck positive chords in the hearts of the Old Guard bureaucrats and conservatives.

Ligachev and Gorbachev had been in close contact during Andropov's short reign. Since Gorbachev's strength lay in behind-the-scenes work, in his prodigious energy, his caution and steady competence, Andropov had placed him in charge of party personnel, or cadres, where he proved a forceful administrator. As Andropov pushed the purge of regional party organizations, Ligachev, the straitlaced puritan, was his main hatchet man. Two months before Andropov's death, he was promoted to the leadership as secretary of the Central Committee. There was at that stage no inkling of disagreement between him and Gorbachev. The two men had first met in the late sixties, when they worked occasionally on youth issues on a committee set up within the Supreme Soviet. Ligachev was the first chief of that committee, and was succeeded by Gorbachev in 1974.

When Chernenko took charge of the Kremlin, Ligachev's career was threatened with eclipse. Indeed, had Chernenko lived longer, he would have most certainly had his own man appointed to the personnel post. But shortly after Chernenko died, Gorbachev promoted Ligachev (along with Ryzhkov) to full Politburo membership without having him go through the intermediate stage as a nonvoting Politburo member. He named Ligachev the party's chief ideologist, or the number-two figure in the hierarchy. Ligachev's enemies later said privately that this appointment was made hurriedly in the first month of Gorbachev's rule, that Gorbachev was paying his political debt, and that if Gorbachev's advisers had had the time to review the situation carefully they would have realized that Ligachev was ill suited for ideological work.[16]

Boris Yeltsin publicly but obliquely voiced this same view when he said that some "skeptics and downright opponents of the new approach" were holding senior positions, adding, "We could have avoided many blunders in appointments."[17]

Ligachev's minimal education and experience made him the least prepared man ever to hold the job, in which his immediate predecessors were Gorbachev, Chernenko, Andropov, and Suslov. He had no intellectual pretensions, nor did his knowledge of Marx and Lenin go beyond the elementary stage. Reformist intellectuals were initially patronizing about Ligachev, portraying him as a man of mediocrity, and it was a widely held belief among Gorbachev insiders that Ligachev's main problem was brain power, that he was just not as smart and knowledgeable as the new people who surrounded the leader.

But this was an error. Others, while granting the absence of imagination and glitz, saw in him a skillful politician who enjoyed the rough-and-tumble of Soviet domestic politics and who moved quietly, often for the jugular, leaving so little impression behind that no one heard him or saw his footsteps except a few real party insiders. Above all, he was a man of the party establishment who believed in the capacity and the right of a party elite to govern on its own terms, the honest party people deciding on the right policies in the proper and established way. Whether he saw his chief as something of an intellectual and adventurer—as many ideological hard-liners privately thought—is unclear. In the new constellation at the top, Ligachev's promotion may have been Gorbachev's concession to the conservatives. The Chernenko faction in the Politburo was still strong at the time, and perhaps eager to have in the number-two post an older and more conservative figure as a counterweight to the younger party chief.

Whether or not Gorbachev anticipated it, Ligachev became the magnet for conservative elements. Already in June 1985, the new chief ideologist addressed the Academy of Sciences saying that Gorbachev's reforms, "which we have developed in our discussions, will take place within the sphere of scientific socialism, without deviation to a market economy or private enterprise." His emphasis was puzzling. Gorbachev had said much the same thing, but his whole outlook rested on the belief that socialism as an economic system contains vast untapped potential, which would be freed by a judicious application of basic economic laws, laws that the command economy had simply denied. Gorbachev was also hinting that he was moving toward market socialism as he repeatedly evoked Lenin's New Economic Policy, which reintroduced small-scale private enterprise in industry, agriculture, and services in 1921, and which was subsequently abandoned by Stalin. There was another difference between Gorbachev and Ligachev, a more subtle one. Gorbachev's whole approach was centered on efforts to energize the individual; he talked about "the value and dignity of the individual." One of the fundamental problems of socialism was to accommodate and provide more room for an individual's personal interests and motivations. In the economy, he wanted to ensure "a more solid and direct connection between the interests of the individual" and productivity through contractual arrangements.[18] Ligachev's approach was more conventional; he saw "individualism" as a phenomenon "alien to socialism."

Ligachev displayed what seemed to be ambivalence about the new reforms in somewhat contradictory statements. In that same June 1985 speech to the academy, he pleaded for stricter controls over the economy, while in an article in the July issue of *Kommunist* he complained about the damaging results of such controls. To many people, this alone suggested that the ideology chief had not yet found the center of his ideological gravity. Unlike Gorbachev, who tended to view ideology as a sterile ritual to which lip service must be given because it was the source of his legitimacy, Ligachev remained the most visible top figure emotionally attached to the old rhetoric of communism. He talked about a "pluralistic society" in the Soviet Union—"we have different classes, different social groups," he told *Le Monde* later, there are ethnic groups, also "professional groups et cetera. Each one has its own interests"—but he saw all these interests as fitting neatly into the "class interest" of the Soviet people and invariably returned to ideology as a means of dealing with all conflicts. There was in this an odd tinge of dogmatism, a jarring note in Gorbachev's pragmatic choir. But that too seemed natural. During the first year, and even after the end of the party congress, political conflicts were not so visible as the entire Gorbachev administration was searching for its bearings.

For Gorbachev, the main objective was to seize control of the Brezhnevite party machinery and energize it. The party, with its nineteen million rank-and-file members (7 percent of the population), permeated all Soviet institutions—every school, factory, organization, institute, collective farm. To mobilize this vast army, to give it direction and make it respond to his wishes, Gorbachev needed to gain control over a smaller army of party officers, about 450,000 of them, the *nomenklatura*. That stratum of cadres, which held positions of power and enjoyed great privileges, was the backbone of the party.

Like any party, it had become corrupt, and many of its members, in Gorbachev's words, were "dishonest, pushy, and greedy people intent on benefiting from their membership."[19] During the Brezhnev years, which could be described as the golden age of the *nomenklatura*, most of these officials held what seemed to them to be lifetime jobs. The key lay in the system of appointments, which strengthened the party's hierarchical lines of authority and paved the way for mafia-type local party establishments which were not bothered by Moscow as long as they reported good economic results.

The intellectual exhaustion of the party expressed itself in the poverty of the official lingo. The bureaucratic patois described any policy approach as "complex," most difficulties as "thought up" (*nadumannoe*). Moscow always stood ready to "rebuff" its enemies and deliver "crushing blows" against aggressors. The party itself was invariably "in the forefront" of each and every issue; the string of self-congratulatory banalities seemed endless. Anything positive was "socialist" in its basic nature; socialism itself was without flaws. Once the problem was "seized," its "resolution" seemed automatic. The holding of meetings and the passage of decrees passed for real work. The party had become less an instrument of action than a way of life. Cautious, mediocre thinkers who shrouded their views in these clichés moved up the ranks gradually, and by the time they received independent responsibility they were often, as Yeltsin put it, too old to exercise it vigorously. An "ossified" Stalinist concept of socialism eliminated all debates and creative ideas from theoretical and social sciences, while "authoritarian evaluations and opinions became unquestionable truths that could only be commented upon."[20]

This was more or less the situation that confronted Gorbachev as he sought to turn the party into an agent of change. He had thought initially that by altering its composition, by bringing in people who like himself were truly interested in public affairs and the betterment of society, he would be able to push his national reconstruction program through. In the Ukraine in June 1985, during an impromptu conversation carried on national television, he talked optimistically about a "powerful economy, the most powerful advanced sciences, a qualified working-class and educated people—a people possessing ample love for the motherland—[and] such a powerful force as the party which is capable of skillfully holding on course our socialist ship."

But, having fought his way inside the Brezhnevite machinery, he found little worth preserving. Beneath the manufactured optimism of the party's public position there was only the manufactured optimism of its internal life. Everybody pretended to toe the line, and any debate or introduction of new ideas was stifled by the careful reticence of members determined to avoid problems and headaches. The hesitation to commit oneself to an opinion was so contagious that it had poisoned the entire apparat.

It was a party incapable of providing firm leadership, which held power for power's sake and failed to see the need for change.

Who was responsible for this situation?

"It is the leading bodies of the party and the state that bear responsibility for all this," Gorbachev answered his own question.[21]

Despite the turnover begun under Andropov and continued by Gorbachev—roughly one-fifth of the cadres were replaced by 1986—the mood of the party had not changed perceptibly. Andropov and Gorbachev brought in a group of people who were undoubtedly anxious to get the economy moving, but they were up against a majority who feared the uncertainties and upheavals that accompany real changes.

Gorbachev had a somewhat ambivalent spokesman in Ligachev, for he sounded more and more like a cautious defender of the existing system, although, on economic issues at least, he was in tune with the goals of perestroika. Ligachev went along with the vast purge of 1985–86, but he was against structural changes such as the proposed policy of early retirement and rotation of officials. "We should not be looking at the calendar but at the true results" of officials' work, he said.

Gorbachev's initial signals also seemed contradictory, as he emphasized local initiative and autonomy while simultaneously relying on political intervention at the highest levels to force changes. Again, Gorbachev seemed to have underestimated the frailty of man and the strength of institutions as his speeches began to reflect his impatience and frustration. His extraordinarily quick rise to supreme power seemed, at least during his first year in power, to have reinforced his self-confidence, his belief in his own capacity to mold events, and his expectations that the party and society would respond to his eminently rational and coherent plan of action. Faced with an intractable *nomenklatura,* he began to blame his predecessors, although he would not stoop to mudslinging and personal attacks. By January 1987, he would concede that "the problems that have accumulated in society [are] more deeply rooted than we first thought. The further we go with our reorganization, the clearer its scope and significance; more and more unresolved problems inherited from the past come out."

In the months after the spring congress, Gorbachev began to look for ways to generate pressure from below, to inspire the rank-and-file members to rebel discreetly against those who opposed his reforms. He still hoped to reform the party by establishing authority over its elite, the *nomenklatura,* but this time he was asking the rank and file to control their superiors.

Gorbachev had sought an open fight of ideas with the old establishment and was armed with arguments and concepts to guarantee that he would come out on top. But the bureaucratic establishment refused to argue. Rhetorically, they went along with his policy; privately, they expressed doubts and reservations, and did what hostile bureaucracies do everywhere: they waged rearguard actions of obstruction; they sought to exhaust the energy and commitment of his team and wear him down. They waited for him to make a mistake, to hang himself with his own rope.

Chapter 7

CHERNOBYL: THE HONEYMOON ENDS

The strange political lull that followed the end of the congress on March 3, 1986, came to an end with a bang, giving Gorbachev a powerful jolt from a most unexpected quarter.

At 1:23 A.M. on Saturday, April 26, an explosion destroyed a nuclear reactor at Chernobyl, in the Ukraine, sending blasts of radioactive fumes and particles high into the atmosphere and setting off fires in nearby buildings. Two persons were killed as part of the control room was blasted away. When twenty-eight firemen from the nearby town of Pripyat arrived thirty minutes later, they saw flames leaping two hundred feet into the air, but they were not aware that under the ruin the graphite core of the reactor was burning too.

There was chaos at Chernobyl during that long springtime night. As Geiger counters climbed off the top of the scale, the firefighters sought to contain the blaze at Reactor No. 4 from spreading to the three nearby nuclear reactors that jointly constitute the Chernobyl Power Station. The blaze was racing toward the turbine room, with the frightening prospect that it could ignite the oil-storage facility and spread to the neighboring Reactor No. 3. Indeed, the roof of the building housing the third reactor block briefly caught fire, but the firemen managed to put it out. As dawn broke, scores of fire-fighting brigades arrived from Kiev, the Ukrainian capital, about eighty miles to the south. Early in the morning, medical teams evacuated the original group of Pripyat firemen and almost all the members of the skeleton crew inside the power station at the time of the explosion. It was not clear who had been exposed to lethal doses of radiation and who had not. Those who knew the most, who undoubtedly recognized that they were in the midst of the worst disaster in the history of nuclear power, simply fled from the scene: the plant's deputy director, several shift managers, and some senior foremen.

Word of the Chernobyl disaster reached Moscow early Saturday. Gorbachev said later that "soon after the first few reports had reached us, we realized that the situation was serious."[1] At least by 6:00 A.M. that Saturday, or less than four and a half hours after the explosion, responsible authorities in Moscow had full knowledge of the disaster.

Academician Leonid Ilyin, director of Moscow's Institute of Biophysics and a top nuclear-safety expert, was woken up shortly before 6:00 A.M. and given the first report. "At that point it was clear what had happened, and we didn't need to take any special radiation measurements," he was to say later.[2] There were frantic efforts to assemble and dispatch specially equipped rescue teams. By midmorning, a government commission had been set up under a deputy prime minister, Boris Shcherbina. One of the first experts to reach the scene of the disaster was nuclear physicist Valery Legasov, who himself received excessive doses of radiation; two years later he committed suicide while being treated in a Moscow hospital.

Legasov and other emergency workers immediately identified more than a thousand people exposed to radiation. By late afternoon, 299 of them had been flown to Moscow. The victims fell into roughly three categories. The most serious had been exposed to fifteen hundred or more roentgens; radiation had destroyed their central nervous systems, and they were lying prostrate, unable to move. Those in the second category—who suffered exposure to two to fifteen hundred roentgens—were vomiting, some of them continuously, for several hours. When they reached Hospital No. 6 in Moscow, late Saturday afternoon, their symptoms had gone into remission; they were euphoric, chattering about the accident as if the worst was behind them, and asking to speak by phone with their families. But it was a cruel illusion. Within hours the symptoms returned. The third and largest category of patients—exposed to less than two hundred roentgens—were treated in Kiev.

In the shadow of the still-burning reactor, a few miles from Chernobyl, life in Pripyat continued as if nothing unusual had happened. On Sunday, the balmy springtime weather enticed people outdoors. Children went swimming in an outdoor pool, and young men played soccer. For almost thirty-six hours, no one was informed of the danger. Not until late Sunday morning did Shcherbina order the evacuation of Pripyat's forty thousand residents. The entire medical profession of the Ukraine was mobilized to check eighteen thousand persons believed to have been exposed to radiation. As thousands of military specialists, technicians, miners, decontamination experts, and construction workers began arriving at the scene, Shcherbina complained that containment efforts were slow; it was, he said, "like hitting an elephant with shotgun pellets." The reactor was still out of control.

By Sunday evening, it was clear to the leaders in Moscow that only more trouble could be expected from Chernobyl. The atmosphere in the upper echelons of the Kremlin was funereal.

When Professor Ilyin flew to the area on Monday, he found the town of Pripyat deserted. "The cherries and apples were in bloom but the town was dead. It was a difficult thing to grasp," he said. High up in a helicopter over Chernobyl, he saw an almost uninterrupted caravan of cars, trucks, buses, and tractors, all going in one direction—away from the disaster. "The strange thing was that there was no panic. But people knew something terrible had happened." Circling over the disaster site, Ilyin watched Soviet Air Force pilots fly their helicopters close to the burning Reactor No. 4 to dump thousands of tons of sand, boron, and lead. Scientists were preoccupied by the specter of a meltdown. The reactor was physically sinking as its heat and the still-burning graphite fires weakened the steel supports inside the concrete floor. Some specialists feared that the additional pressure on the concrete floor caused by dumping tons of sand, lead, and boron on the reactor in an effort to seal off the radiation and extinguish the fire could lead to an uncontrollable meltdown. A melt-through into the water table that irrigated the surrounding land and supplied water to the area's industries and population held the prospect of an even greater catastrophe. Nobody was sure how to cope with it.

On that same Monday, at about 9:00 A.M., workers at the Swedish nuclear power station at Forsmark, about seven hundred miles northwest of Chernobyl, first detected abnormal levels of radiation. Outside the plant, Geiger counters showed radiation four times higher than normal. Other nuclear facilities in Sweden and Finland detected similar radiation, and an analysis of wind currents led them to believe that the radiation had originated in the Soviet Union. But the Swedish Embassy in Moscow received only bland denials to its requests for information. As the Swedes were preparing to issue a radiation alert, Moscow, shortly after 9:00 P.M. Monday, issued a terse statement on the television evening news. "An accident has taken place at the Chernobyl Power Station, and one of the reactors was damaged. Measures are being taken to eliminate the consequences of the accident. Those affected by it are being given assistance. A government commission has been set up."

The statement was little more than a weak cover story. It conceded that which could be hidden no longer.

What did Gorbachev know about Chernobyl, and when did he know it?

There was no one to put this perennial question of American politics to the Soviet leader, the same leader who had asserted, *"S narodom nelzya zaigrivat"* ("One mustn't toy with the people") and whose whole professed political credo was glasnost. Since the Soviet government formed a special commission to deal with the disaster hours after it had occurred, there is no doubt that Gorbachev was informed in detail on the morning of April 26. What he was told about it is not known; but, judging by Ilyin's statement, top experts were fully aware of the magnitude of the disaster on their hands.

It is difficult to imagine a credible explanation for the failure to inform the people of the Chernobyl area, including more than three million residents of Kiev some eighty miles to the south, not to mention the governments and peoples of neighboring countries. Kremlin insiders later said that Gorbachev had wanted to go public right away, but that the majority of his colleagues had urged caution since the ultimate shape of the disaster could not be predicted at that point. If that was indeed the case, why didn't he reject their advice?

Critics everywhere promptly charged, with considerable justification, that even Gorbachev, faced with a crisis of unprecedented magnitude, resorted to the Russian habit of refusing to confront an unpleasant reality promptly, of stonewalling in the hope that the disaster would somehow vanish or that nobody would notice it. It was an old story in the Soviet Union. Moscow stonewalled for days on the fate of the Korean civilian jetliner that Russian pilots shot down in 1983. When Hitler's armies invaded Russia on June 22, 1941, and German planes were carrying out massive bombing raids deep inside Soviet territory, Moscow Radio continued to broadcast its regular program as if nothing had happened, failing to inform the people about the war for nearly twelve hours. Madame de Staël, living in Russia as a refugee from Napoleon in 1812, had complained that she was unable to discover anything about the course of the Franco-Russian war even though Napoleon's troops had reached Moscow. William Richardson, a British traveler who visited Saint Petersburg in the 1760s, described the phenomenon succinctly: "Half of Russia may be destroyed and the other half would know nothing about the matter."[3] But this was Gorbachev, the champion of glasnost, hesitating to tell the people about an accident that potentially affected their health and their daily lives. Not until eighteen days after the accident did he provide an account of it on Soviet television.

Throughout the country and the world, the long silence produced disillusion and incredulity. Even Gorbachev's supporters conceded that Chernobyl had tarnished his reputation for openness. But they stressed that the initial delay was caused by confusion, that nine days after the disaster a coherent information operation had snapped into action, that from that point on the Russians had been exceptionally forthcoming, and that the detailed report they presented to the International Atomic Energy Agency (IAEA) in Vienna four months later was surprisingly candid (which critics also conceded).

Gorbachev may have redeemed himself in the weeks and months following the accident, but by the standards he had set for himself, he fell short in the Chernobyl test. The gap of almost three full days between the accident and the first brief Soviet statement suggested the old instinct for secrecy, and raised doubts about whether any information would have been released if the Swedes had not recorded high radiation levels and issued an official nuclear alert. The initial silence reinforced criticism that Kremlin leaders were more concerned about maintaining their political positions and personal reputations than about protecting their people, in this case from nuclear radiation.

Gorbachev appeared aware of this when he gave his televised report to the nation. His face was haggard. He seemed to have aged in the short span of eighteen days. He sought to project quiet dignity, which came naturally to him, but his arguments were weak. "As soon as we received reliable initial information," he said, "it was made available to the Soviet people and sent through diplomatic channels to the governments of other countries." He did not express any regret or offer any apologies. And he made a great deal out of Western press exaggerations, especially some false and irresponsible reports about tens of thousands of dead buried in a mass grave in the Chernobyl area, expressing anger and dismay at so much "malice and malevolence in the world." But that too seemed like the old Russian ploy of diverting attention from substance to lateral propaganda issues. He was repeatedly to link Chernobyl with the *Challenger* space-shuttle tragedy a few months earlier, to demonstrate that both superpowers had their share of technological disasters. He attempted to seize the initiative by saying, "Chernobyl showed again what an abyss will open if nuclear war befalls mankind," and he advanced proposals to heighten nuclear cooperation and devise a system of information exchanges and mutual assistance if similar accidents were to recur.

Although he would not apologize for his handling of Chernobyl, he was changed by it. From that point on, natural disasters and man-made calamities would be reported promptly in the Soviet media. (The first was the sinking of the passenger liner *Admiral Nakhimov* in the Black Sea, with the loss of more than four hundred lives, the following September.) He also reached some "crucial conclusions" about the continued development of the nuclear-power industry, introducing greater safety precautions and ultimately advocating a slowdown in the country's nuclear-power program.

Although he devoted only forty-one lines of type to Chernobyl in his 1987 book, *Perestroika,* he remained defensive about the issue, and recognized that he had suffered a serious setback, both at home and abroad. A few weeks before the accident, while attending a congress of East Germany's communists, he had talked about the nuclear danger posed by U.S. missiles in Europe, the continent that he called "our common home."[4] Now that Soviet nuclear dust and materials were floating over Europe, Europeans quickly pointed out that the failure to inform them on time about the potential danger to "our common home" showed his blatant disregard for the neighborhood.

At home, ordinary people murmured doubts about his leadership. Historian Yuri Afanasiev, economist Gavril Popov, and other intellectuals openly questioned his performance. Many had initially disregarded broadcasts about Chernobyl that the Voice of America, the BBC, and other Western radio stations beamed into the Soviet Union. Moscow's continued silence had only encouraged these stations to expand their comments about the disaster and fill the vacuum created by official secrecy. Gorbachev described it all as a diabolical conspiracy. U.S. industrialist Armand Hammer, who saw him shortly after Chernobyl, found the Soviet leader angry with top Reagan-administration officials and their criticism of his performance. "What are they trying to do to me?" Hammer quoted Gorbachev as saying. "Create a breach between me and the Russian people?"[5]

The final human toll of Chernobyl is unknown. More than thirty persons died from radiation within the first few months, including a movie director and his cameraman who went in to take footage of the reactor's mangled remains and the cleanup efforts; but the number of persons exposed to radiation in the thirty-kilometer-radius zone around Chernobyl, according to Soviet figures, exceeded a hundred thousand. Robert Gale, an American physician who was called in to help treat the victims, said later that these hundred thousand people would have to be monitored for the rest of their lives, and many of them might develop radiation-induced cancer. What will be the eventual impact of the radiation that entered the food chain, and permeated the earth and water of the region, is another imponderable. "The work goes on," Gorbachev said. "It will take years."[6]

It wasn't until May 4, when a change of winds occurred, that Western broadcasts were confirmed by Soviet broadcasts. On May 5, Ukrainian Health Minister Anatoly Romanenko took to television to inform viewers that, although there was no real cause for alarm, people should close their windows, take showers and wash their hair daily, scrub their apartments, and wash all fruits and vegetables. He advised pregnant women and children to stay indoors, until they were evacuated from the city. Kiev's streets suddenly became virtually deserted, except for the railway station and the airport, where thousands flocked, seeking to flee. Although Romanenko's announcement about the evacuation of children was reversed the next day, thousands of people still sent their children away. Wave after wave of them piled off trains arriving in Moscow's Kievski railway station. Friends, relatives, and acquaintances took them in. At the station's taxi rank, people exchanged such antiradiation "remedies" as drinking large quantities of coffee or, inevitably, vodka. Many expressed anger that they had not been warned earlier of the danger. They were certain that authorities had not told them the full truth.

Some consequences of Chernobyl still remain indecipherable, making it difficult to assess the ultimate damage. The economic price was substantial; the rescue operation cost about $2.7 billion.[7]

Though it started as a public-relations catastrophe, however, the subject of Chernobyl was to fade from the world press, particularly after the Russians began to report in extensive detail about the human failings and misjudgments that led to the disaster, and the subsequent heroic efforts to contain the damage. Gorbachev's aides first said that he saw Chernobyl as a "disastrous episode," not a "cataclysm." And six months later Gorbachev himself described Chernobyl as "a tragedy of relatively local proportions."

It is a mark of Gorbachev's political dexterity and his inherent optimism that he promptly returned to the task at hand, tackling the Soviet Communist Party, and even used what he learned through the Chernobyl disaster to condemn party policies and intransigence. Before Chernobyl he had been showing signs of growing frustration with the party and the system. Now he used the postmortem of the disaster as public evidence of the specific flaws of the system.

The government, it turned out, had less access to factual information than did Soviet newspapers, and proved incapable of responding when information was available. A month before the disaster, experts quoted in *Literaturnaya Ukraina* had ominously warned that the Chernobyl nuclear complex was poorly constructed. Reactor No. 4 became operational in 1984, but two more plants were being built next to it and were due to start operating in 1990. According to the paper, the quality of the cement was scandalously poor: "The construction is not fit for assembly, and never will be. Equipment, machinery, and mechanisms started to wear out, and shortages of basic mechanical devices and instruments occurred. Problems have multiplied and become overgrown with a massive quantity of unknowns."[8] Yet nobody paid any attention to these warnings. Nor did the authorities in Moscow know that there were disagreements among experts, since all reports were designed to indicate complete unanimity on all subjects.

Inertia was the force at work, and Gorbachev knew it. Even before Chernobyl, when he traveled to Kuibyshev, an industrial center on the Volga, and then on to Togliatti, the home of the Zhiguli Automobile Plant, he had vented his frustrations. He wanted rank-and-file party members and ordinary workers to realize that each individual had to put his shoulder behind the wheel. "We have to begin, first of all, with changes in our attitudes and psychology, with the style and method of work," he told the Togliatti workers. "I have to tell you frankly that, if we do not change ourselves, I am deeply convinced there will be no changes in the economy and our social life."[9]

But he needed the party. Formally, as always, party organizations complied with the orders from Moscow. In practice, little was happening. An illuminating example was provided by the case of Osman Khozanov, first secretary of the Ordzhonikidze district in Tadzhikistan, who as part of perestroika was supposed to purge his committee of lazy and incompetent officials. He did so, but put his own relatives in their places.[10]

Other regional committees simply defied instructions. One of the most flagrant acts of open resistance occurred in Rostov-on-Don, where communist authorities gave a hero's burial that summer to a disgraced former senior Communist Party colleague who had been convicted of corruption and who died in jail. In a grand act of defiance, his corpse was borne, in an open coffin lined with red velvet, through the main streets, the way leaders' funerals are conducted in Red Square, with local communist grandees following in solemn procession. At the cemetery, speaker after speaker extolled the man's virtues. A subsequent investigation revealed that, like a genuine underworld chieftain, he had continued to run his corruption rackets from his prison cell. Police records showed that theft and embezzlement connected with the ring had even increased after he and other members were imprisoned and two of them were sentenced to death by firing squad.[11]

In the course of 1986, Gorbachev began to encounter open resistance within the leadership itself. Ligachev's voice was growing steadily louder and more skeptical in the inner circles as his hard questioning exposed one problem after another in perestroika. Conservative misgivings at that stage were succinctly articulated by Fyodor Burlatsky in an imaginary debate, published in *Literaturnaya Gazeta,* between a Gorbachev-style regional party leader and his conservative deputy, a man in the Ligachev mode. The deputy regards all the talk about market forces, competition, cooperative and individual forms of private enterprise, and profit as something incomprehensibly dangerous. "Nothing will come of it," he is certain. He does not quite understand these things, but he is sure that they constitute a retreat from socialism, a "step back from what we have won." He is especially worried that people like himself, who do not "reconstruct" themselves, could be fired. But, most important, the deputy is against political reforms. What will that do to the party? he wonders. If there is to be devolution of decision-making authority, if local factories go over to "self-management," he wonders, "what will there be for us to do?"[12]

By the time Gorbachev addressed the June plenum of the Central Committee, his frustration with the lack of movement was explicit.

He lectured them as they had never been lectured before.

"For a whole year we have persistently sought new approaches that would create the conditions for deepening the process" of modernization, he said, but things had improved only "somewhat." Many plans had not moved "beyond good intentions." Losses due to negligence were exorbitant (thirteen billion cubic meters of gas burned needlessly per year, a million tons of coal lost in transportation, one-fifth of the entire agricultural production). Corruption, cronyism, laziness, resistance to change, and incompetence marked the work of party and industrial managers.[13]

The view of the party and its inadequacies that Gorbachev outlined at the plenum was extraordinarily scathing. The "dominant style" in party work was so thoroughly bureaucratized that the party machinery had become an end in itself. Party officials surrounded themselves with "yes-men" and engaged in deliberate acts of deception and fraud to "conceal failures." Shuddering at the proliferation of paperwork and the expenditure of energy, Gorbachev said that even Cabinet ministers and top managers "have altogether lost the habit of speaking to one another." Everything was done by correspondence. With documents moving for weeks from one desk to another, it was manifestly impossible to take immediate action on a pressing problem. Officials, he said, "are unable to speak to one another over the telephone, to get together and settle problems, [because] they try to shield themselves from responsibility by means of documents."[14]

Worst of all, this "dominant" style encouraged the most defensive and conservative impulses within the party: no new opportunity was worth a risk. He confronted the ultimate expression of this conservatism in the party's determination to protect those who, if wrong, were wrong for the right reasons, and to penalize those who, although right, were right because they were innovative. When individuals do show initiative, he said, "they find themselves in a tight spot and suffer defeat."

To illustrate his point, Gorbachev told a story about the unnamed head of an electrical-engineering institute in Cherkassy. His institute had developed new machine tools and control systems, which it sold to firms at home and abroad. However, a local factory refused to accept the new machinery. When the institute director was temporarily assigned to run the plant, he introduced the new technology, bringing the plant "to life and improving its income." However, he was soon unjustly accused of violating regulations, dismissed from his post, and expelled from the party. Moreover, Gorbachev said, when the man wrote a letter to the authorities in Moscow it was "intercepted at the post office by the local authorities and never reached Moscow."[15]

At times like this it seemed that Gorbachev was beginning to grasp the party elite's unshakable belief that the country's policy was their institutional (if not personal) property and to understand that this belief was the source of resistance to the spirit of perestroika. They paid lip service to his policies, but perestroika could become a mere illusion. "As far as talking goes, everything is fine, but there is no real change."

With inertia the principal force at work, his entire plan could be doomed. Hegel's dictum that "Truth is always concrete" redirected his attention toward a strange irony: he and his closest advisers, as leaders of the Soviet state, had come to regard the ruling Communist Party as an immovable organization wallowing in lies and self-deception. His speech reflected his acute awareness of the degree of the party's degradation.

But, however frustrated, he needed the party. Whatever the disagreements, he believed that the rank-and-file would eventually and wholeheartedly side with him. Not the KGB and not the military but the party was the key because, as he put it, the party "has in its hands powerful levers for influencing social processes." He would fight for the heart of the party, and he was convinced that he would win in an open and fair struggle. Which in turn led to a new feature in his public policy, the invasion of forbidden areas of thought and action that began under the name "glasnost." Glasnost, in its evolving guises over the years, was to become Gorbachev's main legacy, modifying the relationship between ruler and subject. But at that point, in mid-1986, none of his key associates anticipated its eventual impact; nor, probably, did he.[16]

Amplifying the thoughts he advanced in private meetings, Gorbachev effectively launched his glasnost policy at the June plenum as a way to "establish control by the people over the [party] bureaucracy.

"The time that has elapsed since the congress, and the latest developments, have clearly confirmed the vital importance of the lessons of truth of which the congress participants spoke," Gorbachev said. "In all situations we should remember Lenin's warnings: 'Illusions and self-deceptions are terrible, the fear of truth is pernicious.' The party and the people need the whole truth, in big things and small. Only the truth instills in people an acute sense of civic duty. Lies and half-truths produce a warped mentality, deform the personality, and prevent one from making realistic conclusions and evaluations, without which an active party policy is inconceivable."

By exposing the basic defects of the system, Gorbachev presented his case as fully as he could. However frequently he resorted to communist jargon, he left no doubt that he was asking the establishment to give up its hypocrisy, and warning at the same time that if they refused to do so he would force the issue with glasnost from below. In short, this was a declaration of war against the conservative party establishment.

Chapter 8

THE GLASNOST GAMBLE

Despite the power and prestige of his office, Gorbachev had too many officials in high positions whose primary loyalty was not to him or his program. Some of his remarks to the Central Committee showed his disappointment with those of his colleagues who gave him only rhetorical support. More and more he turned away from the people he had inherited toward those he had brought in himself—the people he had worked with, knew well, and trusted most. The conflicts at the top were not only over policy but also over power. He felt hemmed in by the collective control of the Politburo and sought ways to escape.

Gorbachev set out on his glasnost campaign as a committed warrior who wanted to fight his enemies in broad daylight on an open field. "Glasnost" was not his term. It had been a major demand of political dissidents during the Brezhnev years, most eloquently evoked by the novelist Alexander Solzhenitsyn. In an open letter protesting his expulsion from the Soviet Writers' Union in 1969, he wrote: "Glasnost, honest and complete—that is the prime condition for the health of every society, and ours too."

Attempts to find a precise translation of "glasnost" fail to capture its full meaning. It literally translates as "openness" or "publicity." But since it became Gorbachev's war cry, the term has acquired more complex political connotations. It stands for greater openness and candor in government affairs and for an interplay of different and sometimes conflicting views in political debates, in the press, and in Soviet culture. Gorbachev had talked about glasnost from the very beginning, but had spent his first year focusing on his economic strategy for perestroika. It was his frustration with the party, which was either unwilling or unable to enact even modest changes, that made him wave the glasnost banner. Clearly, the unsettling instructions for greater efficiency and accountability were threatening party privileges, habits, and comfort. Clearly, the sprawling bureaucratic elite was resisting the reformist tsar. He'd been in office more than a year, but nothing was moving. Even major decisions were dying a slow death in the bowels of the bureaucracy. One of Gorbachev's first moves had been to pass a decree in April 1985 providing for distribution of private plots to one million families each year; it also instructed local authorities to make available building materials for country cottages and repair services. "We said that no matter how high the demand of our construction organizations for these materials, some have to be set aside for the people and put on sale," Gorbachev complained. "When we checked on how these decisions were implemented, we found that department after department systematically bungled them."[1]

As a practical politician, he turned to glasnost in an effort to increase popular pressure for his program. It was a major decision. To move a nation, he had to gain the nation's ear. The only way to reach large audiences was through the media.

He had already sought to convert his popularity and his office into political pressure, but exhortatory public speeches had limited success. Russians tend to respond to such direct intervention at times of visible and tangible crisis. The crisis Gorbachev was talking about was invisible and intangible, for his concern was the threat of future decline. What was tangible and visible was a shortage of consumer goods; poor services; and a deterioration of the country's welfare system. And there was little he could do immediately to rectify them. His aides felt he was running a risk of dissipating his influence by endless repetition of his message.[2]

A joke that circulated during the summer of 1986 revealed the mood of the population. The joke portrays the Soviet Union as a train that is stopped dead because there are no more railway tracks. Each leader deals with the crisis in his own way: Stalin has the conductor and engineer shot; Khrushchev rehabilitates them; Brezhnev closes the curtains and orders that the train be shaken from side to side to create the illusion of movement; and Gorbachev opens the curtains, leans out the window, and shouts, "We're out of rails, we're out of rails."

By opening up the media, by revealing all the shortcomings and outlining all the problems in the country, by politicizing the population, Gorbachev was assured that his program would touch every family. He had started a "revolution from above"; he wanted now to open another revolutionary front, "from below." His target was the "entrenched, inner, immovable bureaucratic party layer," which *Pravda* in December 1985 said was based on privileges, and which had positioned itself between the leadership and the working people.[3]

The nature of Gorbachev's war was perhaps most succinctly assessed by one of his strongest supporters in the literary world, writer Vitali Korotich, who said that it was a war against the Stalinist system, which has created a huge party bureaucracy that still runs Russia. Whereas the issue of Stalin's crimes still preoccupied the intellectuals, Korotich said, "the fight against Stalin is a fight with a shadow. It's the people who stole yesterday and who are still here that we have to deal with now."[4]

But to view this policy merely as a limited tactical device in a power struggle with the bureaucracy obscures as much as it reveals. Novelist Anatoly Rybakov, whose *Children of the Arbat* was to become the country's best-read book of the eighties, and who had discussions with Gorbachev about perestroika, put it in a broader context. The "lawless, arbitrary rule" of Stalin had inflicted an enormous psychological price on the nation, he said. "Stalin did the thinking for everyone, so everyone stopped thinking." Now "we are not settling accounts with Stalin. We are settling accounts with what he left us, with what he put into our souls." Hence Gorbachev's emphasis on spiritual revival, his belief that the people have to shed the inertia of the past and learn about democracy and civic responsibility, that this process would help revive the economy. The process he had set in motion, Rybakov said, would take a long time.[5]

It is instructive to recall that Soviet communism, except for the initial outburst of energy that comes when men with new ideas get a chance to put them into practice, had degenerated, after Lenin's death in 1924, into a ruthless denial of the very ideals for which high-minded men had shed their blood. Stalin did develop Russia's in-dustry but, with his violence, cruelty, and megalomania, he reduced the country to a vast prison camp, banning thought, eliminating books, substituting naked police rule for government. Truth was the tyrant's first victim. Under Stalin, there were no independent news-papers to expose his fictions, to tell the truth and rouse public opin-ion. And Stalin's successors were either willing or unwilling prisoners of his system. There was no public opinion, only the party's com-mand. The newspapers were monochrome, predictable, and repet-itive; the same propaganda was reported as fact in all of them. Frank discussion was banned, not only in public but within the party itself.

Before Andropov took power in 1982, it was almost treason-ous to raise doubts about the perfection of the Soviet way of life. Criticism became acceptable under Andropov because he himself communicated a profoundly critical attitude toward the ideas and institutions that official Moscow had come to view with such great self-satisfaction. But Andropov was in power for too short a time to introduce a great change in popular attitudes. Only after Gorbachev's glasnost did the public begin to face the facts: that the Soviet way of life was miserable; that the schools were a mess; that officials were callous and ignoble; and that the party was losing its sense of direction and purpose.

Some Soviets and Americans remembered a period of openness in the mass media during Khrushchev's last years in power, sym-bolized by the publication of Solzhenitsyn's *One Day in the Life of Ivan Denisovich* in 1963. But the process of openness was tightly controlled, always in the service of the Khrushchev regime, and even Solzhenitsyn was contained.

Khrushchev's image in the West after his ouster underwent a sig-nificant transformation, and he is now remembered as a liberal, almost benign figure. But this view springs from garbled memories of Khrushchev. Even a cursory glance at old newspapers and books published while he still held sway in the Kremlin shows a different picture. He sent tanks into Hungary in 1956 to crush the rebellion; he executed Imre Nagy and other Hungarian leaders despite his pledge of safe conduct; he built the Berlin Wall and bullied John F. Kennedy in Vienna. "We will bury you" (capitalists) is a quote that appeared with persistent regularity at the time. Even in his own cultural thaw, Khrushchev remained a despot.

It was Khrushchev's government that publicly denounced Pasternak after he was awarded the Nobel Prize for Literature as "that swine who feeds off the enemy's trough." He personally scolded abstract sculptor Ernst Neizvestny and several modern painters, saying their works seemed to have been done by a donkey's tail. Ironically, after his ouster Khrushchev asked his son to have Neizvestny, the sculptor he had publicly denounced while in power, do his gravestone. The sculptor did that after Khrushchev's death, using slabs of black and white marble to symbolize the struggle of good and evil in Khrushchev's soul.

Khrushchev's was a carefully selective truth. He exposed Stalin's crimes because he needed such exposures in his struggle for power; but he would not permit others to question his own policies. He, like most Russians, was uncomfortable with the idea that different and sometimes contradictory arguments could be equally valid.

Gorbachev's glasnost introduced precisely that idea.

The transformation of the press and television that began in the summer of 1986 was quick indeed. What seemed most significant was the sudden plurality of views. Some outlets remained conservative and cautious. Others plunged into the business of more honest reporting with zest, revealing the seamy side of Soviet reality. The scope of mismanagement revealed in the press was staggering. Newspapers and magazines and television started giving space to forceful arguments about the wisdom of some basic party policies.

Even journalists, in the forefront of the drive, were divided in their reaction to glasnost. A prominent Soviet commentator, who began his career during the Khrushchev years, revealed the basic difficulty when he told us, "As a journalist I was taught that the party was correct no matter what, and that my job was to justify all party policies. We did not know of any other truths outside this framework. What truth? Now we are told to report truthfully, to be objective. For many of us, this is a rather difficult turnaround." Glasnost challenged entire lives and careers. One middle-aged journalist confided to us, "It is as if I am told that I have been dishonest throughout my entire professional life."

Younger journalists voiced the countervailing view. Glasnost had not gone far enough. As one told us, "Yes, we can be much more open and forthright now, but you should know that there are still things we are not allowed to print."

What seemed most disturbing for Russians, what made them intensely uncomfortable, was the challenge to every certainty that had been imposed for decades. Economists who had lived all their lives practicing Stalin's voodoo economics were suddenly asked to consider new ideas. One conservative economist, A. Popova, published a scathing article in which she directly lectured Gorbachev and his men, without directly naming them. What they are doing, she said, is heretical and wrong. You can have either a market economy or centralized planning, she asserted. You can't mix them, as Gorbachev's men are trying to do. There is no room for private entrepreneurship in socialism.

From the start, glasnost revealed old wounds and created new divisions. Those who had suffered for their dissenting views in the past were entranced by the new openness. Others, whose numbers were greater and who had been tranquilized by propaganda to regard lies as truth, were keenly uncomfortable. Communist Party members, in particular, were troubled. Could the party handle information technology without a threat to its grip on power? What would be the ultimate effect of Gorbachev's glasnost on the non-Russian republics? Was there a prospect of nationalist outbursts in Central Asia? The old ways provided an element of predictability. Gorbachev jarred their nerves by talking about things they didn't want to talk about.

According to Viktor Afanasiev, the editor-in-chief of *Pravda* and a cautious perestroika-supporter at that point, at the bottom of it all was public uncertainty about whether Gorbachev's reform effort was just another campaign that would ultimately fade away. "People, especially those in the middle and upper-middle levels of the party and state apparatus, are sitting on the fence, waiting to see what's going to happen," he said. "Then there are those who put spokes in the wheels of our policy."

The only social stratum that welcomed glasnost with genuine enthusiasm was the intellectual class. It was an important alliance for Gorbachev.

Alexander Solzhenitsyn may have claimed more than the truth when he wrote in his *First Circle* that "a great writer is, so to speak, a second government in his country." But in Russia, with its history of despotism, writers, poets, scientists, and other farsighted and high-minded intellectuals came to play a larger role in public life than their counterparts in other countries. Categorized by the generic Russian term *intelligentsia,* they emerged as the most important social group to oppose tsarist absolutism in the last century.

The *intelligentsia* is a peculiarly Russian social stratum, a segment of the educated and politically conscious public who represented, or believed they represented, public opinion. Russia's meager political culture revolved around the concept of relations between state and society and placed the ruler in the position of patriarchal despot, who effectively regarded the entire territory of the empire as his property and all its inhabitants as servants. The nineteenth-century state was the source of all material benefits, and all social groups, ranging from the nobility to peasants, looked to the crown as the ultimate defender of their interests. This in turn ensured political rigidity. With various sections of society pursuing their material self-interest through subservience to absolutism, there was no coherent political opposition. Nor did Russia have an emerging middle class that asserted its interests, as did the middle class in other countries at the time. The vacuum was filled in the nineteenth century by the *intelligentsia.*

The *intelligentsia* could be equated with the educated and professional classes or, in its broadest sense, with white-collar workers.

The term's more restricted and perhaps more accurate definition involves the section of the educated and professional classes that is actively and intensely interested in political and social issues. As a social stratum, the *intelligentsia* became commonly associated with egalitarianism, feminism, and progress, and more generally with opposition to absolutism. From the 1860s onward, it generated a drive for change in the name of political liberty, social justice, and human dignity. This was the first time that political opposition had been formed around abstract ideals. The *intelligentsia* included both liberal and conservative segments of the educated elite; it was a fluid and amorphous group, given to political and social theorizing, not to political action. As a nonorganized social stratum it failed to push for constructive political changes, yet the *intelligentsia*'s opposition to the omnipotent state led to a bitter struggle that ended in the collapse of absolutism. Lenin, Trotsky, Bukharin, and virtually all other Bolshevik leaders were intellectuals first, and antitsarist conspirators second.

Predictably, the *intelligentsia* did not prosper under Soviet rule. Lenin's hesitations about freedom of speech were linked to his unwillingness to permit political opposition. Even so, in 1922 Lenin ushered in a period of "golden years" of fertile turmoil in aesthetic experimentation, philosophic debates, and literary-critical theory. Stalin's anti-intellectualism became noticeable in 1928. It was partly pathological, reflecting Stalin's inferiority complex; yet the despot was aware that the revolution was the spiritual offspring of the *intelligentsia* and that the intellectuals could turn against him. He was determined to reduce them to sycophantic impotence and eventually to wipe them out altogether.

The society Gorbachev inherited was significantly different from the one Stalin had left behind more than thirty years earlier. Younger and far better educated, it included the world's largest professional class. Modern Soviet intellectuals maintain differing views as to who really belongs to the *intelligentsia*. Vitali Korotich, editor of *Ogonyok,* saw an intellectual as someone "capable of thinking independently." Economist Nikolai Shmelyov defined him as a person of culture. Yegor Yakovlev, editor of *Moscow News,* saw the term as a "moral and social category": "The first criterion that marks out an intellectual is his determination to make the world around him a better place." Historian Natan Eidelman described intellectuals as those educated individuals who became "superfluous people during the Brezhnev era," or "internal émigrés."

Though politically fragmented, the *intelligentsia* in the eighties played a crucial role in running the Soviet state, occupying middle-level management positions. And Gorbachev needed them badly. Perestroika could not happen without them. It needed managers, scientists, engineers, and poets. Without new novels, poems, and plays, new movies and television programs, he could hardly hope to transmit his message to the people at large and create a positive climate of glasnost.

The memory of recurring disappointments and retrenchment made the intellectuals at first suspicious of Gorbachev. Like Khrushchev in his struggle against Stalinism, Gorbachev needed glasnost for political reasons. It was one of the tools for dislodging corrupt and inefficient officials and replacing them with younger, more dynamic, and professionally better-qualified men and women.

But there were contrasts. Khrushchev was instinctively anti-intellectual. If an intellectual is a person whose primary habit is the realm of ideas, Khrushchev was a rustic given to the crude and brutish ways of a backward Russian village. Gorbachev was not an authentic intellectual either. He was a provincial politician, with only a short tenure in Moscow, and without links to the world of science, culture, the arts, or education.

Yet he professed to be exhilarated by ideas and by the company of those who manipulated them with ease. His thirst for approval from the intellectuals grew over the years. Moreover, Raisa Gorbachev enjoyed the world of ideas far more than the political world of her husband.

The intellectuals were intrigued by the unusual candor Gorbachev showed in his initial speeches as leader, yet they remained reserved. They were the first to detect his uncanny talent for public relations, and they believed Gromyko when he described Gorbachev as a man with a nice smile but with teeth of iron. They were not going to be seduced by calculated gestures such as Gorbachev phoning theater director Oleg Yefremov the day after he had seen the production of Yefremov's play, to praise it.

But in the summer of 1986, even the skeptics recognized that the cultural thaw was real. Gorbachev ordered the release of all previously banned films. Newspapers and magazines suddenly became lively. People began to complain that there wasn't enough time in the week to read all the newly unlocked treasures of Soviet literature that jostled for attention with unprecedentedly candid political commentaries, or to see the new plays that broke most of the old taboos. Novels—some, like Rybakov's *Children of the Arbat,* more anti-Stalinist in tone and substance than the works of Solzhenitsyn—were being prepared for publication. Boris Pasternak's *Doctor Zhivago* was released. Nabokov's *The Defense* and countless other formerly banned works appeared for the first time. Though the apparatus of censorship was not dismantled, the censor's authority was sharply circumscribed.

In addition to lifting longstanding bans on individual books and plays, Gorbachev began to invite prominent intellectuals to the Kremlin for discussions, telling them about the need for democracy and displaying tremendous emotional energy in a setting of open discussion. Raisa, an intellectual in her own right, was drafted to the board of a new cultural fund to promote the arts, and she became the most important route to his ear.

Glasnost evolved from the exposures of injustice and incompetence into a political debate sanctioning criticism of the regime's shortcomings and raising a variety of ideas about the future of the Soviet state. Under the banner of glasnost, various groups sought the right to organize, demonstrate, and publish their views independent of government control. For party members, this was an unsettling experience. Not only did they no longer have a monopoly on truth; they were uncertain what the party line held as truth.

When the intellectuals raised some delicate issues about the country's tortuous recent history, about Stalin's crimes, and about the systematic fabrication of history, the battle lines were formed between the reformers and the conservatives. Each major attack on Stalinism generated a conservative counterattack. The conservatives publicly accused liberal writers and poets of "treasonous" thoughts. Leading the charge was Sergei Mikhalkov, the classic Stalinist mandarin, abusive and rough to those who worked for him, obsequious to those above him. Author of the old Soviet national anthem, which extolled Stalin's leadership and wisdom, chairman of the Russian Writers' Union, and a longtime literary bureaucrat, he brooked no faintheartedness, and believed that real doubters had no place in Soviet literature. Rank and loyalty and discipline, according to Mikhalkov, were as important as talent.

Ironically, market forces became influential in the field of culture far sooner than they were detected in the economy. Mikhalkov and other cultural bureaucrats were facing open competition, as glasnost suddenly provided room for fresh talent. As head of the Writers' Union, Mikhalkov had collected millions of rubles in book contracts for writers whose ideas he could manipulate. Now no one was interested in his books. In the preglasnost era, he skillfully worked behind the scenes to head off any serious questioning about artistic policies. Now, while paying lip service to Gorbachev's new policies, he complained that the names of people "who have contributed so much to Soviet power" were being subjected to public abuse. He conspicuously quoted a line from Ligachev, who had argued that "careful consideration should be extended to proven talents."[6]

Other established writers were less subtle in their attacks, particularly war novelists, who claimed to be artists of proven revolutionary probity and apparently enjoyed logistical support from the military. Writer Pyotr Proskurin assailed liberal opponents as "hooligans" and said that writers who sought to cast new light on the country's Stalinist past were engaged in "necrophilia." One line of counterattack is exemplified by war novelist Yuri Bondarev, who said at a Writers' Union meeting that "liars" and "men without talent" were stealing the limelight under cover of glasnost. Glasnost, he said, resorting to the images of his craft, has produced conditions of "civil war in Soviet literature." He and others like him, he said, were "surrounded by completely destructive forces"—the situation was like that in July 1941, when Nazi armies threatened the existence of the country. The conservatives, he said, were withdrawing before the onslaught of "civilized barbarians," and if this retreat continued and "we don't take a stand as at Stalingrad, the whole enterprise will end up with our national values, the spiritual pride of our people, cast into an abyss."

"When all the nightingales are slain, an owl begins to sing," he concluded.[7]

However, the sound and fury of intellectual debates about glasnost—and made possible by it—had little impact on daily life and the workplace, something that Gorbachev supporters were ready to acknowledge. "It is, after all, easy to decide to publish *Doctor Zhivago*," Sergei Zalygin, the editor of *Novy Mir*, conceded cheerfully. "It is far more difficult to make a single factory more efficient."[8]

Conscious of internal problems, Gorbachev was moving in his foreign policy to try to defuse contentious issues, above all to halt the American SDI program, reasoning that any agreements that would reduce arms expenditures would give him a freer hand at home to pursue his national reconstruction. It was Andropov, in his first policy speech as Soviet leader, on November 22, 1982, who identified Moscow's misguided emphasis on the military and who insisted that economic reforms were the order of the day. "We exercise our main influence on the world revolutionary process through our economic policy," Andropov said. In reshaping the Soviet economy, the Russians had to look at reforms in other socialist countries and draw on "world experience."

Profoundly realistic, Gorbachev saw the arms competition as an expression of political warfare between the superpowers. In order to reduce the intensity of this warfare, he was willing, unlike his predecessors, to offer an attractive and honest basis for negotiations. Those who knew him mentioned another factor in his reasoning. Gorbachev deeply resented the Western image of Russia as that of brooding and malevolent despotism—or Reagan's "evil empire"— and he sought to change that image through his own conduct.

As early as August 1985, he sent a signal to Washington when he told the editors of *Time* magazine that "foreign policy is an extension of domestic policy," adding, "Since we are undertaking such challenging domestic plans, what external conditions can we be interested in? I leave it to you to provide the answer."[9]

But he had come empty-handed from Geneva, and the urgencies of security remained at war with his dream of national reconstruction. His advisers were debating what kind of radical arms cuts might lure the Americans away from SDI at the next summit. When French President François Mitterrand arrived in Moscow in early July 1986, Gorbachev talked about reductions in conventional arms that would accompany a removal of nuclear weapons from Europe, releasing the continent "from the explosive burden of armaments." He wanted to set aside Western arguments that the U.S. nuclear missiles were necessary for Europe's protection because of the Warsaw Pact's superiority in conventional arms.[10]

At the end of July, Gorbachev traveled to the Soviet Far East to announce a new policy toward Asia, and particularly to hold out a branch of compromise to China.

The Chinese had made a modest overture when Politburo member and future prime minister, Li Peng, the leader of the Chinese delegation to the funeral of Chernenko, addressed Gorbachev as "comrade"—the first time such a communist address was made publicly after more than two decades of bitter hostility. Another signal came when he extended greetings from Party General Secretary Hu Yaobang.

Li's mission was almost identical to the one his foster father, Zhou Enlai, undertook in the fall of 1964, shortly after the ouster of Nikita Khrushchev. Zhou traveled to Moscow ostensibly to attend the anniversary celebrations of the Bolshevik revolution, but in fact to sound out the new Russian leadership.

Li was impressed. The gap between Deng Xiaoping and Gorbachev was not too wide. The problem, however, was Deng, who was at the sharp edge of the Sino-Soviet split, and who was conditioned to think of inherent dangers. Deng led the Chinese delegation to Moscow in 1956, at the time of Khrushchev's secret anti-Stalin speech to the Twentieth Party Congress, and again in 1963, at a moment of ideological and emotional crisis that made the breach irrevocable, when he was snubbed by Khrushchev. His deep-seated mistrust of the Russians prevented him from recognizing the extent of Gorbachev's reforms and delayed Sino-Soviet rapprochement by a couple of years. Li, who received his college education in the Soviet Union and was fluent in Russian, proceeded in his speech to offer hopes that the split was bound to heal soon. He explicitly stated Beijing's readiness to proceed with rapprochement by emphasizing the importance of interparty ties between the two countries.

In his first months in office, Gorbachev moved to expand economic cooperation with China rapidly. In June 1985, the two communist giants signed a $14-billion five-year trade agreement, the first such accord since the early sixties. The trade between the two countries up to 1982 totaled about $300 million annually. The Chinese were becoming more responsive. In September, Li Peng again visited Moscow (stopping over on his way home from Europe) and met with Gorbachev. The momentum for accommodation was gaining force.

But Gorbachev waited until July 1986 to come forward with a comprehensive diplomatic package for Asia. The gestures to China had to be set against his firm assertion that Russia was determined to be a power in the whole of the Pacific; "We are," as he put it, an "Asian-Pacific power." And though his gesture was not of the type likely to move Deng, a series of small steps Gorbachev announced did create a positive impression in Beijing.

Most significant was his psychological concession. He described China as "a great socialist country," the first time in more than three decades that a Soviet leader uttered such words. He offered to undertake specific conciliatory steps, including a withdrawal of seven thousand Soviet troops from Afghanistan; the prospect of a reduction of Soviet forces in Mongolia; and a proposal for balanced troop cuts along the Sino-Soviet border. He accepted the Chinese version of the facts in the border dispute over navigational channels and islands in the Amur and Ussuri rivers, a contentious issue that had led to serious border clashes in 1969. There was no indication of Soviet give on the Kampuchea issue, where Moscow supported the Vietnamese occupation. The Russians' leverage on Hanoi was reduced by their use of the Vietnamese bases at Cam Ranh Bay and Danang;

but Gorbachev hinted that the use of Cam Ranh Bay was mandated by the American bases in the Philippines, and if the Americans were to withdraw from these bases, "we should not be found wanting in response."

His grand design for the Pacific included an Asia-Pacific version of the Helsinki Conference on European Security. He let it be known that he intended to visit Japan as soon as the Japanese gave the go-ahead.[11] He was moving from raw power to diplomatic maneuvering to further his country's aims. Some critics argued that he wanted to freeze the United States out of the Far East, but his underlying motive may have been to pursue Moscow's long-term goal on the cheap, making a virtue out of the necessity to reduce the unsustainable percentage of his GNP devoted to weapons. Any increased friendship with China had two advantages: on the one hand, the cost of maintaining a huge Soviet force in Asia was draining; on the other, the Russians sought to enter into relationships with the countries on the Pacific rim to get tangible high-tech benefits from their advanced economies.

Moscow had discovered Asia's economic dynamism. For the first time, it began courting countries such as Thailand, Malaysia, and Singapore (secretly South Korea and Taiwan as well); for the first time, a comprehensive review of policy toward Japan got under way as a reflection of Gorbachev's conviction that the Soviet Union would not be able to share effectively in East Asia's economic boom without Japan's participation. Some officials privately murmured that the logical consequence of this reassessment was to find a way of compromising on Japan's claim to four small islands in the Kurile chain, which the Russians had occupied at the end of World War Two. It became increasingly clear to the new leadership that the dispute over the four islands would block indefinitely any extensive development of political and economic ties between Japan and Russia.

The Vladivostok speech on July 28, 1986, during Gorbachev's first visit to the Soviet Far East, was designed to dramatize his interest in China, Japan, and the Pacific rim. It signaled the start of a new aggressive diplomacy in Asia. But China came first. In addition to diplomatic flexibility to mollify Beijing, Gorbachev also offered Soviet credits for the construction of the Urumqi–Kazakhstan railroad and invited the Chinese to participate in Soviet space exploration.

The same speech showed his growing realization of domestic difficulties. "The further we go," he said, talking about internal matters, "the more clearly we see the complexity of our task and the enormity of the workload at hand." He described his policy as "people-oriented, a policy following in the interest of every Soviet family and every Soviet person."

Before leaving for his annual Black Sea vacation, Gorbachev went on television on August 18 to announce his decision to extend by six months the unilateral moratorium on nuclear testing. The moratorium had been unpopular with the military people when he first announced it a year earlier, and Gorbachev defended himself by saying that the extension, along with other Soviet arms proposals he had advanced earlier in the year—sharp reductions in strategic weapons; readiness to open the country for verification measures; a ban on chemical weapons; and cuts in conventional forces in Europe—was designed to facilitate an arms-control breakthrough before his meeting with Reagan later in the year. Privately, he was troubled by the absence of progress at the Geneva talks; they were "choking on the endless discussions of dead issues."[12]

In his speech he returned to his preoccupation with foreign policy as "an extension of domestic policy" by saying that the United States' military policy, "including the notorious SDI," was designed to "intimidate us [and] to induce us to make needless expenditures." By continuing the moratorium, he was hoping to generate internal American pressures against Reagan's SDI drive.

There was a defensive tone in this speech. Conservative critics viewed his arms policy as one of Soviet concessions. But he was becoming obsessed with the SDI program, which would force him to divert funds and resources to the military and slow down his perestroika. Washington, he said, was using the arms race to "exhaust the Soviet Union economically . . . impose hardships of all kinds on the Soviet leadership to foil its plans, including those in the social sphere and those for improving our people's living standards."[13] He was speaking to his country, he said, but his message was directed also to the rest of the world and "in particular to the government of the United States and the American people."

.   .   .

The likelihood of a fruitful Washington summit diminished radically on August 30, while Gorbachev vacationed on the Black Sea. KGB agents pounced on Nicholas Daniloff, the Moscow correspondent for *U.S. News & World Report,* and arrested him, accusing him of espionage. The KGB obviously planned to use Daniloff as a hostage to secure the release of Gennady Zakharov, a Russian physicist working at the United Nations, who had been arrested by the FBI in New York a week earlier. An inflamed American public opinion almost instantly made it clear to Gorbachev's advisers that Daniloff's arrest was wholly misconceived. "It's the worst possible thing that could happen," a senior Gorbachev aide said privately.[14]

In Gorbachev's absence, the day-to-day operations of the Kremlin were in the hands of Yegor Ligachev, his number two in the party, who, along with KGB Chairman Viktor Chebrikov, was presented with evidence casting doubts on Daniloff's activities in Moscow. In fact, the only incriminating thing Daniloff had done was to deliver a letter from a KGB agent provocateur masquerading as a dissident Russian Orthodox priest to the U.S. Embassy in Moscow. In the letter, the bogus priest sought to establish contact with American operatives, offering to provide them with intelligence information. This had all happened the previous January, and Daniloff had never seen the bogus priest again.

The Daniloff affair revealed Gorbachev's political vulnerability. He had inherited Andropov's reformist coalition, in which the KGB, one of the three main institutional pillars in the system, was an essential component. He had alienated the military, the second pillar, by removing scores of top officers and placing others under strict party control. And he was at war with the conservative majority in the party, the third pillar. Without KGB Chairman Chebrikov's backing, Gorbachev's position would become intolerably precarious. Presented with the *fait accompli* of Daniloff's arrest, he was virtually forced to back the KGB, which, guided by its narrow institutional interest, wanted to secure the release of their man back in New York.

Clearly frustrated by the Daniloff incident, which strained relations with the United States when he was eager for a breakthrough, Gorbachev ended his vacation in mid-September and stopped on his way home to talk with the people and seek signs of support. He chose his native region of North Caucasus, where he was sure of getting a good reception. On September 17, he was in Krasnodar; the next day, in Stavropol. He appeared buoyed by the reception. But while he mingled with the crowds in Krasnodar, Soviet television also showed ordinary people asking challenging questions. "Aren't we too soft in talking to foreign countries?" one man asked the leader. A similar question was debated in several articles in the armed-forces daily *Krasnaya Zvezda*, which ostensibly defended Gorbachev's "consistency" in foreign affairs.

When he returned to Moscow, Gorbachev persisted in his determination to meet Reagan. His own aides suggested an interim "minisummit," and Shevardnadze had suggested it to the Americans. By proposing to meet Reagan at Reykjavík, he sought to defuse the tensions between the two superpowers. He also wanted to give "a powerful impetus to turning the [arms-control] process in the required direction."[15]

Gorbachev got what he wanted: an agreement to meet in Reykjavík on October 11–12 and, after protracted diplomatic bargaining, a resolution of the Daniloff affair. The United States would release Zakharov; the Soviet Union would release Daniloff. In an extra concession, the Soviets would also release Yuri Orlov, the Soviet physicist and human-rights leader imprisoned in Siberia, and would allow him to emigrate to America.

Traditional foreign-policy practitioners argued that Gorbachev should not go to a summit unless he was given to understand that progress was conceivable and something of substance was likely to result.[16] Most questioned whether any possible package of measures could break the impasse at Geneva (where the talks "are practically deadlocked," Gorbachev said at Reykjavík). But Gorbachev's closest advisers favored a bold approach, and he took their advice, preparing a package of "drastic measures" that stunned the Americans when it was put forward at Reykjavík. It was a big gamble. It was also something that incurred permanent resentment of Gorbachev on the part of the Soviet military establishment.

He knew he was gambling. Writing about Reykjavík later in his book, *Perestroika,* he said, "It's hard to say when realism will prevail in our evaluations of each other. But it will come one day, perhaps quite unexpectedly, because life makes us wiser. History is rich in examples showing how abruptly the situation may change." As a student of Hegel, he also was familiar with Hegel's acid remark that "Peoples and governments have never learned anything from history."

Chapter 9

WINTER
OF DISCONTENT

The proposals Gorbachev brought to a drizzly, cold Reykjavík were radical indeed. He also brought along Marshal Sergei Akhromeyev, the Soviet chief of staff, as a form of insurance policy whose very presence seemed to pronounce favorably on the enterprise most Soviet military men viewed with suspicion.

Still worried about SDI, he was going to make an offer Reagan could not refuse. His case was tight as a drum. Almost. He was prepared to disengage himself from the positions that his predecessors had stubbornly clung to. That his position evolved in a small circle of advisers—and not within the political and military establishment—seems evident from his readiness to bargain away the mainstay of Russia's military might and political standing. He proposed a mutual elimination of all strategic offensive arms in a period of ten years.

The package included concessions on virtually all major nuclear issues. He set aside U.S. forward-based systems and weapons that Moscow regards as strategic because they can reach Soviet territory. He expressed readiness to accept intrusive verification procedures— "any form of verification," as he put it. On nuclear missiles in Europe, he accepted Reagan's zero option, allowing the nuclear weapons of France and Britain and thus ensuring Western military superiority in the region. ("This was a very big concession on our part," he told the Reykjavík press conference on October 12.) He wanted to keep a hundred of these medium-range missiles in Asia, while the United States could deploy the same number in Alaska. All of this in exchange for a restriction of the SDI program to laboratory research for a period of ten years—a move he felt would slow down the momentum of SDI development.

But nothing came of the Soviet proposals. Reagan, Gorbachev said, "insisted to the bitter end that America should have the right to conduct research and testing on every aspect of SDI, both in and outside the laboratory."

To the extent that such things can be judged by politicians and press conferences, both sides seem to have been entranced by the prospect of an arms agreement that in scope and importance would dwarf any other such undertaking in history. It was the most remarkable display of improvisation in high places since Tsar Nicholas II and Emperor William II attempted to settle Russo-German differences on a yacht off Björkö in 1905. Secretary of State George Shultz seemed genuinely dejected when he reported the failure. Gorbachev was also "sad and disappointed." He added, "Our positions had never been so close."

For domestic political reasons, both sides quickly moved to put a positive spin on the bad situation. Washington put its public-relations "shovel brigade" into action, while Gorbachev insisted, "Nonetheless, I would not say the meeting was useless. On the contrary, it is a new stage in a complicated and difficult dialogue in the search for solutions."

Back in Moscow, Gorbachev reported the result of the summit to the ruling Politburo, which "approved" the leader's work (in contrast to the "full approval" he received on his return from the Geneva summit).[1] Evidently he had encountered criticism from his colleagues. Some of the major vested interests of power were disturbed. In internal debates over the next months, his supporters defended the gamble as having smoked out the Americans while scoring propaganda points for Moscow. But critics, quick to attack as an act of imprudence any gamble that failed, were joined by conservatives who opposed the policy of glasnost for baring too many of the country's weaknesses.[2]

That same evening, after the Politburo meeting, Gorbachev went on television to present his case to the people. He outlined the proposals he had put forward. They were "truly large-scale and clearly in the nature of compromise," he said. "We made concessions. But we did not see even the slightest desire on the American side to respond in kind or to meet us halfway." The Americans, he said, "had come empty-handed to gather fruits in their basket." He reported Reagan's stated willingness to share with Moscow the results of SDI tests. "I said," Gorbachev continued, "Mr. President, I do not take this idea seriously. You don't even want to share with us oil equipment or equipment for the dairy industry, and still you expect us to believe your promise to share the research developments in the SDI project."

The Americans, Gorbachev continued, were calculating that "the Soviet Union will ultimately be unable to endure the arms race economically, that it will break down and bow to the West. One need only squeeze the Soviet Union harder and step up [pressures from] the position of strength." That was, he said, an illusion. "We do have problems, which we openly discuss and resolve. . . . In general, I would have to say that the Soviet Union's strength today lies in its unity, dynamism, and the political activity of its people." This trend was growing, he said, and the country had the capacity to respond to any challenge. His Reykjavík disappointment was balanced by an almost blind faith in a new proposition on arms control, which had evolved as a result of practical discussions with Yakovlev and others, but which now became the basis of his thinking. He had come to grasp that he could never hope to destroy the enemy's forces and expect to save Russian cities and limit damage; at the same time, Soviet power was strong enough to make any attack an instant catastrophe for the United States. Both sides, he argued, were addicted to secrecy; major decisions were restricted to an exceedingly small number of people on both sides, which in turn inhibited arms talks, since both sides were involved in deception and manipulation of policy. The problem was compounded in the Soviet Union by the military's obsessive stranglehold on policy. He would break this stranglehold. He wanted to expose the policies of both superpowers as having been governed by false perceptions. Reykjavík was the beginning.

Therefore, he said, Reykjavík was "a major event." He saw a qualitatively new situation developing. It was a useful meeting, paving the way for a "possible step forward." He was convinced that he had chosen the "correct" path.

Some days later, on October 18, 1986, the Reagan administration delivered an open blow by announcing the expulsion of fifty-five Soviet diplomats from the United States. From the vantage point of Gorbachev aides, such an action coming in the immediate aftermath of the summit seemed deliberately calculated to undermine their leader. It certainly strengthened the arguments of conservatives. In response to letters published in *Pravda* and other newspapers questioning why he had come back empty-handed from Reykjavík, Gorbachev decided to go back on Soviet television on October 22 to defend his policy. He was convinced, he told his audience, that "we have not fully realized the full significance" of Reykjavík, but would do so in the future and "do justice to the accomplishments and gains, as well as to the missed opportunities and losses." He reiterated his previous arguments, but this time he emphasized that his position was in line with Chernenko's policy, which, in January 1985, linked strategic, medium-range, and space weapons into a package. This package had been the basis of his policy. "Our concessions are also a part of the package," he said, apparently addressing those who had been casting a critical eye on his whole approach to strategic issues. "No package, no concessions."

Reykjavík, he said, had generated "more than hopes." It had highlighted the difficulties. Then he launched into an attack on the Reagan administration for trying to misinterpret Reykjavík and following up with the expulsion of Soviet diplomats, which, he said, "appears as simply wild." Moscow would have an equally tough response (which came a few days later, when more than a hundred Soviet drivers, repairmen, maids, and other support staff employed at the U.S. Embassy in Moscow were withdrawn, an action that severely crippled embassy functions for a while).

He expressed his frustrations later when he said that "every time a gleam of hope appears" in Moscow's dealings with Washington, some "provocative action" would follow and poison the atmosphere.

He felt outmaneuvered by the Americans, who were playing a "cat-and-mouse game" with their arms-control policy.[3] Perhaps inadvertently, he let it be known that he felt like the mouse.

Indeed, his position was beginning gradually to erode, at home and abroad. Reagan was slowly bending his hand, and Gorbachev, when he went to Washington a year later, would abandon the package and sign only an agreement on elimination of all medium-range missiles, agreeing, in a further concession, to give up the hundred missiles in Asia.

The fall of 1986 was unseasonably warm, contributing to an exhilarating mood of freedom in Moscow, where glasnost was hitting its stride. The explosion of truth in the press made the society seem like a drowsy bear emerging from hibernation and making groping responses to the new season. The people who used to live by the old Moscow saying "I don't read the papers; they make your hands dirty" were now lining up for them at kiosks all over the city. The circulation of once-despised magazines like *Ogonyok* and *Znamya* rocketed as they became more forthright and lively. It was impossible to get copies of *Ogonyok* despite its 1.5-million circulation. Edmund Stevens, the veteran American journalist who has lived in the Soviet Union for more than half a century, said the atmosphere in the capital reminded him of the heyday of Khrushchev's thaw.

The press and television had begun to raise people's curiosity but had not yet galvanized them into action. The growing public interest in Gorbachev's program was a curious phenomenon, summed up by a thoughtful intellectual: "The people feel as if they are watching an adventure show. They have yet to be convinced to get up on the stage."

Some of the ferment had spilled over to Leningrad and a few other cities, but the country at large seemed impervious to changes. Resistance to glasnost in the provinces ranged from violence to obstructionism. Journalists investigating corruption and inefficiencies were harassed or beaten up by local police. Sales of *Ogonyok* were banned in some parts of the country by local party chiefs, who regarded the weekly magazine as a carrier of antisocialist if not seditious ideas.[4]

It was an odd situation. The huge apparat of oppression, surveillance, and eavesdropping was intact, ready to be used, while glasnost let the people vent their feelings in a way that only a few years earlier would have resulted in KGB persecution. Now nothing happened when dissident views were featured prominently in the press. An anecdote captured popular uncertainty about the disappearance of retaliation. A senior official, having read an article containing interesting dissident views, phones his wife at home. "Darling, have you read that amazing piece on the front page of *Pravda*?" he asks. "What piece? I've not had a chance to look at the paper at all. What is it about?" she inquires. "Ah," he says, a note of caution creeping into his voice, "let's talk about it later, then. It isn't safe to talk about over the phone."

In his Krasnodar speech on September 17, which was televised live, Gorbachev took a major step on domestic matters by embracing the idea of a market economy and limited private enterprise. He recalled Lenin's New Economic Policy (NEP)—which was subsequently dismantled by Stalin. Lenin's NEP restored a market economy and private enterprise but, Gorbachev emphasized, that did not mean a return to capitalism. "We live in different times and are working out and realizing our plans in different historical conditions. But we can and should utilize Leninist lessons in the way we restructure" the Soviet economy. In early April, he had introduced partial reforms of agriculture, moving a few steps toward NEP. They included a provision that salaries of agricultural workers be in direct relation to output, and called for incentives for 1986 in the form of hard-to-get consumer goods and equipment. Collective farms were permitted to sell 30 percent of their output directly to shops or cooperatives. This program broadened the so-called brigade-contract approach, under which groups of farmers, families, or individuals can contract out to work for farms. In addition to cash incentives, contract workers would have the option of getting 25 percent of their income in the form of automobiles, tractors, and consumer goods.

But glasnost in the press revealed strong bureaucratic opposition to an NEP revival, indicating that many people in the upper echelons of the party were secretly opposed to the leader's perestroika program. A joke circulating in Minsk, in Byelorussia, suggested a coun-trywide public perception that most bureaucrats paid lip service to the new policies but in reality were against them. In the joke, Gor-bachev, Reagan, and Mitterrand meet for a friendly conversation and start talking about their problems. Mitterrand says his problem is that he has nine mistresses, knows one is cheating on him, but cannot figure out which. Reagan dismisses Mitterrand's problem as a trifle and says he has far more serious worries: he has fifty body-guards, knows one is a KGB agent, but cannot figure out which. Finally Gorbachev reveals his problem, which is far greater than either Mitterrand's or Reagan's: he has a hundred ministers, knows one has genuinely adopted perestroika, but cannot figure out which.

News from the perestroika front was discouraging; it seemed to be one muddle after another. Television reporters interviewed the director of an eyeglass factory in Byelorussia that was making too many lenses for the number of frames it received; the director was demanding a standard solution—he wanted authorities in Moscow to take the superfluous lenses off his hands. Gorbachev himself crit-icized the absurdities of central planning that failed to provide proper coordination on a massive scale. Theft of public property continued at previous levels. One newspaper reported that storage workers at the Lenin Komsomol automotive spare-part plant habitually sold $26 parts for $1.30 and pocketed the money from the sales.[5] When police visited the home of a woman who worked in a candy factory to discuss charges that her teenage son had pilfered materials from a building site, they discovered one room of her apartment filled with Misha Bear–brand chocolates; she confessed that she took several boxes home with her every day. We visited one of the pizza restau-rants that had opened with great fanfare in Moscow in the early 1980s; the "pizza" was a thick ball of half-cooked dough topped with raw cabbage and a piece of melted cheese. What, we wondered, had become of the genuine Italian pizzas prepared by Italian-trained chefs? We soon discovered the answer in a newspaper report that said the ingredients were regularly taken home by the restaurant staff.

The antialcoholism campaign was creating different types of prob-lems. Desperate alcoholics began drinking anything with alcohol content, including eau de cologne, antistatic liquid, air freshener, insecticide, window-cleaning fluid, and shoe-polishing creams. In the absence of vodka, some people resorted to sniffing glue. In a period of two and a half months, fourteen cases of group poisoning were reported, more than 350 persons were hospitalized, and about a hundred died from poisoning. In Kuibyshev, on the Volga River, the director of a perfume shop demanded police help because customers insisted on buying eau de cologne by the boxload. Shop managers began limiting eau-de-cologne sales to two bottles per person, and only during licensing hours. A war veteran named as M. Paulin from Kuibyshev wrote to the local trade directorate requesting that all invalids of war be given the right to buy a bottle of eau de cologne every four months without standing in line. The director of a household-goods shop in Perm, in the Urals, refused to accept glue deliveries, because the moment glue went on sale the shop was besieged by customers, who often engaged in fistfights. At a cellulose factory in Arkhangelsk, in the north, there was a serious case of mass poisoning after workers imbibed condensed alcoholic wastes. In the Gomel region of Byelorussia, the sales of window-cleaning fluid doubled from 1985 to 1986. Sales of sugar—a key ingredient in moonshine—also shot up, and some regions introduced sugar rationing.[6]

The press also began for the first time to focus on drug abuse, a symptom of the cynicism and disillusionment that had developed among the young during Brezhnev's last years. A sociological study conducted in Georgia showed that 63 percent of drug users were blue-collar workers; they mostly used hashish, although some used morphine, opium, and heroin.[7]

The anticorruption campaign also seemed to be failing. The full scale of official corruption in the Central Asian republic of Uzbekistan involved losses exceeding $2 billion. A systematic falsification of cotton harvests had brought medals, praise, and fortunes to high officials in a corruption scheme directed by the minister of cotton production himself. The minister was executed by firing squad, and twenty-six hundred other officials were arrested. On his way to India in late November, Gorbachev stopped for a day in Tashkent, the capital of Uzbekistan, to meet with the local communist establishment. He had harsh words for their poor response to perestroika and criticized the many officials who professed to be communists but were to be found praying at mosques in the evenings.

Before he departed for India, Gorbachev conceded that "perestroika is not proceeding easily. The main obstacle is the mentality. The mentality that has taken shape over the years should be changed."[8] Accustomed to following directives from Moscow, local officials and factory managers found it difficult to operate independently in the new atmosphere of perestroika, which essentially required that they take the initiative, rather than depend on orders from Moscow. A cartoon captured this problem succinctly. It showed the director of a provincial factory (who, like all factory managers, had been told to put himself and his operation through "perestroika") dictating to his secretary a telegram to the central authorities in Moscow. The telegram read: "We have successfully completed perestroika. Await further instructions."

Despite these frustrations, Gorbachev and his men pressed on with the program. A new regulation was passed which liberated Soviet firms to deal directly with foreign partners, something that was previously done exclusively through the Ministry of Foreign Trade. (The notoriously corrupt Ministry of Foreign Trade had been dismantled, with many of its officials sent to jail for extortion and accepting bribes.) A new law was drafted to encourage joint ventures with Western firms. In December, a new law allowing very restricted "individual enterprise" was passed by the Supreme Soviet. Angry letters poured in to newspapers, claiming that the legislation was a way for people to get rich quick: "What did we have the revolution for?" said one indignant woman. A system of quality-control inspection was introduced at fifteen hundred major firms in an effort to improve production. Many of the inspectors, however, were bribed by factory managers, and they were given no power to interfere in the way the factory was run.

Throughout the fall and early winter, the old and traumatic issue of Stalin and Stalinism began to emerge in the forefront of public debates. For the first time, explicit public condemnations of both began to appear in the press. Gorbachev had moved gingerly on this issue, aware of the potency of Stalinist backlash. When he first touched on the problem, in his first months in office, he had been cautious, describing Stalinism as "an invention of opponents of communism . . . used to smear the Soviet Union and socialism."[9] But the logic of glasnost and his own perception of Stalin led toward a major public reappraisal of the dictator's role in Soviet history.

Another issue to emerge at the time was Raisa Gorbachev.

Elegant and eloquent, she had early on generated some adverse comments in this society dominated by conservative views on the role of women. Anti-Raisa grumbling came mainly from women who resented her fashionable clothes, her sophistication, and especially her high public profile. In the West she had been an asset to her husband; at home her very presence next to him during their extended tours seemed something of a liability.

As the political struggle in the Kremlin intensified, Raisa's role that fall became a source of controversy. It is difficult in Russia to attack the leader directly, but his wife is an easy target for the opposition. Bureaucrats began to describe her as "imperious" because of her proud mien. A series of hostile jokes began to make the rounds, suggesting she was exerting too powerful an influence on her husband. They were similar to—though more vicious than—the charges made against Nancy Reagan.

A typical anecdote has Raisa in bed with her husband. In a haughty tone, she asks him, "Misha, how does it feel to sleep with the wife of the leader of the Soviet Union?" In the climate of glasnost, critics stood up during public lectures to voice their resentment of Raisa. After the Reykjavík summit, to which Raisa accompanied her husband, the questions of "Who paid for her trip to Reykjavík?" and "Why didn't she pay for it herself?" confronted some prominent political scientists on their lecture tours.[10] The same question was being asked by party bureaucrats.

The winter came late in 1986, but it did so with a vengeance.

The mood at the U.S. Embassy was gloomy. Spirits had been high and combative at first, after October's tit-for-tat maneuverings led to the withdrawal of Russian embassy employees; but they gradually sank lower and lower, as U.S. diplomats combined cleaning toilets, shoveling snow, unloading trucks, and washing corridors with their diplomatic duties. With temperatures dipping to minus thirty, life in the American compound slowed to a crawl.

Russia's political life that December reached new heights of intensity. After months of maneuverings to dislodge the remaining Old Guard figures from the leadership, Gorbachev managed to oust Brezhnev's old friend Dinmukhamed Kunaev, the leader of Kazakhstan, and replace him with an outsider, Gennady Kolbin, who looked like a Russian, though he was, in fact, an ethnic Chuvash. He still could not do the same in the Ukraine, where Vladimir Shcherbitsky clung to power with unusual tenacity. Like most regional party chiefs under Brezhnev, Shcherbitsky had built a feudal machine of his own. But he was particularly strong, and his resistance to Gorbachev's efforts to prize him out exemplified the limits of the new leader's power. Shcherbitsky and his men sought to keep glasnost out of their realm, a relatively simple matter since they controlled the police. One celebrated incident focused attention on the problem. When a reporter for a mining magazine in Voroshilovgrad, in the Ukraine, sought to expose "shortcomings in the work of [local] law-enforcement agencies," he was charged with hooliganism and put in jail for thirteen days. When his friends complained to Moscow, *Pravda* sent two journalists to investigate. They found that a provincial chief of the KGB, identified as A. Dichenko, had personally sanctioned the journalist's arrest. A few weeks later, KGB Chairman Viktor Chebrikov personally announced Dichenko's dismissal in a front-page statement to *Pravda*. The five-paragraph story found an extraordinary resonance in Soviet society, signaling as it did that glasnost was more than a rhetorical slogan. (In further developments, two prosecutors and three police officers were fired and a vice-minister of the interior was given a "severe warning." A few months later the KGB chief for the Ukraine, Stepan Mukha, was replaced by Nikolai Golushko, who had previously served in Moscow. Mukha's ouster was reported in the Kiev daily *Pravda Ukrainy* on May 26.)

Also in December, Gorbachev moved energetically to cement his

relations with the *intelligentsia* and did so in a spectacular manner
that stunned both domestic and foreign audiences. He freed Andrei
Sakharov, the nuclear physicist and Nobel Peace Prize laureate, the
country's foremost political dissident, who had been sent into internal
exile in early 1980, a few weeks after he criticized the invasion of
Afghanistan. He and his wife had been confined to the closed city
of Gorky, on the Volga, about three hundred miles east of Moscow.
They had been repeatedly harassed by the KGB. On two occasions,
when he staged protests by hunger strike, Sakharov was kept alive
by being tied to a hospital bed and force-fed. Although he was kept
in total isolation, his courage and intellectual tenacity had gained
him worldwide fame. Among dissidents at home, he had become a
hero of almost mythical proportions. He was released in a startling
fashion. One cold December day, workmen showed up unannounced
at his apartment and installed a telephone. The next day it rang.
Sakharov picked it up to hear Gorbachev's voice at the other end
of the line telling him to return to Moscow to resume his "patriotic
work." It was an unprecedented act for a Soviet leader. (Stalin used
to phone dissenters for a pleasant chat, but for a different, sadistic
purpose: it was generally a prelude to their being tried, executed,
or sent to Siberia.) Not only had Gorbachev personally ordered
Sakharov's release; by directly phoning the nuclear scientist, he had
made a public act of contrition. A few days later Sakharov was in
the studio of Moscow Television conducting an interview via satellite
with American television networks, criticizing the Soviet occupation
of Afghanistan and the continued incarceration of Soviet political
dissidents. Following his release, scores of other imprisoned political
dissidents were freed.

In one fell swoop, Gorbachev had disarmed his foreign critics and
signaled to the Soviet *intelligentsia* his commitment to liberalization.
More and more, he began to regard public opinion as a basic element
of power. The liberation of Sakharov brought him more international
goodwill than any other single act; he had been repeatedly placed
on the defensive when meeting Western visitors who raised the unpleasant issue of human-rights violations in his country and invariably
brought up Sakharov's name. He had made a conciliatory gesture
during his first year in office when he permitted the physicist's wife,

Yelena Bonner, to travel to the United States for an eye operation. He had also released another celebrated dissident, Anatoly Shcharansky, and allowed him to emigrate to Israel.

In freeing Sakharov, he defused an international irritant and, at the same time, deprived less well-known political dissenters of the symbol of their struggle and their most important voice. But this could have been achieved without Gorbachev's dramatic personal intervention, without his symbolic admission that the human-rights activist had been wronged by his country. Gorbachev's move revealed not only his capacity for bold action but also his readiness to take substantial risks. He evidently studied the KGB's case against the physicist and some of his writings. After his visit to France in October 1985, Gorbachev had felt humiliated by inaccurate statistics he recited at a Paris press conference on the number of political prisoners confined in the Soviet Union.[11] He had angrily demanded an explanation from the KGB for misinforming him. If he had looked deeper into the problem at all, which he most likely did, Gorbachev must have been surprised to discover that Sakharov's writings bore a striking similarity to his own thinking on some fundamental ideas. However critical of the Soviet regime, Sakharov has consistently believed in the possibility of a humanitarian and enlightened government in the Kremlin.

But Gorbachev could not count on Sakharov's goodwill and support. He must have known that his personal intervention would be viewed with suspicion and hostility in many quarters. Over the years, official Soviet newspapers had roundly condemned both Sakharov and Yelena Bonner. Many Russians had come to believe that the physicist had been engaged in treasonous actions, that he was a willing pawn in the hands of Western propaganda against the Soviet Union. The bureaucratic establishment in general held that view.

Gorbachev gambled. He evidently wanted to win the physicist over. With almost everybody else his questioning was hard and relentless, but not with Sakharov. There were qualities that set the physicist apart: the first was his insistence on being free; the second was a capacity—indeed, an instinct—one would not expect from a man involved in the creation of the hydrogen bomb, to see world events not so much as a global chess game but in human terms.

Gorbachev admired both qualities. His intervention carried familiar echoes from the Russian past. Dostoyevsky was sentenced to death for reading seditious literature but was saved by Nicholas I while facing the firing squad. The novelist later turned into one of the staunchest supporters of the autocracy. Though Sakharov did not undergo such a conversion, he became a supporter of perestroika and glasnost, and his word carried such credibility abroad that the West suddenly began to take a new look at the Soviet leader. Some Western critics, aware of the enormous international public-relations success this brought to Gorbachev, began talking of Sakharov as a new stooge of the regime. Some dissidents found it difficult to reconcile the image of the Gorky Sakharov with the man who began to advise foreign leaders to support Gorbachev's policies. Soviet exiles were downright hostile; some charged he had made a "disgraceful fool" of himself and that he failed to see the "difference between free citizens and slaves like himself pledging never to say what displeases their masters."[12]

Sakharov responded to these critics by saying, "I see myself as I saw myself ten years ago. I still say what I think."

Gorbachev's personal involvement in Sakharov's release came in the midst of an intensive political struggle within the party. Throughout the fall and winter of 1986, he had tried to get the ruling elite to accept his plans for what amounted to a far-reaching political reform. Socialism, he argued, was "impossible" without democracy.

As he publicly outlined his arguments, democracy appeared as a form of ideal social order where bitter political struggles were replaced by honest and fair arguments among law-abiding people with the common good uppermost in their minds. This did not mean anarchy, he said. But his entire concept of democracy seemed woolly. Again he seemed to ignore human frailties and the complexities of urban life. Democracy, in his view, excluded personal ambitions and grudges; a democratic press was free and open but would not be used as a forum for people to settle political scores or to slander one another. "Genuine democracy," he said, "is inseparable from honesty and integrity, from responsibility, frankness in judgments, and respect for the opinion of others, and from strict observance of the laws and rules of socialist society."[13]

To unfriendly ears, his words seemed to have a sham quality. He wanted the people to learn a new game called "democracy," but he was drawing up the rules and he was to be the umpire. It was the communist approach with loaded dice. To friends, however, his words marked the beginning of a new process, a process that had so far eluded Russia, and they thought in terms of going to the kindergarten of democracy before moving ahead. Democracy and one-party rule are not wholly incompatible, they said.

Glasnost was the best way to prevent party officials from abusing democracy and to create conditions under which the force of public opinion would keep in check "egoism, demagoguery, and attempts to use democracy for selfish purposes." In order to ensure that "negative past tendencies" not be revived, Gorbachev wanted changes in the unwritten party rules under which party officials at various levels were exempt from criticism. No official at whatever level should be "beyond criticism and outside control." Many of the country's problems "were due to the fact that there were areas that were beyond criticism, beyond control by the people."[14]

The party had to lead the way. Gorbachev defined his concept for its political modernization. The party was to assume a "political-guidance" role and get out of the business of running the economy. A local party committee, he explained, "cannot act as an economic management body—that's what we have to realize. This is not its function, this is a function of management."[15] But the very source of power of regional party officials was their control over the economy; they appointed managers whose careers depended on those of their masters.

Gorbachev was asking the party not only to relinquish its role in direct management of the economy, education, and health care, but also to become involved in the process of democratization and involve citizens in the affairs of government. The party, he felt, had lost ground in the country by ignoring and neglecting the needs and aspirations of citizens. It was merely playing "a game of democracy" by going through formalities that created an illusion of responsiveness. "Democracy is a serious thing. There will be no forward movement if we do not draw people into the democratic process." Party officials hold meetings, he said, at which popular views are expressed, but "no one—not the party bureau nor the executive committee nor any other body—discusses these proposals, and nothing is done to realize them. This is pure deception of the people . . . a profanation and mockery of democracy," he said. "It must come to an end."[16]

Finally, he was moving in the direction of workers' self-management. "The worker and farmer must be given the right to elect leaders on whom they can rely," he said. "This, I believe, is what life really demands."[17]

The public argument foreshadowed the direction he was to take. He had recognized the existence of pluralism; indeed, he sought to encourage different viewpoints. He had also recognized the existence of interest groups, but he evidently felt—in 1986, at any rate—that all viewpoints could coexist within the current political framework. His political reforms would provide needed flexibility and would introduce a meritocracy. One proposal would limit the term of office of party leaders, another introduce multiple candidates and secret ballots in local party elections, and yet another impose a mandatory retirement age. He wanted to enlarge the authority and power of labor unions, now a mere appendage of the party; and he wanted to loosen the party's stranglehold on all positions of power by introducing merit, rather than party membership, as a prerequisite for top positions in all areas.

These ideas were alarming to some Marxist-Leninist traditionalists, who suggested that the Soviet government had been hijacked by a heretic, a devilishly seductive rogue who placed everything in a familiar context but, they felt instinctively, was nudging the whole country in a dangerously strange and unfamiliar direction.

In time, his political rivals began to articulate fears that by toying with the basic principles of Soviet power Gorbachev was approaching rather than avoiding a grievous crisis.[18] Even his limited democracy seemed a threat to their fundamental assumption of legitimacy grounded in the Marxist-Leninist notion that a Communist Party has the right to hold power indefinitely in the name of the socialist revolution. Even among those who saw the need for changes—and Ligachev was definitely in this category—there were genuine concerns. Once initiated, political reforms might acquire a life of their own, with unpredictable consequences.

Gorbachev's attempts to secure a Central Committee majority for such changes were frustrated by the doubting majority. He became involved in one of the most intensive lobbying efforts of his career, inviting each member of the Central Committee for a chat at his dacha in the western suburbs, trying to reason with each. As always, he had two irons in the fire. He was ready to pursue a more limited objective if his whole package was rejected, as it was. But he did not want to be defeated. So his men kept postponing the plenum that was scheduled for December. "Suffice it to say," he conceded, "that we postponed [the plenum date] three times, for we could not hold it without having a clear idea of the main issues."[19]

Whatever his persuasive powers, they were substantially eroded when, following Kunaev's ouster, ethnic rioting erupted in Kazakhstan, and his critics saw the trouble as a foretaste of things to come.

That unrest should erupt in Kazakhstan was a lesson about the extent to which the country harked back not merely to feudalism, but to tribalism as well. What prompted the smiling, dutiful, friendly, and loyal Kazakhs suddenly to assume a new reincarnation, almost overnight becoming anti-Russian toughs and sparking a major internal crisis of the regime? Under Dinmukhamed Kunaev, a Brezhnev crony who had ruled Kazakhstan for the previous twenty years, the province's Communist Party organization had slid into the comfortable *dzuze* (clan) politics of Central Asia. Kunaev put his clansmen and their relatives into top positions, and they in turn put their clansmen and relatives into similar positions down the line. The entire republic was run by a huge "communist" mafia.

When Gorbachev finally moved to ease Kunaev out of his post in Kazakhstan, he probably did not quite anticipate the violent reaction he was going to spark. To make things worse, he had the Kazakhstan Central Committee vote to replace Kunaev with an ethnic Chuvash, Gennady Kolbin. In Kazakhstan, it was not the nationality that played much of a crucial role. Had Moscow selected a Russian member of the Kazakh mafia, there would have been no problem. But

Moscow sent in an incorruptible outsider to clean up the mess. Kolbin, as a Kazakh official put it, was not "one of us."

The rioting began on December 17, 1986, when thousands of young
Kazakhs took to the streets of Alma-Ata, a city of one million, to
protest the forced retirement of Kunaev and his replacement by a
man they regarded as an ethnic "Russian," even though he was in
fact a member of the Chuvash ethnic minority.

Kolbin, fifty-nine at the time, the former boss of the central Russian city of Ulyanovsk—a prestigious post, because Ulyanovsk was
Lenin's birthplace—was an able and vigorous administrator with a
track record of successful crackdowns on corruption, drinking, and
inefficiency. A man in the Gorbachev image, he was recommended
for the job by Shevardnadze, who knew him well. Before Ulyanovsk,
Kolbin served as Shevardnaze's deputy in Georgia. A superb linguist,
he had taken the trouble to learn Georgian well enough to deliver
speeches in that language, and once in Kazakhstan immediately
began taking Kazakh language lessons. Within months he was pro-
ficient enough to converse in Kazakh, and after a year and a half he
delivered a section of his speech to the Kazakh Central Committee
in that language.

Kolbin's appointment had upset the Kazakhs, and the crowds demanded Kunaev's reinstatement. The protest quickly turned into an
anti-Russian demonstration orchestrated by Kunaev men. Police
tried to disperse the crowd after it attempted to march to the Communist Party headquarters. An official version of the incident, distributed promptly by Tass, did not hide the fact that the protesters
were "expressing disapproval" over Kunaev's ouster. It said that
students, "incited by nationalist elements" and joined by "hooligans,
parasites, and antisocial elements," went on a rampage. Tass made
it clear that the protesters were shouting "insulting" anti-Russian
slogans.[20]

Unofficial reports, however, indicated that the riots were far more
serious and violent than Tass had indicated, and that bloody clashes
left seven policemen dead and dozens injured. How many demonstrators were hurt or killed was not known. At the riots' peak there
were about two hundred thousand people milling around in the

streets, watching youth gangs loot food shops and overturn parked cars and set them on fire. After police arrested scores of demonstrators, the crowd marched on police stations and freed them. The police were reported to have been overwhelmed by sheer numbers.

Police reinforcements were rushed to Alma-Ata from neighboring areas, and Politburo member Mikhail Solomentsev and senior KGB officials were dispatched from Moscow to take control. The fact that the army was not called in suggests that the situation was brought under control rather quickly. Kolbin later said that even the police force in Alma-Ata had to be purged of unreliable people: twelve hundred were fired outright.[21]

In line with Gorbachev's glasnost policy, the Soviet media promptly provided accounts of the nationalist unrest, an astounding confirmation of the sincerity of his conviction, even if all the details were not provided and foreign correspondents were temporarily barred from visiting the republic. Anti-Russian and other nationalist outbursts in the Soviet Union had never before been publicly acknowledged.

As a national republic, Kazakhstan is unique. The site of important nuclear, military, and space installations, it is the second-largest of the Soviet Union's fifteen republics (the Russian Republic being the largest, and comprising about four-fifths of the country's territory), but its population is only fifteen million, and although the Moslem Kazakhs are the largest single ethnic group, they are outnumbered by the Slav settlers (Russians and Ukrainians).

The Alma-Ata incident confirmed the fears of Gorbachev's conservative opponents that glasnost would threaten not only the party's monopoly on power but also the cohesion of the multinational empire. What would be the effect of glasnost on nationalism in other ethnic republics?

The multiethnic and nominally federal character of the Soviet state had always been resistant to decentralizing reforms. But not all nations are equal in their importance for the preservation of the empire. With the Russians constituting half of the total population, the Ukrainians and Byelorussians, as the non-Russian Slavs, are the most important. They constitute a quarter of the total population, and account for a larger proportion of the country's economic and military potential. Fortunately, from Moscow's point of view, they are the most Russified.

By opening up the party and society, Gorbachev was also opening up opportunities—in the not very distant future—for nationalist forces in the non-Slav Baltic republics and Moslem Central Asia to challenge the status quo. There were problems even with the Slavs. During a live television discussion, a writer from Byelorussia, the small republic bordering on Poland, suddenly complained about the Russification of the population and asserted, "Byelorussian is not taught in a single school in the republic." A Ukrainian novelist on the panel chimed in that for all practical purposes "Ukrainian is no longer the official language of the Ukraine." The novelist Anatoly Rybakov, who also took part in the discussion, said later that the program had been scheduled to be rebroadcast but was never aired again.[22]

Prospects for the future looked unsettling. The regime's stability rested on the strength of its legitimacy, or popular acceptance of its goals and policies. Authoritarianism, the only model of rule the population knew, had served the party in good stead; it had enforced a sense of cohesiveness and given the country an idea of itself. The crushing dullness and uniformity of public discourse gave way almost overnight to frenetic and freewheeling discussions, and the avalanche of words betrayed uncertainty as to where Gorbachev wanted to go. The party elite now found the leader's talk of democracy and reforms disturbing, because they were dimly aware that he was preparing a good deal more than ideological exercises. They began to talk about the "good days" of Stalin. The yearning for Stalin was the yearning for the status quo and for an autocrat who would at least maintain, if not expand, their prerogatives. Gorbachev was withdrawing these at a terrifying pace.

A substantial section of the population also believed in the firm hand, something that became conspicuously obvious during the last lax years of Brezhnev's rule and that found its expression in a genuine revival of Stalin's cult.

Common citizens were tantalized by liberal ideals of democracy, freedom, and progress, yet their common ethical and political inheritance valued stability. For many, Stalin became the symbol of a simpler world, when prices were stable (in fact, Stalin would occasionally reduce prices on certain basic commodities) and order was maintained. This prettified illusion of the Stalinist past seemed to gain strength from the feeling of vulnerability generated by the talk about changes, higher prices, cost accounting, and efficiency, all of which seemed to foreshadow the loss of the relative security of the Soviet welfare state.

By the end of 1986, most Soviets found Gorbachev's leadership both fascinating and disturbing.

For some time his policy departures were a matter of words alone, the people serving as audience for his vision of the future, and the party consumed by personnel purges. But gradually Gorbachev's reformists began passing new laws and taking new steps, and by 1987 some of these measures were supposed to become a part of life. The question was how to do that. The answer, clear in retrospect, was: by destroying Stalinism.

Chapter 10

EXORCISING STALIN

The political struggle over Gorbachev's reforms entered a new phase in January 1987, when Stalin and his crimes again became one of the central issues in public debate. Within the next two years of raging ideological upheavals, first Stalin and subsequently Brezhnev and Chernenko were completely discredited. Two days before New Year's Day 1989, Moscow Radio was to announce that all references to Brezhnev and Chernenko were to be removed from public buildings and places.

But first came the extraordinary film *Repentance*, which had its premiere in Moscow in January 1987, and about which Gorbachev is said to have remarked that enough copies should be made so that everybody in the country would see it.

Georgian filmmaker Tengiz Abuladze's movie is not an artistic masterpiece. Outside the Soviet Union, it would be barely understandable. Inside the Soviet Union, however, *Repentance* marked a major anti-Stalinist event. The central character of the movie is a not entirely mythical Georgian tyrant, Varlan (Stalin was a Georgian), who is made up to look like Stalin's secret-police chief and fellow Georgian, Lavrenti Beria. Employing the methods of realism and surrealism, the grotesque and the absurd, Abuladze shows the dead dictator in various phases of his life, the phases Stalin went through. Early on he reviews a march-past from a ceremonial balcony while a great portrait of himself is flying like a kite overhead. He brings flowers (Stalin used to send flowers) to the apartment of an artist he is about to have arrested. There are haunting images from the thirties, the time of the Great Terror, such as the red wax seals the secret police used to stamp on the doors of the homes of people they took away, to prevent friends and relatives entering. At one point a woman searches through piles of logs from Siberian forests where prisoners in the gulag worked. She was looking for a message carved by her captive husband. This was the only way that he and other inmates of the gulag could communicate with friends and relatives outside. The enormous emotional impact is not only in the individual scenes but in their sum. The film's power of parable and the extraordinary force of its images instantly convey the context: the film is about the corruption of a generation that is heir to tyranny, and the demoralization of that generation's own children. In the opening scenes, Varlan's body is found night after night propped up balefully against a tree in his son's garden. Some say this is because he mustn't be allowed to rest in his grave, while others claim that it is simply impossible to get rid of him forever. In the final scenes, with an electrifyingly symbolic charge, the tyrant's corpse is cast off a mountaintop by his son, whose own alienated child has just committed suicide after learning the truth about his grandfather's crimes.

It is clear, in retrospect, that this was the onset of an offensive on Stalin that was to culminate at the seventieth anniversary of the Bolshevik revolution on October 5, 1987, when Gorbachev would become the first Soviet leader to denounce Stalin in public by describing his crimes as "enormous and unforgivable." But Gorbachev was proceeding methodically, starting with a powerful allegory and moving gradually toward more detailed condemnations. Between January and November, the offensive against the dead dictator shifted to poems, novels, articles, and historical works. Stalin appeared as the central character in a novel by Rybakov, who shows him in the early thirties as he was planning crafty provocations to destroy his potential opponents physically and consolidate his personal dictatorship. Vasili Belov's book *The Last Day* focused on the mindless destruction of peasants during Stalin's collectivization drive. Alexander Bek's long-suppressed novel *A New Appointment* con-

tained perhaps the most explicit and devastating analysis of the in-
humane system created by Stalin, a system capable of perpetuating
itself even three decades after the death of Russia's pockmarked
Caligula. The previously censored sections of Marshal Georgi Zhukov's memoirs were published, showing Stalin's top military man
fearing for his life in the Great Purge of the thirties, when the dictator
had the entire top echelon of the Red Army executed as Nazi spies.

As it picked up in intensity, the anti-Stalin campaign encountered
fierce opposition, for it opened the way to public debates of other
unpleasant issues in Soviet history, and focused public attention on
Moscow's systematic lying about the country's past, its falsification
and censorship to maintain an illusory image of its society.

But the momentum of glasnost was, by this time, unstoppable—
not simply in the unleashing of criticism and argument but finally,
in late 1986, in a new form of political activism at the grass-roots
level and the emergence of independent clubs and organizations.

Although nothing had changed in daily life, Yeltsin's stewardship of
Moscow had moved the capital into a unique period when the spirit
of the times and the possibilities of life suddenly and discreetly came
together and when the people, in the words of political scientist
Fyodor Burlatsky, were "no longer afraid as before."[1] What Burlatsky had primarily in mind was young Muscovites who began organizing "informal associations" of varying size and orientation.
They began as environmental or historical preservation lobbies, but
were rapidly to evolve into genuine pressure groups. It was glasnost,
of course, that legitimized such political activism.

Never since the tumultuous days of 1917 had the Russians so
openly debated the problems in their country and their hopes for its
future. Within the span of a few months, hundreds of these associations and social clubs were formed. In a country that traditionally
lacked an open clearinghouse for ideas, the independent clubs were
a new phenomenon. The Communist Party had held a complete
monopoly on all public discourse. No organization, whatever its objectives, was allowed to exist without sponsorship and control by the
party. The emergence of these groups was so sudden that the au-

thorities did not know how to deal with them or even what to call them. Either for lack of a better term or perhaps to underscore their tenuous legal standing, they were referred to as "unofficial organizations" in the government-controlled media.

The birth of one such unofficial organization in Moscow gave an insight into the ferment and passions that were emerging in Gorbachev's awakened country.

In late November 1986, Moscow city authorities began the construction of a new inner-city circular highway to ease traffic congestion. The project cut right through an old Moscow neighborhood known as "German suburb," where foreigners lived during the seventeenth and eighteenth centuries, and where Peter the Great spent much of his youth. One after another, the once-stately mansions began to crumble under the onslaught of the wrecker's ball and bulldozers. At first residents started to argue with the demolition teams about the wisdom of their destructive endeavor, pointing out that some of the finest examples of seventeenth- and eighteenth-century architecture were being wiped out for the sake of an impersonal new highway. The workers summoned the police, and soon the argument was placed before City Hall's transportation department and the Office for the Preservation of Historical Buildings.

While the arguments were going on, the demolition teams continued their work, approaching a small palace built in the eighteenth century by the wealthy merchant family Shcherbakov. A neighborhood action committee was organized by Kiril Parfionov, a twenty-two-year-old Bauman Institute student, and Leonty Bizov, thirty-three, an economist, to collect signatures on a petition to preserve the Shcherbakov Palace. The petition, signed by several thousand neighborhood residents, was presented to City Hall, and the following day the demolition company moved its heavy equipment over to the dilapidated palace. Members of the action committee were furious; they decided to guard the palace around the clock.

The demolition company called in police when the activists bodily prevented the machinery from moving close to the building. In the ensuing arguments, several persons were roughed up, and some were detained. That angered the entire neighborhood, and people began phoning prominent cultural and political figures to seek support. Locked in a test of wills, city officials made a semblance of agreeing to back down and stop demolition while the matter was being reconsidered. The heavy equipment was moved away; nerves calmed down. Secretly, however, they ordered the wreckers to do their work at night. The action committee, suspecting that the authorities might resort to such a ruse to create a *fait accompli,* continued to keep the building under surveillance.

When, on a cold January night, the wreckers moved their bulldozers and other heavy equipment to start demolition of the Shcherbakov Palace, committee members were awakened by the lookouts. The decision was made to damage the equipment, an act of civil disobedience. In the darkness, the activists poured sand and sugar into the gasoline tanks of the machinery.

Police were summoned the next day to find the perpetrators. The whole episode was beginning to acquire the proportions of a major scandal. Several persons were arrested, and Parfionov was promptly expelled from the Bauman Institute. But by then the issue had come to the attention of Yeltsin, who sided with the protesters. The arrested were freed; the Shcherbakov Palace was declared a historical monument; and the transportation department was ordered to move the highway into a tunnel under the area.

By this uneven struggle, the action-committee members were encouraged to form a new independent club. They called themselves the Shcherbakovtsi.[2]

No one knows exactly how many clubs were formed during 1986 or how many people were involved in their activities. Official reports in the spring of 1987 mention more than a thousand in Moscow and about two hundred in Leningrad. Similar organizations were formed in Orel, Ivanovo, Novosibirsk, Kuibyshev, Gorky, Sverdlovsk, and other cities. Some clubs, such as Leningrad's Salvation (Spasenie), had well over ten thousand active members; others, such as the Restructuring (Perestroika), formed by young specialists at Moscow's Central Mathematical Economic Institute, had about a hundred members. In the countryside, scores of "social-political correspondence clubs" were formed to conduct political and social debates by mail. The signs, however modest, of the nation's coming out of complacency and lethargy were encouraging for Gorbachev and his supporters. The stirrings at grass-roots level suggested the end of Brezhnev's stultifying policies and the widespread public apathy they produced.

What was Gorbachev's view? He had at this point, we think, a terrible ambivalence about the independent organizations. Though he did not doubt Yeltsin's sincerity in passionately endorsing this grass-roots movement, Gorbachev knew the arithmetic of his Central Committee and concluded that political constraints dictated that he proceed with caution. However commendable, these independent organizations contained the seeds of national discord, at least according to the conservative view, which held that, once people started organizing outside the Communist Party's framework and began struggling for some of their rights, they soon would come to claim *all* their rights. When barriers began to fall, pressures for liberalization would accelerate, since revolutions grow not from despair but from hope. And there was hope in the air.

Inevitably, some of the informal organizations born with the blossoming of liberation and glasnost revived the worst aspects of the Russian character. The largest and perhaps the most sinister of all independent associations was Pamyat (Memory). Openly anti-Semitic, strongly anti-Western, and covertly anti-Gorbachev, it organized street demonstrations in the spring of 1987 against some prominent Gorbachev supporters, including Yegor Yakovlev, editor-in-chief of *Moscow News,* the flagship of glasnost. In April 1987, some fifteen hundred Pamyat activists demonstrated outside the newspaper's offices in central Moscow, accusing Yakovlev of harboring "Jews and Freemasons" on his staff. Other people accused of being "secret Jews" included poet Andrei Voznesensky, journalist Alexander Bovin, and historian Dmitri Likhachev. Police officers were present, but none of the Pamyat activists shouting anti-Semitic slogans was arrested.

Pamyat activists frequently resorted to fascist-style methods of intimidation, including threatening phone calls at midnight and pogromlike actions. The apartments of several Jewish intellectuals were ransacked and their property was demolished by Pamyat gangs.[3]

Though Pamyat was an extremist minority, the distressing thing was that it had been founded with the support of at least some elements in the conservative establishment and in Russian nationalist-intellectual circles. The organization, with affiliates in other Russian cities, was led by two charismatic figures: Dmitri Vasilyev, a photojournalist, and Valery Yemelyanov, the author of a viciously anti-Semitic book.

Yemelyanov, the more bizarre of the two, was convicted by a Moscow court in 1980 of killing his wife, dismembering her body, and burning the remains at a city dump.[4] He had insisted that she was murdered by the Jews. Curiously, he was sent to a mental hospital for treatment after doctors diagnosed him as schizophrenic. One of the many instances of corruption exposed in 1987 by the glasnost-freed media was a report that doctors frequently accepted bribes in return for a false diagnosis of mental illness to help criminals avoid prison and to save young men from the draft. Yemelyanov was released in mid-1986, evidently with the help of prominent Pamyat supporters. In his book *Desionizatsia (De-Zionization)*, ostensibly issued in Paris but said to have been printed in Russia, Yemelyanov praises the anti-Jewish policy of the last Romanov tsars and extols Stalin for eliminating Jews from the Communist Party leadership and restoring the spirit of Russia. (Pamyat was also peddling two other anti-Semitic books, Vladimir Begun's *Creeping Counterrevolution* and Alexander Romanenko's *About the Class Essence of Zionism*.)

Though the extremist groups challenged the tolerance of Gorbachev and his supporters, the vast majority of independent organizations were politically moderate and supportive of Gorbachev's policies. One group, known as the Club of Social Initiatives, stated that its main purpose was to transform Gorbachev's reforms "from being theory from above into practice from below." A club called Glasnost, whose members were former political prisoners, was in Gorbachev's camp. One of the club leaders, Sergei Grigoryants, who became editor of *Glasnost* magazine, a journal issued three times a month in a hundred typed copies and focusing on human-rights abuses and social issues, put it this way: "We support Gorbachev's program and we want these changes to continue and deepen. What we do is what Gorbachev wants to do but is not able to."[5]

Gorbachev opened up the traditional intellectual forums that had been banned by the Soviet regime since 1917, even during Khrushchev's short-lived thaw. The independent clubs were similar to the *kruzhok* (circle), which, throughout the nineteenth century, was a popular vehicle for intellectual activity. The circle involved persons of common intellectual interests who met occasionally to debate issues of common concern. When the tsarist regime became oppressive, the circles were forced underground and acquired a subversive character.

Just as the new, nonparty associations appeared to revive the nineteenth-century tradition of the *kruzhok,* Gorbachev's free press revived another traditional forum for nineteenth-century intellectuals: the debate in periodicals. Eluding tsarist censorship, which proscribed political debates, the great ideological arguments of the nineteenth century were conducted in the form of literary criticism; Russia's greatest literary critic of the time, Vissarion Belinsky, created out of the literary essay and the book review powerful tools of social analysis. The revival of this artful form for debate under Gorbachev was conspicuously strong; one of the most devastating and detailed analyses of the Stalinist system, for example, appeared as a review of Alexander Bek's novel *A New Appointment* in the scientific journal *Nauka i Zhizn.* It was written by an economist, Gavril Popov, who subsequently emerged as one of the most passionate supporters of perestroika.[6]

The proliferation of independent organizations, political-action committees, and lobby groups eventually led to a rift in the leadership and the fall of Boris Yeltsin. Yeltsin felt that, if the leadership properly worked with them, these thousands of independent groups could become the backbone of the process of democratic development. Ligachev, Chebrikov, and others thought differently, and, at least in the short run, their views prevailed.

•   •   •

For three weeks prior to the Central Committee plenum on January 27, 1987, Gorbachev spent almost all his time at his dacha in Barvikha, just outside Moscow, conducting one of the most intensive lobbying campaigns ever mounted by a Soviet leader. Like Lyndon B. Johnson, Gorbachev felt he could convert anyone. He wanted to reason with the doubters, persuade them of the wisdom of his course, get them on his team. It was something he had done well in Stavropol, using his charm and intellect. He believed that, if he confronted each Central Committee member face-to-face, in the privacy of his country home, he would be able to explain the rationale for reforms and impress upon the visitor the urgency of the moment. He still did not know how truly intractable his opposition was, the party insiders who worked privately in closed rooms, always cloaked in secrecy until the deed was done.

In one month, Gorbachev met individually with each of the three hundred Central Committee members. The weather was frigid—the mercury dipped down to $-31°C$.—and the two-lane "government road" through the forests of the western suburbs was kept clear of snow for the interminable flow of black limousines. His aides were out at the dacha, and he called on Yegor Ligachev and other Politburo figures to join some discussions. He wanted to give elective bodies greater authority over executive ones; he needed new rules to reinvigorate the party.

Despite his enormous efforts, both sides stood their ground, and the plenum ended in a stalemate, though it is worth recording that none of the thirty-four persons who spoke at the meeting came out openly against the leader.[7] "No one said a single word against perestroika," Yevgeny Primakov, a nonvoting Politburo member and Gorbachev confidant, said later. "But there were various approaches, various levels of criticism about the sharpness of the policies."

The only senior official who did not address the plenum was Yegor Ligachev, the emerging standard-bearer of the opposition, and his silence, particularly after Gorbachev's efforts to include him in the January dacha sessions, was conspicuous. Though no one overtly challenged the new reforms, when the voting took place the party elite let its views be known. The plenum endorsed Gorbachev's proposal for multiple candidates and secret ballots in local party elections, and agreed in principle that non–party members could hold top positions. But it refused to adopt other political reforms, including the increased power for elective bodies.

In the votes for membership of the Central Committee and Politburo, Gorbachev also got part, though not all, of what he sought. He was strong enough to promote three of his people into top leadership slots: Alexander Yakovlev, already secretary of the Central Committee and his closest political adviser, was given the additional position of alternate Politburo member; Anatoly Lukyanov, who runs Gorbachev's office, formally moved into the leadership as a secretary of the Central Committee; and Nikolai Slyunkov, appointed a member of the Central Committee and alternate Politburo member in 1986, was made a secretary of the Central Committee.

But the senior Brezhnev holdover, Vladimir Shcherbitsky, the Ukrainian party leader, retained his Politburo seat. And Boris Yeltsin—the charismatic communist boss of Moscow, an alternate Politburo member, and the leading reformer on Gorbachev's team—was denied full membership in the ruling council.

Though he had reasoned with each Central Committee member, Gorbachev went into the plenum dubious about the outcome. He wanted to show some muscle, and he did, providing three surprises for the committee, signaling his intention to continue the anticorruption drive against the Brezhnevite officials.

The first surprise was the arrest, days before the plenum opened, of Brezhnev's son-in-law, General Yuri Churbanov, the former first deputy minister of the interior: he was booked on corruption charges.

The second surprise was an extraordinarily tough speech. Gorbachev had circulated a draft of his speech, along with other material (including letters of complaint about the party bureaucracy from ordinary citizens), to all Central Committee members a week before the plenum. But he delivered a different speech. The sheer savagery of his attack on the corruption during the Brezhnev years and his renewed emphasis on political reforms stunned his audience. He criticized "extremely ugly forms" of corruption in the party organizations of Uzbekistan, Moldavia, Turkmenistan, Kazakhstan, and parts of Russia, including Moscow. "You could tell by the looks on their faces that a lot of people in the hall were unhappy, to put it mildly," one Central Committee member said privately.[8] Gorbachev assailed the way the country had been run in the past, and his rhetorical barbs were directed at many figures present at the meeting. The country, he said, was in an even worse mess than he had suspected when he took power. He did not mention Brezhnev by name, but he strongly condemned his rule, saying that "most planned targets haven't been met since the early 1970s." The country, he continued, had been governed by people who had abused their power and privileges. His wholesale attack on the party included criticism of "senior officials . . . who abused their authority, suppressed criticism, sought [personal] gain, and some of whom became accomplices in, if not organizers of, criminal activities."[9]

Political reforms, he said, were needed to carry out perestroika. This meant reorganization of "the activities of the party and its workers at all levels." The introduction of democracy, as he put it, would make the party more efficient, allowing the younger, better-educated men and women of talent and ambition to replace those officials "who view initiative and activism of people as something little short of a natural calamity." Without democratization of social life, he continued, the party would not be able to galvanize people into action.

"We need democracy like air," he said in his closing speech. "If we fail to realize this, or if we realize this but make no really serious steps to broaden it, promote it, and draw the country's working people extensively into the perestroika process, our policy will get choked, and perestroika will fail."[10]

That Gorbachev had anticipated a rebuff by the Central Committee became clear when he sprang his third surprise on the plenum: the idea of an emergency party conference. Gorbachev was not a man to be underestimated; he was mastering a certain kind of power that his opponents did not fully understand, going public when traditional party men expected him to operate behind the scenes. He exercised power differently. When they refused to hear his arguments for political reforms, he announced that he would convene a party conference to seek approval for the reforms.

Under the Soviet system, the Central Committee functions, in effect, as the party's parliament. The leadership cannot change party rules or make any major decisions without its approval. Its three-hundred-odd members are elected by party congresses, which meet once every five years. Normally the leader can maneuver a majority of Central Committee members to back his policies. But Gorbachev was trying to do things many regarded as abnormal and he could not obtain the parliamentary vote of confidence. He was essentially the leader of a minority government doomed to seek consensus each step of the way. He could muster the support at the very top, in the Politburo and the Secretariat, but he could not get it in the Central Committee. Khrushchev's situation was different. He had problems at the top but, on at least one occasion, he was saved by a majority in the Central Committee after his Politburo and Secretariat colleagues had agreed to remove him. (Eventually, when he attacked their privileges, a majority of the Central Committee members did back a palace coup that toppled Khrushchev.)

The change in party rules was an issue directly affecting most Central Committee members, and the conservatives managed to form a majority against the leader's wishes. Rebuffed by the majority, Gorbachev would normally have had to wait until 1991 to try to push his political program at the next scheduled party congress. But there is a device available to the leader to circumvent such an unpleasant impasse and appeal to the broader party elite over the heads of the Central Committee. He can convene a "party conference," or what in practice amounts to an emergency party congress, to seek approval for his program. The five thousand delegates to the conference are elected in secret ballot by nineteen million party members, a deliberate attempt to sidestep the traditional grip of regional party barons on the composition of their delegations to the meeting. The last leader to deploy this device was Stalin, who in 1941 drastically changed the composition of the party's ruling bodies.

January was not a happy month for Gorbachev. He had let it be known that he had little respect for many of the conservative barons he found around him, the people who claimed, when he advanced his reformist ideas, that they had always done things the other, "traditional" way in party business. He had asked his Central Committee colleagues to "speak up" and offer alternatives to perestroika, but nobody came up with a single proposal, and nobody came out against him head on.[11] It was a frustrating experience. He did not blow his cool, yet those who worked with him were surprised by the intensity of his emotion. In his political approach, as in his private life, Gorbachev was a puritan, but the Kremlin was no place for a puritan. He had evidently considered resigning if the Central Committee completely blocked his proposals. Yegor Yakovlev, the *Moscow News* editor, quoted Gorbachev as telling a meeting of news executives that, if the Central Committee had reached the conclusion that perestroika "is not justified and should be rejected, I would have said: I cannot work otherwise."[12]

The idea of failure may have entered his calculations for the first time in the first weeks of 1987. He had been so confident of himself, always climbing upward and gaining honors and positions, always doing the right thing, working long hours so that the long day became a badge of honor, until he reached the peak and became wholly identified with his program. But he would not give up. He had always made it clear that he would not give up, not let his offering to the history of socialism slip out of his hands.

"The year 1987 will be a determining one in many ways, for the fate of perestroika is in fact being decided now," he declared three weeks later at the trade-union congress. "We realize now that only the very first steps have been made." He saw himself waging an "uncompromising struggle between the old and the new."[13]

Almost immediately after the January plenum, journalist Alexander Bovin sounded the alarm. Gorbachev, Bovin wrote in the weekly *Novoe Vremya,* was opposed by the same "socialist conservatives" who had defeated earlier reform attempts by Khrushchev and Alexei Kosygin. "I cannot escape the feeling that we underestimate the scale and power of resistance that is opposed to our strategy." He called on the people to rally around Gorbachev, suggesting that perestroika was not an irreversible process. People of his generation had high hopes after Khrushchev's Twentieth Party Congress, in 1956 (when he launched his anti-Stalin campaign), only to be bitterly disappointed after his fall, in 1964. "My generation and I watched with bewilderment, pain, and a disgusting sense of our own impotence, as the ideas of one of the most historic congresses of our party kept seeping through the bureaucratic sand."[14]

Bovin was a member of the Gorbachev generation. Khrushchev's was the first political voice they had listened to; he had imbued them with a sense of purpose. Gorbachev had also witnessed the way the bureaucracy subdued Khrushchev and engineered his ouster.

Early on Gorbachev had told a group of Soviet writers that the bureaucracy would attempt to "grind up" his administration and break its neck the way "they broke Khrushchev's neck."[15] He would not walk away from this. He would fight. "If not us, who?" he said in the same speech. "If not now, when?"

After the plenum, Gorbachev would more frequently launch into tirades against the party bureaucracy. Reforms, he said, are "resented by those who until now ran the affairs of an enterprise, district, city or laboratory as if it were their own private domain, without the slightest regard for the opinion of the collective, of the working people. Among them are also people who took advantage of the atmosphere of total license for embezzling public funds and self-enrichment. . . . Here lie the sources of resistance to perestroika, of sluggishness and a desire to sit things out."[16] He assailed conservative opponents of democratization as engaging in "pure deception of the people."[17]

More and more he stressed the importance of glasnost in his speeches. "Everything should be placed under the control of the people so as to make the process of perestroika irreversible and to prevent a repetition of what happened in the past." The elite, responding to his leadership, began turning the wheels in the proper direction. The Supreme Soviet began issuing pardons to scores of political prisoners, and American Jewish leaders received assurances in Moscow that an estimated eleven thousand refuseniks, as Jews who had been denied permission to emigrate from the Soviet Union were known, would be allowed to leave. Tass reported that two previously banned films by the late poet and actor Vladimir Vysotsky would be released, adding that they had been kept on the shelf

because of "the opposition on the part of bureaucrats." An icono-
clastic troubadour, Vysotsky was still idolized by millions of Russians
for his satirical ballads, which sharply conveyed the realities of Soviet
life. Officially spurned during his lifetime, he was now nominated
for a state prize six years after his death. A statue depicting him as
an angel with tied wings was erected at his grave, which became a
site of pilgrimage for Vysotsky fans.

But Gorbachev's speeches displayed for all to see the extent of his
frustration, as well as the nature of the questioning he was facing in
Kremlin councils about the pace and scope of his reforms.

Some politicians evidently urged the abandonment of the program.
Others were warning that "democracy will be used by people to
disorganize society and undermine discipline, to weaken the system."[18] In Moscow itself, the party organization, for instance, resisted
Gorbachev's new legislation, which allowed private enterprise on a
small scale. Only one of the city's twenty-seven district party committees endorsed the policy; the others voted against having any
private enterprise in their districts. In some meetings, opponents
overtly argued against cooperative ownership as "Jewish business."
Boris Yeltsin, the Moscow party leader, had to intervene personally
in each of the other twenty-six party committees to push the official
policy.

Yeltsin also waged a frontal assault on the party bureaucracy, one
of the most hazardous moves a Soviet leader could make. In the
wake of the January plenum, he orchestrated a campaign against the
most cherished privileges of the *nomenklatura,* its special shops,
hospitals, and *spetzshkoli,* or special schools.

Yeltsin was a puritan in Babylon, a man in Gorbachev's own
image. He had distinguished himself as the leader of Sverdlovsk, an
important industrial center in the Urals, as an austere, energetic,
and incorruptible administrator who hated grafters and sycophants.
Gorbachev brought him to Moscow first as a secretary of the Central
Committee; since December 1985, he had served as the boss of the
capital, replacing Viktor Grishin. Taking over a thoroughly corrupt
Moscow party bureaucracy, he epitomized the reformist thrust. He
worked a sixteen-hour day and was very much a loner, surrounded
by hostile forces. His loyalty to Gorbachev and his program was

doubly strong because Gorbachev was his only patron, the only source of his power. In his public appearances he seemed well briefed, keenly interested, somewhat humorless, and exceptionally outspoken. He came to his new job, met it on his terms, and began weeding out Brezhnevite holdovers. Not being of Moscow, he faced difficulties in trying to conquer it. The city of eight million had been run for eighteen years by Grishin and his cohorts, who supervised mafia-type district party organizations. Grishin used to have a few drinks with district leaders, frequently oiling the wheels of the city party machinery with vodka. Yeltsin would have none of that. He worked hard; he hoped they could see the rightness of his actions. He was an exceptional man but not a wise politician.

Gorbachev's struggle with the party elite and the onset of the campaign against its privileges suddenly expanded the ranks of Yeltsin's enemies. Moscow is the bureaucratic capital of a bureaucratized empire; officials working in federal, regional, and local bureaucracies number in the hundreds of thousands.

In early March, Moscow city newspapers began to carry articles about "special schools" at which children of the elite could be seen arriving daily in official chauffeur-driven cars. These schools offered tuition in modern languages, most commonly English, German, and French. The facilities were superior, sometimes including saunas and swimming pools. The most devastating exposé, in *Moskovskaya Pravda,* demolished the myth that these schools existed to develop the talents of gifted children from all backgrounds. It said that the ninety special schools were concentrated in Moscow's most prestigious districts and only 6 percent of first-year children at the schools had working-class parents; by the final year, the percentage shrank to almost zero. The newspaper described a typical scene in the school bathrooms: fashionably dressed children bartered and sold foreign goods, from chewing gum to pornographic magazines that they had obtained from their well-connected parents. The attack on special schools was followed by an exposé of special hospitals for the party elite.

Nikita Khrushchev had mounted a similar campaign shortly before his ouster from power. Gorbachev's drive—through Yeltsin—touched off similar resentment in various bureaucracies. The bitter

reaction was summed up in a letter to the newspaper from a middle-
aged Muscovite, wife of a senior official: "Stop fulminating against
us. Don't you see you are wasting your breath. We are the elite,
and you cannot stop the process of stratification in the society. You
aren't strong enough for that. We shall tear your puny sails of your
perestroika to pieces—you won't get far. So you'd better tone down
your ardor."[19]

Yeltsin, whose allies controlled *Moskovskaya Pravda,* had the letter published. Doing so was, in his view, a part of glasnost. "You
can either open all the windows wide and let the fresh wind sweep
away the cobwebs, or once again bolt the door and try to sweep the
dirt under the carpet," he said. He pressed his assault on the party
bureaucracy, criticizing "party executives [who] outdid even the
clergy as far as rituals are concerned." Perestroika, he continued,
was "proceeding at a slow pace, largely because there are quite a
few reefs and even mines on its course. The further we push, the
greater the resistance is likely to become. The people in the central
apparatus who are used to having power and delegating responsibility
have been fiercely resisting this drive."[20]

From the sacred privileges of the elite to their sacred ideology,
Gorbachev and his reformers gave the party leaders no respite. They
pushed the issue of Stalin to the forefront of public debates, starting
a painful re-examination of the "rampage of evil" under the dictator.
Gorbachev led the way by declaring in February that "there should
be no forgotten names or blanks, either in history or in literature."
He called for an open reappraisal of Old Bolsheviks killed by Stalin,
including such figures as Leon Trotsky, Nikolai Bukharin, Lev Kamenev, and many others who made the revolution but who had been
disgraced by Stalin, turned into nonpersons, and obliterated from
history. These names, Gorbachev said, "must not be pushed into
the background." It was "all the more immoral to forget or pass
over in silence large periods in the life of the people," he said,
referring to the Stalin and Khrushchev eras. "History must be seen
for what it is. . . . We are not going to present bad things in rosy
colors today."[21] Gorbachev's allies were more explicit. Georgi Smirnov, the new head of the Institute of Marxism-Leninism, asserted

that the crushing of Khrushchev's reform program had led to the stagnation of the Brezhnev years, and he proposed a major new re-examination of both the Khrushchev and Brezhnev periods. (Khrushchev had been an official nonperson since his ouster from power.) Yuri Afanasiev, the dean of the Moscow State Faculty of Historian-Archivists, raised the same question more directly: "Khrushchev's role in our postwar history requires more precise definition. How much longer can we pretend that he simply did not exist?" Afanasiev pointed out the absurdity of censorship that snipped out frames of Khrushchev in films about Yuri Gagarin, the first man in space.

In March, the "socialist conservatives" reacted to the anti-Stalin campaign with an open and systematic attack on glasnost. Yegor Ligachev joined in the battle by denouncing those who sought to portray "our history as a series of continual mistakes and disappointments."[22] The ongoing re-examination of history, he said, should emphasize "above all the period of triumph of socialist construction," a reference to Stalin's forced industrialization. The furious struggle over history and Stalin was more than polemics over their past; the Russians were debating their future.

In retrospect, the battle lines seemed to have hardened around the Yeltsin attack on party privileges, which came on top of Gorbachev's effort to change party rules formally. But glasnost also was producing fresh political issues that would raise new doubts in the minds of moderates about the wisdom of the Gorbachev course.

By March, Gorbachev aides said they believed that the conservative opposition was beginning to coalesce.[23] Historian Roy Medvedev suggested that Gorbachev at this point was "not a complete master of the Politburo but he is of the Secretariat, which is more important."[24] The two institutions constitute the pinnacle of power, making up what is usually referred to as the Soviet leadership. The Secretariat, usually composed of nine to twelve secretaries of the Central Committee and chaired by the general secretary, prepares the issues for decision by the Politburo, which consists of about twelve officials. The Politburo is also chaired by the general secretary. The mechanics of power provides the general secretary with the capacity to dominate day-to-day politics. But on major issues he can be checked, either in the Politburo or, more likely, by the three-hundred-odd-member Central Committee, which holds regular meetings two or three times a year.

Beyond the institutional checks, there were other powerful forces that have humbled many of Russia's leaders—the bureaucratic behemoth and social inertia.

Chapter 11

NEW THINKING

When Gorbachev took power, as Seweryn Bialer of Columbia University speculated, he probably thought he would face a wall of conservatism that hammer blows would demolish. He encountered instead a spongelike resistance, indifference to hammer blows.

Gogol's *The Inspector General* is the satirical masterpiece on corruption, sycophancy, and administrative irresponsibility in the tsarist bureaucracy of the nineteenth century. The Russian bureaucracy's ability to deprive even the sharpest domestic initiative of its momentum was unparalleled. Ironically, Soviet communism reinforced some of the basest tsarist traditions. Over the past seven decades, the system has degenerated into one that penalizes initiative, efficiency, decency, and responsibility while rewarding opportunism, laziness, sloganeering, and deviousness. With the best will in the world—not just Gorbachev's but that of every party member and every citizen—the entire complex machinery that constitutes the world's second-largest economy could not be changed in a matter of years.

This point was illuminated by the experience of an old friend. Though he fervently wanted Gorbachev to succeed, he was highly skeptical, partly because of his most recent trip outside Moscow. He had been called on short notice, he said with a smile of infinite resignation, to consult with the officials of a textile firm some three hundred miles from Moscow. The officials had signed a joint-venture agreement with a West German firm, such ventures being encouraged by the Gorbachev administration, under a new law, passed only months earlier, allowing foreign capital investments in the Soviet Union. The West Germans were among the first to take the plunge into a potentially promising market.

The German firm had shipped truckloads of the most up-to-date machinery to their new partners several months earlier; now two German executives had arrived to inspect the facilities where the equipment should have been installed. Not speaking Russian, they hired an interpreter in Moscow and took an overnight train to their destination. From that point on, Gogol took over.

The Soviet partners greeted their visitors warmly and immediately took them to the executive office building for a discussion, which lasted the entire morning. Detailed plans and an impressive mockup of the new plant were proudly displayed. The two Germans made approving noises, then politely asked for a tour of the real building site. No, no, the Russians wouldn't hear of it, saying the new partners had to partake in local hospitality.

The management had laid on a special luncheon, including black and red caviar, smoked sturgeon, and Kamchatka crab. Since Gorbachev's crackdown on alcoholism, mineral water had replaced vodka and champagne as the officially prescribed beverage for such occasions. But the inquisitive Germans had created an emergency for the factory management. It decided, apparently with considerable enthusiasm, to break Gorbachev's ban on alcohol. Vodka, champagne, and speeches flowed well into the afternoon. The object was, our friend said, to extend the reveling into the evening, when the Germans were scheduled to return by train to Moscow. The Russians had no plans to show them anything.

But during the feast the Germans became more and more insistent on seeing the construction site. After all, that was the reason for their trip, they kept repeating. When it became clear that the vodka had not achieved its desired effect, a Soviet executive instructed the interpreter to refrain from translating while another Soviet official entertained the visitors with a disingenuous soliloquy on his experiences in the West. Meanwhile, other Russians at the table engaged in a seemingly jovial discussion. "We can't show them the site," the local party secretary said. "They'll see that we're so far behind that we've had to get soldiers in to do the work." Another executive suggested that the soldiers could be ordered to leave the construction site. Yet another official suddenly remembered another impediment. The tour was out of the question, he said, because the crates containing the West German machinery were lying half covered in snow near the entrance to the site. "They can't avoid seeing them," he said.

Somebody suggested that they tell the unsuspecting visitors that an authorization from Moscow was needed for such an inspection. A purportedly feverish series of phone conversations ensued while the baffled West Germans became more and more irritated. "Well, hell, we are business partners, aren't we?" one of the Germans said emphatically. "What does Moscow have to do with this?"

Confronted with such determination, the Russian officials were cornered. The three top Russians excused themselves for a brief consultation in a nearby office. They reached the decision to order the soldiers to leave the site for an hour and to have a bulldozer tear out the fence in the rear of the building and make it look like the entrance to the construction site. The newly created path to the building was to be well trodden so as not to arouse any suspicion. Again, our friend said, the lunch had to be extended while the orders were being carried out. The Russians, now all smiles, returned to the executive dining room and informed their guests that they had obtained Moscow's permission. The group relaxed. They then launched into yet another series of toasts to hail constructive cooperation between countries with different social systems.

Eventually the Germans were given a tour of the empty building. The German machinery, they were told, was safely stored in a warehouse some kilometers away. But just as everything seemed to have worked out, the Germans suddenly expressed the wish to see the Soviet partners' existing mill. Again the Russians sought to distract the visitors while debating the problem in low tones of voice. "Impossible," said the party secretary. "They will see that we have no ventilation system." The plant manager warned of an even greater embarrassment: some unspecified piece of equipment had broken down in the dye division, and workers wearing rubber boots were tramping cloth knee-deep in tubs filled with dye. There was no easy fix for these problems, our friend said, and the German business partners had to be turned down with the promise that they would see the facility on their next visit. The Russians tried to assuage the Germans' ruffled feelings with yet another round of caviar and champagne and gifts of painted wooden folk art.

"The whole thing was an outrage," our friend concluded. "It is so typically Russian. No matter what you decide in Moscow, the folks out in the provinces say enthusiastically, 'Yes, comrade, it will be done,' then continue to work just as they have always done."

Even at the center of Soviet power, in Moscow, where glasnost and perestroika had made some headway, much of the bureaucracy was stubbornly resisting change with all means at its disposal. After the January plenum, the guerrilla war reached well beyond the confines of corrupt inner-city politics, into the heart of the Kremlin.

In the spring of 1987, we called on Gorbachev's special assistant Georgi Smirnov, freshly appointed to head the Institute of Marxism-Leninism. The institute, set in a large park of birch and pine trees on the outskirts of Moscow, looks like a contemporary version of the old Russian Orthodox monasteries. A high brick wall around the sanctuary keeps it secluded from the outside world. The iron gates clanged open to let us into this preserve of Marxist contemplation; we drove down a winding paved road through the carefully tended grounds, dotted with shaded benches. A young, clean-shaven man of modest bearing, with the air of a novice, took us through the corridors of the large building. It seemed devoid of life, as tranquil as a monastery; people moved quietly, almost like monks. But we were soon to discover that there was turmoil behind the doors.

Though Smirnov had long coveted his new job, he had not expected such a fierce battle when he took it on. Within days of his arrival, he discovered that the staff members of the institute, which ever since Stalin's day had been a bastion of dogmatism, were trying to buck him at every turn. Smirnov confided to us, with seeming good humor, that the invidious resistance included "anonymous letters denouncing me" to the KGB and the Central Committee. Anonymous denunciation is a practice of long standing in Russia, but it was startling to hear of such methods at the Mecca of communist faith.

Gorbachev was equally startled as news of such incidents reached him. In a private meeting with prominent Soviet writers, he said that trying to restructure the bureaucracy was proving far more arduous and exhausting than most outsiders appreciated: "If only you knew how painfully it's going!"[1]

The restructuring of diplomacy was only slightly less frustrating. Gorbachev had begun early on to take control of foreign policy by moving Eduard Shevardnadze into the Foreign Ministry. The additional appointment of Anatoly Dobrynin, the veteran ambassador to Washington, as secretary of the Central Committee signaled Gorbachev's desire to make the Secretariat the planning center of foreign and security strategy. He needed someone as experienced as Dobrynin working directly under him. He understood the difficulty of transforming a tradition-bound bureaucracy into a tool for quick action, and he expected resistance from the military high command.

Dobrynin quickly articulated the direction of the New Thinking. In an article in the September 1986 issue of the party journal *Kommunist*, he asserted that "the interdependency of survival is of cardinal importance" in the nuclear age, and that "modern weaponry gives to no state the hope of defending itself by technical and military means only, by building the most powerful defense. National security and international security have become inseparable notions."[2]

In the subsequent issue of *Kommunist*, the man handpicked by Gorbachev to head the political directorate of the armed forces, General Alexei Lizichev, defended Dobrynin's position, butting his head against a majority of the Old Guard military leaders, who were suspicious of Gorbachev's arms-reduction schemes; they opposed his unilateral moratorium on nuclear testing and believed that Gorbachev's new approach made the country look weak.[3]

The Old Guard marshals occasionally paid lip service to arms control, but they did not really believe in it. It was obvious that any closer relationship between Gorbachev and such men as Marshals Viktor Kulikov and Sergei Sokolov was going to be uneasy in the extreme. The only security they were interested in was measured in units of military hardware. In contrast, Gorbachev thought war was not merely a matter of numbers; quality also counted.

Gorbachev was at odds with the military ideologically and personally. He regarded old military professionals as inherently stuffy, narrow-minded, and wrongheaded. Wrapping themselves in patriotism and Cold War zeal, the military leaders had claimed a disproportionate chunk of the national wealth. In Gorbachev's mind, the kudos the nation had heaped on the Red Army's performance in World War Two was not entirely justified: the victory was paid for with too much Russian blood, or, as one of his senior supporters put it privately, "with so much blood, a sea of blood, that we could have drowned the entire German army in it without ever fighting them."

From the very beginning, Gorbachev signaled his coolness toward the military. Possibly that was a result of his analysis of the economic situation, and his realization that Brezhnev's massive expenditures on the military would have to cease. Just four months after taking power, he moved to ease the military grip on the nation's security policy through a series of personnel changes in the upper echelons. His first known major meeting with the armed forces leaders took place in Minsk in July 1985, when he explained the enforced retirements of many top commanders. He was not against the military (as long as it embraced his perestroika), but he wanted a leaner and more effective force. And he knew that the Old Guard marshals would oppose any cuts. Throughout 1985 and 1986, he continued to enforce changes in the upper echelons of the high command and in military districts: by July 1986, he had replaced the commander-in-chief of the ground forces, the chief of the navy, the chief of civil defense, and the chief of the main inspectorate of the armed forces; and First Deputy Defense Minister Marshal Vasili Petrov was replaced by Army General Pyotr Lushev. The top marshals—Sokolov, Kulikov, and Akhromeyev—nonetheless retained their key positions. (Akhromeyev was retired in late 1988, but was retained as an adviser by Gorbachev.)

In early 1987, Gorbachev brought General Dmitri Yazov, the commander of the Far Eastern Theater, to Moscow as deputy minister for personnel. He had met Yazov during his visit to the Far East the previous summer, and the general had impressed him as a military man after his own heart. While Yazov gained firsthand experience in the machinations of high-level military politics, Gorbachev could continue to work with Sokolov as defense minister.

The crux of Gorbachev's New Thinking was that the issue of nuclear arms is "a political and psychological problem rather than just a military and technical one."[4] Soviet security and the "advancement of socialism in the world" no longer were a function of the Leninist "correlation of forces" to be strengthened by military means. The goals of security, Gorbachev said, must be achieved primarily by diplomatic, political, and economic means. Yes, we are encircled, Gorbachev argued at a Central Committee conference in May 1986, playing upon traditional Russian fears of encirclement. "We are encircled not by invincible armies but by superior economies."

The military-industrial complex responded. In June, Premier Nikolai Ryzhkov outlined intentions to involve defense industries more deeply in the production of consumer items,[5] and was echoed by Politburo member Lev Zaikov, who said: "It has been decided that the military sectors of industry will not only take an active part in the production of civilian products and nationally needed goods, but also combine it with the technical re-equipping of light and food industries, public services, and trade."[6]

It was at the February 1986 Twenty-seventh Party Congress that Gorbachev appeared to be rewriting the official dogma for the first time (in order "to rid our policy of ideological prejudice").[7] No longer was communism expected to "triumph" in the struggle with capitalism; Lenin's dream of the "downfall of imperialism" was not even mentioned in the party program. Even Khrushchev's concept of "peaceful coexistence" with the West was softened. It no longer meant "a special kind of class warfare." For Gorbachev it meant dialogue and competition between the two systems. He talked of an interdependent, almost integral world, beset by threats posed by nuclear weapons, ecological problems, and poverty.

Gorbachev's novel approach on SDI at Reykjavík continued the ideas he had introduced in February. The Reykjavík package was based on the "integral" linkage between strategic and medium-range missiles and space weapons. He had offered concessions in the field of strategic and medium-range missiles in order to limit the American SDI program. It was precisely America's effort to reach superiority with SDI that "we perceive as the main danger," he said.[8] He had won conservative endorsement for the concessions providing they were part of the package; but that package was based on a strategy calculated to kill the whole enterprise.

When his Reykjavík gambit failed, when Reagan refused to budge on SDI, Gorbachev tried a new approach. Five months after Reykjavík, in March 1987, he untied the Reykjavík package and offered to reach a separate agreement on medium-range nuclear missiles. He sought to convince Reagan and Shultz of the seriousness of his intentions, and he understood that he had to make concessions—or be "flexible," as his aides described it. This opened the way for a historic Soviet-American agreement eliminating all medium-range nuclear weapons later that year.

Gorbachev's move may have seemed like a slap in the face to military conservatives who had reluctantly endorsed the package. By untying the package and accepting Reagan's zero option on the medium-range missiles, Gorbachev was in effect renouncing the huge SS-20 arsenal that the Soviets had deployed against Western Europe in the 1970s. In explaining his reversal, Gorbachev took the high moral ground, portraying the Soviet Union as the champion of peace. But in reality he was seeking to obscure the essential weakness of his position; success was eluding him both at home and abroad. Nuclear physicist Andrei Sakharov articulated a stronger defense than did Gorbachev. He said that the untying of the package was a way to overcome a "dangerous deadlock" in the negotiations. As a military threat, SDI was, in Sakharov's view, "a kind of Maginot line in space—expensive and ineffective." The ideas behind the Reykjavík package, said Sakharov, were not sound. "I believe a compromise on SDI can be reached later," he said.[9] But according to Gorbachev, he had decided to untie the Reykjavík package after hearing "the thoughts and ideas of an international intellectual elite" that he had gathered in Moscow the previous month, in February 1987.[10]

That meeting of glitterati was an extraordinary event, a display of Gorbachev's flair for public policy, not merely public relations. He had managed to attract more than a thousand international celebrities from eighty countries—businessmen, authors, religious figures, scientists, and actors, including the singer Yoko Ono, the writer Graham Greene, Hollywood stars Gregory Peck, Peter Ustinov, and Kris Kristofferson, the Italian movie star Claudia Cardinale, novelists Gore Vidal and Norman Mailer, former Prime Minister of Canada Pierre Trudeau, Austria's former Chancellor Bruno Kreisky, economist John Kenneth Galbraith, millionaire businessmen Donald Kendall, William Norris, Armand Hammer, and Robert Roosa—to come to Moscow to take part in a three-day seminar "For a World Without Nuclear Weapons, for Mankind's Survival." Among the Soviet participants was Andrei Sakharov, released from exile less than three months earlier.

Moscow had never seen anything like it. Never before had any Soviet leader orchestrated an attempt to identify the Kremlin with such an array of prominent intellectuals. Probably none of Gorbachev's predecessors possessed the imagination to assemble a star-studded international cast to serve as a background for a peace campaign. And perhaps no other world leader would be able to draw such an impressive crowd. There was little doubt that for most foreign participants Gorbachev himself was the attraction.

The purpose of the seminar was to outline Gorbachev's New Thinking about international security before an audience of international celebrities and opinion-makers, hence ensuring maximum worldwide publicity. He turned on his charm for the participants, deploying a mixture of flattery and purposeful discussion. Chatting with Yoko Ono, he told her that both he and his wife liked the Beatles' music, then mused about her late husband, John Lennon, and said he was a fine man. With the fervently antiwar activist Petra Kelly and General Bastian of the West German Green Party, he discussed disarmament; he held Bastian's hand for a long time while

they were talking, as if to impress him with the fervor of his conviction; the retired general was delighted.

The occasion, as he fully realized, offered an opportunity to enhance his authority, not just in foreign politics but on the domestic
front. His enemies, he knew, were lying in wait, ready to turn on
him the moment he blundered on security moves or some other issue.
But he was becoming increasingly confident in his diplomatic skills.
He had restored surface stability in international affairs and he was
regarded with respect by the West. He demonstrated to the bureaucracy that he was the day-to-day captain of Soviet foreign policy,
beyond his foreign minister and his Central Committee aides and
experts. His mastery of detail and the quality of his reflections on
display before a glittering audience in the Grand Kremlin Palace
proved that the Soviet leader was a forceful figure, commanding the
respect of the outside world and thus deserving respect at home.

Introducing the philosophical themes of New Thinking in an elegant speech befitting the forum, he talked about peaceful competition
between socialism and capitalism; about general moral standards of
humanity; about the future of the world in the shadow of nuclear
weapons; about the "balance of interests" among nations and the
need for civilized relations among them. He was a rationalist who
felt that the arms race was senseless and the sooner it was turned
around the better. He resurrected Khrushchev's grandiose "total and
universal disarmament" proposal, which in Gorbachev's vision became "a demilitarized world" to be achieved "stage by stage, of
course." He wanted, he said, to rid the world of nuclear weapons.
"Humanity must become stronger and overcome the nuclear sickness
and then enter the postnuclear age. It will acquire an immunity to
violence and to attempts to dictate to others. Today international
relations are made soulless by the worship of force and the militar-
ization of consciousness." His country was on the right side of all
these issues; it stood for "humanizing" international relations.[11]

Conscious of Russia's traditional vulnerability on humanitarian
issues, he argued that New Thinking involved a new approach toward
human rights. Alluding to the recent releases of political prisoners
and the renewed exodus of Soviet Jews, he said that his approach
"to the Third Helsinki Basket [on human rights] is there for all to

see." The relaxation was not due to Western pressure, he said, but was the result of "our own new way of thinking."[12] Sakharov's presence at the conference was tangible evidence of his conviction.

Gorbachev also took advantage of the opportunity to stress the positive aspects of the Reykjavík summit. "It was not a failure," he said. "It was a breakthrough. What happened in Reykjavík irreversibly changed the nature and essence of the debate about the future world." (By the time he moved toward an agreement on medium-range missiles in the fall, Reykjavík in his rhetoric became "a turning-point in world history.")[13] He had proposed that the sword of Damocles hanging over humanity be removed in two stages within ten years. The Americans, he continued, "were scared by the new opportunities and are now trying to beat a fast retreat." But there could be no going back. The policy of deterrence—or nuclear equilibrium—was "in fact a policy based on intimidation." Considered in a historical context, he said, it does not reduce the risk of conflict: "it increases that risk." The most adamant supporters of the policy in the United States "are those who are inclined to teach us morality" and who believe that "threat, force and the use of force are the only language that can be used in dealing with others."[14]

Gorbachev's thinking was evolving. He had traversed a long road from his spirited defense of the Kremlin Cold War policy before the Canadian Parliament in 1983 to a more complex and revisionist view of the community of nations. His basic philosophical assumptions became more pronounced. He regarded as "unacceptable" the notion that man is violent by nature and that war is a manifestation of human instinct. His Reykjavík disarmament scheme represented a "new political outlook, a way of conducting international affairs." In the nuclear age, security for one nation can only flow from security for all. He was sure that his New Thinking would eventually prevail. Ideas did not belong to one nation. Once born, they grew.[15] He later put it this way: "The world's nations are interdependent, like mountain climbers on one rope. They can either climb together to the summit or fall together into the abyss."[16]

Similar themes, of course, had long been used by Soviet leaders to play on Western yearnings for peace. It was a way to placate Western apprehensions, to improve the atmosphere. Henry Kissinger spoke of Soviet diplomacy as knowing "no resting places" and constantly advancing one scheme after another ostensibly as a contribution to relaxing tensions. Yet they were constantly pushing. Gorbachev's personality and conviction, his eloquence, transcended the routine politicking of his predecessors. He was expressing humanistic concern and thoughtful leadership. By becoming humanity's spokesman for peace and disarmament, he wanted to inflict a moral defeat on the West and force Reagan to justify his policies. Gorbachev too was pushing. But he was better at it.

Gorbachev seemed certain that he was the right man with the right idea at the right moment, manipulating people and events for the good of humanity. When he talked to foreigners, especially during his first two years in office, he was self-righteous, and his arguments were one-sided. Perhaps the traditional Russian inability to concede a mistake in front of foreigners kept him from admitting that many things did not work in his country, or that his predecessors may have overreached themselves by going into Afghanistan. To do so was not merely to acknowledge human frailty, but to fail in his duty.

In private, Gorbachev had expressed different views. Zdenek Mlynar recalled visiting his college friend in Stavropol in 1967, when Mlynar was a secretary of the Czechoslovak Central Committee. Gorbachev, at that point the administrator of the city of Stavropol, expressed his support for the deposed Khrushchev's de-Stalinization program. He complained about excessive centralization and told Mlynar he considered Brezhnev a transitional political figure. Mlynar had the impression that Gorbachev was almost wistful when he, Mlynar, explained the policies of the Prague Spring, a reform movement that Soviet tanks would crush within a year. Before he became Soviet leader, as we know from Canadian politician Eugene Whelan, Gorbachev agreed privately that the 1979 invasion of Afghanistan was a serious mistake. He did not subscribe to the so-called Brezhnev Doctrine of limited sovereignty, which Moscow invoked to justify military interventions anywhere that "the gains of socialism" were threatened.

But now, as general secretary, Gorbachev felt the burden of the empire he had inherited and the burden of his office; he had to uphold the previous policies. Western intellectuals seized upon his defense of these policies as a reflection of his duplicity. When he talked about "humanizing" international relations and spoke with seeming sadness about the "archaic nature of the Iron Curtain," what exactly did he have in mind? Did he grasp that the logical consequence of the rhetoric was, as Norman Stone put it, "to dismantle the Berlin Wall and remove troops from Eastern Europe"[17]? That was something most people at that point believed he would never do. But though they were prescient words, at the time Gorbachev's Western critics suggested that he was as much a prisoner of his background and political constituency as they were prisoners of theirs. And they weren't wrong. Gorbachev had to keep in mind his domestic audience, steeped in the mentality of the Cold War, and the military and security bureaucracies, whose congenital defensiveness automatically dismissed the very notion of "conceptual breakthroughs."

Nonetheless, Gorbachev's New Thinking did introduce a shift in military doctrine. He began talking about "sufficient security," rather than the official doctrine of "equal security," or the requirement to be as strong as all adversaries combined. "Sufficient security" implied reduced military needs, or at least a reorientation of military programs in favor of modern technology. He sounded so convincing that even within the Soviet establishment people began to wonder whether this was a utopian vision of the world, not just a pragmatic public-relations stunt (as was the case with Khrushchev's total disarmament). One Soviet official quoted a senior armed-forces officer as saying privately, "Your New Thinking is fine for international consumption, but don't infect our troops with it."[18] Georgi Shahnazarov, a senior Central Committee official who subsequently joined Gorbachev's personal staff, implicitly acknowledged the resistance of professionals when he insisted that the professional military would "eventually" accept the new doctrine.[19]

At the end of April, at the plenum of the Soviet Writers' Union, three-star General Dmitri Volkogonov, General Lizichev's deputy in the Political Directorate of the armed forces, publicly voiced misgivings about New Thinking, which, he said, was generating pacifism and working to the detriment of vigilance. In the arcane etiquette of Kremlin debates, he was challenging basic concepts of Gorbachev, and specifically his concessions that smacked of unilateral disarmament.

Volkogonov ostensibly criticized "nuclear pacifists" in West Germany whose position was one of unilateral disarmament. But he might as well have been talking about Gorbachev. "In the absence of a foolproof mechanism for blocking wars," he said, "we have to keep in readiness the mechanism of war."

To illustrate the damage glasnost was creating, the general quoted from a published essay in which the author conducted a fictitious conversation with the commander of a Soviet nuclear submarine.

"Imagine," the author said, "that the Americans had launched a pre-emptive nuclear strike and the Soviet Union was a desert. But your orders are to launch a retaliatory attack on the United States. Would you press the button?"

The commander responds by asking the author, "Would you?"

"No," said the author. Then, according to the author, the commander also began to entertain doubts and had no definite answer.[20]

Volkogonov, arguing indirectly against New Thinking, warned against "one-sided understanding of the nuclear era." Some Soviet editors, he said, had gone so far as to "caution Soviet people against their wholly understandable watchfulness toward forces that have repeatedly demonstrated their aggressiveness." He wanted, he said, to reiterate that, "while struggling for peace, we have to be on alert—such is the cruel logic of the nuclear age."[21] (At Alexander Yakovlev's suggestion Volkogonov, an articulate Stalinist, was subtly co-opted by the Gorbachev people, who selected him to write the first biography of Stalin and gave him complete access to the Stalin-era files.)

Volkogonov's arguments were reiterated in internal debates, where Gorbachev and his men encountered stiff opposition to the new concepts, and resentments over what the military men regarded as unwarranted concessions Gorbachev was prepared to make in his dealings with the Americans.[22] A rhyme circulating in Russia at the time made this point: "There is no meat, there is no sausage, there is no vodka, perhaps there will soon be no rockets either" ("*Myasa nyet, kolbasi nyet, vodki nyet, mozhet bit ne budet i raket* ").

His eye on History, Gorbachev stuck to his New Thinking with the fervor of an evangelist preacher. His speech to the international peace forum in Moscow carried visionary overtones. Gore Vidal called it "the most intelligent political speech ever heard." Andrei Sakharov expressed the belief that his proposals were genuine. "Gorbachev and his supporters, who are waging a difficult struggle against ossified, dogmatic and self-seeking forces, have an interest in disarmament, in making sure that huge material and intellectual resources are not diverted to producing new and more sophisticated weapons," Sakharov said.[23] He also shared Gorbachev's view that New Thinking was an integral part of perestroika. The economic, social, and political reforms are intimately linked with international security issues, he said.

Perhaps the best insight into Gorbachev's motives was contained in an April 1987 speech by his closest adviser, Alexander Yakovlev, to the Academy of Sciences. He described the nature of Soviet-American rivalry as essentially not military but economic; the Americans, he said, were waging "an economic war," seeking "to force the Bolsheviks to arm themselves to economic death."[24] The Soviet Union, in his view, should not try to compete in certain areas with the United States. Because economic indices inevitably displayed Soviet inferiority, Moscow's propaganda should put the stress not on economics but on social and spiritual issues. New Thinking, in this view, represented a necessary shift away from the traditional dogmatism in order to secure perestroika. In Yakovlev's view, Gorbachev had intended to buy himself a slowdown—a breathing spell of five years (he had proposed research only, not testing, on SDI for five years)—during which he could concentrate on domestic affairs. In the course of his campaign, he discovered some side benefits in this posture: his aggressive disarmament push weakened the moral superiority of the West.

Gorbachev stressed his commitment to disarmament in early February 1987, when he met with Henry Kissinger, Cyrus Vance, and other members of a Council on Foreign Relations delegation. Peter Tarnoff, the council's president, quoted Gorbachev as saying that he wanted "to be remembered as a man of vision, not illusion, a man capable of transforming Soviet society."[25] A master of one-upmanship, Gorbachev had adopted Reagan's own arms-control ideas—which his Kremlin predecessors had found unacceptable—and served them back to Reagan.

Gorbachev's activism, his faith in his power of persuasion led him to become his own foreign minister and public-relations man. On the major issue of arms control, he was almost playing the role of desk officer, wanting to know everything that was going on, to stay ahead of problems; his aides said privately that nothing exasperated him more than to be surprised by a crisis.

In less crucial issues he was equally involved. During anniversary celebrations of the Bolshevik revolution in November 1986, Gorbachev stopped the line of ambassadors in Saint George's Hall to talk to the Egyptian envoy, Salah El-Din Bassiouny. "Mr. Ambassador," Gorbachev said, "we've got to solve the issue of military debt."[26] Four months later the two sides reached an agreement. Egypt, which had refused to pay more than $1 billion it owed to Moscow for weapons delivered before the break in Soviet-Egyptian relations, resolved that the whole debt would be converted into the Egyptian currency and turned into a twenty-five-year interest-free loan to be paid in Egyptian goods.

Even when confronted by the unexpected, Gorbachev responded immediately. At a Kremlin meeting in the fall of 1987, the Malaysian prime minister, Dr. Mahathir Mohamad, had raised the Antarctica problem, arguing that the region should be placed under the control of the United Nations rather than the great powers. Gorbachev, obviously not briefed on the matter, thought about it, then agreed that it should be discussed. "I thought he was just saying it," said M. M. Sathiah, the Malaysian envoy to Moscow at the time. "But a few days later we were approached by the Foreign Ministry to begin discussions."

.   .   .

Sathiah's positive assessment was echoed by Margaret Thatcher, who arrived in Moscow at the end of March 1987. Gorbachev's eloquent gesture—to stop jamming the British Broadcasting Corporation's Russian-language transmissions two months earlier, a demonstration of glasnost at work—was a propitious beginning, and the visit was useful for both leaders. When Thatcher first met Gorbachev in London in 1984, their personal chemistry had been very good indeed. They were able, as she later put it, to dispense with diplomatic niceties and "get right down to the nitty-gritty." She was more than a gracious hostess; her remark that Gorbachev was the kind of man she could do business with set the tone of his British trip, and his successful entry onto the world stage had a significant positive impact on his domestic political standing as well.

Thirteen hours together in Moscow allowed them to probe their respective positions more deeply. She had never spent so much time, she said, with any other world leader. They argued, grew excited, and interrupted each other; but she formed an impression of Gorbachev that was quite positive. ("If he told me he was going to do something," she said to British journalists covering the visit, "I would implicitly accept his word.")

Again Gorbachev put forward his argument against the nightmare of nuclear holocaust, saying that he had come to understand that nuclear inferiority (or superiority) at this stage had no significant strategic or political effect—only psychological. Moreover, nuclear arms could not be easily used for political blackmail. He seemed to be rejecting Bush's notion of a "limited nuclear war," and he refused to accept the prospect of an indefinite nuclear-arms race. It would be easy to make no changes in the status quo, he said, but there was nothing one regretted more than missed opportunities, and he was not going to miss this one. The real test of political leadership was here. His predecessors had left the issue in the hands of the military, whose mind-set required allocations for more and more weapons—all procurements based invariably on the worst-case assumptions. The false perception of nuclear balance guided military needs, yet the quest for a favorable shift in this balance was an illusion. He wanted to change the goals to which the next generation of man should dedicate itself. If nuclear weapons are never fired off, they constitute a hopeless economic waste; if they are fired off, they mean the end of civilization. He wanted to break the cycle of madness. He returned to the same theme time and again. As he put it in an interview with Indian journalists in November 1986, "The world today is one in which a struggle is under way between reason and madness, morality and savagery, life and death. We have determined our place in this struggle definitely and irreversibly. We are on the side of reason, morality and life. This is why we are for disarmament, most notably nuclear disarmament, and for creating a system of general security. This is the only possible way that mankind can regain immortality."

Thatcher, while wary of Russia, liked the man at the helm, and she understood that the Soviet Union was no longer fixed forever in its Stalinist mode, that here was a leader prepared to explore all possibilities for reasonable accommodation. As long as he was in charge, the West would do well to dispel the hysteria of the Cold War and get down to the business at hand. Thatcher of course saw the continuity of Russian strategic goals in the world and knew that the nuclear effort was costing Moscow ferociously. She was not deluded by Gorbachev's smooth talk, but she recognized the significance of Gorbachev's New Thinking: he was the first Soviet leader to acknowledge the permanence of the noncommunist world.

Gorbachev needed a politician of high reputation to interpret his New Thinking to a skeptical West. Because of Thatcher's standing in the Western community and her closeness to Reagan, Gorbachev knew that she would relay his views in an incisive and fair way to other Western leaders, and Reagan in particular. He outlined for her his New Thinking on Europe. In 1985, President François Mitterrand of France had first suggested to him, he said, the possibility of a gradual advance toward a broader European policy. The next year, when he visited Moscow, Mitterrand said, "It is necessary that Europe should really become the main protagonist of its own history once again so that it can play in full measure its role [in the quest] for equilibrium and stability in international affairs." In his discussions with Mitterrand, Thatcher, and other European leaders, the idea that "Europe is our common home" emerged as a concept in

Gorbachev's mind. He later said, "I had been looking for such a formula for a long time. It did not come to me all of a sudden but after much thought and, notably, after meetings with many European leaders."[27] In his mind it suggested a greater degree of integration, even though the Continent was divided in two opposing military alliances.

In reviving Charles de Gaulle's concept of Europe "from the Atlantic to the Urals," Gorbachev hinted to Thatcher that his policy in Eastern Europe would be different from that of his predecessors. He dismissed as outdated the Brezhnev Doctrine giving Russians the "right" to intervene militarily in their allies' affairs, and suggested that Moscow wanted to expand the East Europeans' room for maneuver, rather than constrict it. It was a philosophical topic they both found stimulating. They were on the same wavelength—though undoubtedly for somewhat different reasons. Thatcher thought in terms of expanding freedom within the Soviet empire, whereas Gorbachev hoped to woo Western Europe away from the American embrace.

Thatcher did not yield on Britain's nuclear-deterrent force, nor did she mince words when presenting Western views on East-West issues. Debate was sharp when she declared that Britain would not join the Soviet Union and the United States in any nuclear-disarmament process. But Gorbachev countered: "Let us assume that we begin the process of disarmament, remove medium-range missiles from Europe and reduce strategic offensive weapons by fifty percent or by another percentage while you continue building up your forces," he told Thatcher. "Have you ever thought what you will look like in the eyes of world public opinion?"[28]

They had a thunderingly good argument over Stalin's pact with Hitler, with Thatcher suggesting that the Soviet Union joined the battle against the Nazis only in 1941; Gorbachev said he reminded her that the Russians had fought against fascism politically since 1933 and joined the armed struggle in Spain in 1936. As for the Hitler-Stalin pact, he said that it would not have taken place had Britain and France agreed to cooperate with the Soviet Union at that time.[29] They had what Gorbachev called a lively exchange on Nicaragua. "You accuse us of solidarity with Nicaragua, but do you consider it normal to render assistance to apartheid, or racists?" he asked her.

Whatever their disagreements—over the Stalin Pact, Nicaragua, or the arms race—they genuinely liked and admired each other, and clearly offered each other support whenever possible. Thatcher was full of praise for his domestic reforms and, after her visit, told Mortimer B. Zuckerman, *U.S. News & World Report* chairman, that Gorbachev was the first Soviet leader to speak openly and freely about almost any subject. "You can deduce quite a lot from what he is already doing. He has one enormous problem, which is how to translate the kind of vision he has of a more prosperous society into action when he is dealing with a people with no history of economic liberty or of [mass] landownership."

For his part, Gorbachev had gone out of his way to make her visit a big success by giving her full access to the Soviet media, something Russians rarely do. She acted as though she were talking to a British audience, arguing for the British nuclear deterrent and saying that U.S. medium-range missiles had been placed in Europe only after the Russians had deployed nearly three hundred of their SS-20 medium-range missiles, the latter point being aired for the first time on Soviet television. The Russians were captivated by her elegance, intelligence, and quick wit, and gave her the nickname Nasha Masha (Our Maggie).

"This has been the most fascinating and invigorating visit I have ever made abroad as prime minister," she told a news conference upon her return home. And her popularity shot up by twenty-two percentage points almost overnight—superb timing given her imminent, successful re-election campaign.

As Gorbachev clearly hoped, Thatcher did play an important role in shifting Western views on the Soviet Union during a summit meeting of seven Western leaders in Venice that June, two months after her visit. It was at this meeting that the seven leaders spent most of their time discussing Gorbachev and, in part because of Thatcher's impressions, decided that it was time to accept the reality of changes in Moscow. And when the seven leaders met again in Toronto in 1988, she inserted words of praise for Gorbachev in her speech to the Canadian Parliament.

In a spirit of friendly reciprocity, in December 1987 Gorbachev stopped off in London on his way to the Washington summit to have a private talk with Thatcher. Though he'd visited her in 1984, he was not then the leader of his country. Now he was creating history: the first Soviet leader to visit Britain in more than thirty years.

Chapter 12

MILITARY MANEUVERS

A
t the center of Soviet foreign policy was Gorbachev's new pragmatism. Moscow, he declared at the party congress in the Kremlin Palace of Congresses, was no longer in the business of exporting revolution. Gorbachev instead placed emphasis on the development of political, diplomatic, and economic ties with all countries.

His speech on Asian security in Vladivostok in July 1986 foreshadowed a greater diplomatic and economic activism in parts of Asia his predecessors had virtually ignored. He made it clear that Moscow wanted to join the Asian Development Bank and to expand ties with all Pacific nations, but principally with China and Japan. Privately his aides told the Chinese that Moscow would facilitate the end of Vietnam's occupation of Kampuchea. The aim of his policy was to broaden steadily the base of contact and cooperation with China and discourage its military and political cooperation with Japan and the United States. Deng Xiaoping immediately signaled his interest, implicitly acknowledging Gorbachev's new flexibility on two of the three "impediments" to better Sino-Soviet relations by saying, "The main obstacle to the improvement of Sino-Soviet relations is the Vietnamese aggression against Kampuchea." (The other two were the concentration of Soviet forces along the border and the issue of Afghanistan.) Deng said that if Vietnam was to withdraw troops from Kampuchea he would "go any place in the Soviet Union" to meet Gorbachev.[1] But Deng had made it clear that his cooperation with Washington and Tokyo would remain an essential part of his drive for security and modernization.

In Latin America, Gorbachev announced a more active Soviet role, although he did not want to "erode the traditional [political] links" between the United States and South American countries. But the Russians would vigorously seek Latin American trade. "For decades we have looked upon Latin America as your doorstep and behaved there accordingly," he told Reagan. "Nations have had enough of this."[2] Africa, for Gorbachev, was a continent "in ferment"; here too he seemed inclined to avoid any high-cost commitments and to exploit opportunities through political and diplomatic means if and when they presented themselves. Like his mentor, Andropov, Gorbachev made China, the United States, Europe, and Japan his priorities.

Gorbachev also had to deal with the political and military commitments of his predecessors. Brezhnev's had been an old-fashioned game of poaching new holdings in distant parts of the world, most of which turned, over time, into costly liabilities. As they grew in number, they seemed to diminish in usefulness. Most intractable of all was the problem of Afghanistan.

It was a heavy political burden. The maintenance costs of the war had risen to the point that they directly impinged on Gorbachev's desire to deal with long-overdue social, economic, and political problems at home.

Unlike his three immediate predecessors, Gorbachev had no public record of commitment to the Afghan war. The most junior member of the leadership, he was not even consulted on the fateful move.[3] It was not his war. He made that much clear in his February 1986 party-congress speech, when he called Afghanistan a "bleeding wound" and said he wanted to withdraw Soviet troops "in the nearest future" if a political solution could be negotiated. But he was in a Vietnam-type situation, looking for a way to quit the war but to do so without public humiliation. No one, especially not the United

States, seemed willing to help him extricate himself without paying a price. So Afghanistan became yet another incentive for Gorbachev to improve relations with Reagan.[4]

Since Brezhnev ordered the invasion in December 1979, the troops had gradually become bogged down in a guerrilla war that the Russians could not win without major new troop commitments. They were sucked further into the quagmire by the prestige question. Brezhnev, immediately after the 1980 Moscow Olympics, let it be understood that his was an open-ended commitment to the puppet regime in Kabul. "No one should have any doubt about it," he added. Afghanistan's communist government acquired an importance far beyond its own existence.

But the war had been going badly. The Kabul government was shaky. Military casualties were high; more than 15,000 Soviet soldiers had already died and the pain inflicted on the civilians was even greater. Moscow's policy of hiding the nature and extent of the war had been quite successful at home for the first few years. The press rarely reported on the war and, when it did, stressed the burden on Kabul, not on the Soviet people. Moscow, according to official reports, was simply providing technical assistance and trying to push for an international conference that would recognize the Kabul government; the press talked about the Afghan communist government and the people as if they were linked: both were being harassed by "bandits," or *dushmani,* who were stooges of Western imperialists. There was no mention of how the war might be affecting the Soviet Union itself: vintage Brezhnev.

With the political turmoil of transition between 1982 and 1985, most foreign-policy issues were pushed into the background. Nobody was prepared to bite the bullet of retreat, though Andropov did begin to distance himself and Moscow from the Kabul regime. In his June 1983 speech to the Central Committee, he alluded to Kabul's claim of building socialism, adding: "Proclaiming a socialist society and building one are two different matters." Gorbachev, as in many other matters, took Andropov's lead and went much further.

Victory seemed more elusive than ever, while costs were spiraling. The pacification program was constantly disrupted by the guerrillas. From the fall of 1986, the Afghan resistance fighters were shooting down more and more Soviet aircraft with U.S.-supplied Stinger missiles. Even Moscow's client communist elite in Afghanistan was divided, adding more fuel to the arguments against committing the power and reputation of the Soviet Union to a weak enterprise. Looking ahead, Gorbachev saw the war as a vast complication of his foreign relationships, a policy that would force him to act from a weakened position. Supporters of Brezhnev's decision had argued that time was on their side, but Gorbachev thought differently: time was working against him. When he took power in March 1985, he tried to intimidate the Pakistanis into shutting off the supply lines and closing the staging areas for the guerrillas. During their meeting at Gorbachev's inauguration ceremony, he warned Pakistani President Zia ul-Haq personally and sternly about possible consequences. As early as April 1985, only a month after he took power, Gorbachev requested a "hard and impartial analysis" of the Afghan situation, starting, as he said later, "even at that time to seek a way out."

A year later he advanced proposals to the UN mediator, Ecuadorian diplomat Diego Córdovez, including the first Soviet troop-withdrawal timetable—forty-eight months from start to finish. When Babrak Karmal, the Afghan leader, showed reservations about Moscow's shift, he was replaced on May 4 by an intelligent, forceful man, Dr. Najibullah Ahmadzai, who used to head the Afghan secret police. By the fall of 1986, an aide to Gorbachev told a member of a visiting American delegation from Dartmouth College's private U.S.-Soviet discussion group: "We know we have to get out, but we don't know how to get out. Please help us."[5]

While visiting India, where he was questioned repeatedly about Afghanistan, Gorbachev said he wanted to see a "nonaligned, independent, sovereign . . . and neutral Afghanistan. It is up to the Afghan people to decide what kind of system of government they will have." He continued: "We have had excellent relations with it regardless of its system of government. We cooperated with kings and prime ministers, and we are cooperating with today's Afghanistan." He was, he said, committed to a political settlement. "We will take an active position on this and invite every party involved in the problem to participate and cooperate."[6]

A serious effort to seek a political solution came in January 1987,

when Shevardnadze and Dobrynin traveled to Kabul to induce the
Afghan regime to seek political accommodation with the leaders of
the Mujahedin guerrillas. A political settlement, Shevardnadze said
publicly, was "close," and the withdrawal of Soviet troops "is utterly
clear . . . and not far off." This was followed by Kabul's January 12
offer of a cease-fire and talks on national reconciliation. Nothing
came out of it except a sense that the communist side was moving
toward some form of compromise. There were no intimations of
what "neutralization" and "nonalignment" might mean, what sort
of a deal could be struck up with the Mujahedin and their supporters,
only a start of political exploration. But Gorbachev was desperately
trying to find a way to pull out his 110,000 troops without bringing
about the collapse of his clients in Kabul. He was searching for a
relatively painless way out, just as Lyndon Johnson and Richard
Nixon had looked for a way to escape Vietnam. So Soviet diplomats
circulated ideas about forming an interim regime including Afghanistan's former king, Mohammed Zahir Shah, and with noncommu-
nists holding half the Cabinet posts. They also envisaged a UN
peacekeeping force to monitor Soviet withdrawals.

But the war had already claimed hundreds of thousands of lives
and driven five million Afghans into refugee camps in Iran and Pakistan. Was a coalition government a real possibility? Gorbachev
seemed conscious that getting out of a quagmire has to be painful.
There were telltale signs he was also entertaining less desirable op-
tions as sentiments grew in his circles of advisers that the war would
have to be terminated sooner or later. Córdovez was told in March
that Moscow was reducing its withdrawal timetable to twenty-two
months, then to eighteen months. By July 20, 1987, when General
Najib was summoned to Moscow, Gorbachev had made up his mind.
Senior officials later said that Gorbachev told a surprised Najib, "I
hope you are ready in twelve months, because we will be leaving no
matter what." Two days later, in an interview with the Indonesian
newspaper *Merdeka,* Gorbachev stated, "In principle, Soviet troop
withdrawal from Afghanistan has been decided upon."[7]

Coinciding with the economic pressure to withdraw from Afghanistan was the new pressure introduced by glasnost. Evidence of negative popular sentiments toward the war began to appear in the press.

Perhaps the most conspicuous sign of gradual disengagement was an October 1987 article in the mass-circulation weekly *Literaturnaya Gazeta* that discussed a division within the Afghanistan Communist Party, describing the split as being so deep that it "reaches down to the family level." Such public description of an allied party, particularly one engaged in a fierce civil war, could not appear in print without prior approval at the highest levels in the Kremlin. The article begged the question of why Soviet boys were fighting and dying in Afghanistan.

The fact that the war was coming home and turning into a domestic political issue was reflected in a new documentary movie, made in January 1987, entitled *Is It Easy to Be Young?* The film included extraordinarily frank views from Afghan veterans about the war. One young veteran commented on his experience in Afghanistan, "Of course it was our duty to go in, but I couldn't help thinking I was involved in dirty business." In April, the Soviet press reported a rocket attack by Afghan rebels on a textile plant in Soviet Tadzhikistan that killed one civilian and wounded two others. It was the first known attack inside Soviet borders. The attack itself was perhaps less significant than the Soviet decision to publicize it. At the very least, this was a concession that the war could no longer be treated as though it did not exist.

Among the numerous independent organizations that emerged in late 1986 were clubs organized by the veterans of the Afghan war, young men who shared a lingo of their own that was becoming less and less a secret at home. The words themselves—"kefir" (yogurt) means "tank fuel"; "berries" is "ammunition"; "zinc" stands for the coffins the dead are sent home in—were enough to preserve the truth of the experience. Soviet reporter Artyom Borovik, among others, began writing pieces about the psychological problems and difficulties faced by returning veterans, the same post-traumatic stress disorders American psychologists had diagnosed in returning Vietnam veterans. Borovik concluded that the root of the returnees' problems lay in the contrast between the world of mutual trust that unites soldiers in combat and the world of falseness and corruption that greeted them back home. "In Afghanistan, soldiers never lie to one another, because they know their lives depend on being able to rely on one another in critical situations. When they come back, they see nothing but red tape and materialism—everyone is out only for himself."

Particularly painful for the veterans and families of soldiers killed or maimed in Afghanistan was the callous way they were being treated by the bureaucracy, and the decision made by the Defense Ministry that the markers on the graves of those killed in action give no indication of where they had died.[8] Cemeteries throughout the country are scattered with graves of men who died young, but there is no mention of Afghanistan on the tombstone, only the cryptic statement that they were "fulfilling their internationalist duty."

In November 1987, protesting the policy, two thousand Afghan veterans held a meeting in the Central Asian city of Ashkhabad, close to the Afghan border, and decided to erect a national monument to dead comrades without government help. Their leaders organized a news conference in Moscow on November 21 to announce that they would collect donations and that their action reflected unhappiness with the lack of recognition for their service.

Despite glasnost, no official figures had been released on the number of dead in Afghanistan. But by 1987, the growing popular resentment of the war was reflected in articles in the press questioning the purpose of the war and the unfair policy that assigned the sons of workers and peasants to Afghan duty. "Only rarely did I come across children and grandchildren of writers, cultural figures, high and leading officials," wrote one reporter, Kim Selikhov.[9] It was the beginning of a long process of disengagement.

In April 1987, Gorbachev went to Prague to deliver his New Thinking on relations between socialist countries. Prague was not an accidental choice of venue. Czechoslovakia was ruled by Gustav Husak and a geriatric group of hard-line communists who were brought to power in 1968, after Soviet troops crushed the Prague Spring reformist regime of Husak's predecessor, Alexander Dubček. Some eighty-five thousand Soviet troops remained in Czechoslovakia.

Although the Prague government was reserved toward Gorbachev, the Czech people were enthusiastic about glasnost and perestroika and gave him a genuinely enthusiastic welcome. It was a remarkable turnaround for people who had scrawled "Ivan, go home" on the walls of their city after the crushing of the Prague Spring. They liked him even though he defended the 1968 invasion. He talked to street crowds and responded to their questions. Gorbachev didn't repudiate Brezhnev's decision, and nobody really expected him to, but the way he defended it was disarming. He did not obscure the fact that the invasion caused him grief. He said he had thought "long and hard about it" and reached the conclusion that it was the right action. He seemed open and aboveboard; the Czechs wished their leaders were more like him.

Long after he left, they were still telling jokes and anecdotes about him. A black joke has Husak convening a Warsaw Pact meeting to discuss Gorbachev's reforms. He and other Warsaw Pact leaders, all of whom have been in power for years, decide that the only solution is to send the tanks into Russia to suppress the heresy—or, in communist jargon, "to lend fraternal assistance." Yet another joke ran, "What is the difference between Dubček and Gorbachev? Nothing, but Gorbachev doesn't know it yet." Gorbachev's spokesman in Prague, Gennady Gerasimov, joined in. Asked during a press conference in Prague to point out the difference between the program of the ousted reformer Dubček and Gorbachev's New Thinking, Gerasimov quipped, without batting an eye, "Nineteen years."

Husak's reaction to Gorbachev's reforms was conspicuously cool. His ideological chief, Vasil Bilak, publicly berated Czechs who were "raving about the so-called new policy—they call for the rescinding of the lessons we learned from 1968. But that is something they will not see." Husak and Bilak were brought to power to stamp out what everyone recognized was a similar reformist program advocated by Dubček. Gorbachev's reform and modernization threatened to pull the rug from under Husak's feet. He couldn't stop Gorbachev, but he could censor some of the new ideas, at least for a while. With noticeable regularity, the Czechoslovak communist press failed to carry full texts of Gorbachev's speeches advocating economic and political reforms.

．　　．　　．

East Germany was equally unenthusiastic about glasnost and perestroika. Its leader, Erich Honecker, stressed his own economic and
political path, never mentioning Gorbachev's initiatives. An East
German Politburo member openly questioned the idea of following
Gorbachev's perestroika. "If your neighbor puts up new wallpaper
in his apartment," he said, "would you feel obliged to rewallpaper
your apartment as well?" Gorbachev's term "New Thinking" was
dropped from East German press accounts detailing his policies.
Romanian President Nicolae Ceauşescu was openly hostile, while
Bulgaria's Todor Zhivkov, in power since 1954, insisted that he had
implemented his own glasnost and perestroika even before Gorbachev came to power.

Only in Poland and Hungary were Gorbachev's reforms met with
official applause. Hungary's János Kádár was the first Soviet-bloc
leader to embark on the path of economic and cultural liberalization.
Poland's General Wojciech Jaruzelski, under pressure from a then
shrinking but still-active Solidarity opposition, had appropriated
many of the economic reforms championed by the banned trade
union as his own, and was backing at least the appearance of growing
democracy.

Gorbachev's populist style itself—his openness—made his conservative hosts uncomfortable. He talked with the Czechs the way
Husak never talked to them. In Romania, looking at rows of silent,
sullen faces, he asked why nobody spoke up, only to provoke nervous
laughter from the crowd. "If you were to tell me that everything was
fine in the country and in every family, I wouldn't believe it. There
are problems," he said. Later he told workers at a Bucharest loco-
motive factory about the official talks. "I criticized the Romanian
side, and Comrade Ceauşescu [criticized] the Soviet side." In his
speech in Bucharest, he also made known his distaste for Ceauşescu's
megalomaniac style and his corrupt leadership. Alluding to the scores
of top positions held by Ceauşescu's relatives, he said that the Soviet
party was purging "those who did not justify themselves in work,
who besmirched themselves with dishonor, lack of principles, and
nepotism." The Romanian press censored his more pointed remarks.

Evidently aware of these reactions, Gorbachev was merely nudging his allies in his direction, not pushing them too hard yet. He sought to inspire them with Moscow's example by telling them about his program and his expectations. But most of his speeches dealt with broader foreign-policy issues. In his Prague speech, Gorbachev talked about Europe "from the Atlantic to the Urals" and the role of the Soviet bloc. In most of his subsequent foreign-policy speeches he elaborated on this aspect of New Thinking. The bloc itself was being "readapted" to the post-Brezhnev world.

It was an accident of history, Gorbachev said prophetically in Prague, that Stalin's Russia had imposed its form of socialism on Eastern Europe. That was because the Soviet Union was "the only country with experience in socialist development." But not any longer. Other socialist countries had gained their own experiences, and Moscow no longer had a "monopoly on truth."[10] Each bloc nation "has its own traditions, peculiarities, and ways in which its political institutions function." The framework of their relations must be "strictly based on absolute independence." Each national government must decide on the scope and pace of its "readaptation." Economic coordination and cooperation in some areas should be strengthened, but without "administrative regimentation. We want fewer committees and commissions and . . . [more] economic incentives, initiative, the socialist spirit of enterprise, and direct links between firms."[11]

He returned again to the idea of a "common European home." He foresaw a degree of integration despite political divisions—in the fields of security, environmental protection, transport, and science and technology. Eastern Europe stood to benefit from an accelerated economic cooperation. "This is not simply a beautiful fantasy but a result of a careful analysis of the situation in Europe."[12]

In effect, Gorbachev wanted to restart and deepen détente in Europe, which had reached its apogee at the 1975 Helsinki conference. At the conference, the United States, Canada, and thirty-three European countries adopted a wide-ranging declaration on improving human rights, communication, and measures to reduce the threat of war on the Continent. But the process of détente subsequently foundered on the hostilities generated by a new Cold War. He viewed his New Thinking as turning into "an actual force" once the disarmament process got under way. Since NATO had raised the question of shorter-range nuclear weapons in Europe as an impediment to an agreement on medium-range missiles, Gorbachev offered in Prague to start talks on cuts in the shorter-range weapons. The Russians had deployed these weapons in Czechoslovakia and East Germany in 1983 as a countermeasure to Pershing deployments; now he said that they would be removed once an agreement with the United States was signed. He wanted to reduce the level of military confrontation in Europe, he said, and was prepared to negotiate reductions and subsequent elimination of tactical nuclear arms and "drastic reductions" of troops and conventional weapons."[13]

Although the foreign-policy and security aspects of his New Thinking went down well in most East European capitals, Gorbachev's domestic policy left his six allies uncertain. This lukewarm reaction was partly due to political succession problems looming in all the East European capitals except Warsaw: in Romania, because of Ceauşescu's ill health; in Hungary, East Germany, Bulgaria, and Czechoslovakia, because their leaders were well into their seventies. Each of these countries was experiencing severe economic problems, and each was subjected to internal pressures. Aware that he could not afford to rapidly force his reforms down the throats of largely conservative East European leaders, Gorbachev had nevertheless drawn up the framework for dramatic modernization of the Warsaw Pact and Comecon, the Soviet-bloc common market. It was an odd situation. For the first time since the war, Moscow was in the forefront of the liberalization drive, while the East Europeans were dragging their feet. But they were all too conscious of the fact that the two previous Soviet armed interventions took place during periods of political redefinition in the aftermath of Kremlin transitions—Hungary in 1956, or three years after Stalin's death, and Czechoslovakia in 1968, or four years after Khrushchev's ouster.

The Prague visit was a success. Television coverage revealed to discriminating Soviet audiences that their leader was received with enthusiasm in a country in which Russians, after the 1968 invasion, had come to be quietly disliked and despised. One senior official and

Gorbachev-supporter remarked acidly after the Prague visit, "Isn't it a shame that Gorbachev is understood better abroad than at home."[14]

Perhaps most skeptical were his own generals, who found his strategic concept hard to take. They had expended a great deal of effort and money acquiring their nuclear punch, and the idea of banning all rockets from Europe was not fully comprehensible to them. Gorbachev was a newcomer to security policy, and although he boldly talked the anti-imperialist game—and indeed he saw as inevitable Moscow's continued rivalry and competition with the West—he did not seem to have anti-imperialism embedded in him as a lifetime mission. The generals, like in fact much of the military establishment, had been nurtured on visceral anti-imperialism; they were prepared to die fighting the imperialists. Theoretical concepts based on rationality—the idea that a more imaginative foreign policy and a sound economy were as vital as weapons to the country's defense—made little impression on the brass. Politically, therefore, the marshals were natural conservatives who were much more at ease with the traditional bureaucracy. The one conspicuous exception, an eloquent voice for modernization, was Marshal Nikolai Ogarkov, the chief of staff, who had enthusiastically supported Andropov's program and was subsequently dismissed by Chernenko. Ogarkov believed that Moscow had more than enough nuclear weapons and that it could afford to cut their numbers and concentrate resources on sophisticated conventional arms. Above all, he felt that the country's economy had to move quickly into the high-tech age. In retrospect, his removal by Chernenko seemed to have been engineered by his traditionalist rivals in the Defense Ministry, who not only regarded Ogarkov as too intellectual but saw him as a forceful figure who wanted to reshape the defense establishment.

Volkogonov, the deputy chief of the political directorate of the armed forces, reflected the intransigence of the military, its deprecation of the New Thinking, when he wrote in May 1987 in the intellectual newspaper *Literaturnaya Gazeta*: "The conceptions of New Thinking do not contradict the Leninist doctrine of defense of the socialist fatherland. But recently publications have appeared in our press that, according to our opinion, distort interpretations of the phenomenon of war, the military-political situation, and the social role of the Soviet armed forces." He continued: "Unfortunately, certain authors are concentrating their efforts merely on condemnations of war in general, on vivid descriptions of its apocalyptic consequences, without clearly pointing at the address where the threat comes from. . . . There are arguments that, in order to eliminate mutual threats between the two opposing systems, we should begin with ourselves. . . . But our class adversaries today are not prepared to live with the other world. . . . Therefore, just as it is impossible to applaud with one hand, it is impossible to create a nonnuclear world with unilateral efforts."[15]

Only after a West German teenager named Mathias Rust humiliated the Soviet military by flying across European Russia undetected and landing in Red Square (an incident that provoked a purge of the high command known as the "Rust massacre") did it become blatantly obvious to what extent the military was an empire unto itself. After the "Rust massacre," Soviet journals and newspapers began to attack the military's secretiveness, condemning the fact that Soviet diplomats and civilian arms-control experts were forced to rely on figures published in the West. They pointed out the irony that these data, well known in the West, are kept from the Soviet people. (Ogarkov himself had provided perhaps the best illustration of this irony when, as a military representative during the early 1970s SALT I negotiations, he took an American delegate aside and reproached him for discussing Soviet weapons in front of the civilian members of the Soviet delegation. Civilians, he said, were not supposed to know details about the weaponry.)

As usual, the phenomenon of military secrecy was illustrated by a popular joke. Several Soviet citizens are answering questions on the popular television quiz program "Who, When, Where." The question: "Where are Soviet medium-range nuclear missiles sited?" The group is given a minute to come up with the answer. They confer, but at the end of the minute reply, "We don't know." The quizmaster smiles approvingly, saying, "Correct answer."

Gorbachev himself promised to do "more work" on military data, including expenditures. "I think that, given proper effort," he said, "within the next two or three years we will already be able to compare the figures that are of interest to us and our partners." Another commentator said that Moscow was preparing to publish the real defense-expenditure figures. For decades, these figures, published annually, bore little relation to reality. For instance, between 1970 and 1982, the Soviet military budget officially stood at 17 billion rubles annually ($22 billion) despite the huge military buildup, the Afghan war and other military aid outlays. But in 1989 the Russians admitted the real figure was four times that amount.

In the meantime the practice of educating the Americans would continue. By the end of the summer, the Russians allowed American officials to inspect their radar complex, under construction at Krasnoyarsk, in Siberia. The new defense minister, Dmitri Yazov, had issued a direct order permitting the inspection only a few hours before the Americans departed for Krasnoyarsk. The senior officers received the Americans politely and showed them around. But a deputy Soviet minister of the radio-electronics industry, Oleg Losev, a civilian who accompanied the U.S. delegation, told friends later that the senior military men were rattled. Only one among them had ever seen an American before—"and that was forty-two years ago, on the river Elbe," where Soviet and American troops met at the end of World War Two.[16] Moreover, the newly emerging Soviet demands for on-site inspection began to make security officials in the United States nervous about the prospect of Russians' being permitted to snoop around secret U.S. installations.

The Mathias Rust incident led to one of the greatest post–World War Two purges of the Soviet high command.

On May 28, 1987, as the country was celebrating the annual Border Guards' Day and thousands of uniformed KGB border guards visiting Moscow flocked into parks and squares to enjoy balmy spring weather, a nineteen-year-old West German youth, Mathias Rust, piloted a rented single-engine Cessna Skyhawk from Finland across the European part of Russia and landed in early evening at one end of Red Square. While looking for a place to land, Rust had circled over the nearby Kremlin, three times buzzing the green-domed Old Senate building, where Gorbachev's office was located. Tourists photographed the plane as it descended to rooftop level; one British doctor was able to videotape the whole event as the plane approached Red Square over the Historical Museum, circled the Kremlin, and finally landed on a bridge over the Moscow River behind Saint Basil's Church. Some Russian girls and other bystanders flocked to the plane, and the youth, who was wearing a red aviator suit, signed several autographs before the security men rushed to the scene and marched him away. The reason for the delay was that the incredulous security people had first tried to check with their superiors whether the landing was perhaps a scene from a movie about which the authorities had mistakenly omitted to warn them in advance.

At the time, Gorbachev, Prime Minister Nikolai Ryzhkov, President Andrei Gromyko, Defense Minister Marshal Sergei Sokolov, and Warsaw Pact Commander Marshal Viktor Kulikov were in East Berlin attending the Warsaw Pact summit. The purpose of the summit was to explain to the Soviet allies Gorbachev's concept of "reasonable sufficiency" and the approach he was taking toward arms control in talks with the Americans. Sokolov and Kulikov were skeptical about the concept, and this skepticism encouraged the orthodox communists in Eastern Europe to start sniping at Gorbachev later in the year.[17]

The news of Rust's feat spread like wildfire through Moscow. The Moscow correspondent of a leading Western newspaper was told about it the same evening by Soviet contacts but refused to believe it: the idea of a foreign pilot's flying his plane for over four hundred miles through the Soviet Union's air defenses and landing in Red Square seemed too preposterous. Moreover, the city itself is ringed by an antiballistic missile system that is routinely described as formidable.

It was one of those "unexpected events" that Gorbachev once said play a determining role in public affairs so often. The military's inefficiency and incompetence were so overwhelmingly obvious that even their conservative allies were unwilling or unable to protect them. Gorbachev was enough of a politician to seize the chance offered by Rust. Unexpectedly, the way was cleared for him to clean house and place his own people in the senior levels of the Defense Ministry.

He acted swiftly, returning to Moscow and summoning an emergency Politburo meeting forty-eight hours after Rust's landing, at which Defense Minister Sokolov, Chief Marshal of Aviation Alexander Koldunov (who also served as deputy defense minister and commander of Soviet air-defense forces), and dozens of other senior Old Guard officers were summarily fired for "a major dereliction of duty."[18] Both Sokolov and Koldunov were Brezhnev protégés, and both were promoted by Chernenko in 1984. Sokolov, a man of compelling mediocrity but a frontline tank commander in the war against Nazi Germany, was spared total public humiliation; according to the official announcement, he had been relieved of his duties in connection with his retirement. (It was the first time that a Soviet defense minister had been fired for incompetence. Khrushchev fired Marshal Georgi Zhukov as defense minister for political reasons.)

The new defense minister was a little-known general, Dmitri Yazov, sixty-three, whom Gorbachev earlier that year had plucked from the Soviet Far East and appointed deputy defense minister in charge of personnel.

The vigor of Gorbachev's reaction stunned the military. With one blow he had cut the military chiefs down to size, both symbolically and politically. The Politburo statement punctured their pride by charging that they "had shown intolerable unconcern and indecision" in the affair, which testified to "serious shortcomings" in the antiaircraft defenses in general.[19] The Old Guard marshals were also humiliated by the appointment of a relatively junior general as new defense minister. It was a violation of the pecking order they were not likely to forget or forgive. Even before the "Rust massacre," they had been unhappy; Sokolov had been kept as a nonvoting member of the Politburo—a reduction of the military's political authority—while the heads of the other two key institutions, Shevardnadze of the Foreign Ministry and Chebrikov of the KGB, were full members.

Gorbachev supporters in the establishment were delighted. Rust, one senior official joked privately, should be awarded the Order of Lenin, the nation's highest decoration.[20] True, the incident raised some touchy security questions. How could Rust penetrate massive Soviet air defenses? Was he genuine when he said that the motive for his mission was to talk to Gorbachev about arms control and help bring peace to the world? What should be done about the culprit, who was only a boy and hardly a spy? (Almost two years later, after Rust was convicted and subsequently released, the January 1, 1989, issue of *Izvestia* called him the "madcap inspector of our antiaircraft defenses.")

The domestic political impact of the cleanup that followed—more than one hundred senior officers eased out of their jobs—appeared to give Gorbachev control over one of the pillars of the system. He had seized the opportunity and shown himself to be a strong and purposeful leader. It was the kind of vigor that the country and party understood and appreciated. And his standing went up on the eve of a crucial plenum in which his economic reform program—which had been drafted, redrafted, amended, and fine-tuned over the previous two years—was finally to be placed before the Central Committee. He was going into the meeting from a position of strength.

Chapter 13

PERESTROIKA BLUEPRINT

In June 1987, Gorbachev's long-debated economic reform program was approved by the Central Committee and passed into law by the Supreme Soviet.

It was a moment of personal triumph.

For more than two years, he had been pushing perestroika and trying to convince the party and country that some serious changes were required to fix an ailing economy because the economy was the chief determinant of the country's strength. Now, finally, a coherent plan of action was in place.

The Law on Socialist Enterprise was the centerpiece of perestroika, overshadowing in its importance all other legislation. It stopped short of a full market reform. But it recognized profit as the mechanism for securing higher efficiency and the production of things people want to buy. Other legislation, Gorbachev said, was being readied—on price reforms, bank reform, industrial reorganization, and central planning. After more than two years of groping, the new legislation not only gave perestroika clear overall direction but specified procedures for the application of the new economic mechanisms. Its essence was *khozrashchot,* the Russian word combining the notions of self-financing and self-management. Gorbachev gave party bureaucrats, industrial managers, and economists six months to go through the thicket of new regulations before they were to go into effect on January 1, 1988.

Politically, his position was strengthened as three of his key aides— Alexander Yakovlev, Nikolai Slyunkov, and Viktor Nikonov—became full Politburo members. Yet all that power at the top would have to be translated into power at the district and local level for the reforms to succeed. "The way the party acts will determine how the restructuring drive proceeds," he said.[1] But he was confident. He set the date for the party conference for June 1988 and made clear what he expected it to do. In the past, he said, this parliamentary ploy was used to make changes "in the party rules and in the composition of central party organs."

The urgency of Gorbachev's demands made it sound as if he expected a dramatic change at the June 1988 conference, but in private consultations, his aides anticipated the extension of political struggle and residual bureaucratic resistance into the 1990s.[2] Abel Aganbegyan, Gorbachev's key economic adviser, said privately that he expected perestroika to take longer than anyone anticipated. The strategic goal of perestroika, he said, was to transform the existing command economy into "a democratic economy." Privately he was hoping that "in ten years we should pass the halfway mark toward this goal."[3] The country's economy had been run by voodoo economists for so long that it would require Herculean efforts to move it in any direction, let alone toward market socialism. "We are going into the unknown, and people are trying to stop us," Aganbegyan said. "It is as if life is forcing you to live in the water and you don't know how to swim. You have to learn different movements, and imagine how it is if someone is pulling you and trying to drag you under because he doesn't want you to swim!"[4]

Each step on the way was a struggle. During the preceding two years, Gorbachev had introduced and pushed through several economic reforms of significance. One reform dealt with foreign trade, expanding the rights of Soviet producers to deal directly with foreign suppliers and buyers and eliminating the necessity of clearing transactions through the Ministry of Foreign Trade in Moscow; under this reform, Soviet firms were allowed to keep money in foreign currency rather than Soviet rubles, which had little real value. Another new law legitimized private activity by individuals and family members in twenty-nine fields, ranging from car repairs and language tutoring to housepainting and dental practice. But with the exception of housewives, pensioners, and invalids, the newly legal entrepreneurs had to work regular hours in the state economy; they could not devote full time to entrepreneurial efforts. In early 1987, differing pay scales were introduced, relating remuneration more directly to individual productivity. Even these relatively peripheral measures received a lukewarm popular welcome and caused considerable anxieties and difficulties within the bureaucracy. The British weekly *The Economist* succinctly summed up the resistance: "In some communist countries, give people an inch of reform and they will grab a yard. Mr. Gorbachev is having to force the first inch into Russia's fist."

Given the reluctant response to minor reforms, Aganbegyan was concerned about society's reaction to the Law on Socialist Enterprise, particularly because Gorbachev had established such a brief interim—six months—before it was due to go into effect (on January 1, 1988). The people were economically illiterate; they were "a product of conditions." They had been deceived often in the past, so they didn't know what to believe. They wanted things to change instantly; and in an economy of shortages, even significant improvements remained unnoticeable. During Gorbachev's first two years in office, the supplies of meat and milk had increased by roughly 6 percent annually, yet no one had noticed the improvement.[5]

The Law on Socialist Enterprise was a deep surgery affecting the entire economy and virtually the entire society. Theoretically at least, it decentralized the economy, and dispersed the power of the State Planning Commission, which had functioned like an economic tsar whose decisions could not be appealed. Instead of taking orders from Moscow, companies were allowed to buy supplies directly from one another and to sell more of their output on the market instead of handing it over to the state. The state itself became a customer, albeit the one with first preference. All managers would have to submit themselves to their employees for election every five years.

These provisions were to be adopted gradually until their full implementation by 1990. The grace period of two years was designed for "psychological adaptation," also providing managers and workers the time to switch over to new work methods. Companies that could not pay their way—and there are hundreds that have never made a profit—would face reorganization or closure. Moscow's old practice of bailing out inefficient firms by taking the money from the profitable companies was supposed to end by 1990, at least in theory. By 1991, the country's industry and agriculture were supposed to be entirely out of the clutches of central planners, whose job was to be mapping long-range strategy.

It was both practically and politically impossible, Gorbachev aides said, to achieve a full market without price reform. Unless prices were set by real costs and real demand, managers were denied the instruments to enforce sensible economic decisions. Gorbachev's advisers contended that the population would have to be prepared for retail-price changes and a reform of wholesale prices. The irrationality of the price system was best reflected in the fact that all of heavy industry had operated at a loss for six years before wholesale prices were raised in 1981.[6]

"Here we have a market mechanism set up," said economist Lev Logvinov. But, he added, it had to be broken in gently. A precipitate action would only lead to unemployment, high prices, and consequently unrest.[7] Aganbegyan also said that several top economists favored "some unemployment" but that he did not share that view. Although moving toward a market, Russia had to retain at least two aspects of its current welfare state—low rents and full employment.[8]

"We have forty-eight thousand enterprises in the Soviet Union, and it would be very useful to close several thousands of them," Aganbegyan said. "I can name several mining enterprises where the conditions of work are intolerable and which have no economic justification at all. I don't understand this kind of situation, because it makes no sense to keep them going. It would be easier to bulldoze them away and build something new. We could all live better. Instead, we use our extra funds to run bad enterprises. I fear we will see only some symbolic closures to encourage the others."[9]

There were economists who advocated more radical reforms. Aganbegyan's friend and colleague Tatyana Zaslavskaya and the less flamboyant Oleg Bogomolov argued for doing away with central planning altogether. Leonid Abalkin, another leading economist who was to become deputy prime minister in 1989, suggested limiting planning to some 250–300 high-priority commodity groups and leaving the enterprises to work out the rest of their production on their own. The most radical was Nikolai Shmelyov, who had once served as adviser to his father-in-law, Nikita Khrushchev, in the 1960s; he called for a full market. "Market stimuli must extend to all stages of the research, development, investment, production, marketing, and service process," he wrote. "Only the marketplace, not mere administrative innovations," could reinvigorate the Soviet economy.[10] But Shmelyov felt the Law on Socialist Enterprise was a major piece of legislation moving the country in the proper direction. "There's no going back now; things have gone too far," he said, evidently recalling the collapse of Khrushchev's reform drive. He also pointed out that Gorbachev had surrounded himself with far more capable advisers than had his father-in-law.[11]

The June 1987 article by Khrushchev's son-in-law in *Novy Mir* caused an uproar. The conservatives were infuriated by his advocacy of the marketplace, his explicit suggestion that Gorbachev was not going far enough, that the leader himself eschewed bold moves. Ligachev's men in the Central Committee raised the issue during a formal meeting, proposing that the publication of such heretical articles be prohibited. Gorbachev rejected the idea. "We have done that in the past, but we are not going to do it any more," he replied. "Why don't you write an article and present your point of view? Wouldn't that be more constructive?"[12]

Shmelyov's article and Gorbachev's reaction kicked off a glasnost free-for-all that summer. Economists, writers, and intellectuals aired heated arguments in the pages of Soviet journals and newspapers. The reformist side held the edge. Reformers were armed with more cogent intellectual arguments, and, in retrospect, it was clear that they also tried to manipulate the public debate, to turn the popular mood against the Stalinist economists.

The underlying struggle, of course, was for control of the nation's wealth. The hard-line party bureaucrats who practically "owned" the state-run economy had no intentions of surrendering without a fight. For a regional party boss, district party secretary, or city party chief, glasnost was one thing, wealth another. They had become used to controlling this wealth, the output of mines, factories, and forest lands, and they were deeply dug in, more deeply than Gorbachev had expected them to be.

The debate about economics soon became a debate about Stalin. It was all so typically Russian, a switch from the rationalism of Gorbachev's economic agenda to the emotionalism of the old debates, in which reason and facts did not seem to matter. Gorbachev's view was that decency and truth demanded an owning up to some of the dark pages of Soviet history; without coming to terms with the Stalinist past, the country could not build its future. And the dredging up of Stalin's ghost was politically useful to him. The exposure of Stalin's crimes and failures provided an all-purpose weapon against the Stalinist system he was trying to dismantle, against the conservatives who resisted his blandishments, and for the continued open debate about every aspect of Soviet life and history: glasnost.

Glasnost stimulated a feeling of buoyant optimism in the *intelligentsia,* creating a sense of vast possibilities. Perestroika was obviously not working yet, and food was in short supply, but the atmosphere was dizzy. There was a sense of freedom in the air, yet uncertainty about how long that freedom would last. The respected novelist Grigori Baklanov summed up the feeling among the liberals when he asserted, "In my entire life I have never lived in such a time as we are living through now, as far as literature is concerned."[13] *Requiem,* by Anna Akhmatova, the most powerful poetic statement on Stalin's terror, was at last published nearly fifty years after it was written. Anatoly Rybakov's *Children of the Arbat,* in which Stalin is a literary character, and which dwells on the roots of his tyranny, was a literary sensation. (Rybakov had completed the book in 1966 and submitted it to Alexander Tvardovsky, the most celebrated of all editors of *Novy Mir*. Tvardovsky liked it very much and announced its publication. "Each writer is seeking material for that main work," Rybakov quoted Tvardovsky as saying. "You have found a rich gold vein, Tvardovsky said, it is the gold vein of your life." But when the novel was due for publication, it was banned by censors.)

Leon Trotsky, Nikolai Bukharin, and other great Bolsheviks murdered by Stalin and relegated to the status of nonpersonhood for decades now strode on the stage of the Vakhtangov Theater as characters in Mikhail Shatrov's play *Dictatorship of Conscience*. The painter Anatoly Zverev and the sculptor Vadim Sidur, who had both died unrecognized the previous year, were suddenly acclaimed in the press as important figures whose genius was unjustly ignored. At the Institute of Marxism-Leninism, the new director, Georgi Smirnov, was preparing a complete edition of the works of Marx, Engels, and Lenin. Despite seven decades of adulation of the three spiritual leaders of Soviet communism, their complete works had never been published in the country. The institute was also preparing a new history. "We should assess historical facts on the basis of objective evidence and analysis," Smirnov said. Trotsky, for example? "He was full of himself and he argued with Lenin, but he was a talented organizer, president of the Military-Revolutionary Council during the revolution, and the founder of the Red Army. You can't ignore these facts."[14]

But was glasnost here to stay? Official optimism notwithstanding, many intellectuals feared the prospect of retrenchment. Another of Khrushchev's sons-in-law, Alexei Adzhubei, who was once editor-in-chief of *Izvestia*, suddenly appeared in print with a cautionary article. It was based on a conversation with the now forgotten novelist Vladimir Dudintsev, whose book *Not by Bread Alone* foreshadowed Khrushchev's cultural thaw. It was as if Adzhubei wanted to remind his audiences that such a retrenchment had occurred within their lifetime, and that the current intellectual ferment again was based on the dubious proposition of Dudintsev's hero, a lonely inventor, who believes that "once man has started to think he cannot be denied his freedom."[15]

• • •

Those were heady days in the early summer of 1987. It must have occurred to Gorbachev that he had already become a historic figure, that in a little over two years he had managed to put together a program of modernization that, now and in the future, would inevitably become the basis of Soviet policy, the standard by which other Kremlin leaders would be measured. It was impossible to see what truly animated the man whose surface we got to know so well; there are few things harder than getting to know the private life of a top public figure in Russia. As if aware that the world was ready to know more about him and his goals, he agreed that summer to write a book about perestroika for an American publisher. (The book, *Perestroika,* was published by Harper & Row in November 1987.)

Going public in this way was an extraordinary thing for a Soviet leader to do. It revealed the risk-taking side of Gorbachev's character as well as his supreme self-confidence. He did not ask for professional help in putting the manuscript together. He did it himself. "If anyone tells you he is writing things for Gorbachev, he is a liar," one of his key aides said emphatically.[16] *Perestroika* became a best-seller perhaps precisely because it is authentic Gorbachev in tone and substance, and not the slick production of a stable of writers. And he was proud of it. "I've sold five million copies as of last month," he boasted to the visiting Egyptian foreign minister six months after its publication.[17]

No sitting Soviet leader had ever done anything like it. After his humiliating ouster from power, Nikita Khrushchev sought historical vindication by publishing his reminiscences in the West. He secretly dictated them into a tape recorder, and his relatives and remaining friends in the establishment helped smuggle the tapes to the United States, where they were assembled and pieced together into the volume *Khrushchev Remembers.* Once the book appeared in the West, he was denounced at home.

Khrushchev's fate, as we know from his repeated references in private and public conversations, weighed heavily on Gorbachev's mind. Was Gorbachev publishing his argument now to secure his place in history? Or seeking to convince the West of the benign nature of his program? Or, by laying it out before the entire world, did he hope to strengthen his position in Russia? Being a total politician, he probably was seeking to achieve all these goals. He had wrought real changes, set into motion real economic forces that he felt would prevent Russia from drifting into a decline. He believed he had set conditions "for a kind of Renaissance" of Soviet society— for the release of regenerative potentials capable of injecting a new vitality into the system.

Initially it was Gorbachev's sense of certainty, the preachiness of his speeches—and his physical vigor—that attracted many people to him. He was a politician determined to move a nation. He painted a picture of a world being infected by an awesome new weapon that threatened everyone; he described the sloth and economic inefficiency at home, which people knew was true and accurate. He was genuinely passionate about perestroika and wanted things to be better. They did too. The problem was that changes demanded exertion and sacrifices, and it was hard to rev up enthusiasm for them. Gorbachev had not filled the shops with consumer goods; despite all the rhetoric, people felt no real changes in their lives. Workers were becoming disgruntled by the new law connecting their pay to productivity—their wages were frequently being reduced. The first strikes were reported in the Soviet press that summer.

Since Russia's political culture is so different from anything Westerners are familiar with—Gorbachev was, ultimately, an autocrat representing a large ruling oligarchy—it was not so apparent to outsiders just how revolutionary his approach was. He was asking the Soviet people to change their ways, and he sought to persuade them that it was for their own good. The question was whether society was ready for it. The people themselves were asking this question. In their collective memory, as one political commentator put it privately, "we remember the approaches of Boris Godunov and Peter the Great. Boris tried to convince the boyars and failed; Peter didn't want to convince anyone, he just ordered changes."

An old Russian proverb says that the Russian muzhik, or peasant, "crosses himself only after he has heard the thunder three times." The saying captures the quintessential bloody-mindedness of the ordinary citizens of a nation whose despotic past has taught it to respond to force or extreme danger but to little else. Sociologist Andrei Zamoshkin pointed to another inherent obstacle to change: "The value of stability in the Russian mind is greater than in other countries. This is why the bureaucracy can keep things together as in a military garrison. We possess a strong fear of change because changes always appear to us as catastrophic."[18]

Another sociologist said studies reveal that support for perestroika existed in all classes and at all levels of society, but it was diffuse; each person seemed to have his or her own agenda of priorities. On the other hand, the forces of resistance were united by a common and simple idea—to water down or block changes. They also held the mechanism of power at the lower levels.[19]

Gorbachev evidently was conscious of the problem. "Generations must pass for us really to change—generations must pass," he said almost despairingly to a group of Soviet writers and intellectuals. His hope was the people. "There's nothing more potent than the force of public opinion, if only it can be realized."[20] It was a big if. He established the first Public Opinion Institute in the Soviet Union in order to help him assess public moods and attitudes, and gauge to what extent his message was being absorbed by the country. Was he way ahead of his country and his times?

There was another problem. Perestroika was so intimately linked with Gorbachev and his personal power that it was all too vulnerable. What would happen, we asked a senior official, if Gorbachev were to disappear from the scene? Would that mean the end of perestroika? He paused for a moment, and his face assumed a grave expression. "The impulse, the energy, the driving force would be diminished overnight," he said.

Nothing gave Gorbachev and his men greater distress than their sense of the administrative impotence of the government in face of the despotic past and the way it had stunted the country's democratic development for centuries. Gorbachev's speeches reflected his dream of civilized relations between the rulers and the ruled. But how to forge such a bond? He well understood that the real challenge to his program was in the homes, factories, collective farms, and offices of Russia. Ultimately, the people mattered.

Fyodor Burlatsky, a Gorbachev confidant and the country's leading political scientist, seemed to reflect the leader's thinking in an article published in *Pravda* on July 18, 1987. Burlatsky was close to Gorbachev and often floated the latter's views on delicate matters of political theory. In the *Pravda* article Burlatsky proposed a new social contract between the government and the people based on democratization, and patient "step-by-step" resolution of problems and disputes by "contractual" agreements at all levels.[21]

It was an extraordinary article, advocating in burning language some things that hadn't been said publicly in decades, and pointing to the flaws that led the nineteenth-century political theorist Pyotr Chaadaev to conclude that "Russia is a country without a future." Burlatsky wanted to prove Chaadaev wrong. This was a moral issue; the time had come for the nation to abandon token gestures and move on to a new plane of political growth. Buoyed by the surge of spontaneous democratic pressures, the radical reformers saw a unique moment for liberalization. This surge was starting with direct local action—ordinary people taking things into their own hands, generating their own leaders, asserting their own rights—on such matters as environmental problems and historical preservations. In the past, the Kremlin's first response was to curse such initiatives. The Gorbachev men wanted to assume the leadership of this movement, in which they saw the germs of political reawakening. After decades of numbing silence, the political conversation was recommencing, and such collective discussion was a prerequisite for serious government. There was hope, Burlatsky wrote, that the people would disprove Chaadaev's curse as well as Jean-Jacques Rousseau's observation that "Russia will never have democracy; it is a country of slaves. The Russian people have the kind of government they deserve."

A year later, poet Yevgeny Yevtushenko made the same point even more forcefully. "Let's be honest and admit that it was not only the ruling clique that was guilty, but the people as well, who allowed the clique to do whatever it wanted. Permitting crimes is a form of participating in them, and historically we are used to permitting them."[22]

Burlatsky's article sought to rekindle a new spirit after decades of complacency and sullen misery. The development of democracy, he proclaimed, was "the main and even the sole way to implement perestroika." In short, the fate of perestroika was in the hands of each Soviet citizen.

It was probably at this point that Gorbachev first began to contemplate a radical political change of the system. The real issue was the management of industrial society—a problem of administration more than of ideology. The problems were technical, and their solutions required individual initiative at all levels and readiness to make sophisticated judgments. Gorbachev talked about making perestroika "more stable and irreversible" by introducing democracy through new legislative acts. Many Soviet observers, of course, assumed he was talking about the sham democratic ideals held out by his parochial and mediocre predecessors. The words have been so abused that they had lost their meaning. The West was skeptical too; it still viewed him—in George Bush's words—as a fine "idea salesman," a slick communist pitchman capable of gliding away from his own formula.

What did the Gorbachev men mean by democracy? There were intimations as to the turn Gorbachev's mind was taking, although his thinking would be revealed fully later. He began to look at politics as a way of coordinating "the interests and will of all classes and social groups"—a striking departure from the Marxist-Leninist concepts of class struggle and classless society. No one can claim a monopoly on truth, Gorbachev argued, and dissenting views must be heard, because even the most extreme contain "something valuable and rational."[23] The new generation had to disenthrall itself from an inheritance of myths and stereotype, and abandon the clichés of their forebears. He had earlier envisioned "the whole system of guarantees of political and civil rights and freedoms."[24] But while he was writing his book, these rights and freedoms were debated in the context of economic reform, not in terms of the bourgeois notions of individual liberties. Indeed, Gorbachev does not speak of liberty in his book, and he rarely mentions individual rights.

Yet a philosophical debate in scholarly journals at the time showed intimations of fundamental liberalization. One of the most forceful voices was that of historian Andranik Migranian, who insisted that perestroika's principal goal was to reduce government interference in economic and social life while providing individuals and groups with the legal means to act independently of the state. In this fashion, he said, Gorbachev could create a "new civil society." The protection of individual rights and liberties was fundamental to this process. Democracy requires a strong and institutionalized civil society, which cannot be achieved without "radical extension of the autonomous sphere of the personal freedoms of the individual."[25]

To what extent the debate influenced Gorbachev's thinking is unclear. Migranian's position reflected Yakovlev's thinking to a considerable degree, a fact that could account for Gorbachev's later interest in safeguarding the rights and freedoms of citizens. But one had the impression that he came to his later libertarian position not as result of philosophical soul-searching but for practical reasons. The economy was not moving upward; the party, in its languid mode, was stonewalling his policy; perestroika was not working against what seemed to be intractable problems. His intimate acquaintance was with agricultural issues; he wanted to decollectivize the countryside but could not do so. He did not possess administrative or executive authority to force the issue. The party held fast to the clichés of the past, which meant that all facts and proposals were filtered through a prefabricated set of Marxist-Leninist interpretations. Only a political reform—one that would invest old concepts with new meanings and in general focus on pragmatic matters involved in the management of modern society—would allow him to accomplish his goals. In one stroke he could deprive the party of weapons of ideological monopoly which once lay so easily at hand. The idea of political pluralism, an open quest for truth, the answerability of the rulers to the people, and the constitutional guarantees of individual rights and freedoms—all were novel notions in Russia, and they began seeping into the national debate as never before. Gorbachev and his aides kept insisting that they were talking about *socialist* democracy and *socialist* pluralism, but their language and their subsequent actions suggested ideas very similar to Western bourgeois concepts.

In the skeptical West, Gorbachev's words now gained additional weight. Even émigré critics of the Soviet system were taking a second look at Gorbachev in early 1987. Professor Vladimir Shlapentokh of Michigan State University compared him to Alexander II, the "Tsar Liberator," who ruled Russia from 1855 to 1881, and found striking parallels.[26]

Both leaders inherited a floundering economy, stagnating agricultural production, and a growing technological gap. The economic problems in both instances were a direct result of extremely conservative policies. The technological backwardness of Russia in the nineteenth century could be illustrated by the extremely slow growth of railroads. In 1861, Russia had only one-tenth the length of railroad track of England, a country two hundred times smaller than Russia. In the 1980s, the Soviet Union's gap could be seen in its lag behind most advanced countries, and even the newly emerging industrial nations of Asia, in the production of high technology.

There are other similarities: the crushing of the Hungarian rebellion in 1848 by Alexander's father, Nicholas I, and Brezhnev's invasion of Czechoslovakia in 1968. Both had significant effects on the social and political climate in Russia, leading to intellectual stagnation. Pushkin's words seemed to apply to Soviet intellectuals after the crushing of the Prague Spring—"Our public life is a sad thing—this lack of public opinion, the indifference to justice and truth, the cynical contempt for human thought and decency!" Both Alexander and Gorbachev promoted sweeping reforms for fear that Russia would become a second-rate power. Alexander's defeat in the Crimean War was a direct result of Russia's technological backwardness. America's SDI was seen by Gorbachev as a way for the United States to gain enduring military superiority over the Soviet Union.

Both rulers viewed the egotistical behavior of the dominant class (Alexander's nobility and bureaucracy; Gorbachev's party and state bureaucracy) as the main cause of stagnation. Both felt that the country's survival depended on a release of human energy hampered by an archaic economic system. Both sought to lessen the administrative regulation of the economy and to expand individual initiative, including private enterprise. Both released political dissidents imprisoned by their predecessors. Alexander's reforms abolished serfdom and reduced state controls over management in industry and commerce. Gorbachev, by introducing the profit motive and promoting the "family farm" and "cooperative" commerce and services, wants to move in the same direction.

The two rulers seem even more similar in their political reforms. Both gradually reached the conclusion that it was impossible to control bureaucracy and sought to involve the masses in the political process as a way of curbing its arbitrary rule. Both sought to promote justice. "Glasnost," Shlapentokh said, was a popular term in the 1850s. Alexander freed the great satirical writer Mikhail Saltykov-Shchedrin from exile; Gorbachev freed Andrei Sakharov. Alexander allowed the publication of previously banned books by such writers as Gogol and Pushkin; Gorbachev did the same with the works of even more writers, ranging from Pasternak to Andrei Platonov.

In both instances, the reforms aroused fierce resistance, primarily from conservatives. "The fate of Alexander's reforms is instructive," writes Shlapentokh. After a few years, they began to run out of steam. The first blow was delivered by the 1863 Polish uprising (Poland was a part of the empire). This was followed by an assassination attempt on the tsar by a leftist radical. The monarch eventually withdrew most of the political reforms he had initiated. "Only the economic reforms, having radically changed the country, managed to survive." Glasnost could not survive, because there were no democratic institutions independent of the tsar's power to protect them. Alexander was assassinated in 1881 by leftist revolutionaries, ushering in a period of political reaction and decline.

Although Shlapentokh's lesson from Russia's past was illuminating, it was based on an incomplete assessment of Gorbachev's style and character. No one in early 1987 could have confidently forecast the degree of energy, courage, and even perhaps desperation that propelled Gorbachev to push his revolution into high gear and come forward with increasingly more radical proposals for political reforms.

Chapter 14

CONSERVATIVES BAY FOR BLOOD

Subtly but inevitably, in the late spring and summer of 1987 a change began to take place within the party bureaucracy and society. A flurry of articles and interviews, including one with Gorbachev's top economic adviser, Abel Aganbegyan, raised a series of unsettling questions. They talked of bankruptcies of inefficient firms, price hikes, and wage fluctuations. Ordinary people were worried. They sensed that Gorbachev meant business and that all the articles and interviews were preparing the public for things to come.

Economists understood the problems posed by inevitable price rises. Prices are political dynamite in any system. "The psychology of this change will be very hard for us," said Vladimir Gorshev, rector of the Institute of the National Economy. "I can remember, as a boy in Stalin's time, how every April 1 there would be an announcement of new price cuts. This was the symbolism of success in building communism. And now prices have to rise."

The public debate, however, was dominated by ideological clashes. The debate over history was so fierce that in September 1987, for the first time in memory, schools opened their doors without history textbooks. History teachers were told to improvise. "Of course, those who had taught for twenty years one way were going to continue the same way," Alexander Yakovlev said. "You can't expect them to change their lectures."[1]

The debate about Stalin's crimes was the litmus test. The reformers wanted to expose them; they called for rehabilitation of the Old Bolsheviks murdered by Stalin: Nikolai Bukharin, Leon Trotsky, Lev Kamenev, Grigori Zinoviev, and many others. The conservatives, who had been battling for cultural orthodoxy and challenging the scope of glasnost, fought back. Their argument was that Stalin, though certainly guilty of "repressing" some genuine Bolsheviks in the thirties, had presided over a glorious period of Soviet history and that nobody should be allowed to discredit it. As in other countries, the conservatives knew their best weapon was the charge of betrayal or outright treason; they understood that all the painstakingly assembled evidence probably carried less weight than the simple accusation of a sellout to the West. ("Don't think for a moment that you've got the world monopoly on Jesse Helms," one liberal writer remarked privately, referring to the conservative senator from North Carolina. "We've got our own Jesses, and we've got some Neanderthals that make Jesse Helms look like a paragon of liberalism.")

The conservatives maintained that something verging on the treasonous was afoot in the land. Rock groups, which were emerging from underground into the klieg lights of official stages, drew some of the conservative heat. They represented an insidious Western effort to undermine Russia, the conservatives argued. With glasnost in full bloom, nobody came right out and talked about banning rock and roll, only about giving it a "proper" amount of time on television, and only to those groups that were "decent." Yet another dispute involved the publication of émigré Russian writers. Acrimonious charges back and forth raised the temperature of public discourse.

On the face of it, all of this carried little significance in and of itself; it seemed to be the jealous intellectuals continuing their endless rivalries in a more public fashion. But the polarization of views reflected two things. One was that there were sharp divisions within the establishment; the other was a new, transmuted form of that old Russian division between the (conservative) Slavophiles and the (reformist) Westernizers that had pitted Russian intellectuals against one another for centuries. What was not clear was whether this was a result of doubts about the fate of perestroika or of individual political ambitions. The conservative assault was inspired by Gorbachev's number-two man, Yegor Ligachev, who in a private meeting with writers expressed his concern about the scope of glasnost in literature. He cited several leading novelists but focused in particular on Chingiz Aitmatov, Gorbachev's favorite contemporary Soviet writer, to illustrate the ideological heresy involved in exploring religious and spiritual themes. Aitmatov's novel *Execution Block,* one of the most popular books of 1986, not only portrayed explicitly the Soviet drug culture and the background of corruption against which it thrived; it was also a powerful account of a young man's search for God.

Conservative writers took their cue from Ligachev. Ivan Stadnyuk, Sergei Mikhalkov, Valentin Ustinov, Alexander Mikhailov, and Yuri Bondarev assailed liberal editors for publishing the works of Russian émigré writers such as Vladimir Nabokov; it was, they charged, an act of "literary necrophilia." They refused to recognize any Russian who had emigrated from his country. When Andrei Voznesensky sought to establish a museum for the work of Marc Chagall, whose work had been officially unrecognized in his own country (Chagall was a native of Vitebsk, though he spent most of his life in Paris), he was attacked for his alleged lack of patriotism. In the realm of contemporary visual arts, the struggle was equally fierce. Valentin Sidorov, the chief of the Russian Artists' Union, assailed "the blossoming of dubious flowers of antirealism, which are the direct antithesis to all principles of Russian and Soviet fine arts." In fighting for socialist realism (the realistic portrayal of inspirational Soviet communism), he declared at a union meeting, "we are, in fact, fighting against the reactionary forces of the world."[2] Ustinov claimed that the Soviet cultural world had been hijacked by a clique of untalented self-promoters who were introducing pernicious Western ideas and styles, and who were doing so for personal financial gain.

Yegor Yakovlev, the leading reformist and editor of the *Moscow News,* came under a particularly vicious attack for publishing a letter by a group of Soviet émigré intellectuals under the title "Let Gorbachev Give Us Proof." Signed by Yuri Lyubimov, Vladimir Bukovsky, Ernst Neizvestny, Yuri Orlov, Vassily Aksyonov, Eduard Kuznetsov, Vladimir Maximov, Alexander Zinoviev, and Leonid Plyushch, the letter assailed Marxism-Leninism as false teaching which brought the country ruin. It called for genuine glasnost and said that, since the system did not work, "isn't it time to try something else?"

Conservative assaults on editors and journalists intensified in 1987. Viktor Afanasiev, the editor of *Pravda* and now a Ligachev supporter, indirectly assailed Alexander Yakovlev's office for alleged harassment and intimidation to strangle conservative criticism, "directly or indirectly." The moment a correspondent is given an assignment to collect critical material, he said, "telephone calls follow. . . . Attempts are made to prevent a correspondent's work and publication of their material." He talked about numerous instances of journalists' being fired, dismissed from the party, or imprisoned.[3]

Far more contentious was the question of history, for it touched upon the fundamental intellectual split in the party.

The traditional argument between the Slavophiles and Westernizers, now surfacing in a new form, was about Russia's future. In an old debate that had torn Russia ever since Peter the Great forcibly opened the country to the West, the conservative Slavophiles, by grotesquely idealizing their past, contended that Russia was the country of the future and that it was her destiny to solve mankind's problems. For the Slavophiles it was the Russian Orthodox faith that, by remaining true to Christian ideals, distinguished Russia from the West, which they viewed as poisoned by rationalism and individualism.[4]

In the modern context, instead of the Russian Orthodox faith it was communism that became the rationale of the conservative position. They revived the old Slavophile argument that the communal spirit *(sobornost)* was the quintessential aspect of the Russian national character, whereas the foundations of Western political life were individualistic and legalistic. In Russia, every individual submerges into the community. In the West, which had succumbed to rationalism, each individual was isolated from the community and followed his or her own understanding of life's purpose. But that led to alienation and the excesses of Western democracies, which made Russians wary. This poison of Western ideas and styles was what the conservatives saw in the new openness of the eighties. Hence the problem of history, the quest for truth about Stalin's crimes, which the conservatives assailed as a "literary Chernobyl." Yuri Bondarev, the novelist whose theme is World War Two, used military images familiar to him, such as the 1942–43 battle of Stalingrad that turned the tide of war against Nazi Germany, and publicly called for a conservative counterattack to save socialism.

"If we continue to withdraw, if we don't make [a stand as at] Stalingrad, then everything is going to end up in a disastrous collapse of national values, and everything precious in the nation's spirit will be pushed into the abyss. False democrats have lit up the stolen torch of glasnost and are using the means of information for their purposes, the aggressive ones, destructive, throwing the doors wide open to grayness, vanity, and phony Jacobins."[5]

The conservatives' target was Gorbachev himself. They were clearly disturbed by the trend he had set. Unlike previous Soviet leaders, who were deeply xenophobic and suspicious of foreign influences, Gorbachev seemed genuinely interested in Western ideas and practices. At least theoretically, he was a proponent of free inquiry; his attitude toward the past was almost diametrically opposed to that of the Slavophiles. He argued that "a nation disregarding its history puts a question mark over its future."[6] He wanted to have a new history of the Soviet Union written—"an honest, courageous, and fascinating book throwing light on a great and heroic road traversed by the country and the party, the road of trailblazers. This book must not be shy of the drama of certain events and some individuals' destinies. It must be free from blank pages."[7] He urged historians to write genuine political biographies of Stalin and other leaders; nothing like that had ever been published in the Soviet Union.

He rejected the "half-truths" that filled most existing Soviet works on history. "A half-truth is worse than a drug," he said. "This applies

both to contemporary problems and to the history of our society."[8]
He dismissed the traditional conservative concept that a citizen is
"either with us, or a leper," and tried to extend a friendly hand
toward Soviet artists in exile, something that was symbolized by an
official invitation to ballet star Mikhail Baryshnikov to make a guest
appearance with the Bolshoi Ballet.

The Russians were startled. In the past, people like Baryshnikov,
Yuri Lyubimov, Mstislav Rostropovich, Solzhenitsyn, and others
who defected or who were forced to emigrate to the West had been
regarded as nonpersons in Russia. But for Gorbachev, they were
the people who should be courted and brought back into the fold.
Prominent Gorbachev-supporters openly demanded that the authorities formally reconsider the decisions under which they had
deported Solzhenitsyn in 1974, and stripped Rostropovich of his
Soviet citizenship.

Some matters in these disputes that raged under the banner of
glasnost touched on fundamental political judgments. The question
of Bukharin's exoneration, for instance, was not merely a matter of
historical justice (he had been convicted on trumped-up charges and
executed in 1938). Since Bukharin had vigorously opposed Stalin's
forced collectivization of agriculture, his rehabilitation also would
signal a condemnation of Soviet agricultural practices under Stalin,
precisely the collectivization Gorbachev was trying to break down.
Gorbachev and his men, in their attempts to revive agriculture, had
been seeking to restore the family farm as a basic unit of production, with the collective farm providing support and marketing facilities.

As a rationalist and an empiricist, Gorbachev evidently felt that
public debates would promote a rational consensus. Reason had to
prevail. He believed in the force of ideas. He knew, as he put it,
that "we are an emotional people, we lack the culture to conduct
debate and respect the viewpoint even of a friend, a comrade."[9] But
in the July 15, 1987, speech he asked the party's intellectual elite to
"rise above emotions and convenient stereotypes."

"We will tell the truth and nothing but the truth," he said. "I think we must never forgive or justify what happened" during Stalin's reign of terror. "Never." He continued: "I have no reason to make any big political rebukes. If there were any extremes—and, incidentally, there have been and we have noted them—this took place, after all, within the framework of a struggle for socialism, for perfecting it, within the framework of a struggle that is in the interest of the people." When passions ran high, he said, everyone should remember that these were family disputes, because they were all "in the same boat; we have always been on the same side of the barricades."[10]

It would be inaccurate to describe Gorbachev simply as a Westernizer. He is deeply steeped in his country's traditions and customs, but his pragmatism and rationalism run against the conservative grain of the country. He abhors a vision of Russia based on ignorance and utopianism, and is deeply sensitive to the fact that since the time of Peter the Great the country's modernization has depended on the acquisition of technology through the West, and that Soviets lack the inner growth and understanding which come through the process of conception and production.

He knew that the engine of modernization was military.[11] But merely to imitate the West was not the solution. He wanted to set in motion genuine processes to nourish what he called "a kind of renaissance," not simply technological mimicry. He often talked in public about the Russians' being able to send rockets to distant planets while not being capable of making a decent electric stove. And he repeatedly returned to the issue of the intransigence of the regime. Yakovlev pushed that issue even further in an address in 1987 to the intellectual leaders and opinion-makers, cautioning against self-intoxication and self-deception. Why, he asked, did they perpetuate their "ritual chant" about a homogeneous Soviet society filled with examples of the "ideal Soviet man"? If the description was true, he added sarcastically, where do all the "dishonorable people, corrupt bureaucrats, embezzlers, and frauds come from?"[12]

Was Gorbachev trying to change the nature of government, or merely its style? He felt that the nation had to be sufficiently educated to play its part in the choosing of its leaders, and that that was a long process. He wanted a gradual broadening of privileges and duties, the combination being crucial for an effective perestroika. Yet even this seemed threatening to many Russians. Even nationalistic dissidents were ambivalent about democratic processes. Solzhenitsyn, who suffered at the hands of the system and who was a strong critic of communism, did not advocate a Western-style democracy but pondered what sort of authoritarian order Russia should have. "It is not authoritarianism itself that is intolerable, but the ideological lies that are daily foisted upon us," he wrote in his 1974 *Letter to the Soviet Leaders.* In this view, an authoritarian order could be the foundation of a society based on laws that reflected the will of the population.

The ultraconservatives used Pamyat, the stridently nationalist organization, to stage noisy demonstrations throughout the spring and early summer of 1987. After Abel Aganbegyan gave several interviews in the spring to talk about the forthcoming economic reforms, Pamyat accused him of being a "Freemason" and said he harbored "too many Jews" at his institute. Similar charges were hurled at other prominent reformist figures during a Pushkin Square demonstration by Pamyat members. Yeltsin himself had met with Pamyat members in May after five hundred of them marched outside his office. They complained to him that unspecified forces "linked to Zionists, Freemasons, and imperialists" were trying to destroy the culture of Old Russia and "Americanize" Soviet society.

This view also began to appear in the press. A letter by someone who had been a Communist Party member since 1939, published in *Moscow News,* denounced "unwise glasnost" as unnatural and foreign, something foisted on the leadership by an international conspiracy. To illustrate the point, the letter emphasized the Jewish names of several prominent perestroika-supporters. Among those singled out for denunciation were playwright Mikhail Shatrov (the letter gave his real Jewish name—Marshak) and the country's leading comedian, Arkady Raikin, also Jewish, who had joined the fight for perestroika with articles scathingly satirical of economic mismanagement and drunkenness. "One would think that even the most vicious opponents of the Soviet Union would be ashamed to say such things about our motherland," the author said.[13]

• • •

In the summer of 1987, Ligachev was evidently emboldened enough by the resistance to openly challenge glasnost, which, in his view, was a mistake and threatened much grief. When Gorbachev went on vacation to complete his book *Perestroika*, Ligachev, as acting general secretary, took the offensive, issuing conflicting instructions to cultural and media executives. Glasnost, he told them, was throwing up some "froth and filth." Though he was in favor of glasnost, he was cringing at the Western influences he saw seeping into Russia. "No matter what novelties are offered to us by homegrown innovators and foreign advisers, we shall not deviate from the principle of socialist realism in the arts, from a communist direction in culture, in the moral sphere, and in Soviet education."[14]

Ligachev's assertive opposition presented Gorbachev with a problem to which there was no clear and easy answer. Radical reformists argued that Ligachev was thirsting for power, that he enjoyed rumors of his growing influence (indeed, one senior official said, Ligachev delighted in them), and courted a reputation as the key conservative figure. This would allow him to bind the Brezhnevite bureaucracy even more closely to him and thus restore some of the political ground he had lost at the June plenum. While putatively supportive of the fundamental elements of Gorbachev's agenda, he was quietly sending signals that in fact his position on economic issues was more cautious and traditional, and that he didn't like glasnost at all.

Things were brought to a head later in the summer at a conference of representatives of independent organizations in Moscow. It was a striking scene. About three hundred delegates representing forty-seven major independent organizations met in Moscow's Novator Hall of Culture from August 20 to 23. Yeltsin had sought ways to gain influence over the independent organizations and clubs, to harness them behind the perestroika movement by drafting a blueprint for their cooperation with the system. He failed. The conference, in fact, produced the most terrible dilemma for glasnost, something that frightened the establishment and produced a conservative backlash. As the conservatives had argued, glasnost, taken to its logical conclusions, led inexorably in the direction of a political challenge to the system. The stormy all-night closing session ended in an uproar over whether a Final Declaration should include a provision endorsing a "socialist model of development for our country." Some radical groups were unalterably opposed to it. Even the moderate majority would not give a blanket endorsement of the Communist Party, though it did give unconditional support to Gorbachev and his supporters, described as "the healthy and progressive forces in the party." Unanimity was reached on one decision only: to establish a fund for a monument to the victims of Stalin.[15] (A year later Gorbachev arranged that the state would build such a monument.)

Representatives of Yeltsin's party committee, who attended the conference as observers, were bewildered. They had sought the support and loyalty of these groups, and they had been careful to gather only moderate organizations to the conference. The extremist organizations such as Pamyat on the right and Glasnost, organized by former political prisoners, on the left, had been excluded. Yeltsin and his colleagues expected that these organizations would be reasonable. By the Moscow party's terms, they were not. Nothing like this had been heard in a public forum for decades: the radicals claimed that perestroika was a false new dawn and put forward demands that were heretical. Some delegates wanted to make an alliance with the Christian church. One representative of the group Humanism and Democracy, Natalya Novgorodskaya, in a thundering speech, denounced the entire Soviet period since the death of Lenin in 1924 as one of "crimes and mistakes." The group Left Explosion, from the city of Ivanovo, advanced an anarchist program, questioning the party's political role. The whole thing was a fraud; instead of withering away, as Marx and Engels had forecast, the socialist state had become stronger and more overpowering in daily life, they argued.[16]

Party delegates at the meeting were impotent. They had no say in the shaping of the Final Declaration, which argued that constitutionally, since "all power belongs to the people," they had the right to express and defend their interests "independently and without any intermediaries." While bowing to the party's constitutional role in Soviet society, it insisted that "the party is not united—its ranks include those who bear responsibility for the abuses and miscalculations of the past." Perestroika was meeting "fierce opposition" from the privileged bureaucracy, which was "eager to hold on to its monopoly of information and decisionmaking. They either ignore or counter [Gorbachev's] new beginning and any popular initiative."

The principal aim of Yeltsin's men in organizing a Federation of Socialist Clubs had been to support Gorbachev's program, not merely to provide a forum for even more radical views. But what started as a tactical ploy developed a momentum of its own, and Yeltsin would be held responsible by some. The radicals had no natural leader, but their political demands were clear. The majority demanded that the clubs be accorded legal standing, with the right to propose legislation, field candidates in all elections, and have free access to the mass media. They advocated workers' self-management, an end to censorship, and "full constitutional rights and freedoms such as speech, press, street marches, and demonstrations."[17]

Conservatives in the establishment panicked.[18] Press accounts gave only an emasculated account of the meeting, without mentioning the substance of the debate. The conference was portrayed benignly as a "kindergarten of democracy." But to senior conservative officials it was clear that glasnost had given rise to embryonic grass-roots political activism outside the framework of party-controlled political life, and that the attempt to gain influence over these independent groups had backfired. Some thought Yeltsin had gone too far. By providing the Novator Hall of Culture for the plenary sessions, as well as the Kurchatov Hall of Culture for political and other seminars, the Moscow party had practically extended recognition to a curious assembly of virtually all strains of the radical *intelligentsia*. Groups throughout the country became bolder.

Ligachev understood the conservative alarm better than anybody. Only a couple of days after the conference, speaking to workers of the Elektrostal works outside Moscow, he seized the occasion to establish fully an alternative position. He was unequivocal on the emotional issues of the Soviet past, assailing his chief, without mentioning his name, as one of those who wanted to expose the lawlessness of Stalin in the 1930s. "Some people in our own country tried to denigrate the entire path of the building of socialism in the Soviet Union and present it as an unbroken chain of errors," Ligachev said. "As far as the thirties are concerned, it was the period when our country moved up to second place in the world in terms of industrial production, when we carried out the collectivization of agriculture, and when we reached unreachable heights in the development of culture, education, literature, and the arts. This is a fact, without any doubts. And one more thing. The vast majority of repressed Bolsheviks remained faithful to Lenin and socialism to the end of their lives." It was, he said, "completely unacceptable to talk about the tragic mistakes of those years with malice. . . . One has to tell the young people about the heroic history of the party and the state with responsibility and competence."[19]

Ligachev also distanced himself from Gorbachev's condemnation of the Brezhnev-era stagnation by rattling off a series of "real accomplishments" during those years. The Soviet Union had achieved strategic parity with the United States. "Life grew richer, spiritually and materially." The national income quadrupled. "If you ask me about those years," he continued, "that was an unforgettable time, when we lived a genuinely full life" and made great accomplishments in western Siberia, where he had lived throughout the period. Almost as an aside, he noted some negative tendencies during that time which led to a misuse of power and a decline in the discipline and international authority of the country.[20]

It had become quite difficult to figure out the Kremlin line. Outsiders found this exciting; political struggles were less cloaked in the shadows than before, and one could begin to forecast future moves with some accuracy. But rank-and-file Communist Party members were bewildered. "For you it's like a theater," one senior Soviet journalist told us with surprising bitterness. "But you are in the galleries, you are spectators, while we are playing on the stage. And let me tell you, it's a deadly serious show—no jokes for us."

The debate over glasnost was becoming more entrenched, the conflicting signals from within the Kremlin more pronounced. In September, KGB Chairman Viktor Chebrikov weighed in on the side of the conservatives. It was an ominous sign. Even if Chebrikov remained loyal to Gorbachev, it was clear that he was at the very minimum asserting strong institutional doubts about glasnost. From that point on, Gorbachev's aides became increasingly apprehensive about the possibility of a Ligachev-Chebrikov deal, and many began to say privately that Gorbachev would have to name his own man as KGB chairman if he wanted to feel secure over the coming years.

Chebrikov's speech in which he parted ways publicly with Gorbachev for the first time contained a direct warning to the *intelligentsia,* which, he said, included people whom Western intelligence services were hoping to use in their efforts to undermine the Soviet state. He cautioned the politically active people who were emboldened by glasnost. "One gets the impression," he said, "that these people have understood the process of the broadening of democracy as the freedom to do anything that comes into their heads without punishment and act against the interests of Soviet society."[21]

Gorbachev was still on vacation at the Black Sea. Taking advantage of his prolonged absence, the conservatives began to plot in earnest to remove Yeltsin.

If there was a single issue that made many Russians wary of Gorbachev's glasnost, that issue was ethnicity. Their reservations were reinforced by the sham nature of the multiethnic federation; more than 100 national and ethnic groups are theoretically equal but in fact are almost all at different stages of socioeconomic development, and burdened by different historical traditions.

The storm clouds were gathering, predictably, in the non-Russian republics. Glasnost had encouraged nationalist ferment. In June, Latvian nationalists staged a demonstration in Riga's central square to commemorate victims of Stalinist repression. The police did not interfere. In Armenia, a group of intellectuals formed a committee whose goal was to petition the Soviet government for redress of an old grievance, namely the administrative separation of a predominantly Armenian area, Nagorno-Karabakh, from the Armenian Republic. It all seemed proper and in tune with the new times; they started collecting signatures to push for the return of the disputed area, which is a part of the Azerbaijan Republic, to Armenia.

Also using proper channels, several hundred Crimean Tatars demonstrated peacefully in July in Red Square to press their demand for permission to return to their old homeland in the Crimea. They brought with them a petition signed by thirty thousand Tatars who asked Gorbachev to intervene in their behalf. After the second day-long demonstration in Red Square, Tatar representatives were received by President Gromyko, who told them that a commission had been set up to investigate their demands. The entire Tatar population of the Crimea, about a quarter of a million people, had been forcibly deported to Soviet Central Asia by Stalin because several thousand of them had served in six German-officered battalions that fought against the local Soviet guerrillas in Nazi-occupied Crimea during World War Two.

Russians are always worried about precedents. Letting the Tatars have their way could reopen the issue of mass deportations of Lithuanians, Latvians, and Estonians in 1940, after the annexation of their countries. If one grievance was recognized, how many more would be raised? The airing of these issues posed a long-term danger.

Predictably, there was more nationalist agitation in August in Riga, Latvia, and Vilnius, Lithuania. Throughout the fall, there were nationalist rumblings in the Caucasus area, and especially in Armenia, which eventually erupted into a massive outbreak of communal violence between Christian Armenians and Moslem Azerbaijanis.

Glasnost and the relaxation of rigid controls appeared to threaten the political order. The view of men such as Ligachev, Solomentsev, Chebrikov, and others was that things were moving further and faster than was tolerable. Some supporters were turning against perestroika, but they could hide it; others, who were running major newspapers and magazines, could not.

Viktor Afanasiev, the editor-in-chief of *Pravda,* was cool, intellectual, quick-witted, and urbane. He talked like a reformer, but the more he did so, the more distance he was putting between himself and the reforms. Viktor represented a particular Soviet breed, an intellectual-apparatchik and master of well-crafted indirectness. Journalists who worked for him knew his mode of operation. One could never find a single phrase or sentence from him that contradicted the chiefs, yet he knew how to present the opposite point of view as if it were an abstraction, standing up in closed Central Committee meetings and introducing a brilliant rebuttal by saying, "Critics, of course, could say . . ." Those who disliked him called him a chameleon. He could be enormously entertaining and gay, or grimly humorless and sober. He knew how to make friends with key persons around the leader; more important, he knew how to humor Brezhnev, Andropov, and Chernenko, and he flattered Gorbachev when he took charge. The very fact that he managed to survive as *Pravda* editor under four different general secretaries supported the claims that Afanasiev was typical of a certain caste within the Soviet officialdom who could always detect which way the wind was blowing and were never caught going against it alone. Now he began to side with people in the establishment who were concerned about the growing political activism outside the party, sensing, not entirely inaccurately, that the social groups and political clubs might be dangerous to the existing order. Either *Pravda* began to vacillate and so did Afanasiev, or Afanasiev began to vacillate and led the paper behind him.

Boris Yeltsin became something of a lightning rod for conservative ire. He now went to the grass roots to figure out how to revive political consciousness and activism. In the summer of 1987, Yeltsin tried to come to grips with the independent political activities and to channel them in support of perestroika. He evidently hoped he could rein them in, then apply the spur when necessary. He knew how to talk to them, and they liked him, his approach.

To them he looked like a leader of men—lean, forceful, handsome, a man with a high moral tone; a striking contrast to his predecessor, the sleazy Grishin. He was charismatic, his public arguments sounded right and honest, and his presentation was compelling. Intellectuals suspected that his presentations were better than his true grasp of ideas, as if he had not deeply thought through the ultimate consequences of his views. Conservative critics went further, to accuse Yeltsin of facilitating—unwittingly, to be sure—a collapse of the party's monopoly of power. They argued that his understanding of perestroika would eventually lead to the destruction of the party.

Yet Yeltsin became a hero for young Russians, a cult figure to those who were not necessarily anticommunists but who were filled with bitterness and apathy caused by the "period of stagnation," as the rule of Brezhnev now became known. Unlike other Politburo members, who met with people accompanied by high officials and dignitaries and who simply did not know any more how to talk to the people, Yeltsin took some time to identify the members of these unofficial organizations and to find out what they wanted.

Yeltsin became infected by their ideas. His instinct was sound. Here was a force that could become an instrument of perestroika, let loose to break corrupt institutional networks. It was a tricky proposition, and Yeltsin was increasingly frustrated by the guerrilla tactics of his conservative enemies.

Yeltsin's involvement in the independent political organizations provided the opening to undermine him and his allies in the inner councils of the government, perhaps even to nudge Gorbachev back to a more orthodox policy. A new front had been opened, and, at least initially, it seemed that the conservatives were bound to be victorious.

By September, as Gorbachev's vacation drew to a close, Moscow was awash with rumors. They all had one theme—divisions and clashes among the top Kremlin men—and they persisted even after Gorbachev returned to the capital. Meeting with a large group of visiting French politicians, businessmen, and public figures on September 29, Gorbachev felt compelled to tell them, "There is no political opposition in the Soviet Union, no opposition" to his leadership."[22] But indirectly he acknowledged the problem. Like a stern schoolmaster, he warned unnamed people against using glasnost for "subversive activities": "Those who would like to use democratization as an opportunity for social upheaval, I say to them that their hopes are in vain." The Frenchmen must have been baffled by his reference to unnamed "subversive activities," a phrase he had rarely used before, but the words were clearly understood in the establishment. Gorbachev referred to the affair of the independent organizations, which had united the conservatives with some elements of the KGB.

Now the loyalty of the KGB became an issue. As Andropov's protégé and part of his coalition for change, Gorbachev had inherited their support. But many in the secret-police apparatus were concerned about the course of events since he had taken power. Gorbachev's relaxed policy toward political dissidents and Jewish refuseniks had provoked resentment. Up until now, the KGB had escaped purges and turmoil. But in a June 1987 address to a conference of scholars, Anatoly Lukyanov, Gorbachev's chief of staff, made ominous noises about perestroika of the KGB itself. He argued for the need to "strengthen socialist legality," and said that perestroika would be applied to "the entire totality of bodies" of law and order.[23]

KGB Chairman Chebrikov's assault on glasnost could not be taken lightly. After two decades at the KGB, he knew how to maneuver. He had been among Gorbachev's key supporters, but increasingly he found himself agreeing with Ligachev and other doubters. He was caught between the conflicting pressures of two very different constituencies: the Gorbachev team, pushing glasnost and perestroika to revive the nation, and the KGB establishment, with its fierce commitment to the lessons of the Cold War and its unshakable conviction that coercion was the only thing that mattered when it came down to maintaining domestic order.

Chebrikov's hard-line speech in September of 1987, revealing that he was not the supporter he had been supposed, shook up the Gorbachev men. They knew that the men at the Lubyanka had been rattled when Gorbachev, in early 1986, established a security detachment charged with the protection of the party leader that was outside the total control of the KGB. The move was followed by speculations in the press about the need to curb the KGB's power, but nothing had happened to validate those speculations.

Because of his friendship with Andropov, Gorbachev had inherited the loyalty and support of a number of key members of the KGB establishment, including Chebrikov's first deputy, Vladimir Kryuchkov, the man in charge of the agency's foreign espionage. (Kryuchkov had worked for Andropov from 1959 to 1967 on the staff of the Secretariat of the Central Committee, and then followed Andropov when he was appointed KGB chairman in 1967.) Gorbachev had enough allies in the KGB to forewarn him, but not enough to prevent a change of attitude toward glasnost.

Gorbachev's tactic in response to Chebrikov's betrayal of glasnost was to strike pre-emptively to disarm his KGB opponents. The reply to Chebrikov's September 1987 speech was delivered by Chief of Staff Lukyanov, who phoned Valentin Falin, chairman of the Novosti Press Agency, and said he was ready to give an interview to a Novosti correspondent.

In the interview, which was distributed widely, Lukyanov discounted, perhaps too demonstratively, the role of the KGB in Soviet politics. The agency had no special domestic functions whatever, he said. Its job was to guard the nation against foreign spies. In fact, the Gorbachev administration had been imposing stricter controls on the KGB, and "Since more rigorous control was introduced over its work by the party and our supreme bodies of power, the Committee [of State Security] has been performing its functions properly," he said.[24]

Lukyanov's tone was dismissive as he asserted that the KGB is not a "body of state authority" but, rather, "part of the mechanism of state administration." He then defined the KGB's role. "Its main function is to safeguard our country against subversive actions from outside," he said. "It would be absurd to speak of the KGB as having some special powers in current conditions," he added when asked by the Novosti interviewer whether he feared the KGB could "step in and use their muscle" to curb perestroika's course. Yet this last question underscored the precariousness of Gorbachev's coalition and betrayed the real motive for the interview: the fears of Gorbachev, Yakovlev, and Lukyanov that Chebrikov and Ligachev might be contemplating the use of KGB "muscle" to divert the course of perestroika.

Gorbachev knew that the KGB had to be handled delicately, not provoked into action. He was biding his time. His was still a minority government, dependent upon husbanding his bargaining power for its most effective use. There was no sense in putting his prestige on the line and then being defeated. By delivering his message through Lukyanov, he was maintaining some distance. He also knew that the opposition had to become accustomed to unfamiliar concepts, and he was willing to wait a bit.

The Yeltsin affair further complicated Gorbachev's relations with the conservatives and the KGB. The conservatives were accusing Yeltsin of being an ambitious populist politician determined to set up his own political base among independent groups. Recognizing the discontent in the Politburo and upper echelons of the leadership and a need to do something if he was to preserve his control, Gorbachev ultimately let Yeltsin go, forcing his resignation after a stormy leadership meeting in which Yeltsin made a vicious personal attack on Ligachev and accused him of undermining perestroika. Unable to keep his petulant ally in check, Gorbachev was forced to sack him from the Politburo. Yet his resignation did nothing to eliminate the root of the crisis: the proliferation of independent political groups and clubs. By the end of 1987, there were about thirty thousand independent organizations, and a year later there were over forty thousand of them.[25] The Soviet Union was no longer a totalitarian system but a hybrid pluralistic society entering a long internal crisis and trying to correct the failings of the political process.

But few people could foresee how events would snowball. In the fall of 1987, the country seemed stuck in a quagmire. The conservatives were strong. Perestroika was going nowhere. And nobody was more alarmed than Gorbachev. Speaking in Murmansk, the northern port, in September, Gorbachev proclaimed that perestroika was based on "new socialist principles" to refurbish "our common home." He urged his audiences not to give up when perestroika ran into painful problems and difficulties. "I tell you honestly, it is going to be difficult," he said. "You must keep yourselves in check, comrades, and you must not panic. Never."[26] He touched on the sensitive issue of food prices, saying that increases "cannot be avoided" if the country is to move forward and raise standards of living. The prices issue, he said in a nationally televised speech, also in Murmansk, will be "brought up for the discussion of the working people."[27]

It was not a popular speech, and throughout October 1987 Moscow was rife with rumors about price increases and difficulties at the top, including the unmistakable signs of the imminent ouster from the Politburo of Geidar Aliev, former KGB chief of Azerbaijan, who had been brought into the ruling council by Andropov in 1982. Gossip involving Raisa Gorbachev and her alleged influence on policy gained new intensity, always showing her role as somehow insidious. The dubious veracity of the Raisa rumors was irrelevant; what mattered was that they were deliberately generated as an expression of discontent with her husband. His enemies resurrected the memory of Nicholas and Alexandra, and the invidious comparison to the last Romanovs was designed to make Raisa look like a new tsarina.

Aliev was indeed retired "for health reasons" when the Central Committee met in closed session on October 21, a move of no particular significance except as a demonstration of unease at the top. The official accounts of the session were circumspect about the ouster. But they were thunderously silent about a fierce dispute that erupted between Yeltsin and Ligachev.[28]

Yeltsin accused conservatives, and specifically Ligachev, of blocking Gorbachev's reforms, and warned the party against promising more than it could deliver. Perestroika, he said, has yet to do something for the average man. "Among other things," Yeltsin recalled later, "my speech included criticism of the leadership, namely Comrade Ligachev, because the processes of change in our party are still slow, because the party lags behind, because the processes of democratization in our party do not develop, and because the style and methods of work lag behind."[29]

It was a totally unexpected assault, as Gorbachev recalled later—

"Nobody knew about it in advance, it was something completely spontaneous"[30]—and it ignited an uproar among the conservative majority in the Central Committee. In the heat of the debate, finding himself vastly outnumbered, Yeltsin offered his resignation. The victorious conservative majority had even more reason to gloat. They managed to strike a blow at one crucial aspect of glasnost—they voted to order a halt in the creation of independent publishing and printing cooperatives, protecting the party monopoly on books, magazines, and newspapers.[31]

Yeltsin's resignation was not immediately announced because of the approaching seventieth anniversary of the Bolshevik revolution and the upcoming Washington summit. Gorbachev imposed a veil of secrecy on the dispute. Yeltsin assumed his normal seat in the leadership lineup at the parliamentary session the next day, as if nothing out of the ordinary had happened.

For Yeltsin, it was the end of one life and the beginning of another, from which he would continually try to make a political comeback. More important for his country, it was the beginning of open dissent in the Central Committee, something very new, which was not immediately apparent but which was soon to put a fresh stamp on Kremlin politics.

When Secretary of State George Shultz met with the Soviet leader the next day to finalize arrangements for the Washington summit, Gorbachev's mood was bad. As one American put it later, he bore the special pain of a man determined not to show pain. Frustrated by his domestic opponents, he hit out at the Americans, unexpectedly raising a new objection to Reagan's SDI position, telling Shultz that he wanted more concessions on SDI before he would set the date for the summit. It was odd; both Shultz and Shevardnadze had said previously that an agreement on elimination of medium-range nuclear arms had been completed. Unaware of the fierce internal struggles, the Americans saw his behavior as rash and mercurial, or, more likely, as a ploy to extract—by bluff—last-minute advantages. The American administration was still reeling from Black Monday, the disastrous Wall Street selling panic four days earlier, and Gorbachev may have been tempted to exploit Reagan's political vulnerability.

But there can be little doubt that the overriding concern was his trouble in the Central Committee, and possible future moves by his conservative enemies.

A few days later, Gorbachev reversed himself. Shevardnadze flew to Washington and reached an agreement that the third Reagan-Gorbachev summit would take place December 7–10. Tentative plans were set also for a Reagan visit to Moscow in 1988.

While Shevardnadze was in Washington, leaks evidently emanating from the conservative camp and designed to inflict more damage on Gorbachev reached Western correspondents in Moscow. The stories depicted Yeltsin as breaking ranks with Gorbachev over the slow pace of change and accusing the leader of developing a "cult of personality" that threatened to undermine the program.[32] Rumors suggested that Yeltsin had also accused Raisa Gorbachev of meddling in affairs of state—a point the conservatives had been making for months. Much later, while speaking privately with a prominent American, Gorbachev conceded that he had great difficulties in keeping together the "center-left" coalition to hold off his enemies on the conservative right. Both were for reforms, but whereas the left wanted more glasnost and democracy, the center wanted merely economic modernization. "My enemies are on the right," Gorbachev said, "but the ammunition is provided by the left."[33]

The Yeltsin affair, ignited by Yeltsin's assault on the conservatives, had weakened Gorbachev's position. Four days after the November 7 holiday, Yeltsin was publicly dismissed and replaced by Politburo member Lev Zaikov as Moscow party chief. Two days later, November 13, the entire Soviet press carried two pages of bitter denunciation of Yeltsin as a man who could only criticize destructively and who placed personal ambition above party interests. Despite such massive and unprecedented publicity given to a leadership argument—which some claimed as a victory for glasnost—the whole business smelled of old Kremlin clique politics. The voluminous charges contradicted everything that was previously known about Yeltsin, creating a crisis of confidence with the public. "How could it be that the man we all admired suddenly turns out to be an enemy of the people?" one Muscovite commented. The language used by some conservatives was so outrageous that it shocked many people instead of convincing them. Many were reminded of Stalin-era trials when "traitors" were vilified at hate meetings. Yeltsin was accused of vanity, political adventurism, and demagoguery; he was described as a man of "feudal revolutionary talk" and "pseudo-decisiveness." Many speakers described him as the old-fashioned Brezhnev type that he had constantly criticized. One of the recurring charges was that Yeltsin had delivered "a calculating stab in the back of the party" with his speech on October 21. But the speech that sparked the controversy was not published—another echo of the clique politics of the past.

The announcement of Yeltsin's dismissal coincided with an ominous development on the cultural scene. That very day, the Moscow authorities suddenly closed down an exhibition of works by avant-garde sculptor Vadim Sidur. Officially derided by the Soviet Union until his death in 1986, Sidur had been rehabilitated in the summer of 1987 and hailed as one of Russia's greatest artists. Asked for an explanation of the sudden decision, Sidur's son was told, "We have to consider the interests of the state first and foremost."

The Yeltsin affair was a blow to Gorbachev's authority. His process of political democratization had come under severe attack. A one-line joke that was a play on two similar Russian words—*perestroika* and *peretryaska*—summed up the popular feeling: "Restructuring *(perestroika)* is dead; now there is Shakeup *(peretryaska)*." As he struggled to advance his policy, Gorbachev knew his dream was being thwarted by his own party. Most likely it was at that time that he realized that the task of reforming the party was too daunting and intractable and that, to use Lenin's concept, he had to find "another way to go" around it. He had already called for a party conference, an equivalent to a party congress, to adopt political reforms the following June. And though he would struggle to win control over the conference and have it bend to his wishes, Gorbachev was haunted from that point on by the imperative to find a way to get around the party and its Central Committee. Eventually he would come up with what he thought was the answer.

But, for the moment, he accommodated himself to the realities of Soviet politics. "Politics is the art of the possible," he had written just that summer. "Beyond the limits of the possible begins adventurism."[34] He had to suppress his litigiousness. Having to choose between Yeltsin and the powerful Ligachev group, he chose the politically expedient course of jettisoning Yeltsin without siding with Ligachev.

Having to lose such a loyal and honest supporter was a personal setback for Gorbachev. He acknowledged that he had known beforehand of Yeltsin's intention to resign, but said that he thought he had persuaded him not to rock the boat just before the November 7 celebrations. One thing that seemed to hurt Gorbachev personally wsa that Yeltsin could not wait. What made Yeltsin assail the conservatives just at that moment is a puzzle. There is no question that the opposition had drawn a net around him and was itching to settle accounts with the man who had gone after their privileges. Perhaps his frustrations just overflowed. Worn out by his endeavors and by the unending intrigues against him, which were accompanied by a vicious campaign of slander, he simply decided he had had enough. Or perhaps, a complete maverick, he decided it was precisely the time to draw attention, with his suicidal speech, to conservative attempts to halt perestroika. He conceded later that he was disappointed that Gorbachev had not forcefully come to his rescue.[35]

Yeltsin's main sin was that he was too passionate about perestroika, that he had embarked on a wholesale housecleaning in Moscow and begun a serious attack on party privileges. Of all the people in the Politburo, he was the figure most clearly in Gorbachev's own image. For a majority of people, he was exactly what glasnost and perestroika stood for. He became most vulnerable because he was ebullient, almost outrageously open, because he actually believed in Gorbachev's proposition that it was "either democracy or social inertia and conservatism—there is no other way, comrades."[36] But Gorbachev without Yeltsin would have to find another way, one that lay between the two. In the meantime, almost overnight, Yeltsin became a factor in national politics and a folk hero, particularly among the young.

There were attempts to gather signatures for a petition in his behalf, and independent clubs organized street marches to protest his dismissal; police broke up several meetings organized by independent clubs and organizations to discuss the incident.[37] A few days later Yeltsin was appointed first deputy chairman of the State Construction Committee, a ministerial position. It was another incomprehensible outcome of the turmoil.

Now, under crisis conditions, Gorbachev's standing seemed precarious, and glasnost in jeopardy. The change in atmosphere was painfully obvious. Students at the Moscow Pedagogical Institute who had collected signatures on a petition demanding the whole truth about the Yeltsin affair were summoned before the party committee and chastised. The cooler climate was heralded in a *Pravda* article about party discipline. "Playing into democracy may result in catastrophe," *Pravda* warned. "It is often forgotten that discipline means obligatory submission by everybody to the established order and rules."[38]

As if Yeltsin had been only a stand-in for Gorbachev, Ligachev shifted his tactics in the new atmosphere. He no longer sought to portray himself as only a well-disposed critic of some aspects of perestroika. He was its enemy. He felt that Gorbachev was too enthusiastic about market socialism, which Ligachev regarded as unsocialist and likely to produce chaos—unemployment, wage differentials, bankruptcies, and other destabilizing effects. He also viewed Gorbachev's flirting with workers' self-management as dangerous and smacking of anarchy. But his principal concerns were glasnost and democratization, which he felt would lead to a dangerous loss of party control. He came out openly against such schemes as freedom of choice in party elections, secret balloting, multiple candidates, and a compulsory retirement age. And he came back time and again in the second half of 1987 to his concerns about the emergence of organized groups outside the traditional political system, something Gorbachev supporters, Yeltsin in particular, had encouraged.

Given the stalemate at the top, Gorbachev too began to change his tactics. He gradually eased up on his criticism of the party. He knew that perestroika had no future without political reforms, and since the party was not able to reform itself he had to find a way of curbing its power, and he had to move it altogether from the business of managing the economy.

It was at that time, in late 1987, according to political scientist

Fyodor Burlatsky, who was close to Gorbachev, that the idea of presidential government was first discussed seriously in the small circle of Gorbachev advisers. Nobody knew how to go about it, but one way to get around the top echelon of the party bureaucracy was to change the constitution and create a strong executive. Some advisers argued that the president should be elected by popular vote. Nobody knew at that point what was in Gorbachev's mind.[39]

Chapter 15

CONFRONTING THE BIG LIE

Gorbachev used the seventieth anniversary celebrations of the Bolshevik revolution to break new ground on the troublesome question of Soviet history. He wanted to deliver his own speech, outlining his broader sense of history, but his enemies would not have it. He had to speak on behalf of the Central Committee, which meant that the speech had to be approved by the ruling group, and thus watered down by the conservatives. Despite the intervention, it was a courageous speech in which Gorbachev restored official respectability to Khrushchev and to Stalin's earlier opponents, Bukharin, Lev Kamenev, and Grigori Zinoviev (all murdered by the dictator). Gorbachev declared Stalin's guilt "before the party and the people, for the wholesale repressive measures and acts of lawlessness are enormous and unforgivable." He said that the process of rehabilitation of innocent victims of Stalin's terror, which was "actually suspended" by Brezhnev, had been resumed. (The Supreme Court chairman, Vladimir Terebilov, told *Pravda* on December 5, 1987, that 240 innocent victims of Stalin's terror had been rehabilitated.)

It was the first time a Soviet leader had spoken publicly about Stalin's terror, and to open old wounds on national television was extremely bold. But Gorbachev was distressed by the reaction to his speech.[1] His supporters were disappointed, felt that he had not gone far enough, that he had made substantial concessions to the conservatives by acknowledging Stalin's contribution to the country's development. He had charted the middle course and left both his supporters and his critics dissatisfied. Too battered by the Yeltsin affair to put up another fight, he had accepted the Central Committee's interference without much enthusiasm and with a good deal of misgiving. He had compromised, according to an aide, because he realized that the conservative opposition was burning with a special fuel of its own and he wanted to defuse it—defuse both bureaucratic momentum and individual ambition. The weapon he chose against them was movement. As long as he was constantly in motion, perestroika had a chance.

It was not quite clear whether Mikhail Gorbachev had finally begun to accept the fact that his political interests were not necessarily the same as those of other senior Communist Party officials, or whether he had known that all along but had realized that winter that there was little he could do to change their views.

For the first time, speaking to a conference of editors in December 1987, he openly hinted at his dispute with Ligachev, his ideology chief, by saying that "there is a certain intensification of resistance by conservative forces" to perestroika. "Naturally these people never say that they oppose perestroika," he continued. "Rather, they would have us believe that they are fighting against its negative side-effects, that they are guardians of the ideological principles that supposedly might be eroded by the increasing activities of the masses." Equally, he said, reiterating his earlier criticism of Yeltsin, there are those who are "overly zealous and impatient" and who thus harm the program. The party, he declared, "will not allow any departures from the principles of economic reform that we have adopted."

The more open disputes were apparent at the ancillary meetings of communist leaders during the celebrations of the revolution. Gorbachev personally presided over a meeting that gathered representatives of 178 various communist, socialist, and social-democratic parties and national liberation movements at the top floor of the Kremlin Palace of Congresses. (The Chinese Communist Party did not attend.) In an atmosphere of remarkable tolerance, communist and leftist leaders debated issues frankly—so frankly, in fact, that it was clear that the international communist and workers' movement at the end of the twentieth century was deeply divided on a number of basic issues and that Moscow would never again be able to control and dominate it completely, as they had done in Stalin's day. When a Swedish social-democrat firmly and directly condemned the Soviet invasion of Afghanistan and demanded an unconditional withdrawal of Russian forces, Gorbachev quipped, "We listened to you very carefully, Comrade Erickson." Other members of his delegation—Ligachev, Yakovlev, Ryzhkov—sat expressionless, as if nothing unusual had happened.

In his address, Gorbachev steered the gathering away from the doctrinal debates and polemics that had characterized similar consultations in the past and urged his colleagues to face the major issues of the twenty-first century. He stressed his New Thinking on relations between communist parties by criticizing the "arrogance of omniscience" practiced by his predecessors. What he was talking about, he said, was a "tenacious habit of rejecting other points of view out of hand," meaning that "there can be no dialogue, no productive discussion, and worst of all, the cause [of socialism] suffers." He was moving away from the old-fashioned interparty diplomacy, which often "sugar-coated the truth or, worse still, dealt in Aesopian fables."[2] It would be hard to imagine a more terrible blow for Moscow's old clients in Eastern Europe such as János Kádár of Hungary, Erich Honecker of East Germany, Todor Zhivkov of Bulgaria, or Gustav Husak of Czechoslovakia. With unsettling rapidity, Gorbachev was changing the rules in the middle of the game, as far as they were concerned. (Within less than a year, Kádár and Husak would be gently nudged out; by the end of 1989, all Warsaw Pact leaders with the exception of Poland's Jaruzelski would be disgraced. One of them, Nicolae Ceauşescu of Romania, would be executed.)

•   •   •

Not for the first time, Gorbachev dropped a political bomb on his allies, and then thrived on the foreign front. The December Washington summit was a success. Gorbachev and Reagan signed the first arms-elimination agreement of the nuclear age. Gorbachev had made major concessions. Moscow was to give up three times as many medium) and short-range missiles in Europe as would the United States. The British and French nuclear forces would remain intact, giving the West a margin of superiority in Europe. He accepted verification procedures so intrusive they astounded his military. (For thirteen years, teams of up to forty inspectors from each country were to monitor a missile plant on the other's territory, with the right to short-notice inspection of facilities.) The marshals had earlier complained about "unilateral disarmament," but Gorbachev's new defense minister, Dmitri Yazov, firmly supported his leader. He endorsed the concept of "strategic sufficiency" in a July 27 article in *Pravda*, although his notion that it meant "precisely the magnitude of the armed forces necessary to defend oneself against an attack from the outside" was sufficiently vague to suggest at the very least the military's lack of enthusiasm for the shift.

Gorbachev's concessions, however, successfully served his goal of snaring SDI. He had subtly exploited internal American disputes, particularly the differences between Senator Sam Nunn, chairman of the Armed Services Committee, and the right-wing hawks on Capitol Hill, and in the administration, over the interpretation of the 1972 Anti-Ballistic Missile (ABM) Treaty.

Part of Gorbachev's strategy was to ease tensions, making people in the West feel that he was the man they could do business with, a reassuringly reasonable leader. Gorbachev had carefully read David A. Stockman's *The Triumph of Politics,* and had grasped the essence of the American debate.[3] Given the fiscal problems, he understood that only in an atmosphere of anti-Soviet hysteria would Congress be moved to vote huge funds for SDI. It was therefore his primary objective to cool passions and make the concessions the Americans wanted; in the long run, these would strengthen his country rather than weaken it.

• • •

The treaty eliminating all medium-range nuclear missiles, which Gorbachev and Reagan signed on December 8, 1987, was hailed by both as a milestone in the nuclear age. For the first time, the two superpowers had agreed to eliminate an entire class of weapons, which accounted for about 3 percent of the nuclear potential in both countries—a slight downward adjustment in the amount of overkill.*

The Washington agreement was a major political step, and it stirred hope, both for an easing of the Cold War and for the possibility of a withdrawal from Afghanistan.

Talking with NBC's Tom Brokaw in a major televised interview on November 30, Gorbachev broke new ground by saying that he was prepared to accept a reasonable timetable for the withdrawal of Soviet troops if Reagan would accept a political solution of the problem. In that case, he said, "it could be done very quickly." Australia's prime minister, Bob Hawke, who met Gorbachev the next day, said the Soviet leader told him he considered a shorter timetable than twelve months. Gorbachev said he was in touch with Afghan leader General Najib and that "there might be an earlier withdrawal than contemplated." Australian diplomats accompanying Hawke right then noted that the Soviet leader was talking about the Afghan pullout as if it were something he had firmly decided to do, no matter what other parties did or said, and that he was going to do it soon. Two things held him back. One was the prospect of a total humiliation; the other was the fear that, if he pulled the troops out, his Afghan loyalists would be massacred. On these points he needed Reagan's help.

---

*The main points of the treaty include commitment by both sides to destroy all their missiles with ranges of three hundred to thirty-four hundred miles. The Russians have to scrap 683 missiles, about fifty of which were in Czechoslovakia and East Germany. The United States pledged to eliminate 396 Pershing Two and Tomahawk cruise missiles deployed in West Germany, Britain, Italy, and Belgium. In addition, West Germany agreed to dismantle seventy-two Pershing 1A missiles equipped with U.S. nuclear warheads. The longer-range missiles had to be destroyed within three years after the ratification of the treaty by both sides. The shorter-range missiles, deployed only by the Russians, had to be destroyed within three months after the ratification. The Russians had to give up far more nuclear warheads because their mobile SS-20 missiles carried multiple warheads.

Reagan at first asserted emphatically that the United States would not cut off supplies to the Afghan guerrillas while the Russians were withdrawing their forces. But subsequently a new policy of "symmetry" was worked out under which the United States would stop military aid to the resistance only as Moscow stopped military aid to the Kabul government; otherwise fresh aid would flow to both sides. Both leaders talked about another summit in 1988, to be crowned with further cuts in strategic missiles. Gorbachev ended his toast to Reagan with the words "Until we meet in Moscow." Reagan saw the treaty as "the beginning of a working relationship."

"We make history," Reagan said. "Changing its direction is within our power. However, such change is not easy and can be accomplished only when leaders of both sides have no illusions, talk with candor, and meet differences head on."

Abroad, Gorbachev was generally perceived as the driving force behind these changes, something conspicuously recognized by *Time,* which made him its Man of the Year for 1987. And the summit helped restore some of his political standing at home. The Russians were startled by his popularity in the United States and in the West in general. On the eve of his American visit, his 54-percent approval rating in the Gallup Poll was higher than that of most U.S. officials. American newspapers even talked of "Gorbymania" sweeping the United States. Americans were surprised by his confidence and self-assuredness, and his shrewd and skillful efforts to captivate the public by presenting himself as a new and different Soviet leader.

He engaged in retail politics, stopping his motorcade to shake hands with Washingtonians, an old Stavropol habit that had become the hallmark of his political style. He was passionate, combative, and frequently defensive during meetings with congressional leaders and U.S. media executives, and testy when questioned about the Soviet human-rights situation. "I told the president," Gorbachev said to the executives, "I'm not on trial here and you are not a judge to judge me. Let us treat each other as equals, or we will make no progress." Out of the range of television cameras, however, he was far more doctrinaire. "You don't hear in the meetings what you hear in the public commentary by Gorbachev," commented one U.S. official.

Gorbachev constantly displayed his tolerance and his familiarity with American studies of his country. When Marshall I. Goldman of the Harvard Russian Research Center presented him with a copy of his book critical of Soviet economic performance, Gorbachev instantly noted that he was familiar with its contents and that Soviet specialists had studied it closely. Meeting Stephen Cohen of Princeton, he voiced respect for his work, including a study of Bukharin. And he greeted one of the outspoken critics of the Soviet state, Richard Pipes of Harvard, by pointing out that he was familiar with Pipes's critical review of his own book *Perestroika*. "I see you didn't like my book," Gorbachev joked.

His American critics ascribed his success to his flair for public relations. (As Richard M. Nixon put it, Gorbachev "was born with a master's degree in public relations.") But there was, of course, more to the man than merely public-relations gimmickry. He was a charmer capable of intellectually seducing doubters, always trying to co-opt them, or at least to blunt the sharp edge of their criticism. He had listened to Reagan, and they had developed some rapport. Perhaps more significantly, he had won the hearts and minds of the majority of American people.

Buoyed by his success in Washington, Gorbachev badly wanted to work his magic on Deng Xiaoping, convinced that this was the way to a closer relationship with China. But Deng was having none of it. Gorbachev offered to meet with the Chinese and brief them on the outcome of the summit (as Khrushchev had done after his visit to the United States in 1959), going out of his way to point out that Moscow's differences with Beijing were not as great as those with the United States, but Deng turned him down. Instead, Gorbachev briefed his East European allies, and the Chinese received Soviet Deputy Foreign Minister Igor Rogachev. (The Americans sent Ambassador Edward Rowny to do the same.)

Nonetheless, the Chinese indicated some potential for dialogue. As if they recognized that they might become odd man out in the Washington-Moscow-Beijing power triangle, for the first time in three decades the Chinese media focused their full attention on the Soviet leader, and published an interview with Gorbachev in January 1988.

The summit euphoria carried over into 1988. Reagan and Gorbachev greeted the new year by exchanging televised addresses to their respective populations.

Success abroad, though it had an impact on the Soviet people, was not enough to spur them on to change. Gorbachev entered the year with perestroika moving in fits and starts. It had taken two and a half years, as Leonid Abalkin, the reformist economist who subsequently became deputy prime minister, acknowledged, "to reach an overall conception of the economic reform." The beginning of 1988 marked the second and crucial stage, when perestroika was expected to move "from word to deed." This stage, he added, would last until 1991, when the entire economy would shift to "completely new principles."[4]

The new year ushered in economic reforms in earnest. The reforms called for the creation of markets for goods in which prices are determined by costs, the output mix determined by supply and demand, and individual initiative rewarded by pay and status. This time changes were to happen on the national scale. As of January 1, the enterprises that accounted for 60 percent of nonmilitary production gained freedom to operate without day-to-day interference from Moscow. Once again, Gorbachev was up against formidable obstacles.

A military empire like Russia functions adequately as long as the towering magnificence of its leader is coupled with his stiff resolve to uphold the order. But Gorbachev's main objective was to dismantle the hierarchical military society at home and abandon the grand-style, costly, expansionist imperialism abroad. The latter had proved easier than the former.

Gorbachev was almost fifty-seven and physically vigorous, but he was showing the strains of endless political infighting, to say nothing of his self-imposed resolve to reorganize a country that had steadfastly refused to be organized. Most managers resisted attempts to take part in an experiment that was only vaguely outlined, and most bureaucrats were not about to force them. What was supposed to happen was not happening. Wholesale markets should have sprung up spontaneously, but buyers and sellers were not allowed to set prices. In the absence of wholesale markets, the ministries in Moscow remained the sole brokers. Enterprises continued to be dependent on ministries for scarce supplies and markets. Where ministries were eliminated, as was the one handling foreign trade, local enterprises simply did not know how to trade.

In the first months of 1988, it looked as if perestroika could be fatally crippled. Gorbachev argued vociferously with the conservatives about the need to encourage quasi-private agriculture and private and cooperative ventures to fill the gap in consumer services and light industries. No one argued against him. But, as poet Yevgeny Yevtushenko put it, "The first method of slowing down perestroika is sabotage in the guise of support. The second is stifling with embrace."[5] Many of Gorbachev's initiatives were losing force, diluted and distorted by entrenched interests, and especially as a result of political uncertainty at the top. Ligachev's victory in the Yeltsin affair and his opposition to the political component of Gorbachev's perestroika left most party apparatchiks reluctant to implement the reforms as long as there seemed to be a chance that the general secretary could be deposed.

Despite his great power, Gorbachev was the prisoner of his Central Committee; he dared not move head on against its conservative majority. Khrushchev's fate was on his mind, and he repeatedly mentioned it in various closed forums.

Indeed, in early January there was open speculation in Moscow that Gorbachev could be deposed at the forthcoming party conference in June, that this in fact was the objective of the conservatives, although one should not "underestimate the power and ability of Gorbachev to fight back."[6] Ligachev had dropped hints of his enhanced position while attending a congress of the French Communist Party in Paris in December 1987. He and Gorbachev were on the same wavelength, Ligachev said. "Following our Marxist-Leninst theory, it is impossible to have economic progress without democratization, and democratization without glasnost. It would be a joke." But he added that the Politburo had instructed him to "organize" the work of the Secretariat, the hub of power, which runs the day-to-day business of the country and which is the general secretary's source of power.[7] He was, Ligachev said, chairing the meetings of the Secretariat.

By early 1988, the conservative resurgence seemed to be getting the better of Gorbachev. More and more he appeared, even to his supporters, as a man facing pressures beyond his control, pushing ahead with new regulations and decrees, but giving the impression of having lost a sense of direction. Wags immediately came up with a riddle: "What's the difference between perestroika and chess? In chess you have to think before making a move."

Even as he appeared to be flailing, Gorbachev was looking for a new way to approach the question of political reforms. Searching for allies, he found the Russian Orthodox Church. From his experience in Privolnoe, he knew that Christianity remained remarkably tenacious, despite seven decades under the heel of an invariably hostile state. His own grandparents were religious; he said in a visit to Britain in 1984 that his grandparents had kept icons in their house, hidden behind portraits of Lenin and Stalin.[8]

In the spring of 1988, he seized the opportunity for a dramatic gesture of reconciliation with the church. He sent the signal with an unexpected live national television coverage of midnight Easter services at the Yelokhovsky Cathedral in Moscow. The gesture could hardly have been more spectacular; Easter is the most important holiday for Russian Orthodoxy. In the past, Easter and other religious holidays had made the Yelokhovsky Cathedral look like a church-state battleground. (Apart from uniformed police and plainclothesmen in the cathedral grounds, mounted police were deployed to keep believers from approaching, and the entire neighborhood was closed to traffic just to make sure that things were kept under control.) State television customarily ran its most popular programs during the Easter services, to encourage people to stay at home.

Following the Easter broadcast, Gorbachev made several other bold gestures, tying many of them to the recognition of the upcoming celebrations in 1988 of one thousand years of Christianity in Russia. A master of symbolism, he invited the seventy-seven-year-old church primate, Patriarch Pimen, and other members of the Church Synod to the Kremlin, to signal a more relaxed climate for the faithful. It was the first publicized Kremlin reception of the Russian Orthodox hierarchy since the days of World War Two. The only precedent was a meeting on September 4, 1943, between Stalin and the church leaders, at which Stalin formally recognized the church's help in the war effort.

In welcoming the prelates, Gorabachev talked about the faithful in terms indicating that they were full-fledged citizens of the country and that they would be protected by a "new law on the freedom of conscience, now being drafted, [which] will reflect the interests of religious organizations as well." This, he said, was a "tangible" result of his new approach to state-church relations. Believers were also beneficiaries of and responsible for "perestroika and democratization—in full measure and without any restrictions." He wanted them on his side. Gorbachev condemned past antireligious repressions as a "departure from socialist principles." Past mistakes, he added, "are being rectified." His administration wanted to reintegrate the church into the nation's life. "Churches, which are meant to perform purely religious functions, cannot keep away from complex problems that worry mankind or from the processes taking place in society."[9] He seemed to recognize that the best way to the people might be through the church, not the party.

Displaying a similar intent to woo the people, Gorbachev made a foreign-policy decision that was extremely popular at home. On February 8, 1988, he announced that he would start withdrawing Soviet troops from Afghanistan on May 15, and that all troops would be home by February 15, 1989.

By April 15, 1988, after weeks of feverish and complex diplomatic activity, an accord for the pullout of Soviet troops from Afghanistan was worked out and signed in Geneva. It was a face-saving document. Gorbachev, in fact, accepted the Soviet Union's defeat in the war, just as France had accepted defeat in Algeria, and the United States in Vietnam. Almost precisely two years after he publicly described Afghanistan as a "bleeding wound," he was beginning to cauterize it.[10] He also started the process of gradual disengagement from Kampuchea and Angola.

In yet another bold move, Gorbachev allowed the publication of Nadezhda Mandelshtam's memoir *Hope Against Hope* in the monthly journal *Yunost*. Her searing indictment of the Stalinist system, published in the West in 1970 but denounced in Brezhnev's Russia, was now hailed as "an epic description of the 1920s and 1930s." Her husband, poet Osip Mandelshtam, had been a victim of Stalin's purges. Now she was no longer condemned as a dissident or a traitor, but was hailed as a distinguished chronicler of her times who "unconditionally condemned the moral and cultural barbarity of those years."

The avalanche of events made it difficult to sort out what spelled genuine change and what might be a public-relations gimmick, and watching Gorbachev himself seemed the only clue to understanding. Gorbachev was entering his fourth year in power as a world figure. Even those who had known him well before he moved into the top slot were surprised by his sensitivity, his majesty, his arrogance, his boundless yet shrewd ambition, his capacity to grow. There were many Mikhail Gorbachevs. Like any successful politician, he had schemed to enact his policies and enlarge his authority. He had learned whose egos to stroke and when. His bluster, if he was given to garrulousness, was largely on the outside; on the inside, he was tough, considerate, thoughtful, he did his homework, and he could be reasoned with.

But there was also in him something of the provincial boy's illusion that the world was made of wax that could be shaped. He wanted to shape a better future. He came across as an incorrigible optimist. But, spectacular though they were, his reforms were not moving the country. Glasnost, which had initially opened up the world of polit-ical and moral ideas, had begun to degenerate into traditional Rus-sian intellectual feudings, which were bound to undermine the very purpose of his policy.

One has to assume, since he retained power, that Gorbachev had a better sense of the balance of conflicting forces than did most of his opponents. That he had turned toward foreign policy at this stage was only partly explained by his yearning to deal with issues where he could seize the initiative, display imagination, and control events. The other side was that he wanted to open up Russia to the outside world, to show his citizens how those of other nations live. Slowly,

Soviet television began to display a realistic picture of Western living standards, which were higher than Soviet standards. Gone were the doctored versions of the past, when the screen showed life in the West as one of penury and injustice.

Gorbachev was changing in front of the nation's eyes. The growth of his mind was best reflected in his ideological approach. With the exception of Lenin, all his predecessors had gone into the past to seek a philosophical basis for their actions. Gorbachev, while trying to link his policies to Lenin's teaching, was heading toward something new. In his future, no icons of the past were as holy as they used to be.

There was an important stylistic change too. He gradually came around to accepting the ironies of the modern age and the absence of permanence. One of the characteristics of the long Brezhnev era was its yearning for stability in a world that was rapidly changing. Gorbachev was a product of that era, which valued stability and regularity. Yet he was introducing upheaval and instability in Soviet life, taking down the fixed guideposts, generating a spasm of self-doubts, a reinterpretation of the nation's past, so that even Lenin, the sage who had remained inviolate after the initial ravages of glasnost, now came under public scrutiny. One wide-ranging debate in the pages of the communist youth weekly newspaper *Molodoi Leninets* focused on an incident involving two young men who angrily destroyed with their fists a portrait of Lenin. Some letters to the editor charged this was an act of hooliganism, while others supported the destruction. "I am completely on the side of" the two young men, wrote Sergei Chepesyuk, twenty-four, from Shadrinsk. "I think that the youths had punched nothing 'sacred' but merely the portrait of a man whose teaching brought us to what we have today." Chepesyuk broadened the argument to say that Lenin himself was against public adulation of his personality, and that it was the party bureaucracy hiding "behind the leader's name" that was engaged in the lawlessness of the 1930s and which in the fifties, sixties, and seventies "did their dirty deeds pushing the country to the level of economic stagnation and political demagoguery." New generations should not allow the party bureaucracy to use Lenin as a "shield" for its actions.[11]

Perhaps his view of himself was changing too. On the one hand, he had become much more a politician (in the Western sense of the word) than any of his predecessors, adapting himself to evolving situations and using different tactics. He was trying to put together a grass-roots coalition, and having great difficulties with it—a curious coalition, consisting of the intellectuals, young people, women, the Russian Orthodox believers, and a progressive minority of the party. But his political jargon and his ideas were more American than Russian, reminding many observers of John F. Kennedy. Even his themes were Kennedyesque, dealing with the limitation of power and focusing on human destiny in the postnuclear era. He advocated nuclear disarmament and collective security, for they constituted "the only possible way that mankind can regain immortality." He believed in the force of ideas and reason, no matter how impractical.

On the other hand, the longer he stayed in power, the more he tended to identify himself with the office of the Kremlin tsars. He appeared to be losing his Stavropol touch, his knack for simplicity. He was very much aware of the power he represented, and usually received guests in Saint Catherine's Hall in the Kremlin. In dealing with the American president, the Gorbachevs chose the even grander Saint George's Hall and waited at the entrance as Ronald and Nancy Reagan climbed the long marble staircase. It was clearly a calculated scene, the imperial splendor of Russia weighing on the insignificance of the individual.

By the spring of 1988, Gorbachev had acquired the stature of a major statesman in the field of foreign affairs. But if his dealings with foreign potentates gave him a degree of majesty, his domestic opponents took it away.

Divisions in the Kremlin and in the party bureaucracy seemed bound to sap his energies. The continual struggles between reformers and conservatives over virtually each significant issue made Gorbachev appear as a man incapable of delegating authority and running a modern government. Sophisticated forces within the leadership itself were now arrayed against him, quietly contradicting his publicly stated views and challenging his position. This led him to seek more power, and he began to rationalize it by using the logic of another pioneer communist reformer, the late Marshal Tito of Yugoslavia, who had argued that "Economic reforms are impossible in Communist systems; what is possible are political reforms with economic consequences."[12] The way out was to create a strong executive that would take day-to-day decisionmaking away from the Politburo and the Central Committee, a French-style presidential system of government that would permit him to circumvent the Politburo consensus and the endless arguments and compromises it involved.

If he was to succeed, he had to be given full powers, which meant a reform of the political system. He wanted to have this resolved at the June 1988 party conference. He used to have an obsession with consensus; he had been trying to sign up as many people as possible to his policy, wanting to make it a policy that the broadest range of Central Committee members and other party worthies found acceptable and bearable. But consensus, he began to realize, was an illusion as far as economic and political reforms were concerned. A consensus might make him and others feel safer and more comfortable, but would not move perestroika forward. Once in power, he was no longer a consensus man, because he realized that, if he allowed someone like Ligachev to decide what was feasible and what was not, he would lose control over his own program. More and more, Gorbachev began to lean toward those in his entourage (among them Yakovlev) who argued the superiority of the politics of combat over the politics of consensus. The political scientist and *Literaturnaya Gazeta* columnist Fyodor Burlatsky, a Gorbachev confidant, a few months later provided a hint about "serious deficiencies" of consensus when he observed that Soviet leaders, because of the tradition of Politburo consensus, have to "fight for real authority"—and that this fight resulted in either "expedient and one-sided solutions or a paralysis of power." Each Soviet leader spent "about five years to gain one way or another the supremacy" over his other Politburo colleagues. This struggle brought about an atrophy of the political brain. The implacable consensus was also at the root of the problem of succession. Burlatsky savagely attacked the fact that a Politburo consensus was crucial to one's chances of becoming the country's leader. "Our experience shows that this is fraught with serious shortcomings. Otherwise it is impossible to explain how a great country like ours could have such leaders as L. I. Brezhnev and K. U. Chernenko."[13]

Yakovlev's view was crucial to Gorbachev. He favored the politics of combat only as a tactical device to break the impasse. He had developed strong admiration for his chief, whom he saw as a man who had a sense of history, who knew that the best decisions are often the loneliest ones, and who now wanted to be a strong executive. He felt that Gorbachev could be trusted with power. Gorbachev detractors argued that he wanted to become an autocrat.

The conservative challenge came in March 1988, with perestroika making no visible progress and Gorbachev's reformists in disarray as a result of the Yeltsin affair. It came in the middle of one of the fiercest political battles in decades.

Chapter 16

AN ABORTIVE PUTSCH

Gorbachev began to curb the power of the party bureaucracy in earnest at the start of 1988. On the last day of January, a government announcement decreed a drastic reduction in the number of limousines servicing party and government officials. As of July 1, 1988, about four hundred thousand persons would lose one of the most sought-after symbols of the privileged bureaucrat—the ubiquitous black Volga sedan and chauffeur. The decree specified that the official cars were to be either sold to the public or turned into taxis. Another decree set July 1 as the day when Soviet citizens who possessed hard currency could no longer use it to shop in special hard-currency shops for foreigners.

Despite the wounds he had suffered in the trench warfare with the conservatives, Gorbachev had to plunge forward. His moves were similar to those taken by Khrushchev before his ouster. Recognizing the potential for similar recriminations against Gorbachev, his supporters in the media promptly stole the bureaucrats' fire. Khrushchev, a January article by the Novosti Press Agency said, was ousted in 1964 because "he had caused considerable pain to the bureaucracy by depriving it of a number of the privileges it had until then enjoyed."[1]

Also in January, monuments to the late leader Leonid Brezhnev began to disappear. They vanished during the night, as did signs spelling out his name on metal-and-concrete billboards. The fall from grace in this fashion is a peculiar Russian rite and served as a prelude to the discrediting of both Brezhnev and Chernenko. Stalin had denounced his political rivals and turned them into nonpersons; Khrushchev did the same to Stalin when he took charge upon the dictator's death. Brezhnev and his confederates took the same course when they ousted Khrushchev in a palace coup in 1964. The cycle was broken when Andropov succeeded Brezhnev in 1982. Despite its conspicuous compensatory merits—such as blaming all wrongs on discredited predecessors—Andropov felt it to be one of the reasons for the failure of the Soviet state to develop civic respect for its own institutions.

The removal of Brezhnev monuments could not occur without at least the tacit approval of Gorbachev, and the fact that he allowed his supporters to resort to this odious rite (which was, by its very nature, contradictory to the ideology of perestroika and glasnost) revealed the weakness of his position. He had previously sought to provide a balanced assessment of Brezhnev's long rule. In December 1986 *Pravda* noted the eightieth anniversary of Brezhnev's birth by addressing directly the failures of his leadership. Almost a year later Gorbachev himself criticized Brezhnev by name, saying that much of what he had proposed to do "remained on paper—was left suspended in the air." Yet he had resisted the howls of vengeful reformists calling for retribution against the Brezhnevites. Historians—not the government—should assess his predecessors. But now, despite all his talk about truth and reason, about breaking precedent, Gorbachev showed himself the prisoner of tactics he professed to disdain. Now the code phrase for Brezhnev's era was the "period of stagnation," and verbal salvos against it became more and more frequent. (Chernenko was almost totally ignored, as if he had never existed, as if Gorbachev had only contempt for the man who had defeated him in 1984, the same Chernenko whom Gorbachev had described as "the soul" of the Politburo in his February 1985 Supreme Soviet election-campaign speech.)

To diminish Brezhnev's stature, the Gorbachev administration did not confine itself to words. Brezhnev's son-in-law, General Yuri Churbanov, the former first deputy interior minister, was in jail awaiting trial on corruption charges—allegedly for having taken bribes in excess of $1.1 million. Brezhnev's private secretary for thirteen years, Gennady Brovin, was sentenced to nine years in prison, also on corruption charges. The scope of mismanagement during the "period of stagnation" loomed larger and larger as perestroika's problems became more difficult.

The conservatives were not taking the stepped-up criticism lightly. For months, tensions had been building between Gorbachev's increasingly radical group of reformers and the conservatives led by Ligachev. Though concerned about the threat to their power and privileges, the conservatives were waiting for an opportunity to stage an anti-Gorbachev putsch, staying viable by proclaiming faith and hiding doubts. By the spring, glasnost had become a weapon used by the enemies of glasnost.

The clamor within the party establishment for a resolution of political uncertainties took the form of an attempt to abort the scheduled Nineteenth Party Conference in June. Gorbachev managed to beat back the conservatives.[2] But he had little ammunition. Perestroika was at a delicate stage. Economic indicators were not encouraging. The GNP rose in 1987 by 3.3 percent over 1986, but Tass conceded that the figure was lower than expected. And other events—particularly the growing unrest in the southern republics—slowed down Gorbachev's drive.

First came Armenia. A group of Armenian intellectuals gathering petitions to press for reunification of Nagorno-Karabakh with Armenia had collected ninety thousand signatures, or about 75 percent of the entire adult Armenian population in the province. Armed with such evidence of grass-roots backing, the group traveled to Moscow in January 1988 and was received by Pyotr Demichev, an alternate member of the Politburo and deputy head of state. He saw nothing particularly sinister in this. Gorbachev people were later mortified to hear about Demichev's remarks, for they clearly sent a wrong signal. But that was in retrospect. Another delegation went to Moscow in early February and got an even warmer reception. The word had spread through the Armenian community in Nagorno-Karabakh that their petition would be accepted, and town councils one after another voted to rejoin Armenia. On February 20, the Council of People's Deputies, the region's highest governing body, dominated by the local branch of the Communist Party, formally approved a request to Moscow to redraw the internal political boundaries.

The Armenian action coincided with demonstrations in Yerevan, the capital of Armenia, against a plan to build a chemical plant in that city. Word of the Nagorno-Karabakh decision excited the crowd of protesting Armenian environmentalists who were gathering in Yerevan's central square, inspired by a clarion call to nationhood. Soon hundreds of thousands of Armenians in the central square practically shut down the business of the city. In neighboring Azerbaijan, however, the nationalist fervor of Armenia produced alarming rumors of Christians murdering and raping Moslems. The chief of the Azerbaijan Communist Party, Kyamran Bagirov, rushed to Nagorno-Karabakh, which is under Azerbaijan's jurisdiction, stopping off on the way in Agdam, a predominantly Azerbaijani town, in an effort to calm the situation. But the emotions ran too high to curb. Two days later, on February 22, thousands of Azerbaijani Moslems from Agdam organized a protest march on the provincial capital of Stepanakert; they overturned cars, destroyed fences, and started burning things that stood in their way. The violence had started; unreason threatened to rend the skin of civility.

Moscow rushed in party inspectors to Baku and Yerevan, appealing for calm. The Nagorno-Karabakh Communist Party chief was dismissed. He was replaced by Ghenirki Pogosian, who had voted for rejoining the region to Armenia. Planeloads of soldiers arrived in Yerevan and were deployed around key strategic points in the city. The crowd in the city's central square continued to swell, and reports estimated a gathering of five hundred thousand. Some claim one million people were in downtown Yerevan at the peak of this uncannily peaceful protest. The crowds remained disciplined. Katolikos Vasgen I, the head of the Armenian church, had appeared on television, calling for restraint. So did Gorbachev, speaking through his aides. He was conscious that glasnost had unleashed a grave political quandary for him in Armenia, and he summoned prominent Armenian intellectuals to Moscow for a conversation.

Poet Silva Kaputikian and writer Zori Balaian came away impressed by his grasp of the convoluted history of the region and his pledge to seek a resolution of the problem. They also felt he was well disposed toward the Armenian cause, although Gorbachev had made no specific promises. Balaian told the crowd in Yerevan's central square that Gorbachev understood their problem, and they subsequently voted to disband.

Just when things seemed to be calming down, an explosion of ethnic resentment occurred on February 28 in the Azerbaijani city of Sumgait, about fifteen miles from Baku. Sumgait, the petrochemical center on the bank of the Caspian Sea, had a large percentage of Christian Armenians living among the Moslem Azerbaijanis. The two communities were so fatefully enmeshed in underground fears and antagonism, so entrapped by history in the ethos of violence, that the destructive instincts in an atmosphere of wild rumors could be touched off by almost anything or anyone.

A federal prosecutor's report was the spark. It announced that two young Azerbaijanis had been killed two days earlier in the ethnic disorders in the town of Agdam. The inadvertent implication was that they were killed by Armenians. A crowd of wild Azerbaijanis went on a rampage in Sumgait, looking for Armenians. More than thirty persons were brutally murdered.

Although the violence was subsequently contained and the communist leaders of Azerbaijan and Armenia replaced by new figures, the dilemma remained. Gorbachev seemed unwilling to tamper with the boundaries, something that would set a disturbing precedent in his multinational country. Rather, he thought in terms of concessions to Armenians in Nagorno-Karabakh, such as more control over schools and TV broadcasting—which proved to be unacceptable both to the Armenians and to the Azerbaijanis. A few months later Nagorno-Karabakh was accorded special status: formally, it remained under the administrative jurisdiction of Azerbaijan; informally the disputed enclave was brought under Moscow's direct control. But this was done after a great deal of violence and tragedy.

The specter of ethnic turmoil disturbed the country. Russian nationalists, professing concerns about possible repercussions for the stability of the empire, privately blamed Gorbachev. Conservatives did so openly. That some issues could be settled without much fuss—such as the Crimean Tatar problem—only seemed to annoy the conservatives. Eleven months after their July 1987 protest demonstrations in Red Square, the Tatars were granted the right to return to the Crimean homeland from which they were forcibly deported by Stalin in 1944. A state commission headed by Gromyko, however, ruled out the possibility of the re-establishment of an autonomous administrative unit for the Crimean Tatars. But the commission made the assertion that "the present administrative-territorial division of the country, which came to exist many decades ago, has been sealed in the Constitution" and could not be changed by a government decree; this annoyed the Armenians.

In the aftermath of the Nagorno-Karabakh dispute, the national minorities question was of particular importance. In essential ways, it suddenly become Gorbachev's biggest single issue, as well as his most acute point of vulnerability. The dispute gave a foretaste of supremely difficult issues to come. The problem was how to manage them. Glasnost had unleashed the novel concept of popular will in a country lacking experience with and machinery to accommodate it. The reformers had been too busy with a host of other problems to deal with that of national minorities. Even after the first anti-Russian disturbances in Kazakhstan, they did not develop a coherent policy for reconciling the inevitable emergence of nationalist aspirations with glasnost, democratization, and economic decentralization.

Gorbachev would have to find a way to satisfy at least some of the aspirations of non-Russians while keeping the structure intact. The only solution was more decentralization, but the conservatives grumbled. Khrushchev, they said, had destabilized Eastern Europe with his de-Stalinization; now Gorbachev was destabilizing the Soviet Union itself.

The disarray of the Gorbachev camp became even greater as the June party conference approached. He had been firmly convinced that democracy in the party would favor his program. He had fought a long and bruising battle the previous winter to have the party select delegates by secret ballot, only to discover that most people were concerned with their narrow interests and that secret ballots favored the established party machinery. Unless the rules were changed, Gorbachev partisans argued, the June conference would be dominated by a "conservative minority."[3]

"Democracy," it became apparent, worked in favor of the established Brezhnevite party members, who knew how to manipulate the bureaucracy and who knew clearly what they did not want. That Gorbachev's belief in orderly procedures and fair means was misplaced became clear when he and his aides were forced to resort to deception and vote-fixing to ensure the selection of Gorbachev supporters as delegates to the party conference. Here they were trying to do the right thing, one senior official confided, only to see democracy work against them. This was because the conservatives were not reasonable; the whole system was not reasonable; they could not afford to be reasonable either.

Gorbachev was committed to using his office to educate the country, but his faith in his ability to "reason" with the people was shaken by the ethnic turmoil, and the enemy camp was growing. Some of the key figures already at odds with Gorbachev were grumbling in the background. Vitali Vorotnikov had distanced himself; so had KGB Chairman Viktor Chebrikov and Mikhail Solomentsev. Gromyko supported him, but it was a qualified support. "I am too old," Gromyko told an American visitor, "and I don't understand much of what they are doing. But we have to give the younger people a chance."[4]

Increasingly, Gorbachev was distracted from his strategic objectives by details. He was involved in everything, and he prepared for Politburo meetings as he had once prepared for exams, cramming facts and figures, thereby forcing ministers and other high officials to follow suit prior to their appearances before the ruling council. Top officials privately grumbled. He was too exacting a taskmaster.

From the outside, it seemed that Gorbachev had difficulties delegating power. In fact, he did not have enough people who could manage the pace and ambition of his program. Apart from Yakovlev, Shevardnadze, and Lukyanov, personnel chief Georgi Razumovsky and ideology secretary Vadim Medvedev had become intimates whom he consulted on a daily basis. But the more one contemplated Gorbachev's advisers, the more one was struck by their incessant and restless soul-searching. These men, with an immense and under-developed country to run, to bring forward into a modern world, spent a great deal of their time arguing theoretical and philosophical issues, and their uninhibited theorizing deadlocked Gorbachev's policies.

There were doubters even in Gorbachev's inner circle. A prominent American academic reported a fascinating insight from his private conversation with one of Gorbachev's top advisers and his scientist son. The son was putting forward arguments as to why perestroika was not getting anywhere and why its chances for success were diminishing. "Why don't you tell that to Gorbachev?" the son demanded. "I know that you are right," the Gorbachev adviser replied. "I know we can't succeed. But when I get in front of that warm and charming man who wants so much to do something for the country, I have no heart to tell him that we can't succeed."[5]

The public mood had changed too; perestroika was no longer an exciting challenge, but a difficult—some would say impossible—job to be done. Despite the great powers of Gorbachev's office, he did not possess the mystique of the Romanov tsars and their mandate from heaven, which served Alexander II when he carried out the emancipation of the serfs. Gorbachev was the first among equals, and he had to listen to his Politburo and Central Committee. They could remove him from office, unless he found a way to secure his power and diminish his dependency on the Politburo and the Central Committee.

The gravest challenge to Gorbachev's leadership came in March 1988, when he was in Yugoslavia on an official visit and his closest ally in the leadership, Alexander Yakovlev, was also out of the country, visiting Mongolia. Gorbachev's defense minister, General Dmitri Yazov, was also away, in Geneva for an extraordinary three-day meeting with United States Secretary of Defense Frank C. Carlucci. Ligachev and other conservatives launched "an uprising against Gorbachev and perestroika."[6]

The putsch began somewhat inconspicuously on March 13—on the eve of Gorbachev's departure for Belgrade—with the publication of an unusual article on page three of *Sovyetskaya Rossiya,* the organ of the Russian Republic's government, which is headed by Politburo member Vitali Vorotnikov. It appeared under the headline "Letter to the Editors from a Leningrad University Lecturer," and was signed by Nina Andreyeva.

Nobody in Gorbachev's immediate entourage focused that day on the meandering criticism of modernistic tendencies brought about by glasnost that spread over the entire page. Andreyeva was upset with rock-and-roll music, with new books and plays, and particularly with efforts to debunk Stalin. She denounced glasnost as a source of "ideological confusion" that had led to the "loss of political bearings" among students.

But within a day or two it became clear that the letter made forceful criticism of positions on which the reformers were most vulnerable. It suggested that the government had been hijacked by politicians with dubious communist credentials, whom it identified as adherents of "left-wing liberal intellectual socialism." Such people, it continued, "eschew proletarian collectivism in favor of the notion of 'the intrinsic value of the individual,' " refusing to recognize "the leading role of the party and the working class in building socialism and in perestroika." The question is, "Which class or stratum of society is the leading and mobilizing force of perestroika?"

The tone of Andreyeva's letter bore Ligachev's imprint. Indeed it was discovered later that the document had been heavily edited by journalists with links to Ligachev. It extolled Stalin as a leading "trailblazer" of socialism and generally struck the themes that Ligachev himself had emphasized previously:

> I can neither accept nor agree with too much that has appeared [in the press]. Talk about "terrorism," "the people's political servility," "spiritual slavery," "universal fear." It is not surprising that nihilistic sentiments are intensifying among the students and there are cases of ideological confusion, loss of political bearings.
>
> For example, what can young people gain from revelations

about "the counterrevolutionaries in the U.S.S.R. in the late twenties and early thirties," or about Stalin's "guilt." . . . Or the public reckoning of the number of "Stalinists" in various generations and social groups. Take, for example, the question of Stalin's position in our country's history. The industrialization, collectivization, and cultural revolution which brought our country to the ranks of great world powers are being forcibly squeezed into the "personality-cult" formula. All this is being questioned.

There is no question that this period was extremely harsh. But, then, we prepared young people for labor and defense without demoralizing their spiritual world with masterpieces imported from the other side or homegrown imitators of mass culture. Imaginary relatives were in no hurry to invite their fellow tribesmen to the "promised land," turning them into "refuseniks" of socialism.

It is the champions of "left-wing liberal socialism" who shape the tendency toward falsifying the history of socialism. They try to make us believe that the country's past was nothing but mistakes and crimes, keeping silent about the greatest achievements of the past and the present.

The authors of time-serving articles under the guise of moral and spiritual "cleansing" erode the dividing lines and criteria of scientific ideology, manipulate glasnost, and foster nonsocialist pluralism. Principles, comrades, must not be compromised on any pretext whatever.

It was, as Gorbachev supporters later called it, an "antiperestroika manifesto" calling for a decisive turn against the established policy.[7]

Emboldened by the victory over Yeltsin and by signs of weakening in the Gorbachev camp (some moderate figures in the leadership had grown resentful of the leader's repeated attempts to push policies before obtaining collective endorsement), and taking advantage of the absence of Gorbachev and so many of his key aides, Ligachev called a meeting of Soviet editors on March 14 to discuss party policy. As acting general secretary, he praised the *Sovyetskaya Rossiya* article and criticized glasnost. Tass, the official news agency, the same day drew the attention of editors across the country to the *Sovyetskaya Rossiya* piece, in effect instructing them to reprint it. At least forty-three newspapers did so.[8] Some editors refused to run the piece, and some even attacked it.[9] Heartened by the piece, the hard-line East German regime reprinted it in the party daily *Neues Deutschland. Pravda* editor-in-chief Viktor Afanasiev, who was now supporting Ligachev, called a staff meeting and chastised his subordinates for ignoring a piece as important as the Andreyeva letter. Ivan Laptiev, editor-in-chief of *Izvestia* and a strong Gorbachev supporter, called in the senior editors and announced that he would stick with Gorbachev all the way. But he seemed to be in the minority.

Ligachev's meeting with key editors helped propel the putsch into a more dangerous phase. The conservative right moved into action. Party lecturers hinted that the Andreyeva message represented the new line, a victory for Ligachev and his supporters, and roundtables were organized to discuss its ideological content in a positive light (one of them was even televised). One lecturer speaking to the party organization of Leningrad Television criticized Gorbachev by name, saying he was partly responsible for the ethnic unrest in Armenia and Azerbaijan. Gorbachev's economic adviser, Abel Aganbegyan, an Armenian, was accused of having made nationalistic comments that encouraged Armenian demands on Nagorno-Karabakh. (*Moscow News* said later that some people in the military also gave their support to the Andreyeva message.) The conservatives seemed to be moving toward a showdown.

Gorbachev, traveling in Yugoslavia, was alerted on the second day of his visit about Ligachev's gambit. Yugoslav hosts noted that each evening, after the official program had ended, the Soviet leader worked for at least three hours into the night, and talked at length with Vadim Medvedev, who was accompanying him.[10] If privately worried about the dangerous signals from Moscow, publicly he endured all with total stoicism. He was steady in his intent to bury the concept of the "Brezhnev Doctrine," asserting that East European nations were free to choose their own political systems. (He reaffirmed this in his May 22 interview with the Washington *Post,* saying, "I can only confirm what I said. . . . I would only add that interference is unacceptable from any country.")

Neither Gorbachev nor Yakovlev seemed eager to react to Ligachev's manipulation of the journalists when they returned to Moscow on the 18th and 19th respectively. The mood in the capital had changed starkly, however. Ligachev supporters were on the offensive. Among the intellectuals there were widespread speculations that Gorbachev's bold new policies had already been crushed.

Yakovlev assessed the damage. He could take heart from the fact that Ligachev and his allies had ineptly chosen to take a stand on the pro-Stalin platform, presumably anticipating that a conservative groundswell would force a change in the party line and even the removal of the general secretary. An investigation determined that Andreyeva had indeed written a letter denouncing glasnost and sent it first to *Pravda* and *Izvestia,* the two principal newspapers, the previous December.[11] Neither paper paid any attention to it, and Andreyeva then sent it to *Sovyetskaya Rossiya,* whose conservative editor, Valentin Chikin, seized on its contents for a potential anti-reformist salvo. The link to Ligachev was rumored to have been a journalist on Chikin's staff, Vladimir Denisov, who served as the paper's correspondent in Tomsk between 1978 and 1982, and who became closely acquainted with Ligachev during his last four years as Tomsk's party chief.[12] Some said Denisov was sent to Leningrad to work with Andreyeva on the article; others said the letter was expanded by Ligachev himself and embellished by his aides and then sent back to the paper.[13] Whatever the details, the piece summed up Ligachev's thinking on glasnost and perestroika.

Armed with this assessment, the Gorbachev people began preparing for a showdown. They were now in a position to decide when to bring the issue to a head. In purely procedural terms, Ligachev had been so sloppy as to leave himself open to attack. He had interfered in Yakovlev's official domain without advance consultation, a clear case of usurpation of authority (Yakovlev was in charge of the press and propaganda). Even those in the Politburo who sympathized with Ligachev's policies were unlikely to endorse the precedent he was setting. It was not merely a matter of Politburo courtesy. To endorse Ligachev's action would mean giving carte blanche to any Politburo member to go over, for example, to the KGB and issue orders whenever Chebrikov was out of town, undermining the KGB chief. It is an unwritten rule that members not interfere in one another's areas of responsibility.[14]

The issue was supremely difficult. Gorbachev wanted to finish Ligachev as a player, but, given Ligachev's bureaucratic support, Gorbachev knew that this had to be done gradually. He had to restrain some of his people, who yearned for a brutal assault on Ligachev. He wanted to solve the problem rather than create a Ligachev issue that might become a truly divisive battle.

An air of Byzantine intrigue hung over the Kremlin as Gorbachev waited for the moment to reassert his authority. He had consulted with General Yazov, the defense minister; Marshal Sergei Akhromeyev, the chief of staff; and several other ranking officers, to ensure the support of the armed forces. Word quickly filtered out to Gorbachev supporters that the crucial showdown was under way.

When Ligachev left for a scheduled trip to the Vologda region, north of Moscow, on March 27, Yakovlev summoned top editors to reassert the liberalizing course. He acknowledged the differences between Gorbachev and Ligachev and said that *Pravda* would run an authoritative response to the Andreyeva piece. On Thursday, March 31, the response, drafted by Yakovlev, was delivered to *Pravda*'s office. But there was nothing in *Pravda* over the weekend, and the reformers in the know were alarmed.

It was at this point that Gorbachev had to make a decisive stand. Once again he fell back on his most powerful weapon: his own willingness to quit if necessary, and his determination not to compromise the essence of his policy. He had to force a clear decision from a bitterly divided top bureaucracy.

In early April, after talking privately with each member of the leadership, Gorbachev brought the matter before the Politburo. The Marxist historian Roy Medvedev, who had been exonerated as a result of Gorbachev's victory, saw the events as a measure of Gorbachev's weakness. Medvedev, suddenly a respected and nationally recognized figure after two decades of officially imposed oblivion, pieced together the following account of Gorbachev's gamble:

After presenting to the members the facts about Ligachev's role in the Andreyeva affair, Gorbachev argued that he could not continue without an unequivocal endorsement of his policy, which included the publication in *Pravda* of the reply drafted by Yakovlev. (The text of Yakovlev's article was given to each member.) Conflicting signals, he said, threatened to derail the entire perestroika. Resting his case, he told the assembled leadership, "You should discuss this thoroughly, and you may decide that you want to have a new general secretary." Then he dramatically left the meeting. He went to his dacha to await their verdict.[15]

Gorbachev placed his career in the balance. His colleagues' limited commitment to his program was becoming increasingly questionable; his own position, increasingly untenable. And yet, as a gambler, he knew that none of his rivals could offer an alternative to his program, that a majority of his colleagues, even if they had serious reservations, knew deep in their hearts that the Soviet ship of state had reached the point of no return, and that any effort to reverse the course could ultimately prove disastrous.

What precisely happened inside the Politburo is not known. Despite the existing split, the Politburo backed the leader. Ligachev was given a mild formal reprimand for his role in the Andreyeva affair. Nothing was said in public about the Politburo decision, but the victory became clear on April 5, when the reply drafted by Yakovlev took up the entire second page of *Pravda*. Under the headline "Principles of Perestroika: Revolutionary Nature of Thinking and Acting," the document vigorously restated the need to press ahead with glasnost and perestroika. It called the Andreyeva letter a "manifesto" of antiperestroika forces "who bluntly propose stopping or else turning back altogether." Learning to live under conditions of broadening democracy and glasnost was "no easy learning process," the article said. It continued:

Some people have become confused and perplexed. The launching of democratization, the rejection of edict-based and command-based method of management and leadership, the expansion of glasnost, and the lifting of all manner of prohibition and restrictions have caused concern: aren't we shaking the very foundations of socialism and revising the principles of Marxism-Leninism?

"Don't rock the boat," others say intimidatingly. There are also those who bluntly propose stopping or else turning back altogether. [The Andreyeva article] was a reflection of such feeling.

The article is dominated by an essentially fatalistic view of history, which is totally removed from a genuine scientific perception of it, by a tendency to justify everything that has happened in history in terms of historical necessity. But the cult [of Stalin] was not inevitable. It is alien to the nature of socialism and only became possible because of deviations from fundamental socialist principles. The article expresses concern about the well-known spread of nihilism among a section of our young people. This disease is rooted in the past. It is the consequence of the spiritual diet that we fed to young people for decades and of the discrepancies between what was said on rostrums and what actually happened in real life.

Although disturbing questions lingered, the public mood after April 5 changed dramatically. The intellectuals were jubilant. The great Gorbachev victory ushered in a "Moscow Spring" of previously unknown freedoms.

But the internecine war was not over. Ligachev's supporters sought to push Gorbachev in a more radical direction, apparently figuring that this would prompt more moderate figures in the leadership to join the conservative resistance.

On April 13, KGB chairman Viktor Chebrikov joined the debate. In a speech in the Volga River city of Cheboksary, he complained about an "excess of attention" given to negative aspects of the Soviet past. But was he challenging the leader? The chasm was not clearly visible, although Gorbachev observed in a speech in Tashkent on April 15 that some figures were uncomfortable with his policy course. "The scope, the novelty, of problems along all the directions of the new stage of perestroika have, frankly speaking, frightened some people."[16]

The skirmishing also continued in the press. Even after *Pravda* printed Yakovlev's unsigned editorial, the party daily and the rest of the press went on to publish reader comments arguing with the denunciation. But that was the price Gorbachev had to pay to remain credible. And it was his willingness to pay that ultimately made an impact on the nation, ushering in a genuine and fierce political debate.

In the midst of these debates, Gorbachev supporters called for a change in the rules of delegate selection for the June conference. Unless that was done, they said, the conservatives in the Central Committee could "oust" Gorbachev. "The support of the party apparatus for our leader is by no means general or unanimous, or always sincere."[17] Never before had the Soviet press aired the idea that a Kremlin leader could be ousted. The sharpness of the political struggle was almost palpable.

The delegates' selection process became the legitimate arena for open battles as the conservatives sought to assemble an anti-Gorbachev coalition.

In several areas, only insurrections could dislodge the Brezhnevite machine. In the Siberian city of Omsk, about eight thousand angry citizens staged a demonstration after the local paper published the list of people (Brezhnev holdovers) elected to the conference.[18] On the island of Sakhalin, eleven and a half time zones east of Moscow, citizens took to the streets of Yuzhno-Sakhalinsk and at a rally in the central square voted no confidence in the Sakhalin party leadership. The crowd of more than a thousand then elected a group of eight deputies to act as an alternative government. After a "tumultuous week" of crisis, the reformers won, with backing from Moscow. The local party chief, Pyotr Tretyakov, was forced to resign, and corruption charges were raised against him and other members of the old committee. Gorbachev publicly endorsed the insurrection when he told a June 2 news conference that the decisions made were "necessary for the process of democratization on the Sakhalin island."

Under Gorbachev's very nose, however, in Moscow, his allies could not get nominated by their own local party organizations. Some of the most celebrated perestroika-supporters—among them the editor of *Moscow News,* Yegor Yakovlev, *Ogonyok* editor-in-chief Vitali Korotich, economists Leonid Abalkin, Tatyana Zaslavskaya, Nikolai Shmelyov, and Gavriil Popov, historian Yuri Afanasiev, and playwright Mikhail Shatrov—were rejected by local and district party committees, an indication of the conservatives' entrenchment and the fallout of the Yeltsin affair. The prospect of the most eloquent intellectual reformers' being barred from the conference posed so acute a problem that Gorbachev, at the last moment, personally attended the June 3 meeting of the Moscow city committee. He managed to have some of the rejected candidates added to the list of Moscow's 319 delegates, but he could not get the committee to accept writer Alexander Gelman, whom Gorbachev liked and praised publicly.

Despite the intensity of the political battles, outer decorum was being preserved. The only public occasion demanding the presence of all twelve Moscow-based Politburo members was the May 1 Red Square parade, and it was smiles all round. Gorbachev, dressed in a gray topcoat and trilby hat, struck up an animated conversation with Ligachev for the benefit of television cameras scanning the leaders atop the Lenin Mausoleum. On a VIP stand next to the mausoleum, Raisa Gorbachev, talking to reporters, expressed her satisfaction with the presence of Western ambassadors, who had been boycotting Red Square parades since the 1979 Soviet invasion of Afghanistan.

The next day, *Pravda*'s front page carried a long letter from a middle-level official denouncing Stalin, secrecy in Communist Party affairs, the absence of free debate, and careerism and corruption. The country's current predicaments, he said, are a result of dictatorship and the absence of accountability that led to the creation of a "parasitic" class of party bureaucrats. "The truth is that our errors and failings are, in the first instance, the failings of our party." And on May 7, while addressing top editors, Gorbachev acknowledged disagreements in the Kremlin. But, as he put it, there was "a real turmoil in the minds of many people," including those "at the top," but this was due more to "confusion and panic than to outright opposition."[19]

. . .

The reformers were gaining momentum, reflected in ever more force-ful attacks on Stalin by passionate perestroika-supporters. "I want to drive a stake through his heart so he can never rise again," said novelist Anatoly Rybakov, seventy-seven, explaining why he wanted to live a few years more. "I want to help kill once and for all the system he created." Among the many anti-Stalinist plays and books was a scathing satire staged by the student theater of Moscow State University, in which Stalin and his police chief, Beria, are the prin-cipal figures. The music was written by the country's leading com-poser, Alfred Shnitke, who put together an ironical mix of officially touted melodies from the Stalinist era to underscore the farcical character of the play, written by poet Viktor Korki.

Virtually all shadowy aspects of Soviet life came under public scrutiny through a chorus of old and new supporters of glasnost and perestroika, including Alexei Adzhubei and Nikolai Shmelyov, both sons-in-law of Khrushchev; writers Chingiz Aitmatov, Vasili Belov, Alexander Gelman, Grigori Baklanov, and Valentin Rasputin; poets Yevgeny Yevtushenko and Robert Rozhdestvensky; Dr. Slava Fy-odorov; space expert Roald Sagdeyev; writers Daniil Granin, Vla-dimir Drozd, Vasili Selyunin, Anatoly Strelyani, Leonid Pochivalov, Maya Ganina, and Larisa Vasilyeva; historian Yuri Afstafiev; and many others.

But the most conspicuous symbol of a new intellectual climate that spring was the return of celebrated defectors to the West. Yuri Lyubimov, seventy, the country's most prominent cultural fig-ure to defect (while visiting Great Britain in 1984, under Cher-nenko's rule) was soon followed by dancers Natalia Makarova and Rudolf Nureyev. The Soviet press began running interviews with those who remained in the West, such as novelist Georgi Vladimov and cellist Mstislav Rostropovich, and *Izvestia* called for the restoration of Soviet citizenship to Rostropovich. But Lyu-bimov's return was the most significant. Only Solzhenitsyn's pop-ularity and prestige loomed larger, and the Gorbachev people began talking about asking the writer to return home from his ex-ile in Vermont. Solzhenitsyn's eventual readmission to the Soviet Writers' Union—which in turn formally requested the Soviet Parliament to restore his Soviet citizenship—was to become the most unequivocal sign of change and fluidity.

With glasnost blossoming as never before, the entire country seemed to have become a vast debating society. From the point of view of the Brezhnev era, the Soviet Union was in the grip of an almost subversive spirit, lacking in due respect for Bolshevik propositions, and toying with dissident ideas for which people only a few years earlier were sentenced to long prison terms.

It was no longer clear what constituted the party line, since the party itself was bursting with polemical arguments. The debate over the proposed reforms started an avalanche of new ideas. One was to create local commissions to control the activities of the police and the KGB, and to remove the KGB entirely from the business of domestic law enforcement. Another was to establish the legal right for citizens to create any kind of public organization "provided their objectives and actions are not in contradiction" to the constitution.[20]

In Pushkin Square, intense young men and women argued politics in small groups and large, touching on all formerly taboo topics, as uniformed policemen watched and plainclothesmen pretended to be merely interested bystanders. This was a new experience for the country, a Hyde Park Corner in the center of Moscow. What was apparent was that the ability to speak openly had fortified the citizens' self-respect. Even those who were critical of Gorbachev felt a sense of reluctant kinship with him.

Opposition groups and independent clubs also debated the agenda for the forthcoming party conference as if they were going to take part in it. Nuclear physicist Andrei Sakharov, in fact, suggested that nonparty people be invited to the conference; the suggestion seemed ludicrous at the time, but it is a measure of the astonishingly rapid change in some aspects of Gorbachev's Soviet Union that six months later Sakharov was formally proposed to stand for election to the Supreme Soviet and was re-elected to the ruling council of the Soviet Academy of Sciences.

An alliance of independent Moscow clubs met at the Energetika House of Culture to debate political changes in the country and to push for changes such as the establishment of free trade unions, freedom of religion, abolition of travel and emigration restrictions, and new pension and consumer-protection legislation. The five-hour session was held with the knowledge and approval of Moscow party authorities, but most of the three-hundred-odd participants were young people in their twenties and thirties, many of them looking like a part of the beat generation, and most given to fiery rhetoric.

While new ideas were in the air and on the printed page, the leading reformist sociologist Tatyana Zaslavskaya and other key intellectuals in Gorbachev's camp publicly advanced proposals for the creation of "new social formations" outside the Communist Party, a sort of popular front or union, to promote perestroika. These new "formations" would not constitute a political opposition but, rather, would "supplement" the party's "established structure and its bureaucratic nature."[21]

Zaslavskaya's ideas were amplified by Boris Kurashvili, a senior member of the Institute of Government and Law, who proposed the creation of a Democratic Union to represent the interests of people who were not members of the Communist Party, who, he noted, "constitute the majority of the population." The proposed Democratic Union would provide an organizational home for many of the independent political and social groups. Though not a second political party, he said, the Democratic Union would be a new social organization performing "some of the functions" of a political party (and would field candidates in elections for local soviets). The Democratic Union would have its own national and local organizations and its own newspapers, and would carry out lobbying efforts, initiate legislative actions in the Supreme Soviet (parliament), and in general, scrutinize and criticize the performance of the government and party bureaucracy. In the course of 1988 and 1989 such political formations emerged in the Baltic republics and received the formal backing of local communist parties.

Kurashvili also became a strong advocate of the presidential system, but his concept differed from that favored by the majority of reformers. Kurashvili argued that "the general secretary of the Communist Party should be elected president of the Presidium of the

Supreme Soviet directly by the country's population," rather than by an expanded new parliament.[22] What about fears that the shift would deposit too much authority and power in the hands of one person? Kurashvili's answer was to strenghen the Presidium of the Supreme Soviet. "Thus the weight and role of the president of the Presidium will considerably grow, yet the collective head of state will remain. The Presidium will pass its decisions collectively," while the president would have a right of veto.

Coinciding with the stunning proliferation of open debate was a staggering transformation of television. On a single night in May, economist Gavriil Popov debated before a national audience the advantages and drawbacks of the two-party system, with the advantages outweighing the drawbacks, and Grigori Baklanov, editor of the literary journal *Znamya,* talked about people in the bureaucracy who wanted to oust Gorbachev.

Underlying glasnost was a broader strategy of power management. Power itself was not Gorbachev's objective, or an end in itself; rather, he exercised power to achieve certain long-term objectives—to make his country viable, more efficient, and ultimately stronger. He had insisted all along that perestroika was a process, and that glasnost was an instrument of policy, not its ultimate objective. But Gorbachev and his men were also aware that, if they could not impose perestroika and get the economic results they sought immediately, they at least could help change the climate and make perestroika inevitable at some later stage.

In that sense, the Moscow Spring of 1988 was heartening. It gave the first inkling of revival of public interest in politics, and thus raised hopes for a possible transformation of national values and purposes. Gorbachev was right in believing that national argument was the way to dispel national apathy and to focus attention on problem-solving. The people, he said, "are emerging from a state of social apathy and indifference."[23] He had won over the intellectuals and the believers, and made his most penetrating appeal to young people, who were most free of the legacies of the past. The gospel of glasnost and hope had stirred their finest instincts. The Russia of the spring and summer of 1988 was quite different from the Russia of the previous year. The country had come alive again, groping for its future.

On May 26, the reformers scored a major victory over the conservatives by convincing the normally docile Supreme Soviet to vote for a review of the tax law. Conservative bureaucrats had fought Gorbachev's efforts to promote private entrepreneurship by taxing individual and cooperative businesses at a top marginal rate of 90 percent. The punitive taxation forced many closures of businesses. The old law was repealed. On the same day, the parliament passed a new law designed to improve the status of cooperatives and to encourage their proliferation and growth. As of July, cooperatives, at least theoretically, were given equal status with state enterprises. Gorbachev had managed to lift restrictions on their size, reduce stipulations about which industries and services they could be involved in, and eliminate limits on personal earnings. The original law on private businesses, passed in 1986, had restricted cooperative membership to pensioners, students, and others without a regular job in the state sector. Now anybody could join.

The law itself, although radical, was no guarantee that the problems of private business would vanish. Bureaucratic resistance and ideological antipathy remained strong. A prosperous private pig farm in the Moscow area was burned down by arsonists who were envious of its owner's wealth. Yet the interesting thing about the law on cooperatives was that it advocated perestroika from the bottom up; the Law on the State Enterprise was being imposed on recalcitrant managers and bureaucrats from the top down. It was one solid step toward the institutionalization of perestroika.

In the midst of the "glasnost spring," Ronald Reagan arrived in Moscow. "There is no way I really can explain how I come to be here," Reagan told *Time* columnist Hugh Sidey on the fourth day of his May 1988 Moscow visit. There was an almost dreamlike quality to the visit. This was the man who five years earlier had declared Russia an "evil empire." Suddenly he had become Gorbachev's friend, his potential partner for a joint mission to Mars. Since both countries were already thinking about sending unmanned missions to the planet, Gorbachev said, why not do it jointly and make it cheaper? At the very least, the proposal made good public relations.

While there was little of substance that he and Reagan could discuss (he could not revive East-West talks on reducing conventional arms in Europe in the closing days of the Reagan administration), Gorbachev saw enormous propaganda benefits in the homage paid the Kremlin by such an extravagantly anticommunist figure as Ronald Reagan. This was a moment when pomp becomes substance. When they first met at Geneva in 1985, their relationship was tentative. At Reykjavík in 1986, Reagan suggested a peaceful private chat, and their talk marked the beginning of a personal relationship. By the time he came to Washington to sign the INF treaty, Gorbachev knew that Reagan would help him in Afghanistan, even though the Soviet Union itself would have to cope with the grave political consequences of the defeat there.

On the eve of Reagan's arrival in Moscow, Gorbachev publicly paid him an unusual tribute. "I would like to say that realism is an important quality in President Reagan as a politician," he said. "Who would have thought in the early eighties that it would be President Reagan who would sign with us the first nuclear-arms reduction agreement in history?"[24]

That the most conservative of postwar U.S. presidents should be ending his White House tenure with a visit to Moscow, describing the Kremlin leader as a "friend," seemed to confirm Gorbachev's course. He wanted the visit to symbolize the end of the Cold War and to define the framework of future relations. He and Reagan ushered in an "era of nuclear disarmament" on June 1, 1988, by exchanging ratification documents of the Intermediate-Range Nuclear Forces Treaty, which they had signed in Washington the previous December. The Cold War was not over, but the two men had agreed to an intermission, and the intermission was important.

The summit series, from Geneva to Reykjavík to Washington and finally to Moscow, was part of a process Gorbachev had set in motion as a means of gaining international acceptance for himself and his country. And it had worked. Now he could reap some of the benefits. In Washington he had to be on the offensive, making sure that the folks back home saw him as a forceful defender of Soviet interests. In Moscow he could afford to relax. This was clearly a more assured man than the Gorbachev of six months ago. He even looked different, seemed to have lost a little weight. His speech was more vivid and his manner more patient and courteous. He was a solicitous host, yet firm in dismissing Reagan's sermons about human rights and American values. He scored propaganda points by his physical vigor and the fact that he was twenty years younger. He was constantly animated, bursting with ideas and emotions, and generous enough at one point to rescue a tired and disengaged Reagan by cutting off reporters' questions.

He handled Reagan's transformed attitudes with directness, grace, and wit. "Somebody asked the president whether he still considered the Soviet Union to be an evil empire," Gorbachev said in a dinner speech, with an absence of gloating so conspicuous that he must have practiced it in advance. "He [Reagan] said no, and he said that within the walls of the Kremlin, next to the tsar's gun, right in the heart of the evil empire. We take note of that. As the ancient Greeks said, 'Everything flows, everything changes.' Everything is in a state of flux."

It came as a surprise to official Russians just how warmly Muscovites received Reagan. They lined the streets to cheer his motorcade. As the presidential car moved down Kalinin Prospekt, young people waved enthusiastically. When the Reagans made an impromptu visit to the Arbat, a pedestrian mall in the heart of Moscow, they were literally mobbed by friendly crowds. The speeches he delivered to the students of Lomonosov University and to the Soviet writers and intellectuals were perhaps his most spectacular performances and touched the deepest chords of the Russian psyche. The Russians loved him.[25]

"I'm not religious," commented a Muscovite, "but I was delighted to hear him end his speeches by saying 'God bless you.' We never heard it said before on television."

Much of the credit for a judicious selection of themes and the overall approach to Russians undoubtedly goes to Ambassador Jack Matlock. In Matlock, the United States had as its envoy a man who was not only a superb diplomat but also a superb student of the Soviet Union.

With Russia turning inward and absorbed in its own self-exploration, Matlock saw the openings available to Reagan for reaching the ordinary people. Under his guidance, the president hosted a meeting with dissidents and refuseniks, and he forcefully defended religious freedom when meeting with the church leaders at the Danilov Monastery, which had recently been returned to the church. ("We pray that the return of this monastery signals a willingness to return to believers the thousands of other houses of worship which are now closed.") Yet in every speech Reagan took care to compliment Gorbachev on the liberalization already achieved, deliberately trying to give his host a boost prior to the June 28 party conference.

But before the conference took place, there was one more major round with Ligachev, so charged that it almost eclipsed the summit. As Reagan's visit progressed in an orderly way, the already bitter political debate over the conference suddenly escalated when Boris Yeltsin assailed Ligachev in an interview with the British Broadcasting Corporation and called for Ligachev's removal.

However humiliating his ouster from the Politburo a year earlier, Yeltsin remained loyal to Gorbachev. Chafing in isolation when his nature yearned to act, he remained a respected figure in the country, and his views were certain to influence the atmosphere at the party conference, if not its outcome. Vendors in the city's Izmailovo Park sold buttons with his picture and a caption that translates as "Tell 'em Yeltsin." Still a member of the Central Committee, he had also been elected to attend the party conference as a delegate from Karelia, a province near Finland.

Yeltsin had already identified the problem of Ligachev at the Central Committee meeting the previous October, but his speech was never published. Now he took advantage of foreign television to force the issue. Ligachev was responsible for the slow pace of perestroika in the party, he told the BBC interviewer. "It would be possible to develop the process more actively with someone else in his post." Pressed to answer whether he believed that Ligachev should be removed, he said, "Yes." Ligachev was the reason that democratization in the party had not developed properly. The style and methods of party work remained authoritarian, Yeltsin said. This was Ligachev's responsibility. He was an opponent of social justice; he did not support the elimination of privileges for the party elite.

Ligachev was stung. With the world press focusing on the Moscow summit, he became news throughout the globe. On the last day of the summit, when Gorbachev was asked, during a live, nationally televised press conference, about Yeltsin's BBC interview, he was forced to reaffirm his support for Ligachev and to call on the BBC to provide an unedited tape of Yeltsin's interview so that the Central Committee could establish exactly what he had said and "demand that he explain his position." But this backhanded support did even more damage to Ligachev. The very fact that his authority was publicly questioned placed him in an untenable position, and it was a key moment in the battle between conservatives and reformers. The reformers were trying to whip up support for the blueprint for political reforms at the party conference. Endorsed by the Central Committee in late May, the blueprint included a number of proposals that Ligachev opposed—limited terms of office, a shift of power from party committees to elected councils, and competitive elections at all levels. They were Gorbachev reforms, and Gorbachev rightly described himself during the June 1 press conference as "the main author" of the document.

Ligachev fought back. In a speech in Togliatti, the industrial city on the Volga, he contended that "adversaries in the West and some people in our country too" were resorting to "a notorious trick" by making allegations about differences in the Politburo. He and all other Politburo members were fully committed to Gorbachev's perestroika, he said, and its success depended on Communist Party control. But then, no longer resorting to the Aesopian language of opposition, Ligachev assailed the essential aspects of Gorbachev's program: "Foreign voices want the Soviet Union to have a political opposition and are dishing up to us the idea of a multiparty system. But if we consider the 'advice' that our country's economy be placed on the footing of Western market economies, little remains of socialism. All that is aimed at weakening the political stability in the country, upsetting social justice, and stimulating a far-reaching social stratification of society."[26]

The party was approaching the Nineteenth Party Conference in an unfamiliar atmosphere, quite unlike the carefully stage-managed affairs of the past. Ligachev's public humiliation had left his supporters confused and distressed. But they felt that time was working for them and for the millions of bureaucrats and ordinary people who had been appalled by the extent of the Gorbachev revolution. On the other side of the barricades, intellectuals were in turn alarmed, mystified, and exhilarated. The conference, they hoped, would be a decisive turning point of perestroika.

Chapter 17

THE MAKING
OF A PRESIDENT

The Nineteenth Conference of the Soviet Communist Party was the high-water mark of Gorbachev's reform. It was a time of transformation—a transformation potentially so far-reaching as to frighten both his supporters and his critics.

His admirers feared that he was trying to do too much too quickly, to introduce too many new ideas in too short a time. He was, they said, imprudently ignoring the mood of the country, severing himself from the people.

Critics saw him as a relentlessly ambitious man whose reckless ideas and policies were a threat to socialism in Russia. Writer Yuri Bondarev obliquely likened Gorbachev to an airplane pilot "who has taken off, but does not know where he is going to land,"[1] and Ligachev, presenting himself as the defender of "old values," immediately threw his "full and total support" behind Bondarev and used a similar metaphor to articulate his reservations about the leader's course. "As folk wisdom has it," the husky-voiced, feisty, implacable Ligachev said, "before entering the place, know the way out."

Well before the opening of the party conference, as is customary, the two main camps had reached a tenuous compromise on the guidelines and objectives for the conference. These decisions were made at the May Central Committee plenum, and Gorbachev had been in a position of strength in the wake of the reformers' victory in the Andreyeva affair and the orgy of glasnost it had unleashed. At that point Ligachev was vulnerable, so the plenum adopted many ideas more radical than would have been thought possible a year earlier. But the price was high. It was agreed that the party conference would advance only ideas and "recommendations"; implementation would. be left to later meetings. A part of the compromise was to forgo any personnel changes in the Central Committee, although the Conference was empowered to change up to twenty percent of the Central Committee's membership.

These were setbacks for Gorbachev. A year earlier—in his report to the June 1987 plenum—he had specifically singled out "changes in the composition of the central bodies of the party" as one of the tasks of past party conferences and one he hoped to perform at this conference. Under the terms set at the May plenum, the conference became more of an educational forum, but one in which he thrived. Despite the obsessive commitment to his vision, Gorbachev was a modern man who knew his limitations and could clearly see the possibilities open to him. Both his mind and his means were flexible. He was prepared to negotiate the means, but not the ends. Only perestroika was nonnegotiable.

Gorbachev sought to carve out for himself a "centrist" position. Like Stalin forty-seven years earlier, he used the device of a party conference as a surrogate forum for major decisions that otherwise would have to wait for the next five-yearly party congress, in 1991. Hence the occasion resembled a constitutional convention led by Gorbachev, and he was able to set up the basis for a new constitutional arrangement, adopted less than six months later.

In fact, the country was showing that it had outgrown the Brezhnevites. The communist-style organization notwithstanding, the conference demonstrated political stirrings of quite a new kind. It was a new political exercise, a reaching out on the part of the younger, better-educated administrators and intellectuals toward the concept of consensus.

For the first time in more than six decades, a good number of the five thousand delegates who gathered in the Kremlin Palace of Congresses on June 28 had been elected in real elections (for months, conservatives and reformers had struggled over local candidates in certain districts). They were a visible symbol of the fact that public opinion was a new (if fragile) factor in Soviet politics, and they gave the gathering its uniquely freewheeling tone.

The majority of conference participants, however, were there simply as part of the establishment chorus—if a divided one. But even these delegates, anxious to side with authority and showing sycophantic deference to their patrons, reflected the real balance of forces in the party itself. The mix provided for political theater that, while carefully choreographed, left enough room for unprecedented spontaneity. Several delegates openly disagreed with Gorbachev. And some real internal party arguments exploded on television screens, the most dramatic one on the last day, when Boris Yeltsin once again assumed his gadfly role in Soviet politics by openly assailing Ligachev and his conservative supporters as enemies of perestroika.

Gorbachev was in the thick of the action throughout the four days, as a somewhat domineering director, alternately coaxing, prodding, and hectoring his actors to achieve the desired effect. The party elite revealed itself in a dialogue with the leader and, by virtue of television, with the nation itself. It was a spectacle any orthodox communist would regard with the greatest of discomfort.

Gorbachev saw the open debate as an important precedent preparing the country for a transformation of national expectations and attitudes. It was another gamble, another extraordinary display of glasnost at work, in this case under the exacting conditions of TV broadcasts. Gorbachev could proudly say, as he did in his concluding remarks after four days of unequaled candor, that "this Palace of Congresses has not known such discussions, and I think we will not be mistaken in saying that nothing of the kind has occurred in our country for nearly six decades."[2]

Gorbachev understood that, in order to move the country, he had first to engage the imagination of the people. Education alone was not enough. The danger was the threat of fueling rising expectations. As an old Russian saying goes, "The question for reforming Russian rulers is how to build a fire that will not produce flames."

The conference, with all its turmoil and divisions, turned out to be an almost ideal setting for Gorbachev. He captured the nation's ear, using both spontaneous and engineered confrontations to make the failure of past policies manifest to people. The open confrontations would prepare the people for the new style of political activism he wanted to introduce—not necessarily democracy, but at least a system in which there were a number of players with different interests.

Gorbachev wanted a genuine national consensus for his proposed changes in the system, and winning that was not easy. Russia's government was founded on the rule of man, not of laws; the figure of the tsar or the general secretary was all-important. Since Stalin, general secretaries had been limited by the concept of "collective leadership," which was instituted to prevent the recurrence of bloody terror, but which at the same time seemed almost ideally designed to block the kind of reforms Gorbachev was promoting. The very nature of his program made it necessary for him constantly to defend his personal authority against opponents seeking to limit the scope of his decisions. Unless he achieved real reforms in the political system, he would be constantly at war with his opponents, and vulnerable whenever he left the country (as Ligachev had proved in April).

The conference revealed new as well as familiar temperamental traits. Gorbachev repeatedly succumbed to the temptation to use emotion as a tool in politics. He adroitly exploited people and events to make his views prevail. But all along he clung to the middle ground, an actor in continuous interaction with his audience, professing an aversion to the authoritarian tendencies of his conservative opponents, yet manipulating and hectoring others to do what he wanted done. He knew his program was worth fighting for, even fighting hard and a bit dirty. He had ensured that several perestroika-supporters would be on the rostrum, and they worked for his program.

One of the first speakers, actor Mikhail Ulyanov, made an impassioned speech against Stalinism, using the Andreyeva letter—the intimidation tactics that led to its broad publication—as an example of Stalinist authoritarianism now. "Do we today have such legal, juridical, political, constitutional guarantees of rights, laws which would protect us from possible uncontrolled administration by injunction or some other cult?" No, Ulyanov answered. Which means that evil forces that wish to "intimidate" people are real, something that "has been shown by the bitter and rather dreadful story of the article by Nina Andreyeva. Many—not all but many—stood to attention and waited for their next instructions." "It is to do with us," he added, after an interruption; "the fact that we took fright at her letter, that's what's terrible!"

Ulyanov made a forceful argument for freedom of the press. "We have a one-party system. But in nature, after all, everything is arranged according to the principle of the battle of opposites. And this is where we need the press, as an opposite force that can perfom the role of an opposition, if a need for this arises. . . . But in our country, some comrades would like to keep the whole of the press in their pocket."

Ulyanov was interrupted by Gorbachev, who sought to establish the middle position: "We should not give up the press, this national forum, to the domination of one group after another. Earlier there was one group, now we have another." His remark could be interpreted in several ways, but the main point was that he occupied the middle ground, frustrating the conservatives and forcing them further to the right. The writer Bondarev, spokesman for the right-wing conservatives, denounced the press for its "anarchic chatter, cheap sensations," and argued, "Through the press, we give the young not the truth, bitter though it may be, but a succession of disappointments flavored with cynicism." Bondarev attacked "our extremist criticism" for creating an atmosphere in which the "main postulate is—Let all the weeds flourish and all the evil forces compete."

Gorbachev claimed the middle ground the way a squash player claims the T. On the delicate question of personnel changes, again, voices more radical than his allowed him to respond as a moderate. This was essential, since a majority in his party supported the conservative faction in the leadership. Hence "the people" spoke in favor of a purge of Brezhnevite officials while he showed tolerance and moderation.

A delegate from Stavropol criticized Gorbachev for trying to "educate the bureaucrats with humane methods [when] in fact they ought to be stripped of their functions, quietly pensioned off, and [let us] be rid of them." Gorbachev interrupted the speaker, asserting, "If the Central Committee again starts to purge bureaucrats, we won't get anywhere." He was trying, he said somewhat ambiguously, to put the whole society "into motion, and then the bureaucrats will not know where to go."

At the afternoon meeting that same day (June 28), another delegate, Viktor Melnikov, became even more strident in demanding that party leaders who were identified with the "period of stagnation" be fired.

"Are you talking about me, or Ryzhkov here?" Gorbachev interrupted: who were the "stagnation leaders" who had to go? There was a sudden hush in the cavernous hall. Nothing so daring had ever been asked publicly at a party meeting of any kind.

"Both of us know who they are," Melnikov said, and the television cameras recorded his turn to Gorbachev as he ticked off the names of President Andrei Gromyko, Politburo member Mikhail Solomentsev, *Pravda* editor Viktor Afanasiev, and Georgi Arbatov, the director of the U.S.A. and Canada Institute as those among the "stagnation leaders."[3] (The inclusion of Arbatov was confusing since he was a perestroika supporter. He has served as adviser on U.S. policy to Brezhnev, Andropov, Chernenko, and Gorbachev.) Attention was instantly focused on Gromyko, who sat in the front bench next to Gorbachev, but his stony expression suggested pure indifference. At seventy-nine, he looked like an old man, his energies depleted, his engagement minimal.

Once publicly aired, the words acquired a life of their own. Later in the day, another delegate proposed not only that the "stagnation leaders" be dismissed but that their pensions be reduced. Asked at a press briefing about his attitude toward the proposals, one Gorbachev supporter, Roald Sagdeyev, the director of the Soviet Space Institute, looked into the television cameras and said he did not agree with the proposal that pensions be reduced. "I think their pensions should be increased," he said, "provided that they leave their posts as soon as possible. The sooner the better!" Russian journalists and officials inside the auditorium of the Foreign Ministry Press Center broke into thunderous applause.

Perhaps more than any other open conflict during the conference, the dramatic televised duel between Ligachev and Yeltsin generated an unprecedented surge of spontaneous mass interest in politics. Yeltsin had exposed the right problem—Ligachev—in October 1987. But he had done so at the wrong moment, doubtless doing a disservice to Gorbachev. Ever since, however, he had been performing a useful role for the reformists' cause, becoming a popular figure with the masses, especially the young. Again, his own radicalism allowed Gorbachev to claim the center of the political spectrum, to project himself as a sober figure who could not be blamed for being "leftist" and who was clearly not a conservative "rightist." The spectrum on the right ran from the amiable skepticism of Gromyko and Solomentsev, to the active conservatism of Ligachev and increasingly, Chebrikov, to the outright hostility of such figures as conservative Ukrainian party leader Vladimir Shcherbitsky, the most visible exponent of Stalinist-style politics in the country.

Still looking boyish and earnest despite his heart attack, Yeltsin addressed the conference and demanded his rehabilitation. The party, he said, should concentrate all its efforts on the problems that affect people's lives—food, consumer goods, services—or perestroika will turn "more and more into chatter." He attacked the conservatives, and singled out his nemesis, Ligachev. He felt exonerated by the tone of the conference, he said. "The issues I raised at the October 1987 plenum have been fully reflected in the speeches at the conference." ("I am asking for rehabilitation, at least while I am still alive," as Yeltsin put it acerbically.)

The clarity of Yeltsin's position made him look good in the eyes of the average Soviet citizen. (In early 1989, he was drafted by popular acclamation as candidate for a new parliament.) But his reception at the conference was less favorable. When he began his plea for rehabilitation, there were shouts in the hall demanding he be interrupted.

Gorbachev, unperturbed, promptly injected himself into the debate. "Say what you have to say, Boris Nikolaevich. . . . Let's remove the mystery from the Yeltsin affair. Let him say everything he believes he should say." And later Yeltsin defended Gorbachev: "I know he was sorry to condemn me and that at the time he was the comrade with most faith in me."[4]

When Ligachev took the rostrum, he addressed Yeltsin directly.

"You and I," he told him, "already differ not only on tactics but also on strategy." But Ligachev did not elucidate the differences, attacking Yeltsin personally rather than the ideas he represented. (In an attempt to establish his own credentials, Ligachev revealed that members of his own family had been either shot or jailed by Stalin, an extraordinary position for the party's chief ideologist, who has been publicly arguing against Gorbachev's wholesale assault on the late dictator. It was as if this fact alone gave Ligachev's views greater value and balance.)

As an incredulous nation watched this remarkable debate among its leaders, it was apparent that Ligachev was losing ground. He was a decent and well-meaning man, but his uncritical commitment to the conceptions of the past hardly equipped him to compete with Gorbachev or Yeltsin for the allegiance of a nation in ferment. And the virulence of his attack—he resorted to Stalinist witch-hunt rhetoric—did not go over well on live TV. There was too much venom, not enough subtlety, even for the rustics in his audience. Ligachev charged that Yeltsin was an inefficient and incompetent administrator of Moscow. Moreover, the people of Sverdlovsk had been starving during the years Yeltsin served as that Ural city's leader. He was a "destructive person" whose refusal to take much interest in Politburo discussions (before being ousted from the Politburo) was "monstrous." Ligachev presented Yeltsin's BBC interview, although it was arranged and approved by Soviet authorities, as his satanic link to the "bourgeois press." Ligachev, turning to his enemy, hurled a sarcastic barb that might also have been aimed at Gorbachev: "Do you like having all the foreigners pay attention to you, Boris?"

Finally, Ligachev decided to remind Gorbachev that he owed his post to him and other conservatives on the Politburo who had supported him following Chernenko's death in March 1985: "We have to tell the full truth: We were living through difficult days. I found myself at the center of these events, so I can have an opinion. Radically different decisions could have been made; there was a real danger. I can say that it is thanks to the firm position taken by Politburo members Chebrikov, Solomentsev, Gromyko, and by an important group of *obkom* [regional party committee] first secretaries that the March plenum made the only correct decision."

Under different circumstances, even a few months earlier, Ligachev's defense against Yeltsin and his evocation of the conservative stronghold might have worked. But they did not. Gorbachev's standing grew. In his closing speech, he criticized Yeltsin's tactical mistakes but not the strategic thrust of his proposals despite their radical tinge. Significantly, he failed to utter a single word of praise for his party deputy, Ligachev.

Here was Gorbachev's new politics. People had never seen anything like it before. The dramatic and open struggle between the reformers and conservatives provoked widespread discussions. Those citizens who did not see the exchanges on television rushed to buy newspapers to read the speeches. It was impossible to find a copy of *Pravda* or *Izvestia* in Moscow during the party conference (they were the only newspapers that printed all the conference speeches in full). Every speech at the conference was read avidly and analyzed religiously. For the average Soviet citizen, the conference clarified the issues and provided a clue to Gorbachev's vision of the future.

In the weeks preceding the conference, Gorbachev had read Klyuchevsky's *History of Russia*,[5] and it reinforced his conviction that the absence of an established constitutional order was the source of the country's weakness and perpetual predicaments. Klyuchevsky also reinforced Gorbachev's determination to concentrate on domestic reforms, avoiding at all costs foreign entanglements that would require the squandering of resources that were needed at home, and his determination to break the power stagnation by encouraging active and able men, natural leaders, to emerge at the local level and compete for higher offices.[6]

Gorbachev's immediate goal was constitutional reform, without which there could be no perestroika. He wanted a transfer of power from shadowy Communist Party committees to an elected parliament and an executive president and to elected local councils. His vision was a country based on the rule of law—the emergence of a "civil society" with legal safeguards protecting individual rights, and a political system accommodating plural interests.

He outlined his vision in his June 28 opening speech, an inspiring rhetorical masterpiece in a week of extraordinary speeches. The existing system, he said, was based "on command-style methods," including numerous bans, petty regimentation, and legal instruments designed to "hinder social development."[7] All new legislation, he said, must "unswervingly observe the principle that everything not prohibited by law is allowed"; the judges must be "independent and guided only by the law"; and there could be "absolutely no departure from the principle 'innocent until proven guilty.' "

Gorbachev placed the individual at the center of the system. The entire legal system, he said, was designed to protect a person's dignity and guarantee the "inviolability" of the privacy of his home, and the confidentiality of telephone communications and postal and telegraphic correspondence. Political freedoms had to be implemented to enable an individual "to express his opinion on any matter." He reiterated his commitment to ensure freedom of conscience for religious believers.

Referring to the ethnic turmoil in the Transcaucasus, he called for a re-examination of regulatory "instruments" dealing with the relationship between the federal state and its components to come up with a more precise definition of the status, rights, and duties of the federal state, its autonomous republics, and other ethnic entities. He urged patience, tolerance, and devolution of power to national republics. "Certain collisions may occur, and they can be only settled one way—by ensuring, within the exisiting state structure of our union, the greatest possible accommodation of the interests of each nation and nationality. . . . In our specific situation any other approach is simply impossible, and any attempt at moving in a different direction would lead to disaster."[8]

The entire political system had to be remolded and imbued with a sense of civic responsibility and tolerance. "It is high time we learned to listen closely to what an opponent is saying and not to regard him with invariable prejudice," for that was the way to find the best possible solutions.

A decentralization of power had to be pervasive. At the moment, he said, the Politburo and other top executive bodies "are forced to make decisions" on multitudes of questions that could be decided at local or regional levels. "It is just that everyone has grown used to the existing arrangement"—sending cables to Moscow for decisions on matters that "in fact should be settled locally." People, he said, should decide "those issues that are of direct concern to them" by using a "public vote at the village, district, or city level." Which meant that a "powerful political impulse as well as a clear legal basis" were needed to shift authority to local governments.

"Effecting a large-scale decentralization means to pump life-giving fresh blood into the capillaries of our political and economic system—but obviously without in any way disrupting the blood intake of the brain and the heart of our body politic."[9]

When Gorbachev unveiled his plans for the creation of a "fundamentally new state," he surprised virtually eveyone in the hall by proposing that a reinvigorated Supreme Soviet should be headed by a new executive chairman, or president, a job that was clearly tailored for himself. As general secretary, he would still be the country's ideological chief, but foreign affairs and defense would be the territory of the president. Yet he hinted that he would take both positions, noting that Lenin had combined the two roles as party leader and prime minister. "We must have the courage to admit that, if the political system remains immobile and unchanged, we will not cope with the task of reform."

His instinct was to seize all the power he could, because he knew the strength of opposition he had to overcome. But he sought to "democratize" the party itself, force genuine elections, and institute accountability. He wanted to move power into the hands of government units and leaders, thereby eliminating control and interference by the party bureaucracy. Gorbachev was taking the traditional Soviet theory of power one step further. The general secretary derives his power from being the representative of his party, the country's only legal political party, whose claim to legitimacy rests on the idea that it has a special understanding of what needs to be done to run the Soviet Union properly. Now Gorbachev himself was putting forward the claim that he knew better than anyone what had to be done to save the country.

Among Gorbachev's new ideas was a plan to make the party itself seek public support for its policies; another was to make it accept a form of meritocracy. During the debate, he offered a curiously diffident explanation of his party's claim to power: "We are a ruling party, and in any country it is the ruling party that forms the government at all levels, the executive and regional authorities. Some parties arrive there through revolutionary processes, by peaceful and nonpeaceful means; others arrive there through election—so to speak—campaigns. But it is the party currently in power that forms, that advances all cadres, so to speak, through democratic mechanisms, through relevant voting and so on, and it is the party that puts forward these proposals."

What upset the party bureaucrats was Gorbachev's insistence on "democratization" within the party. Under the new system, party secretaries at all levels would be elected by secret vote of party members. Then they faced another vote to become head of their local soviets, in which (if the traditional composition of the soviets was any guide) Communist Party members were outnumbered four to six by non–party members. Given the proliferation of informal groups and organizations, each of which was likely to field its own candidates to local soviets, party members saw the prospect of genuine competition and challenge to their authority.

The party, Gorbachev asserted, must go "through democratic verification procedures" and elections, because "this is necessary to tackle matters with the support of the will of the people." At that moment, he stopped and surveyed the hall. Many delegates looked puzzled; some shook their heads. "Well, I can already see that the Moscow secretaries are dissatisfied, shaking their heads as if, in all probability, to say, That's going too far. But that, comrades, is the only way."[10]

The backbone of the new "verification" procedure was a legislature that Gorbachev envisioned as more independent than the existing fifteen-hundred-strong Supreme Soviet (its members in the past were voted in in elections marked by ballot-rigging and apathy). He proposed to abolish the Supreme Soviet as it existed, but not to abolish the posts held by deputies. The Supreme Soviet would be replaced by the new body of 2,250 to be known as the Congress of People's Deputies, a type of electoral college that would meet once a year and elect about four hundred of its members to serve on a year-round sitting parliament. All deputies would be elected for a five-year term. The Council of Ministers, or the Cabinet, which had nearly a hundred members, would be pruned drastically. The president would nominate his own prime minister, who would be accountable to the Supreme Soviet. Cabinet members would be answerable to the parliament and would have to appear before it to explain or defend policies and actions. In the past, various Russian rulers tried similar schemes to circumvent the bureaucracy and established interests. Peter the Great introduced his new *kollegii,* or ministries, but was unable to alter the ingrained habits of the administrators. Alexander II introduced *zemstvo*s, or elective local councils, but they never managed to seize control from the bureaucracy. Khrushchev decided to break up the ruling Communist Party into two parts, but was equally unsuccessful.

For Gorbachev, the speech reflected more than three years of careful maneuvering. He sought to create an atmosphere in which change would not be an upheaval but an inexorable unfolding of the promise of perestroika—a "revolution without shots," as he had put it three years earlier.

Chapter 18

UNDER SIEGE

Gorbachev's assumption of the presidency was a deft political maneuver. According to the timetable adopted at the Nineteenth Party Conference, he was to take over the country's newly defined presidency in April 1989. But Gorbachev didn't want to wait. He moved to take over the post of president in its old form in late September 1988, and in the process staged the biggest Kremlin shakeup since Khrushchev's ouster in 1964. His precipitate move, in retrospect at least, seemed like an act of desperation, reflecting his frustration with the failure of perestroika to produce economic improvements more swiftly.

His irritation was understandable. Almost everything that could go wrong during the summer had gone wrong. He had hit an iceberg in Armenia. Only the military was able to keep peace in the disputed Nagorno-Karabakh after renewed ethnic violence. While Gorbachev was vacationing on the Black Sea in the summer of 1988, new grass-roots mass political movements sprang up in Lithuania, Latvia, Estonia, Armenia, and Georgia, all calling for "perestroika and national renewal" and all establishing formal nationalist mass organizations. Nationalist groups were also established in Karelia, which was once a part of Finland, and in Moldavia, which once belonged to Romania. The avalanche of factory sit-ins, demonstrations, and hunger strikes by nationalists soon escalated to ethnic unrest from the Baltics to the Transcaucasus.

The signs of incipient labor unrest prompted the Gorbachev men to start work on strike legislation. Trade-union chief Stepan Shalaev told industrial workers that, although "we do not need strikes, the right to strike must exist. If workers cannot make their voice heard through their factory's production committee or their trade union, they must have the chance to strike."[1]

The economy was in an ever more dire state. The latest State Central Statistical Committee figures revealed a disappointing harvest and massive financial losses from unprofitable enterprises. Figures published by *Izvestia* on October 3 indicated that 13 percent of the country's major industrial enterprises experienced losses during the previous year, amounting to a total of about $19 billion. Despite all of Gorbachev's efforts for economic reform, the party bureaucracy retained its stranglehold on economic decisionmaking.

Although the reformists continued to push the anticorruption campaign as a means of keeping the Brezhnevites off balance, the most conspicuous crackdown on chronic political mismanagement and graft, plunder, and crime was the case against Brezhnev's son-in-law, former First Deputy Interior Minister Yuri Churbanov, fifty-one. His trial opened in September, and confirmed some of the most notorious rumors of the early eighties. Churbanov admitted that he had accepted a briefcase stuffed with the equivalent of $200,000 from former Uzbek party leader and alternate Politburo member Sharaf Rashidov. He said the briefcase was delivered by an official named Umarov who told him that it was a present from Rashidov. "I opened the briefcase and inside there turned out to be 100,000 to 130,000 rubles [$170,000 to $220,000]. I wanted to return the money, but to whom? Umarov had gone, and it was awkward for me to raise the question with Rashidov." Hence he was "forced" to keep the money. "I was told it was a present, and I accepted it as such." Churbanov was subsequently convicted and sentenced to twelve years in a labor camp.

Gorbachev's problems extended beyond the borders. In Poland, an internal crisis was developing amid signs that the banned trade union Solidarity was regaining influence and exploring the limits of freedom in the Gorbachev empire. In Afghanistan, the withdrawing Soviet forces were subjected to repeated attacks and harassments.

(Rebel pressures diminished following the assassination of Pakistani President Zia ul-Haq on August 17, but then picked up again in the late fall.) A top Soviet diplomat, Yuli Vorontsov, first deputy foreign minister, was assigned temporarily as ambassador to Kabul to supervise the withdrawal and maintain a diplomatic grip on the evolving situation there. Gorbachev was committed to the February 15, 1989, date for the removal of all troops, but he was losing his ability to influence subsequent events in Afghanistan.

On September 2, while Gorbachev was still on summer vacation, KGB Chairman Chebrikov gave an interview to *Pravda* in which he renewed his attacks on grass-roots activism and independent political groups. The Western secret services "and subversive ideological centers," he said, "seeking to complicate perestroika, are trying to stimulate the organization of various kinds of clandestine, semilegal, and even legal associations in our country which would act at their bidding." He had to admit, Chebrikov said, that, as a consequence of these activities, "our political, military, and economic interests have suffered damage." All informal, nonofficial groups were suspect. They were being infiltrated by Western agents—and, fortunately, by KGB agents as well, Chebrikov noted—who were urging Soviet citizens "to take the road of direct struggle against the Soviet state and social system." This, he added, should be a warning to those who say that "we are becoming victims of our own spymania."

Gorbachev allies at the evening paper *Izvestia* came up with a quick and elegant riposte to Chebrikov that same day. Deriding his comment about the victims of the KGB's spymania, *Izvestia* published an interview with the country's chief cartographer, Viktor Yashchenko, who admitted that for half a century the Soviet people had been deliberately denied elementary knowledge about their own country. All public maps were falsified on the orders of the KGB; "almost everything was changed—roads and rivers were moved, city districts were tilted. . . . For example, on the tourist map of Moscow only the contours of the capital are accurate." This is senseless, Yashchenko said, because "the advent of satellite photography had allowed other countries to make their own accurate maps."

Ligachev, also taking advantage of Gorbachev's absence, first challenged Gorbachev's New Thinking on foreign affairs when he said in an August 5 speech that Moscow must base its policy on "the class nature of international relations. Any other formulation," he said, "only introduces confusion into the thinking of the Soviet people and of our friends abroad." Shortly afterwards he renewed his opposition to market socialism in a speech in Tula, south of Moscow. "Some people abroad very much want us to embrace a market economy," he said. "This would inevitably lead to the existence of a reserve pool of jobless and homeless."

Beyond such avowals of socialist orthodoxy was the intent to portray perestroika as a Western-inspired program and to cast the existing disputes into the traditional Slavophiles-versus-Westernizers mold. The Ligachev people too had gone after Abel Aganbegyan, who is an Armenian, blaming the economist for sparking nationalist unrest in the province. It was a ludicrous charge. The eruption of communal violence between Christian Armenians and Moslem Azerbaijanis in February 1988 reflected long-standing grievances and hostilities kept in check by strong-arm policies of the Kremlin; with glasnost in full bloom, Armenia only gave a foretaste of more ethnic discord to come.

That Gorbachev had thought long and hard about his next moves became apparent when, after returning to Moscow, he took off on a weeklong tour of Siberia and confronted complaints about the poor living conditions and absence of food. You must, he pleaded in Krasnoyarsk's Revolution Square before an angry crowd, "believe in our policy and in the leadership which is being formed."[2]

In the course of meeting ordinary people on the street and at work, Gorbachev discovered the depth of public resentment over food shortages. People demanded he visit the shops to see the dearth for himself. He was stunned by a firestorm of angry criticisms (the worst scenes were not shown on Soviet television). Ordinary people blamed him for the deteriorating food supplies. Some blamed his glasnost policy for creating nationalist unrest in the Baltics and the Caucasus. (A joke circulating in Moscow that fall revealed the depth of cynicism and doubt. "How do you translate 'perestroika' into English?" the joke goes. The answer is, "Science fiction.")

Nothing was functioning properly. People complained about severe housing shortages, a "disastrous" public-transport system, the lack of kindergartens and medical facilities. Industrial workers angrily charged that they were working under "inhuman conditions" because of the lack of ventilation. This was seen in the country for what in fact it was—Gorbachev was losing public support. His aides speculated that some of the attacks were orchestrated to show him up as an unpopular leader. This, in turn, could be a prelude to a coup. Either way, he was in trouble.

The clearest manifestation of Gorbachev's concern about his status with the people was his sudden retreat on his three-year-old anti-alcohol campaign. On September 16, Prime Minister Nikolai Ryzhkov announced in Moscow a relaxation of restrictions on the sale of beer, wine, and brandy at grocery shops. A government decree ordered an increase in the output of alcohol to meet demand. In a critical situation, this was the most expedient way to regain popular support.

The sounds of mutiny sent a shudder through the reformist camp. While Gorbachev was still touring Siberia, Fyodor Burlatsky published the first Soviet account of KGB involvement in the 1964 palace coup against Khrushchev.[3] It was a veiled warning that Gorbachev might be at risk. This was immediately followed by Sergei Khrushchev's serialized reminiscences in *Ogonyok* about the plot against his father that eventually led to his downfall.[4] His father, Sergei recalled, was seventy years old and tired. His eyesight was failing, and he no longer had the stomach for infighting, so even before the final showdown he laid himself wide open to total defeat by telling his colleagues, "I will not struggle." (In November, *Izvestia* published the first high-level account of Khrushchev's ouster, in the form of an interview with Gennady Voronov, who had been a Politburo member at the time. Acccording to Voronov, Brezhnev personally organized and led the coup. Voronov was not an impartial witness, however, since he was ousted from power in 1970 by Brezhnev.)

Infuriated by rumors of a coup against Gorbachev, his aides attempted to use the televised popular anger to their advantage. Gorbachev allies at Central Television cut some of the worst scenes from his Siberian trip and focused on those in which people demanded forceful action. Moscow Television showed crowds at Norilsk urging Gorbachev to "open fire at headquarters" and simply sweep away the opposition. Gorbachev insisted that he was not going to resort to Maoist techniques or to "apply the methods of 1937," a reference to Stalin's purges. (Mao Zedong's slogan "Open fire at the head-quarters" was used by the Red Guards during the Cultural Revolution, against critics of Mao's policy.)

The television screen revealed a shaken Gorbachev. It was as if, for the moment, he had lost his certainty about his own destiny and his own views. On the rebound, however, he was more articulate and more vivid than usual, and it was in Siberia, under enormous pressures, that he again proved himself an adroit politician. He defended his conciliatory approach. He did not want to become a tsar or dictator. Instead, he argued, the people should act. He was trying to help reverse the torpor of a society that had been abused, misruled, and deprived of the incentive to work or change. But the turnaround had to come from the people themselves.

"Every leader would like to open a box and offer the people the contents," he told chemical-factory workers. "But we have nothing to open." The people, he said, should no longer look to a tsar for help; rather, they should roll up their sleeves and start over. "It is time to abandon tsars and dictators," he said. "We need, of course, authoritative people and leaders, but [we need them] at all levels, from the bottom up."

On returning to Moscow, he was confronted by more trouble in the south, as ethnic violence between Armenians and Azerbaijanis escalated to severe outbreaks of gunfights and vandalism. Workers' strikes paralyzed industries in the area. Here, in an area where two ancient peoples lived at a claustrophobic range, the ancient ethic of "An eye for an eye and a tooth for a tooth" had led both into an impasse. The ethnic unrest now loomed larger than ever over Gorbachev's program. To curb the tumult, he decided on September 21 to declare a state of emergency in Nagorno-Karabakh and the neighboring Azerbaijani district of Agdam. At the same time, he ordered troop reinforcements dispatched overnight to Yerevan.

• • •

Gorbachev used his September 1988 speech at Krasnoyarsk, near the Chinese border, to make a new and forceful appeal to China. Conditions were ripe for the solution of the Kampuchean problems, he said. He was ready to meet Deng. But he also developed ideas first expressed at Vladivostok in 1986, reaffirming that Moscow wanted to play a useful role in the rapidly developing region. He wanted better relations with China and with Japan, and he emphasized the complementary nature of the two economies: Japan needed resources while resource-rich Siberia was next door. More and more he saw Siberia's development over the intermediate term as a broad program funded by foreign investors. He had to develop what Deng had pioneered: "special economic zones" with tax and regulatory easements that would provide a modern scientific and technological infrastructure for the processing of Siberian raw materials. The Russians increasingly looked at Singapore, Taiwan, and South Korea as well as Japan as partners in such ventures.

As he had at Vladivostok two years earlier, Gorbachev advanced a compehensive plan for strengthening security in the Asia-Pacific area, designed to improve Moscow's political ties with a minimum of damage to its military positions. One imaginative ploy involved his offer to abandon naval facilities at Cam Ranh Bay in Vietnam if the United States scrapped its bases in the Philippines. Another dealt with the controversial radar facility at Krasnoyarsk, which the United States contends was built in violation of the 1972 ABM Treaty and which Gorbachev offered to turn into an international space center (Washington demanded its dismantling). The other proposals called for multilateral talks to reduce the level of military confrontation in the area where the coasts of China, Japan, North and South Korea, and the Soviet Union converge. When the Vietnamese leader Vo Chi Cong flew to Moscow on September 20, Gorbachev told him firmly that he wanted the Kampuchean conflict settled. The only question remaining was the timing of Vietnamese withdrawals. The Chinese position was also shifting, especially after the soothing ministrations of Soviet Ambassador Oleg Troyanovsky, who asserted in two interviews with a Shanghai paper that an improvement in Sino-Soviet relations was not directed against the United States but would, rather, contribute to an improvement in Soviet-American relations. Beijing was sensitive to the concept of the "China card" and anyone's playing it.

At home, Gorbachev had to demonstrate that he would brook no more interference in the adoption of the decisions of the party conference.

In the fall of 1988, with Ligachev on vacation, Gorbachev caught his opponents off guard when he suddenly called for an emergency plenum of the Central Committee. Surprise was the weapon. They were preparing for a showdown later in the year; he would present them with a *fait accompli,* expecting that a majority would give in, as they had done before, and approve giving the leader a broader mandate. If he accepted the status quo even for a few months, it would mean a grave threat to his entire program and to his authority as leader. He was coldly determined to mobilize all the resources of public pressure and personal power to force the pace of change.

Gorbachev's address to Soviet editors on September 23 was one of his most sparkling talks, feigning a casual confidence while in fact coming close to conceding despair. Perestroika did not work, he said. "We are going slowly, we are losing time, and this means we are losing the game. In short, it turns out there is a gap between our goals and our work." He talked of a "complex mosaic of moods, confusion . . . illusions, impatience, and irritation" that perestroika was confronting, and then added, somewhat ominously, that his opponents on the right and the left were working together to exacerbate confusion. He was held responsible for the mismanagement of his predecessors. But he would stick it out. "Partial, isolated measures" would never drag the country out of stagnation, he said.

A couple of days later, he reiterated his determination to impose his will in a television report that included a conversation with East German leader Erich Honecker, the staunch conservative who was then still fighting a rearguard action against perestroika. Honecker and Gorbachev were visiting an East German exhibition in Moscow, accompanied by most other Politburo members except Ligachev.

Gorbachev was a polite host, but adamant. "Every one of the present burning problems underlines the necessity for radical change," he declared in his toast to Honecker.[5]

The emergency meeting of the Central Committee, set for September 30, followed by an extraordinary session of the Supreme Soviet on October 1, were given an alarming sense of urgency by the fact that they were made public on Wednesday, September 28, in violation of parliamentary procedures requiring a month's advance notice so such meetings could be announced in the press. Many top officials were abroad on official business: Shevardnadze was in New York attending the UN General Assembly session; Defense Minister Yazov was in India; Marshal Sergei Akhromeyev, the chief of staff, was on a visit to Sweden. Akhromeyev left for Stockholm on Wednesday as scheduled, only to turn around immediately and return to Moscow. Senior Soviet ambassadors who were members of the Central Committee had to break their schedules, alerting host governments that something unusual was afoot in Moscow. Shevardnadze, who had been due to remain in New York until October 3, hastily sought to reschedule several important engagements there before leaving. A meeting with China's Foreign Minister, Qian Qichen, was pushed forward and produced the dramatic announcement that Qian would visit Moscow later in 1988, the first such visit in more than a quarter-century.

In less than sixty minutes on Friday, September 30, the Central Committee accepted Gorbachev's agenda. Much attention, naturally, focused on personnel changes, especially the retirement of Andrei Gromyko. But the most significant changes involved the ostensible promotion of Chebrikov to head a new Legal Commission (thereby forcing him to relinquish his job as KGB chairman) and the shifting of Ligachev to a new position, a shift that experts saw as a "lateral move downward." Both men were neutralized. Their new positions were announced at a press conference by Vadim Medvedev, the newly elected Politburo member given the role of ideological spokesman, replacing Ligachev. (Also sent into retirement were Politburo member Mikhail Solomentsev, nonvoting Politburo members Pyotr Demichev and Vladimir Dolgikh, and Central Com-

mittee Secretary Anatoly Dobrynin. In addition to Medvedev's promotion, Anatoly Lukyanov, Alexander Vlasov, and Alexandra
Biryukova were elected nonvoting members of the Politburo.)

When the rout of perestroika opponents was announced by radio,
Moscow's intellectuals were jubilant, their mood matching the
splendid Indian summer. The next day, in a short, forty-five-minute
session of the Supreme Soviet in the Grand Kremlin Palace, Gromyko, whose career spanned five decades of Soviet power, retired
as Soviet president at the age of seventy-nine, and Lev Zaikov proposed Gorbachev as the only candidate for the post. The predictable
endorsement was greeted by stormy applause.

Gorbachev smiled broadly. When he took the floor to thank the
delegates, he paid a warm tribute to Gromyko "for his tireless work
in the interest of our people and our country." Although much of
Gromyko's handling of foreign policy had been implicitly renounced,
he was given a dignified send-off. Gorbachev saw to it that the old
man, who had played a key role in his own election to the post of
general secretary four years earlier, was extended all the courtesies.
What happened behind the scenes is murky, although Gromyko,
who ostensibly asked to be relieved of his duties as president, stared
passively during the vote and demonstratively failed to raise his hand
in support of the motion. He was, he said later, sad to leave the
leadership, "but age is a stubborn thing and one has to take it into
account." (Gromyko died several months later, sixteen days before
his eightieth birthday.) Pyotr Demichev, the old Brezhnevite who
had served as minister of culture until he was made first vice-president, was unceremoniously relieved of his duties and replaced by
Gorbachev's Law School colleague Anatoly Lukyanov. By Monday,
Vitaly Vorotnikov was kicked upstairs and replaced as prime minister
of the Russian republic, the largest of the fifteen that make up the
Soviet Union, by Alexander Vlasov, fifty-six.

Although it was the personnel reshuffle that caught the headlines,
Gorbachev's structural changes were far more important. As a grand
design it was impressive; however, a closer look at the details raised
questions about the ultimate soundness of the structure. Here was,
finally, a genuine assault on the party monopoly of power, which
was the very essence of the Stalinist regime. And orchestrating po-

litical reforms was a game of endurance, as in soccer, Gorbachev's favorite sport, your defense may be beleaguered and straining, but you've suddenly got to turn positions around to your maximum advantage. And score. That's what mattered.

Gorbachev had scored. Until then, the October 1 unanimous endorsement of his proposals, the Soviet economy was run by a plethora of ministries, but the real power was in the hands of ten departments of the Central Committee which "supervised" their work. The two chains of command (with the party's secretive and unaccountable "departments" having the final say) ultimately meant the absence of accountability. Gorbachev's changes were supposed to remove the party bureaucracy from economic decisionmaking, and thereby liberate his economy. Real power was to be transferred to the ministries. "Guidance" of the economy was given to two newly established Central Committee commissions, which replaced the ten Central Committee departments. One commission, for agricultrue, was headed by Ligachev; the others, on socioeconomic policy, by Nikolai Slyunkov, fifty-nine, a Gorbachev ally. The number of government jobs to be cut was in the thousands, but nowhere near the forecast seven hundred thousand. His sickle did not go deep, and the purge affected mostly senior ranks.

But the reform of the decisionmaking process went deeper. Under the old system, the Politburo decided policy while the Secretariat was in charge of day-to-day affairs. The Secretariat, which consisted of eight to twelve secretaries, prepared issues for Politburo consideration. Overlapping responsibilities frequently led to inaction or confusion. Some Politburo members were also secretaries, which broadened their authority and power. The apparatus, thus diffused, often strangled the leader's true intentions. All decisions came to represent the lowest common denominator of bureaucratic thinking.

Under the new system, there was no Secretariat as such. Instead, on the pattern of "Cabinet" responsibility, each Politburo member was assigned functions and responsibilities that were clearly defined and publicized. Apart from Gorbachev, who was president and general secretary, there were the prime minister, the leaders of Moscow and the Ukraine, the foreign minister, and the heads of the six new commissions dealing with agriculture, socioeconomic policy, international affairs, ideology, internal affairs, and personnel—the last headed by nonvoting Politburo member and Gorbachev protégé Georgi Razumovsky, fifty-two.

The reforms erased the established patterns of authority. Only Lukyanov was clearly Gorbachev's deputy, as first vice-president. The position of "second secretary" in the party hierarchy was dissolved. Ligachev, who was Gorbachev's deputy by virtue of his previous role as chief ideologist, was now in charge of agriculture. To underscore the demise of the second-secretary position, Ligachev was seated on the front bench at the next Supreme Soviet meeting but there was a conspicuously empty chair between him and Gorbachev and Prime Minister Ryzhkov.

And yet Ligachev retained his Politburo seat. His long struggle with Alexander Yakovlev over the ideology portfolio was resolved by compromise. Ligachev's job as chief ideologist was given to Vadim Medvedev. Yakovlev was made head of the new International Affairs Commission, which was designed to supervise foreign relations, while Chebrikov was placed in charge of the Legal Commission, set up to oversee the formation of legal infrastructure. The new KGB chairman was Vladimir Kryuchkov, sixty-four, former first deputy chairman in charge of foreign intelligence and an Andropov loyalist. He had served in Budapest when Andropov was Soviet ambassador to Hungary and subsequently worked for Andropov first in the Central Committee and later in the KGB. An indication of Gorbachev's personal links to the new KGB chief was the fact that Kryuchkov accompanied Gorbachev on his December 1987 visit to Washington.

The retirement of Solomentsev, seventy-four, left open the post of chairman of the party's Control Commission. Solomentsev had been under heavy pressure because investigators into the massive corruption case involving Brezhnev's son-in-law Yuri Churbanov had complained that they could not get Solomentsev's commission to act in time. Solomentsev was replaced by the Latvian communist leader Boris Pugo. Ivan Kapitonov, head of the party's Auditing Commission, also a Brezhnev-era official, retired as well.

The removal of Dobrynin as Soviet ambassador to Washington was a mystery. Dobrynin had cast his lot with the reformers. But he and another veteran Central Committee foreign-affairs expert,

Vadim Zagladin, were subsequently appointed the sole two foreign-policy advisers to Gorbachev, an indication that he was trying to build up his own presidential staff, patterned on America's National Security Council. Yet another reformist figure, Valentin Falin, former ambassador to Bonn, was appointed chief of the International Department of the Central Committee, though he was only a candidate Central Committee member. During Brezhnev's last years, Falin had been demoted to political commentator for *Izvestia*.

The entire swift maneuver placed Gorbachev in the role he was to have taken in April 1989, effectively setting up a presidential system that gave him the post of executive head of state. As the Supreme Soviet was winding down its business, he said, "There is no need for a long-winded policy speech." He was in the saddle. Once the reforms were complete, they would formalize what had already taken place. The new president would have the right to appoint his own prime minister; he would head the country's Defense Council and represent the country abroad. He would serve a maximum of two five-year terms, which would mean that he would be out of office by 1999. No other Soviet party leader has concurrently acted as executive head of state, although Lenin, Stalin, and Khrushchev assumed similar powers by taking on the premiership. After Khrushchev's fall, the Central Committee decided that the two posts should never again be held by one man. Brezhnev, Andropov, and Chernenko all assumed the presidency as a ceremonial job, but the source of their power was the post of general secretary of the Communist Party.

Two years were to pass before the convening of the Twenty-eighth Congress of the Soviet Communist Party. But Gorbachev had set into motion new policies and instituted systemic changes that by 1991 would stamp the great empire with his image.

In winning this victory, Gorbachev asserted his personal power at a cost, but the cost of not acting would have been greater.

Newspapers around the globe applauded Gorbachev's action. The whirlwind reshuffle not only neutralized the two main opponents of perestroika but also shifted them to vulnerable positions. Ligachev, without experience in agriculture, was now presiding over the gradual decollectivization of farming, which Gorbachev had initiated by allowing peasants to set up private farms and lease state land for up to fifty years. Ligachev shared the position with Politburo member and Agriculture Secretary Viktor Nikonov. As head of the legal commission, Chebrikov shared the assignment with Lukyanov.

The new Soviet president left no doubt that he was a forceful figure determined to carry out his program. His decisiveness and deft political maneuvering won new trust for his leadership in foreign affairs, and the benefits were tangible: a flood of West European investments. By October 1988, West German, Italian, French, and British banks had offered or were planning to offer new credit lines totaling about $6 billion. During Chancellor Helmut Kohl's visit to Moscow that fall, the West Germans signed more than thirty major cooperative agreements with Moscow.

But while the world celebrated his victory, Gorbachev was privately less sanguine. His public comments were impersonal and revealing. In his maiden presidential speech, he talked not about foreign policy but about the economy, and did so in admonitory tones. Perestroika had to shift from words to deeds. "We need practical movements ahead" and a genuine improvement in living standards. If perestroika was to endure, large numbers of citizens would soon have to see it as good for them.

But there were other invisible domestic costs. His initial concept of pushing changes through consensus and reasoning—an almost obsessive effort which repeatedly brought him into collision with the attitudes he sought to transform—had proved unworkable. For a long time, he seemed to oscillate between doubt and confidence in his original tactics. But finally, even as he was declaring that he did not want to become a "tsar or dictator," he had seized power, seeking to become a virtual autocrat—a benevolent one, yes, but still a powerful leader in the Russian tradition, seeking power to do good yet in the process abandoning the lofty principles he had espoused with such conviction.

Such concentration of power had disturbed some of his supporters, ranging from enlightened communists such as the new Estonian leader Vaino Valjas, to radical intellectuals such as economist Leonid

Abalkin and physicist Andrei Sakharov, all of whom came out publicly to state their reservations. Questioning the wisdom of the proposed constitutional changes for concentrating too much power in the hands of one man, the reformist legal specialist Boris Kurashvili proposed on the pages of *Izvestia* that an executive president would have to be controlled by Parliament: "To have effective parliamentary control, one needs a multiparty system. And that means parliamentary opposition. We are trying to set up an office equivalent to a president under a one-party system," Kurashvili said. This should not be done before a system of socialist opposition emerged. "This system is one of the key elements of a future widely developed socialist democracy, but we have not reached this stage of development yet."[6]

The constitutional changes suddenly emerged as the focus of mass agitation for greater autonomy in the three Baltic republics, where mass movements known as the Popular Front in Latvia and Estonia, and Sajudis in Lithuania, had become new political factors. When the Estonian Supreme Soviet overwhelmingly approved a "declaration of sovereignty"—an act that stopped short of asserting total independence but called for a new treaty to "determine the further status of Estonia in the composition of the Soviet Union"—the crisis demanded Gorbachev's personal involvement. (The Estonian vote on November 16, 1988, was 258 to 1, with 5 abstentions.) It was an ominous precedent, and he was forced to disown the spirited rebels who were trying to expand their political and economic autonomy under the perestroika banner. The Balts were his allies, and perestroika had a greater chance of taking root in the three small republics—which became independent after the 1917 Bolshevik revolution but which were incorporated into the Soviet state in 1940—than in any other part of the country. But the Estonian legislature voted to amend the republic's constitution, giving itself the right to refuse to apply Soviet laws in Estonia, and this appeared most clearly to impinge on the long-term interests of the Kremlin. The Latvians, Lithuanians, and Georgians did not go so far, but they had cautiously joined in the trend. There were people in the reformist camp who began to wonder whether Gorbachev was not overextending himself a little. For tactical reasons he had to back down to calm public furor; the proposed amendments were modified to meet key Baltic objections. But he had to uphold the Soviet Constitution and firmly force the defiant Estonians into the fold.*

When the Supreme Soviet approved his proposals in December, the vote for amendments was not unanimous—five deputies voted against and twenty-seven abstained, virtually all of them from the Baltics. The new legislation created a powerful new post of state president; established a new national legislature with broad authority; limited terms of office for government officials to ten years; required competitive elections; and strengthened the independence of judges. If instituted in full, the package of measures would produce the most extensive realignment of power in Soviet history. Gorbachev was legalizing a hybrid pluralistic system in which he as president was the locus of power amid a maze of bureaucratic and power centers; he alone had access to all of them.

For better or worse, Gorbachev had opened up some hazardous national questions that his predecessors had kept suppressed for years, and it was only a matter of time before even more troublesome questions would come to the fore. Despite martial law, the ethnic troubles in Armenia and Azerbaijan escalated through 1989 to a religious war and mass killings, which in turn led to huge population migrations in both directions between Moslem Azerbaijan and Christian Armenia. The crisis was temporarily checked by a disastrous earthquake, which devastated Armenia and killed thousands of people. Gorbachev, who was at the United Nations in New York at the time, promptly seized the initiative, canceling the rest of his American visit and the trips to Cuba and Britain and returning home to take charge of the Armenian rescue operations. Here was almost an

---

*The amendments made to the Estonian Constitution conflicted with the Soviet constitution on a number of counts. For example, Estonia recognized the right to private property (the Soviet constitution only allows "personal" property). The land, air, minerals, natural resources, and principal means of production were declared the exclusive property of Estonia (the Soviet Constitution says all these things are the property of the Soviet people). From a strictly legal point of view, the Estonians had no hope of outmaneuvering Moscow at the constitutional game. According to Article 74 of the Soviet Constitution, in the event of a deviation of republic law from federal law, the law of the Soviet Union prevails.

act of God; the scope of suffering and destruction forced the restive Armenians and Azerbaijanis to shift their attention away from the nationalist passions, at least for the moment.

To his credit, Gorbachev would not draw back, appalled though he was by the radical and nationalist forces he had unleashed. As he said in his closing passages at the Twenty-seventh Party Congress in February 1986, he would not back down; he knew of no way but the one he had embarked on. It was clear that he recognized the inevitability of continued ethnic strains. The reformers argued that this was to be expected, that the small nationalities and ethnic groups should be allowed to let off steam, that a better and more equitable arrangement between the federal and republican authorities was bound to emerge before the end of the century. But nobody could foresee the shape of such arrangements except that they would profoundly affect the nature of the country.

Gorbachev's quest for an executive presidency was an effort to restore some control over a situation that was virtually out of control. Key institutions were showing signs of discontent. He seemed to have asked too much from them—from the party to dismantle its own supervisory role, from the government to relinquish its administrative dominance, from the KGB to accept reforms that undermined civil order, and from the military to pay for perestroika with a sharp diversion of funds to the civilian sector. Some of his critics said he was no longer leading the country but merely trying to stay ahead of the rush of events, thus creating an illusion of leadership.

The conservatives opposed anything that would strengthen Gorbachev's grip on power, and many argued that Gorbachev, in his ambition, would pervert the great powers of the office to his own political ends. His natural supporters argued that, although Gorbachev was ambitious, his ambition was benign; but even they were concerned that the new constitutional changes would give his unknown successors too much power and authority.

Here was the central paradox of Gorbachev's rule—the more he sought to disperse power, the more he found it necessary to concentrate power in his own hands. He ultimately succumbed, critics could say, to Russia's history, which makes it clear that modernizers have to be ruthless and dictatorial if they hope to get results. He was trying, as Sakharov chided him publicly, "to get a democratic process through undemocratic means."

But Sakharov, the proud man who had demonstrated that he could not be bought for personal privilege or even for his life, was a firm supporter, knowing that only through Gorbachev's success would his own hopes for his country's regeneration stand any chance of being achieved.

Theirs was a fascinating partnership. Gorbachev had personally freed Sakharov from a cruel exile, and now the eminent physicist was symbolically freeing Gorbachev by providing him the moral authority to govern. It was very much a Russian affair, starting with a connection between a tsar and one of his subjects, but ultimately drawing upon a strain of deep common patriotism. Both men shared a genuine passion for reform; but reforms must come from the visionary tsar advised and constantly prodded by his faithful critic, who was, in effect, the tsar's conscience.

An unsympathetic observer might have put this another way: both men were elitists at heart, both knew that the system was rotten, but both had an exalted concept of their own roles and felt they were the ones who could do something about the situation.

Chapter 19

AN EMPIRE
IN TURMOIL

The final months of 1988 were an interlude of extraordinary political and intellectual turmoil, with the reformers locked into a struggle against their authoritarian tradition and groping toward concepts of free speech, elected government, and civil liberties. For all the exhilarating dialogue between the rulers and the ruled, reverberating as it did with various ideas bearing on the most fundamental issues concerning the individual and the state, perestroika's practical impact was still negligible. Nor did glasnost exert any major impact on Soviet life outside the narrow circle of the *intelligentsia*. The Soviet debate, which outsiders found so fascinating, had little relevance to the realities of provincial life.

A new "cult of personality" was conspicuously growing around the man from Stavropol, and he no longer seemed bothered by the adulation and flattery with which he was surrounded. When he traveled abroad, three or four Zil limousines were ferried by plane so that the power and prestige of Soviet presidency would be properly demonstrated. Some of his critics now openly talked about Gorbachev's visions as a dangerous form of apostasy, professing to see a tinge of self-worship in his pronouncements, the proclivity for breathtakingly bold, risky, or even heroic rhetorical flourishes that revealed the sense of his own lonely destiny. The imperial "we" became more pronounced. He may have raised his eyebrows at some extravagant praise of his leadership in the Soviet media, but the mood of euphoria affected him all the same. At least this was what his enemies in the party, the military, and the KGB began to highlight subtly, drawing the picture of a beleaguered leader in desperate need of foreign successes to compensate for domestic setbacks.

In part, at least, they were correct. The greater the difficulties at home, the greater the temptation to use foreign initiatives to calm the "turbulent seas" of change in Russia. Gorbachev's trip to the United Nations in early December offered him the world stage.

Once again he drew on his talent for public relations, as well as his fine sense of timing, to fill a vacuum with fresh diplomatic initiatives. He was, for all to see, a new breed of Soviet leader, an image that he reinforced with his fifty-five-minute UN oration, during which he behaved with studied dignity, as if deliberately trying to strike a contrast to the last and memorable UN appearance by a Soviet leader, shoe-banging Nikita Khrushchev, in 1960.

It was, in fact, an old and rather tedious speech, not up to his own high standards. His delivery was poor. He made too many mistakes reading the text. But that did not seem to matter. Here was Gorbachev the gambler at his best, commanding the global audience with his visionary enthusiasm. American editorial writers likened his program to Woodrow Wilson's Fourteen Points in 1918 and to the 1941 Atlantic Charter promulgated by Franklin D. Roosevelt and Winston Churchill.[1] This was splendid for Gorbachev, now at a pinnacle of glory unapproached by any Soviet leader. His New Thinking was being put forward as the grand design for a more peaceful world, and his TV audiences at home must have found some satisfaction in watching their leader introduce a measure of moral stiffening to the cynical and shortsighted councils of the West.

Gorbachev was also gracious. He went out of his way to praise Ronald Reagan and George Shultz. And he created a sensation by springing his surprise "Christmas gift" to the world. As a proof of his sincerity in striving for a new kind of international order, he announced his unilateral decision to cut Soviet military forces by half a million men before the end of 1990 and to begin changing an "economy of armaments into an economy of disarmament." Not only were Soviet forces to be cut, but the remaining units in Eastern Europe and Mongolia were to be relocated and restructured so as to assume a defensive configuration.* This was followed up by another surprise: in early 1989, Shevardnadze announced that Russia was unilaterally starting to destroy a portion of its chemical arms.[2]

Gorbachev's speech confounded many people in the West and elsewhere, simply because they had not previously listened to him; or if they had, they had refused to hear him. Suddenly it was discovered that he had abandoned some of the basic tenets of communism, that he wanted his country to become a full-fledged member of the family of nations, that he wanted to help protect the global environment, promote freer trade, diminish the threat of nuclear war. What the rest of the world wanted, he wanted. He had said all this countless times before, but many Western audiences had been conditioned—for good reason, and with considerable assistance from Gorbachev's predecessors—to dismiss Kremlin rulers as liars and propagandists. This time the unilateral arms reductions forced an astonished world to look at him anew: was he a villain or a hero?

The answers differed. There was no doubt that the world had a favorable view of the Kremlin leader, no doubt that he had changed international relations, ushering in a time of greater fluidity as well as fragility. Such shrewd figures as Henry Kissinger and Zbigniew Brzezinski promptly suggested that Gorbachev was cutting superfluous troops and old tanks as a trick to get the West to lower its guard. The West, according to them, should maintain the pressure and continue defense spending to make sure that Moscow did not turn swords into plowshares and back into swords, to the West's eventual peril. Gorbachev's sincerity was immaterial; he must fail. The West must keep Russia weak. Our best hope was that behind him there

---

*In addition to the five hundred thousand troops, he pledged to eliminate ten thousand tanks and eight hundred aircraft. The arms cuts were of symbolic value, since they would involve obsolete systems such as T-54 tanks, produced in the 1950s, and MiG-23 jets, made in the 1960s. The cut of Soviet troops in Asia by more than 250,000 was particularly significant, because it meant a profound and long-term strategic change along the Sino-Soviet border. Given the inhospitable terrain and lack of roads, the Soviet troops deployed along the border in the late sixties and early seventies cannot be withdrawn to new positions deep inside Siberia and then redeployed should emergencies require. The promised cut, part of a secret deal between Moscow and Beijing, signaled that the two nations were earnestly going about demilitarizing their long frontier.

were hundreds of Brezhnevs and Chernenkos eagerly waiting for him to collapse.

Gorbachev, obviously stung by these comments, quipped a month later in Moscow, "The West has attempted to compromise our action by putting out rumors that we are planning to get rid of only [ten thousand] outdated tanks. So I can say that fifty-three hundred of our most modern tanks will be removed from our forces." Gorbachev was addressing an audience of Western dignitaries that included Kissinger, former French President Valéry Giscard d'Estaing, and former Japanese Prime Minister Yasuhiro Nakasone.

Other people took Gorbachev at face value. Paul Warnke's dismissal of the Kissinger-Brzezinski line was typical of the liberal reaction. To imply that the West's best interests lie in sabotaging Gorbachev's policy carried cynicism to the extreme. The cold warriors were incapable of seeing the new situation Gorbachev was creating, said Warnke, who had been President Carter's arms-control chief, adding: "They can't live without the Soviet threat. It's been the dominant ruling element of their lives. If Gorbachev deprives them of an enemy, what can they do?"

What these Western arguments reflected more than anything else, as Stephen S. Rosenfeld of the Washington *Post* pointed out, was the lack of a sense of history—"the deeper understanding that the postwar era is coming to an end and there has not in two generations been a greater need for a major redesign"—or perestroika—of U.S. foreign policy.[3]

This was Gorbachev's strong point. He could conceptualize, see how pieces fit together. He had made a crucial concession seem an act of nobility and statesmanship. It was, in fact, the price he had to pay to reinforce his European positions and to secure a summit with Deng Xiaoping. Gorbachev saw Western Europe and the Pacific rim—not the United States—as Moscow's source of the credits and technology he needed to bolster perestroika. The arms race had been bleeding his country white. He wanted the world off his back so he could direct resources to home investment. But he recognized that he could pursue his European policy only if he had good relations with Washington; and he could approach the Pacific rim only with

Beijing's blessing. In a single imaginative stroke, Gorbachev ensured both.

However, Gorbachev also had his little men counting tanks and missiles and viewing each summit as a zero-sum game where each concession must be paralleled by a gain. There were Soviet Kissingers and Brzezinskis who criticized their president's unilateral arms cut as a sellout. The day after Gorbachev's UN General Assembly announcement, the country's top military officer, Marshal Sergei Akhromeyev, resigned as chief of the General Staff for "health reasons." Even Akhromeyev, who had supported him all along, had to take a distance from Gorbachev's policies publicly, although he remained as a personal adviser to the president on military matters. Marshal Akhromeyev, Defense Minister Dmitri Yazov, General Ivan Tretyak, and other top commanders had gone on record in the preceding months attacking the idea of unilateral reductions. In Akhromeyev's words, Gorbachev's doctrine of "reasonable sufficiency" should not be mistaken for a "unilateral lessening of our defense efforts." Tretyak, commander of air-defense forces, recalled that the last attempt to pare down the size of the military was carried out by Khrushchev and was "a terrible blow to our defense capacity." Unilateral cuts, Tretyak said in an October 1988 article in the military newspaper *Krasnaya Zvezda*, must be examined "a thousand times over."

Gorbachev partisans countered by citing the benefits from Gorbachev's move: first, the rapprochement with China, and, second, the fact that Gorbachev's move had made it infinitely more difficult for the Bush administration to cajole NATO partners into spending more on the common defense. Gorbachev himself defended his position in a speech to writers, editors, and other intellectuals on January 8, 1989.

He seemed to have reached the point where the opinion of generations to come mattered to him more than that of his contemporary domestic critics. Publicly, some of his positions had become more sharply defined. From the moment he assumed power, he had made it clear that one of his main objectives was to rein in the military and curb its excessive spending. This was a prerequisite for turning a military empire into a civilian society. He was now finally making unequivocal moves in this direction. The military budget, he said, would have to be cut without lessening the nation's security. The Soviet Union needed a smaller but more modern army. For years, he said, the government had been hiding the fact that it was running huge deficits. This had had a "pernicious effect" on the whole economy. There were other events that made the military cuts mandatory—the cost of the Afghan war, Chernobyl, the Armenian earthquake.

Before chanceries around the world could assess the full import of Gorbachev's UN speech, a major earthquake hit Soviet Armenia, killing thousands of people and inflicting physical destruction on a vast scale. It was eerie that he should have been summoned back by a natural catastrophe in a Transcaucasian republic already in deep turmoil over ethnic disputes with a neighbor.

With the lesson of Chernobyl in the back of his mind, Gorbachev rushed back home to take personal charge of the relief effort. He was visibly shaken while touring the disaster areas. Apart from the horrendous loss of human life, the disaster had set back all his perestroika plans by at least a few years. (The Chernobyl nuclear disaster cost the Soviet Union more than $12 billion and was described by Soviet economists as a severe blow to perestroika. Damages caused by the Armenian earthquake were expected to be even greater. The central government promptly decided to shut down and phase out a nuclear-power plant outside Yerevan. It was not immediately apparent whether the plant's safety was compromised, but the authorities were not taking any chances. They subsequently ordered five more atomic-power plants shut down.)

Unlike Chernobyl, the Armenian earthquake was an act of God; like Chernobyl, it once again revealed the country's limited capability to respond to disasters, the weakness of its communication network, and the inefficiency of its administration. God and man were both conspiring against perestroika. Man's role in the whole affair was by no means small—why were the old buildings still standing while the new ones were flattened? Even the Soviet press asked some disturbing questions about the design of new buildings, their construction, the sluggishness of local authorities in setting up shelters and medical stations. How could tens of thousands of people die in an earthquake that, measuring 6.9 on the Richter scale, was considered by seismologists a medium-size tremor?

For the first time since World War Two, the Soviet Union openly accepted foreign aid. The magnitude of the tragedy in Armenia was staggering and was bound to exact political costs. In the past, Gorbachev had shown uncommon skill in turning embarrassments to political advantage, but it was not possible to do so this time. Whereas his domestic critics grumbled that he was using the calamity to restore his standing in Armenia, the crisis could not really ease strains running in the region. In the two weeks preceding the earthquake, more than thirty persons had died in violence in Armenia and Azerbaijan; during 1988, more than 150,000 people had left their homes to escape ethnic feuding. Now the earthquake had wiped out several communities, killed more than twenty-five thousand people, and inflicted horrendous costs.

The flow of bad news had made him more distraught than indignant. "There are no grounds for pessimism or despair, let alone for panic," he declared in early 1989. "Perestroika, although not without difficulties and contradictions, is moving firmly ahead."[4]

In fact, his position at home was becoming desperate. Amid signs of mounting inflation and failure of factories to meet production targets, a wide range of consumer durables, clothing items, and household goods—frequently in short supply in the past—had disappeared altogether. People blamed his administration for ever worsening shortages of foodstuffs and consumer goods.

Gorbachev ushered in the new year, 1989, with a somber televised address in which he gave a "maximally objective and truthful" account of the country's economic difficulties. Even at holiday time, he said, "it is nevertheless necessary to tell people about reality. This may not cause any joy, but I think that the truth is the highest satisfaction for our people."

Fyodor Burlatsky, by now the most popular journalist in the country and Gorbachev's most articulate voice, led the New Year's issue of *Literaturnaya Gazeta* with a long editorial calling on the country to take a fresh look at Lenin's promise of "land to the peasants" and to admit that collectivized agriculture was a colossal failure. "Can we continue to ignore the fact that the American farmers, who account for 2.5 percent of the population, not only feed their country but are selling huge amounts of food abroad," whereas nearly twenty times more Soviet collective farmers are unable to produce enough food for their own country?

Nineteen eighty-nine, Burlatsky said, would be "a year of trouble and a year of hope." Food was the main problem. But even more serious were rising nationalist passions; "we have to admit" the fraudulent aspects of Soviet federalism—political power in the hand of Russians while smaller nations were exposed to Russification and the destruction of their cultural, spiritual, and architectural heritage. "The dramatic paradox of perestroika is the fact that all these problems erupted at the same time and at a point when the country's leadership had confronted and was starting to deal with the issues of genuine democracy, genuine federalism, and genuine socialism." Burlatsky also hinted, more strongly than ever before, that Gorbachev was considering the idea of a multiparty system. "We need people who are capable of living together with opponents, not the kind who, supposedly defending the correct positions, are yearning at minimum to suppress their opponents, at maximum to send them to concentration camps." Burlatsky was describing a Catch-22: "To democratize the society, we have to democratize power; but a democratization of power requires a democratic society."

The continued problems with agriculture, as Gorbachev well understood, could not be sustained for much longer. His first major act as president was to recast his agrarian policy, drafting legislation on new land-leasing arrangements whose aim was "to return to the peasants their position as masters of the land."[5] There was some talk of breaking up most of the country's collective and state farms and handing the land back to the farmers on leases of up to fifty years (with the right of inheritance). Eliminating the food shortages quickly, he said at a special food conference, is the "most important question of internal policy." His political fate hinged on his ability to deliver food to the citizens. But when the Central Committee met in March 1989 to adopt a new agricultural policy, Gorbachev had to compromise—the lease idea was adopted, but the collective farms were to remain as the mainstay of the country's agricultural production.

The harvest of 1988 was a disaster, under 195 million tons. Figures Gorbachev cited on January 25, 1989, showed the transport-and-supply system as abysmally inadequate. One-half of all the fruit and vegetables brought into Moscow rot before reaching the shops. (In the country as a whole, he said, the figure was 40 percent.) Another, even more remarkable statistic he cited was that in the Soviet capital there is only one fruit-and-vegetable shop for each twenty-four thousand inhabitants, and the ratio gets worse if the two to three million additional provincial shoppers who invade Moscow every day are counted. As for grain, economist Nikolai Shmelyov claimed, "We spoil one-quarter of what the country produces," or more than the total annual imports from the West.

Gorbachev hoped that, like China's Deng, he could revive agricultural production. Since Deng disbanded collectivized agriculture in 1979, the Chinese had been producing an abundance of food and the consumer sector in general was prospering. How could Deng do it? This was the question Gorbachev posed to a number of perestroika supporters who visited China to study its reforms. Nearly all key economic advisers and top officials, including Deputy Premiers Nikolai Talyzin and Yuri Maslyukov, had made the journey. At first, the Russians publicly sought to discount the importance of China's reform. The old rivalries still came through in public debates, along with an implicit fear of China's developing faster and becoming stronger than the U.S.S.R. in the next century. But soon the Russians began to debate publicly the merits of Deng's reforms. Gorbachev saw the reforms of socialist societies as the critical battleground for the remainder of the twentieth century. "We should show people what the Chinese are doing," he quipped when urging Yakovlev to have Moscow Television open a bureau in Beijing.[6] Moscow Television sent two correspondents to Beijing in the summer of 1988, and their reports on the successes of Chinese economic reforms became a part of Gorbachev's efforts to change the psychology of the country—until late spring of 1989, when Deng's reforms were overshadowed by his crackdown on the democracy movement.

Gorbachev personally witnessed the mass revolt against Deng and his prime minister, Li Peng, when hundreds of thousands of demonstrators disrupted the official agenda of the Deng-Gorbachev summit in May 1989. Gorbachev's reaction was a mixture of incredulity over what he saw as the paralysis of the Chinese leadership and unease over what he regarded as an economically driven discontent. "Who the hell is in charge here?" Gorbachev asked his ambassador, Oleg Troyanovski, as they were being driven by circuitous routes around a town in which student protesters carried his picture and shouted perestroika slogans. This remark, although offered in private, soon reached wider circles. Publicly Gorbachev expressed the hope that Chinese authorities would seek solutions through a political dialogue. And when Deng used the army a few weeks later, Gorbachev cautiously distanced himself from the Chinese. His supporters argued that the Tiananmen massacre demonstrated the need for political reforms, droving home the point that freer markets need freer politics if they are to work.

The 1989 Soviet budget signaled a declining role of the state in the economy—the volume of state orders in virtually all key heavy-industrial sectors, including energy, was lowered. The budget was clearly set to favor light and consumer industries over the traditionally promoted heavy industry. Most significantly, a budget deficit of $59 billion was revealed for the first time. Finance Minister Valentin Pavlov acknowledged that similar deficits had been run in previous years but never publicly disclosed.[7] (Later a senior economic adviser to Gorbachev, Leonid Abalkin, disclosed that the actual budget deficit amounted to $161 billion, or about 20 percent of all government spending).[8]

This only underscored the desperate need for foreign investments. Gorbachev promulgated new laws to attract foreign capital, and foreign investors were allowed control and management of joint ventures. The self-contained, autarchic world was collapsing, and Gorbachev's foreign-policy objectives—"a world of cooperation in diversity"—reflected his growing dependence on the West. Underscoring the radical departure from Bolshevik attitudes toward the West, Nikolai Slyunkov declared in a major address on November 4, 1988, to a rally marking the anniversary of the Russian revolution, that the advancement of "common human values" was at the core of Soviet foreign policy.[9]

Western skeptics saw Gorbachev as charging at America with an olive branch, and, more disturbingly, gaining ground. Kremlin hardliners argued that he was giving away everything merely to gain a pause in the arms race. Foreign praise only raised conservative suspicions. Reagan left the White House in 1989 saying he viewed the Soviet Union as less threatening than he had feared eight years ago, when he denounced it as a country whose leaders would lie, cheat, and willingly commit crimes to pursue their goal of world domination. Gorbachev was convinced that the Moscow-bashing extravaganza of the initial Reagan years was more the result of mood than of doctrine or discipline, and therefore he had successfully sought to encourage mood swings in the opposite direction. With Reagan himself softening Cold War myths and stereotypes, George Bush could not be expected to reverse the process.

Seasoned diplomats privately marveled at the skill with which Gorbachev molded his optimism and projected it onto the world. Russia's new image had the desired effect in the West, giving Gorbachev a free hand to build relations with important partners in Western Europe and elsewhere. He could tell such visitors as Chancellor Franz Vranitzky of Austria, Premier Ciriaco De Mita of Italy, Chancellor Helmut Kohl of West Germany, President José Sarney of Brazil, and President François Mitterrand of France that his relations with the United States were on a steadily improving course. He courted key regional powers such as Argentina, Brazil, Mexico, Saudi Arabia, Egypt, and Indonesia. He visited Cuba, Britain, and West Germany. On the way to Cuba, he stopped over in Ireland for talks with Prime Minister Charles Haughey.

In Cuba, Gorbachev spokesman Gennady Gerasimov publicly declared that the Soviet Union was "against export of revolution," thus abdicating its claim as the wellspring of the revolutionary ideology that had swept through the world for much of the twentieth century. It was not really a new statement. Gorbachev had said as much in February 1986 at the Party Congress, but Gerasimov was now openly trumpeting Gorbachev's bold retreat from the revolutionary epoch in Russia and the international tensions it has generated.

Gorbachev would frequently put his policy in perspective by telling visitors that his thrust was to expand trade and economic cooperation. In a variety of ways, he played for the long term. He was concerned about the shape of European politics and economics after 1992, and sought real adjustments. He joined the Organization of Petroleum Exporting Countries as an observer, discussing joint action on curbing output so as to buoy prices. Our goal, he said in private conversations, was to join GATT, the General Agreement on Tariffs and Trade, and establish working ties with the International Monetary Fund and the World Bank. (Reagan had been more receptive to this argument than Bush. "There is evidence," Reagan said, talking about Gorbachev in his last presidential press conference, "that they don't like being the pariah, that they want to join the family of nations." Bush's national security adviser, Brent Scowcroft, however, still saw Gorbachev's goal as being to divide the West.) Gorbachev already had acquired powerful allies in the West, perhaps most significantly Foreign Minister Hans-Dietrich Genscher of West Germany, who saw nothing wrong with Russia's becoming a genuine partner in the international community.

Initial progress was slower in the Pacific area, although Gorbachev had succeeded in forging fresh ties with Australia, Thailand, Malaysia, and several other countries. His basic message at Vladivostok in July 1986 had been understood in the region—namely, that new forces had been unleashed that required a more businesslike, pragmatic approach in which sentiment and ideology played little role. Gorbachev wanted at all costs to keep his special relationship with India intact. His second visit to India, in November 1988, ostensibly to receive the Indira Gandhi Prize for Peace, Disarmament and Development, was in fact designed to assuage Indian concerns about the impending Sino-Soviet rapprochement. He also wanted better relations with Japan, and when Shevardnadze visited Tokyo in late December, he for the first time publicly announced readiness to talk about the Soviet-occupied "northern islands," foreshadowing future compromises with that country.

But China was the key. And once a normalization of Sino-Soviet relations was agreed upon, albeit on Beijing's terms, Moscow's participation in the region's political and economic affairs was assured. Even before the May 1989 Deng-Gorbachev summit, his New Thinking unlocked the massive ideological logjam that has kept Asia in its grip for decades. Suddenly old enemies were talking to one another; the improbable was being achieved, and the impossible being considered. In the short period of two months between December 1988 and February 1989 there was an unprecedented flurry of diplomatic activity: India's Rajiv Gandhi made groundbreaking visits to two old enemies—China and Pakistan; China started direct talks with its old enemy Vietnam; Thailand sent its foreign minister to Hanoi; Moscow and Beijing established trade relations with South Korea; Australians made first diplomatic contacts with North Korea; and the insular North Koreans sent their first delegation to Japan. Serious discussions were raised about the possible joint exploitation of Siberia by China, Japan, South Korea, and the Soviet Union! The combination would have been deemed impossible only a few years earlier.

Observing the dizzying jockeying for new alliances and positions, and shaking their heads in disbelief, Asian diplomats ascribed it to what they were calling the Gorbachev Effect. Nobody could predict how far things would move. For decades, Asia had been locked into a fixed pattern of relationships based on strategic interests, which owed their ultimate logic to the antagonism between the United States and the Soviet Union. Each country belonged to one camp or the other, and the patterns were defined and cemented by wars—first in Korea, then Vietnam, and finally Afghanistan and Kampuchea. Suddenly Gorbachev's rapprochement with Washington and Beijing had ushered in a new power game, in which commerce rather than ideology was the determining factor.

The 1989 economy was meant to operate on the new principle—*khozrashchot* or self-financing—but it did not. Without price reforms and other essential components, it could not perform as the Gorbachev people had imagined it would, which in turn was discrediting perestroika. The old economic system, which Gorbachev wanted to replace but which was still in operation, became even more inefficient because of the absence of direction and the sheer inability to get the new system off the ground. Foreign businessmen with long experience in Soviet trade also discovered that the decentralization of decisionmaking had generated a good deal of confusion; it was difficult to find people with real authority. This in turn intensified the very stagnation that perestroika was supposed to cure.

At the onset of 1989, economic adviser Abel Aganbegyan privately conceded that the country had entered a far deeper crisis than the leadership was prepared to concede, and that only outside purchases of food and consumer goods and other emergency steps could save perestroika.[10] The experiment with limited private enterprise ran into more trouble as conservative pressures and public discontent over high prices again brought forward restrictive regulations on cooperatives. Public opposition to private entrepreneurs was extraordinarily strong. High salaries earned by cooperative workers did not help; just a whiff of social differences was sufficient to revive the politics of envy. The ban covered the sales of jewelry, religious artifacts, and alcohol, also the sale, rental, or copying of videotapes, as well as publishing and certain medical services. This in turn led to a sense of unease among the relatively small number of entrepreneurs who were prospering.

The howls of despair from the provinces that were printed as letters to the editor in the press carried echoes of Dostoyevskian torment. "There is no purpose in life," wrote a girl from Ulyanovsk. A man from a village in the Urals was more to the point. "Recently all you hear is perestroika, glasnost. But what has changed? Why is sugar rationed? Why are school uniforms rationed, shoes expensive, and wages low?" It turned out that more than forty-three million people, or about 20 percent of the population, lived in poverty, according to official Soviet accounts. "Poverty," said the newspaper *Komsomolskaya Pravda,* "is a reality, our national tragedy."[11]

The Gorbachev people blamed food and consumer-goods shortages on Brezhnev and Chernenko, on the Stalinist system, and on natural disasters. But there was far more to it. The country lacked the basic human and market infrastructure; what was required was to edge toward a more open economy while simultaneously developing managerial talents and industrial texture. And here Gorbachev had run into the very Slavophile core of the country, the eternal Mother Russia, whose history and traditions had left her burdened with a collective incapacity to respond to changes without a theoretical (or religious) basis and without the approval and supervision of authority. He had no simple magic formula promising future happiness and wealth. Nor did he have enough support. The reformers were a minority, so small that they could not possibly reach all levels of the society to provide leadership and energy.

Gorbachev was intelligent enough to know that his program would have to be a lifetime's work for any man, and that the domestic tasks facing him were daunting. He was asking his people to change the way they lived and worked. He would have to wait for another generation. Under the best of circumstances, real economic and social changes would not become evident before the year 2010.

Indeed, for the rest of the twentieth century there were unlikely to be any more revolutionary economic legislation laws and initiatives in the Soviet Union, It was enough to try to implement those already introduced. This was a drama to be played out by many forces—the massive Communist Party bureaucracy; the military; the KGB security establishment; the emerging professional classes; technocrats; newly established unofficial organizations; environmentalists; Russian nationalists; Baltic republics; Central Asian Moslems; the Armenians, Azerbaijanis, and Georgians; and many other groups.

Gorbachev already had admitted limits to his ambitions when he postponed the most difficult economic changes for the five-year plan covering the period 1990–94. But that was before the nationalist unrest and demonstrations began to tear at the central core of the Soviet state, and before the Armenian earthquake inflicted horrendous financial punishment on it. The centrifugal forces had to be managed and controlled. The forward motion would have to come from activism in foreign affairs.

Having established a personal stake in the shape of future U.S. policy, Gorbachev followed Bush's pronouncements with special care. A few years older than Gorbachev, Bush had come to office after having extensive exposure to international relations, and as a result might prove more difficult to deal with than Reagan. Bush's style was more deliberate; he was not a charismatic figure, and he distrusted the flamboyant approach to foreign policy.

At the same time, Bush's conception of America's mission to "make kinder the face of the nation and gentler the face of the world" and to continue "the new closeness" with the Soviet Union indicated to the Russians a subtle shift in American policy. The cautionary signal was the new president's assessment that "our new relationship in part reflects the triumph of hope and strength over experience, but hope is good and so is strength and vigilance."

Bush's key foreign-policy appointments helped bring things into proportion. Secretary of State James A. Baker III was a reassuring figure—the choice of a former secretary of the treasury underscored Bush's preoccupation with American economic and trade problems and suggested that Washington had taken notice of the changes in the international environment in which economics—rather than ideology—offered profitable routes to achieve national goals. The other key men were tough professionals. The new deputy secretary of state, Lawrence Eagleburger, who had served in top State Department jobs in the Nixon and Reagan administrations, was a known and respected figure. General Brent Scowcroft, as Bush's national security adviser, was someone the Russians were most comfortable with. He had held the same job during Gerald Ford's White House years, and embodied that blend of military understanding, academic acumen, and political experience required for a difficult and ill-defined position. He was someone the Russians respected, even though he was going to be a hard bargainer when it came to any future strategic-arms talks. Indeed, Scowcroft was more cautious about the pace of arms control and less starry-eyed than Reagan about the prospect of drastic cuts in strategic nuclear arms, which meant that the prospect of halving all strategic arms in one go was becoming more remote, but so were some of Reagan's most ambitious schemes, such as the SDI program.

Gorbachev sought to engage Bush from the very beginning, striving to underscore that his revolution was designed to modify, not abandon, communism, and that it would not prejudice American interests or infringe on the West's interests. His predecessors' lack of judgment, of instinctive balance, manifesting itself in the wholly disproportionate expenditure of energy and resources on unprofitable imperial expansion, created fears and hostility in the West. His policy was different. Yes, he wanted to say, he knew that a country that does not move forward must move backward. For the rest of the twentieth century, there was nothing he could do to make Moscow's weight felt in the world until the country had overhauled its economy and domestic political arrangements.

Soon, however, Gorbachev was telling Margaret Thatcher, during his visit to London in April 1989, that the Bush administration's foreign-policy review was taking too long, and that this was endangering the momentum of arms negotiations. The tone of Gorbachev's complaint suggested that he viewed Bush's delay as a potentially serious reversal. Gorbachev was exposing his own vulnerabilities. He needed the West's support to get perestroika off the ground and also to tranquilize his domestic critics; they knew that Western investments and goodwill were granted on condition that perestroika continue and succeed.

In Britain, while delivering his Guildhall speech on April 7, 1989, he unexpectedly announced that the Soviet Union would halt production of uranium used to make nuclear bombs. But the West was no longer overawed by such gestures; indeed, by treating serious arms-control matters as public-relations gifts to be distributed on his journeys abroad, Gorbachev was devaluing much of his earlier promise. Even Thatcher was not buying it. And she promptly rejected his request that NATO forgo modernization of its short-range nuclear weapons in Europe. While appreciating Gorbachev's intentions, Thatcher said, "one cannot in fact create a defense system on good intentions."

Gorbachev did leave England with an important symbol, however. After he and Raisa lunched with Queen Elizabeth at Windsor Castle, it was announced that the queen would pay an official visit to the Soviet Union. Both the queen and her husband, Prince Philip, have family ties with the Russian imperial family that came to a terrible end in a bloodstained cellar in Ekatarinburg. Her acceptance of Gorbachev's invitation formally ended the estrangement between the

British throne and the Soviet state since the murder of Nicholas II and his family. (Queen Elizabeth's grandfather King George V had once told his prime minister never to put him in the position of having "to shake hands with the murderers of my relatives.")

The tranquillity in the West was symbolized by the agreement among Western capitals for an international conference on human rights in Moscow in 1991. Western leaders had bridled at the idea when it was first advanced in early 1988, but their change of heart reflected both changing perceptions about Gorbachev's Russia and new possibilities for extracting political advantages. After the successful conclusion of the Vienna follow-up meeting of the European Conference on Security and Cooperation in the spring of 1988, Gorbachev issued a statement hailing the outcome as a step closer to the idea of a common European home. The Soviet "apartment in this home," he said, would be a socialist one, "but we are not going to isolate ourselves, fence ourselves in, and stand in opposition to the outside world." Gorbachev further expanded his vision during triumphal tours of West Germany and France, pleading for a Europe in which "the only battlefields will be markets open for trade and minds open to ideas." Speaking before parliamentarians from the twenty-three-nation Council of Europe at Strasbourg, he solemnly renounced the use of force by one alliance against another and proposed "a doctrine of restraint to replace the doctrine of deterrence." As a sweetener, he announced readiness to make a unilateral cut in tactical nuclear missiles if the West agreed to open talks on mutual reductions.

The peace on the Western front was matched in the east by the formal rapprochement with China. Ever since the 1969 clashes on the Ussuri River, a hostile China had provided the Soviet military-industrial complex with an emotional rationale for a buildup that sapped the country of its vitality and resources. A hostile China meant a weak strategic position for the Soviet Union, a fact initially obscured by the Vietnam War. Some of Gorbachev's key advisers also argued that the Soviet economic crisis at the onset of the eighties was in great part the result of the Soviet military buildup along the long Asian border.[12] His predecessors were unprepared to pay the psychological price demanded by Beijing; they hoped that the Soviet Union would be able to muddle through on its course without serious damage to the economy. It was a mistaken assumption. The Chinese demanded to be dealt with on an equal footing; they insisted on a drastic cut in the number of Soviet troops deployed in the two military districts east of the Urals, and particularly in Mongolia (the fifty well-equpped Soviet divisions, including six tank divisions, faced more than seventy Chinese divisions along the border). At Vladivostok in 1986, Gorbachev signaled readiness to pay the price (by calling China a "great socialist country") and hinted that he would reduce Soviet military strength along the Sino-Soviet border. In talks with the Chinese leading up to the summit meeting, he made it clear that the Soviet divisions would be cut almost in half; the troops in Mongolia were to be reduced by 75 percent.[13] The process, which he set in motion, now yielded practical benefits.

Already Gorbachev had given his citizens extraordinary latitude in criticism and self-expression. In the first months of 1989, during election debates, citizens in major urban centers were publicly raising all sorts of once-taboo questions: Is Marxism dead? Was the 1917 revolution a national tragedy? Should the Soviet Union adopt a multi-party system? Was there an alternative leader to Gorbachev?[14]

In the outlying reaches of the empire, the questions were somewhat more muted but equally disturbing. In volatile Moslem Central Asia, discontent crystallized around explosive environmental issues. In Kazakhstan, which has been the site of almost all Soviet underground nuclear-weapons tests, reports of genetic deformities prompted demands for financial compensation for victims, and triggered campaigns to end all nuclear testing in the republic. In Uzbekistan, the federal policy of using Agent Orange–type defoliants on cotton crops has led to a staggering 25-percent infant-mortality rate and prompted Uzbek candidates to demand a halt in the use of such defoliants.

The environmental concerns were advanced against the background of nationalist reawakenings in the Baltics, the Ukraine, Moldavia, Transcaucasus, and Central Asia. The Afghan defeat and the fury and fanaticism of the Ayatollah Khomeini's Iran next door helped produce an Islamic revival with an uncertain impact on the ultimate shape of the Soviet empire. By 1990, Azerbaijanis began riots along the border with Iran, demanding reunification with ethnic Azerbaijanis in Iran. In other parts of Central Asia, there were calls for Islamic-based autonomy, and this was done in the name of Gorbachev. "We pray Allah to set him on the right road," Uzbek Islamic activists said, repeating with smacking relish the words of a Tashkent mufti. "He [Gorbachev] has given us freedom, and we support perestroika."

Will the Central Asians be content with the revival of the symbols of their ancient national identities, their languages, and the Arabic alphabet abolished by the Soviets? Or will they reject entirely the phony federalism of the Soviet state? Some extremists were already calling for the establishment of an Islamic Republic in Uzbekistan. In 1990, ethnic Russians constitute just under 50 percent of the Soviet Union's population. What would happen if the Ukrainians, the second-largest ethnic group after the Russians, were to demand independence? With fifty million people and one-sixth of the Soviet Union's GNP, the Ukraine would be Europe's second-largest nation.

The logical consequence of glasnost was the right to national self-determination. If permitted, strong nationalist political parties would quickly gain power in free elections in many non-Russian republics. The Islamic revival has ushered in a new era of disturbing uncertainty for Central Asia's Russian minority. In Uzbekistan, where the ethnic Russians account for less than 10 percent of the population, Russian nationalists blame the situation on Gorbachev, often in terms as shrill as those of any Moslem extremist. "Gorbachev is a Jew," said Mikhail Mazol, an unemployed Russian glassblower and native of Tashkent who viewed glasnost and perestroika as part of a Zionist conspiracy. "You have no idea what is going on here. The Russians have become the most degraded nationality." It is not possible to say with any degree of certitude that Gorbachev had considered, even when he publicly mused about the absence of a loyal opposition to keep the government on its toes, the notion of an organized political opposition competing for power with his own party. Nor did he develop a clear concept of federalism, an essential component of any policy dealing with the nationalities question. The tanks in the streets of Baku, Yerevan, and Tbilisi bore witness to the intractability of the issue, and he did not have the courage or the conviction to face it head on. This became clear during a trip to the Ukraine in the spring of 1989, when Gorbachev appealed to the Ukrainians' Slav background to keep the country's unity. "We Slavs must stick together," he said in Kiev. "The future of the Soviet Union depends on our unity."[15]

Setting aside the rhetorical pretensions of all communist regimes, the legitimacy of Russian communists to rule a vast empire rested on a dubious Marxist-Leninist assumption that they had the right to hold power indefinitely in the name of the socialist revolution. Gorbachev clung to this fallacy even as he was democratizing Soviet policies, and this meant that he was building layers of clear rationality upon an unsustainable proposition, all the time counting on the control of the security police and the media to perpetuate his party's grip on power. Power meant control over the economy, which in turn translated into privileges for those who made decisions about how the resources and wealth were distributed, which in turn meant that those in power were not likely to part willingly with power irrespective of the tsar's wishes. This made the other aspect of Bolshevik legitimacy—Lenin's original pledge of "Land to the peasants, factories to the workers, power to the soviets [councils]"—impossible to impose. The pledge never had been carried out; the people had been betrayed; and no amount of legalism by the same old party hacks could restore the people's trust as long as the government did not live up to Lenin's pledge.

There was little in his public pronouncements to suggest that Gorbachev had wrestled with this problem. Initially he construed his mandate narrowly, concentrating on repairs to the Marxist-Leninist system. In his Prague speech in 1987, he talked about perestroika as the reconstruction of a socialist house, which had solid foundations and good walls, but its flooded basement, leaky roof, and broken windows needed repair. Glasnost, though, had shown the house to be a wreck, which many people wanted to abandon altogether in favor of building a new house on the old site. The clash between troops and civilians in Georgia, which left nineteen Georgians dead, put this matter into a sharper perspective.

More and more, and especially after he entered his fifth year in power, Gorbachev began to think of using the hands and votes of citizens to destroy the power establishment. The forces he unleashed were destroying the Stalinist system. And that, it seemed, was Gorbachev's goal. One of his most prominent radical supporters privately argued that Gorbachev had "infiltrated" the system to reform it from within—the only way possible short of a revolution.[16] In this view, the developments in Hungary and Poland could be taken as evidence of his thinking on the issue, since neither country could have made its decision without consulting Gorbachev.

Eastern Europe was supposed to have been the fulcrum of socialism, and the testing ground for Marxism-Leninism, which revealed itself as inadequately simplistic and messianically obscurantist in the last decades of the twentieth century. The bankruptcy of the ideology was more evident here, but so were regenerative efforts to salvage something of the idea.

This was a political minefield for Gorbachev. He was still the master of a European empire, but an empire that was decaying quickly to become, in William Hyland's words, "the new sick man of Europe." He was searching for a way. The British had the imagination, while forced to dismantle their empire, to replace it with the idea of the commonwealth; the Russians had only the Brezhnev Doctrine and tanks.[17]

Strategically, and over a long term, the lands behind the Iron Curtain remained the area where the danger of a war was the greatest. Gorbachev staked his authority and his political future in behalf of a new relationship between Moscow and its East European allies. He repudiated the Brezhnev Doctrine. He urged Comecon, the Soviet-bloc trading association, to shift trade to convertible currency.[18] He decided to cut down drastically on Soviet military presence in allied countries and unilaterally reduced the number of tactical nuclear weapons stationed in Czechoslovakia and East Germany. His hope was that the "biological factor" would solve the problems of fierce resistance to change put up by East Germany's Erich Honecker, Romania's Nicolae Ceauşescu, and Bulgaria's Todor Zhivkov, all old-guard communists in their seventies. The conservative British weekly *The Economist* said that a growing number of people saw Gorbachev as "Mikhail the Liberator" for allowing greater freedom in the eastern half of Europe. No one could have anticipated how accurate that description turned out to be.

Karoly Grosz, the new Hungarian leader, publicly asserted that he enjoyed Gorbachev's blessing for Hungary's political reform. So did Prime Minister Miklos Nemeth, who said Gorbachev "welcomed the idea of pluralism, since he considers the [process of] representation, institutionalization, and confrontation of opinion and interests to be at the core of democracy." Imre Poszgay, member of the Hungarian Politburo, said the system imposed on his country by Stalin "has proved to be a false path in its entirety." In a conversation with Joseph Fitchett of the *International Herald Tribune,* Poszgay forecast that Hungary would be a democracy by the mid-1990s. If the Communist Party loses in an election, he said, "it will have to lay down power."

In Hungary, the experiment with power-sharing was and is extraordinary. When Politburo member János Berecz told the parliament that power belonged neither to the communists nor to any one cause but to all working people—that this was not a "present" from the party but a "basic right"—he was doing an ideological somersault that would have been impossible only a year earlier. But this was the new trend in the Soviet empire. One leader of the opposition Democratic Forum, the writer Istvan Csurka, conceded that much when he said, "I am not sure that either the party or society understands the situation. We have gone so quickly from one extreme to another." The Hungarian communists took the first step toward a genuine political pluralism by passing legislation to allow independent parties and public demonstrations.[19]

In Poland, General Wojciech Jaruzelski, after imposing martial law in 1981 to suppress the independent trade union Solidarity, legalized the independent trade union in 1989.

These were landmark moves, amounting to the communist parties'

offering their opponents a junior partnership in running their countries. Whether this was an act of desperation to help shore up crumbling communist positions or a genuine recognition of evolutionary
forces at work was not possible to say. It will be years before the
results of these experiments become apparent. What is significant is
that the more enlightened among the European communist leaders
have been prepared to concede the failure of Marxism-Leninism, or,
rather, its irrelevancy to the contemporary conditions. The Russians
were groping in the same direction, but more cautiously. Even Gorbachev's opponents saw merit in the part of his political reforms
involving a revitalized Supreme Soviet. By sharing a bit of power
with an increasingly dissatisfied population, they were hoping to co-
opt it into the search for a solution and also remove responsibility
for the inevitably painful remedies from the party's shoulders.

Just how painful those remedies have been can be seen from *Izvestia,* the government newspaper, which in early 1989 demolished
the official pretense of the superiority of communism in Russia. The
Soviet system "originated by Stalin and borrowed from the tsars does
not bring anyone any closer to power by the people than does bourgeois democracy," it said. Indeed, Western societies, for all their
shortcomings, had outstripped the Soviets in ensuring a proper standard of living, education, and medical care for their citizens.[20]

Gorbachev was also engaged in shadowboxing with Lenin, the
national icon, whose vision of the future is still emblazoned in huge
letters right across the Grand Kremlin Palace: "Socialism," it says,
"equals electrification plus Soviet power." With "electrification" so
obviously belonging to another age, the meaning of "soviet power"
had to be invested with new content. Nobody, not even Gorbachev,
was quite sure as to what new content it should be. One thing was
clear. The system of authority by which the Soviet Union has been
held together since 1917 was disintegrating.

Gorbachev has changed before the nation's eyes, becoming more
careful and controlled, a master of his own personality, able to slip
on the masks as occasions or policies demand. He has aged visibly,

but age has added to his statesmanlike posture. He has trained himself to work the crowds, use photo opportunities, hector his opponents. Occasionally flashes of the old Gorbachev come through.

In early 1989 a note of despair slipped into his speech as he blamed misfortunes for the hard times. "It would have been good had we been lucky," he said. But things were not going his way. The treasury was empty, partly because of more than $60 billion in lost revenues from vodka, and partly because they were visited by "our old sins"— he named the drop in world oil prices, Chernobyl, the Armenian earthquake, and the Afghan war.[21]

Two days after the Armenian tragedy another earthquake struck Soviet Central Asia, causing considerable damage in Tadzhikistan. Again the nationalist unrest in the Transcaucasus erupted, and he had to send tanks to the streets of Baku, Yerevan, and Tbilisi to maintain order. But the sight of troops confronting the people was an ominous sight indeed, and the blood spilled since the first flush of tensions has led to disillusionment that could no longer be resolved by any conceivable administrative actions short of more devolution of power.

Even his supporters began to suspect that the endless frustrations with perestroika had wrought meaningful and permanent changes in Gorbachev's character. While he has been able, with his imagination and personal idealism, to give an affirmative impulse in foreign affairs, his ceaseless efforts to do the same in domestic affairs have met with repeated failures. Henry Kissinger found him "less ebullient, more reflective—more thoughtful than" two years earlier. Kissinger ascribed the change to Armenia and the cumulative troubles of perestroika.[22] Sakharov bemoaned the deepening gap between Gorbachev's rhetoric and his actions: "It's hard to say just who Gorbachev is now."[23]

In the country at large, Boris Yeltsin has emerged as a more popular politician—in an open contest there was no doubt that Gorbachev would take second place. Yeltsin, since his ouster from the Politburo, has become more wily. His wife has been shopping in ordinary stores, and in 1989, although still a member of the Central Committee, Yeltsin gave up the right to be treated at the elite Kremlin hospital in favor of the local polyclinic. He has become an "old pro"—honing his political message, peppering it with jokes. His audiences eat out of his hand. His public statements tended to focus on a few simple ideas, and, like opposition politicians in any country, he enjoyed the luxury of being able to criticize and make bold promises without assuming any responsibility. His reputation became legendary—and grossly exaggerated—and his huge following had catapulted him into the position of the putative leader of a "leftist" opposition. He was against corruption and injustices, and for decency in public life. He was a true working-class hero.

Yeltsin's notion that multiparty politics should at least be discussed in the Soviet Union was a clear challenge. Gorbachev resented it. He dismissed another argument by Yeltsin—that the Communist Party should concentrate on just one or two tasks (he named the food crisis as one)—rather than expend energy on everything. Gorbachev's repsonse to this was to criticize "subjectivism and ambition" without naming Yeltsin. Yeltsin's passionate supporters, in turn, have publicly advanced their man as an alternative to Gorbachev. Mikhail Poltaranin, a journalist and Yeltsin man, told a campaign meeting in Moscow: "I can think of quite a few alternatives to Gorbachev. We must look at everybody's program. The present situation is very dangerous; we must prepare ourselves for the possibility of dramatic events."[24]

A somewhat different challenge came from the conservatives, who have begun gradually to build up the stature of Premier Nikolai Ryzhkov as a potential Alexei Kosygin, a sober, knowledgeable man known to favor perestroika and glasnost, yet someone without Gorbachev's vision and excessive personal commitment. Ryzhkov, who for more than four years had been in the background and a loyal supporter of Gorbachev, was suddenly seen as an alternative, a man the conservatives hoped could be advanced in an emergency to meet the hour.

It was a risky adventure. A young artist named Mironenko captured the broad distrust of the entire ruling establishment with a large canvas bearing the following slogan in big white letters on a red background: "Bastards, what have you turned the country into!" The painting, including six portraits of an imaginary candidate, was part of an avant-garde show in Moscow; it represented Mironenko's comment on the new, "free" elections in the Soviet Union. The authorities were discomfited by seeing Gorbachev and his colleagues called bastards, but did not prevent the work from being displayed. However, the visitors' book contained entries such as "Bastards, what have you turned art into!," "Lock them up in a loony bin," and "Send them all to Siberia!"[25]

But even the most sophisticated and frank analyses of the country's predicament, conducted on the pages of *Novy Mir,* revealed old limitations. The open denunciation of the "ideology of war communism" and calls urging the "collapse of the Administrative System" seemed to be left suspended in the air.[26] For there was an element of self-delusion here, the absence of new ideas.

Unlike the commercial West, Russia is a country that fervently needs an ideology, a set of beliefs, a religion—and Gorbachev was offering his people a set of laws, accounting procedures, and efficiency standards and urging them to demolish the "Administrative System" without giving them a clear sense of what would replace it. Glasnost and perestroika were, for many Russians, reflections of anarchy and of the uncertainties of the market that dominate the modern age—the very forces that were alien in a country where it has been inconceivable that any action should be taken without a theoretical foundation and a hierarchical system of authority. In such upheavals, what did it mean to be a communist? Was perestroika merely a romantic dream of Russia's renaissance? What was to be done with a nation frightened of its own potential? Could the conflict between the Slavophiles and the Westernizers ever be definitely resolved? How was anyone to make Russia gain a new sense of itself and its relations with the rest of the world?

Gorbachev apparently came to the conclusion that the only way to succeed would be to revert to the classical "revolution-from-above" tactics. He was to hold power in his own hands; he was to be the source of all reforms, and these were to be worked out and applied by his men. But, more and more, he was not leading; rather, he was engaged in tranquilizing a multitude of situations threatening perestroika. Of course he was cutting moral corners; he had to resort to an unusual degree of cunning. He used many of the techniques he deplored in his political opponents. He expounded his viewpoint with superb style but contrived to leave the impression that anyone who disagreed was a dunce or a muddlehead. His candor, skeptics said, was an act of political expediency; his outward calm a matter of cosmetics.

In the last decade of the century, the Soviet Union is in a period of deep economic and social crisis, which most likely will last well into the twenty-first century. Crime statistics show an alarming rise in the number of robberies, thefts, and break-ins. Consumer-goods supplies are chaotic. Food shortages, the aftermath of the defeat in Afghanistan, the loss of prestige and illusions of prestige, all feed popular resentment. The "level of hatred" in a multiethnic Soviet society is very high, because the authorities over the previous seven decades have destroyed "religion, family, property, national self-awareness . . . and other traditional forms which protected man from the totalitarian system."[27] People in the non-Russian republics are turning against the Russian people, "associating [with them] all miscalculations and vices" created by the system. The rise of Russophobia has even reached Byelorussia, whose people were ethnically and psychologically closer to the Russians than any other nation.[28]

Nationalism is a strong wind in the country. People are trying to establish their identity, not necessarily break up the empire, and the ruling establishment in Moscow cannot recognize the difference. Perhaps, under different circumstances, Gorbachev could have come up with an imaginative new concept of the federation. But he has been hard pressed from all sides, especially by the continued deterioration of the economy. He is so thoroughly identified with the ongoing changes that any failure of the reforms would be his failure. Gorbachev has done what few political leaders dare do: instead of distancing himself from the uncertain enterprise, instead of having his top aides do the public prodding of a baffled population and an obtuse bureaucracy, intervening publicly only to back them up, he chose to preside over the gargantuan struggle to move the Soviet behemoth himself, thus establishing himself as the chief protagonist in the drama. He was indeed, as Margaret Thatcher described him, "a man of destiny." Personally and politically, he could not look back any more. He is a trailblazing statesman trying, with considerable success, to change his country and all of Eastern Europe, and bring them into the modern age.

Chapter 20

AGAINST ALL ODDS

Historians in the twenty-first century undoubtedly will search for the real pattern of events that, with the accession of Gorbachev, ushered in a new historical period. In fact, there may have been no such pattern, even if he and his aides sought to cast snatches of policy into a coherent plan. But there is a vision of a different, freer, and more prosperous civil society, a vision of the country undergoing a true renaissance and joining the rest of the world, from which it had detached itself in 1917. Just by articulating a vision, a charismatic leader can generate currents of vitality and create a sense of vast possibilities. Gorbachev did it. Even if he were forced to leave the political stage prematurely, his legacy would retain a stranglehold on the imagination of his people for generations to come. This much can already be said with certainty.

But visions are often impractical, sometimes unworkable. Rarely are they converted into a reality. Gorbachev initially assumed that a Stalinist, centrally planned economic system could reform itself without great pain and trauma. The idea seemed plausible, if one excluded everything but the system's obvious disadvantages and overwhelming need to keep up with the technological advances of the West. Most of the intelligent people in the establishment listened transfixed to his superbly clear, organized, and articulate exposition of arguments for perestroika.

The conservatives fought Gorbachev each step of the way yet agreed to keep perestroika alive because of the lack of a viable alternative. The reformers, becoming more aware of enormous difficulties ahead, expected that the majority would not permit perestroika to fail once it had passed the point of no return. But perestroika was a surprisingly delicate plant. What was practical and logical at the macro-level became, in the traditional Russian fashion, meaningless by the time it filtered down to the micro-levels of the society. Indeed, perestroika and glasnost had aggravated many of the problems they were supposed to cure.

The initial flood of buoyant optimism began to subside soon after the reforms encountered serious difficulties and it became clear that perestroika was going to be a far more protracted process than anyone had anticipated. Gorbachev was first given two years to show results, but two years were extended to four, then to six, now to ten. His personal credit rating declined. Gorbachev's arguments also started to lose their strength once the focus was enlarged to include all aspects of the empire's restructuring—and that came later with the collapse of communism in Eastern Europe and nationalist outbursts in the Soviet Union.

But then Gorbachev shifted the ground away from the economy into the field of political reforms, although the two were intertwined. The struggle over economic reforms was a struggle for political power. It was fierce. With glasnost having almost destroyed the conventional instruments of Soviet politics, the Kremlin infighting revealed the full extent of the institutional softness of Russia—the absence of any body of solid democratic experience, or tradition of political responsibility, the vulnerability of a mismanaged economy kept isolated from the world for seven decades, and the predatory institutional interests of the bureaucracy, the military, and the police.

The grimness of the situation was captured by conservative novelist Yuri Bondarev's metaphor: was it wise to entrust the aircraft (the Soviet state) to a pilot (Gorbachev) who did not know his destination and lacked maps and charts? But the question provoked other questions. Was it safe to replace the pilot in mid-air without a replacement who possessed the sense of direction and the charts required? What about those who argued that the aircraft should turn back? Was that still possible? Events in Eastern Europe alone indicate that turning back is no longer an option.

Even without knowing the workings of Gorbachev's mind, we find it obvious, at least in retrospect, that his thinking has undergone radical evolution in the course of the eighties. Democracy? When he uttered the word as a Politburo member in the early eighties, no one expected it to mean what Gorbachev seems, ultimately, to have intended. The same word in his mouth once he became Soviet leader seemed to regain some of its original meaning, although critics saw in it merely a propaganda ploy. By 1987, the West began to pay attention when he was telling a group of writers, "They [our enemy] are not frightened by our nuclear might. . . . They're worried about one thing—if democracy develops here, if we succeed, we will win." Democracy, in his mind, became a synonym for social modernization. Gradually he began to think in terms of political pluralism. By 1989, he was publicly endorsing Hungary's reformist leaders, who were, amazingly, initiating political changes that, after a spell of power-sharing, were to lead to immediate and genuine political pluralism and democracy. In his New Year's address ushering in the last decade of the century, he sought to explain the spectacular changes in Eastern Europe in the preceding six months as "the necessity to combine socialism with democracy." Now he could afford such talk politically, having finally managed in the fall of 1989 to neutralize his conservative opponents and push from power Politburo members Viktor Chebrikov and Vladimir Shcherbitsky and scores of Brezhnevite Central Committee members. Viktor Afanasiev was retired from the editorship of *Pravda* and Ivan Frolov, a Gorbachev aide and amateur futurologist, took his place. Yegor Ligachev was still in the Politburo, but seemed like a straw man. Vladimir Kryuchkov, the new KGB chairman, was raised to full membership in the Politburo; Yevgeny Primakov, the parliamentary president and increasingly a close confidant to Gorbachev, became a nonvoting Politburo member.

The sad thing was that perestroika was dying and its architect was fighting mightily to stave off collapse. By insisting on democratic procedures and respect for "universal human values," by endorsing the principle of self-determination and allowing his former satellites to shape their distinctively different multiparty future, he embarked on a course that it was his fate to undermine since there was no halfway point between authoritarianism and democracy. Liberalism abroad did not mean that the same rights of self-determination and pluralism were to be granted within his own borders. He had to become a tsar liberator abroad in order to save perestroika; and Gorbachev did relinquish most of Stalin's conquests in World War Two that were formalized at a wartime summit meeting in Yalta. The Malta summit in December 1989 symbolized a sharp curtailment in Soviet commitments abroad, a step that Gorbachev had indicated to his Warsaw Pact allies in the summer of 1989 when he let it be known that Soviet military force would no longer shore up the Communist regimes which resisted change—in effect writing off Eastern Europe. At home, however, he had to avoid any democratic tests; in a free election he could be defeated, with his compatriots blaming him not only for falling living standards but also for the general failure of socialism.

Gorbachev spokesman Gennady Gerasimov began to publicize the impending change in the summer of 1989 by making joking references to Moscow's new "Sinatra doctrine," a reference to Frank Sinatra's song "My Way," to suggest that all satellite countries would be allowed to go their own way. While this may have sounded like a joke in the West, it was instantly perceived by East Europeans as the death knell to Brezhnev's concept of "limited sovereignty," which was used for the 1968 invasion of Czechoslovakia. (After Malta, Gorbachev formally condemned the Brezhnev Doctrine when conceding that the 1968 invasion of Czechoslovakia was wrong.)

Eastern Europe's response was timid and tentative at first, then recklessly bold. Only Albania, sealed in its hermetic world, eluded liberation as East European communism collapsed in less than six months. Poland got its first noncommunist government; Hungary's Communist Party disbanded and changed its name in an effort to increase its appeal at the forthcoming free elections. One after another the other dinosaur communist regimes were toppled. The Iron Curtain was no more. Gorbachev's personal intervention and pressure forced the dismantling of the Berlin Wall and brought about the abdication of the once invincible Erich Honecker of East Germany. (In September, Gorbachev went to East Berlin and pointedly said that those who did not change with the times would see life punish them; by mid-October Honecker was out.) Bulgaria's Todor Zhivkov and Miloš Jakeš of Czechoslovakia were removed without resistance while the hard-line Czech president Gustav Husak was allowed to swear in a coalition government and then resign, to be replaced as president by the dissident playwright Vaclav Havel, a man who had spent almost five years in prison for his human-rights activities. Alexander Dubček, the leader of the 1968 Prague Spring reforms, was brought back from obscurity and elected president of the Czechoslovak Parliament. Finally, the last Stalinist dictator, Nicolae Ceauşescu of Romania, was ousted in a bloody military coup and executed by the new reformist leadership headed by a dissident communist, Ion Iliescu, who was a student at Moscow University with Gorbachev.

The sight of Moscow in full retreat was comforting to the West. The Cold War was over. The competition between communism and private enterprise was over, too. The West hailed Gorbachev as the tsar liberator, a political magician, or—in the words of a January 1, 1990, *Time* magazine editorial—as "the Copernicus, Darwin and Freud of communism all wrapped in one." Even President Bush, who had insisted for more than four years that Gorbachev was merely a smooth "idea salesman," joined the Western chorus heaping praise on the Soviet leader. "Yes, I think I can trust Gorbachev," he told *Time* columnist Hugh Sidey after the Malta summit in December 1989. "I looked him in the eye, I appraised him. . . . He is a guy quite sure of what he is doing. He has got a political feel. . . . When I first met him in Moscow when I was Vice President and brought up human rights, he grew very heated. This time he talked very rationally, not rancorously."[1]

Gorbachev's popularity abroad did not count for much at home; nor could his foreign triumphs offset the squeals of pain over a declining economy. Talking with Bush over lunch aboard the *Maxim Gorky* off Malta, he was concerned that his capacity to bring food and consumer goods to his people would prove "the ultimate test" of his leadership. He still lacked a convincing plan for reversing the economic decline. His supporters argued that he had to move slowly at home. After the dramatic changes in Eastern Europe, one of his closest associates, Vice President Anatoly Lukyanov, raised the possibility of pluralism in the Soviet Union by indicating that the way would be open at some future date for a revision of Article 6 of the Soviet Constitution, which grants the Communist Party a monopoly on power. This and another major problem—the issue of private property—have been subjects of strenuous debate, and Gorbachev charted his own approach. He was moving away from the traditional Marxist-Leninist positions, but attempting to protect himself at the same time. His supporters floated far-reaching proposals on both these issues while he appeared to stake out a centrist position, arguing that the country was not ready for competing political parties or private property but leaving the door open for both in the future. Simultaneously, one of his key personal aides, Georgi Shakhnazarov, publicly endorsed a draft law that would remove legal barriers to the registration of new political organizations, an issue which has been the main bone of contention between Gorbachev and Kremlin conservatives.

It was not only the conservatives he had to worry about. Even more stringent criticism was increasingly coming from the radicals in the new Congress of People's Deputies who created an opposition caucus known as the Inter-Regional Group. The caucus comprised about four hundred deputies of the 2,250 members of Congress, but among its members were Boris Yeltsin, Gavriil Popov, Roald Sagdeyev, Yuri Afanasiev, and other leading reformers. Nobel Peace Prize winner Andrei Sakharov, one of its leaders, was drafting a speech advocating political pluralism when he died of a heart attack on December 4, 1989. He was sixty-eight. Gorbachev's eulogy revealed genuine feeling for the nuclear physicist; the two were often at odds, yet they managed to carry on a dialogue amid all the clamor. "It is a great loss," Gorbachev said. "You could agree or not agree with him, but you knew he was a man of conviction and sincerity. He was not a political intriguer. I valued this in him."

The tribute to Sakharov provided a hint about Gorbachev's state of mind. Increasingly he treated with disdain anyone who opposed him, and those who vigorously advanced different ideas he viewed as intriguers. When a conservative Siberian party official, Alexander Melnikov, criticized him at a December 9, 1989, meeting of the

Central Committee for seeking popularity in the West and even "blessings" from Pope John Paul II, Gorbachev responded by saying that if the party wanted a different course he was prepared to step down. Ivan Frolov, the *Pravda* editor, described the resignation offer as "an orator's device"; it was the third time, however, that the Soviet president had threatened to step down. Like Romanov reformist tsars of the nineteenth century, he wanted to have a real parliament, but only if this would not lead to the collapse of authority and the ruin of the state. But it was as if politics and ideas had developed more quickly than anyone could have foreseen, turning onetime fervent supporters into merciless critics. The liberal intellectuals, once solidly behind him and normally savage in their views on the conservatives, were now pressing him to move faster and uproot the most deeply held ideological assumptions. Boris Yeltsin became an active competitor, openly criticizing Gorbachev for using foreign-policy "fireworks" to conceal domestic failures.

Yeltsin publicly parted ideological ways with his former mentor. "Those who still believe in communism are moving in the sphere of fantasy," he said in an interview with the Athens daily *Kathimerini*. "I regard myself as a social democrat."

Less than two weeks later, Gorbachev responded in public, deliberately echoing the words used by Yeltsin from the opposite corner of the ring, with an impassioned statement of a personal political creed delivered to the December 20 session of the Congress of People's Deputies: "I am a communist, a convinced communist. For some that may be a fantasy. But for me it is my main goal."

Other radicals, such as economist Nikolai Shmelyov and historian Yuri Afanasiev, did not go as far as Yeltsin, but they criticized the "limits of Gorbachev's model of reforms" and contended that his version of perestroika had played itself out. Their argument was that Gorbachev, at the root of his political being, was committed to the preservation of the Soviet empire and a Marxist-Leninist version of socialism, that he was trying once more to create a model of an ideal society and impose it in practice. But this was an enterprise without a future. Was it possible to create a "better empire"? The old multinational and multilingual state spread over eleven time zones was held together by violence and centralism. Without violence it was bound to collapse. They also regarded as wrongheaded Gorbachev's determination to salvage something of the "culture of Marx and Lenin"—that culture was vanishing before their eyes. Why not give it up? Why not admit that the past seven decades of sacrifices and efforts had been based on a flawed notion which inflicted agony and suffering on several generations and all for nothing?

Gorbachev's reaction was predictable: he accused Afanasiev and his supporters of disloyalty. Such public tribunes bore no responsibility for their words and actions. What they advocated was easier said than done. In the same December 20 speech he denied the right of self-determination invoked by Baltic republics. "I am convinced that nowadays to exercise self-determination through secession is to blow apart the [Soviet] Union, to pit peoples one against another, and to sow discord, bloodshed and death."

He was hurt and angered when an opinion poll revealed that these radical tribunes were more popular than he. He lashed out at liberal editors after the hugely popular weekly tabloid *Argumenti i Fakti* reported in the fall of 1989 that he was not among the ten most popular figures in the Supreme Soviet, a smaller chamber of the Congress of People's Deputies that was to become the real locus of power under Gorbachev's reforms. Two months later *Time* magazine made him its most prominent cover celebrity of the second half of the century; instead of naming him Man of the Year for 1989, it designated him Man of the Decade—the only precedent having been set in 1949, when Winston Churchill was *Time*'s Man of the Half-Century.

But the agonizing debates of liberals and radicals seemed increasingly irrelevant beside the popular feeling of hopelessness and despair. Once again, a joke, circulating in Moscow in early 1990, captured the mood: "There are two ways—one realistic, the other fantastic—for resolving the crisis of the Soviet economy. The realistic way is to have people from outer space come and straighten out the mess. The fantastic way is for the Soviet people to sort it out on their own."

All these turnabouts were not as sudden as they appeared. All had been foreshadowed several years earlier. But even the most farsighted analysts never envisioned that Gorbachev would embark on a foreign-policy course so radical and so swift that it seemed the work of a desperate gambler or reckless adventurer.

After five years in office, Gorbachev was in a mood of very considerable frustration. He was fifty-nine, but he was feeling the self-imposed strains of his perestroika, to say nothing of his determination to modernize a country that steadfastly refused to be organized. Perestroika had become a personal challenge, as he explained it to the Central Committee on December 9, 1989: "It's my lifework. It's my way of seeing things and I am not giving up." Yet barking critics easily got under his skin and he kept lunging into foreign affairs to hide his own inner uncertainties about perestroika. So he found it necessary to be in the limelight; he had to dazzle the world in order to believe in himself. People who had seen him in earlier years were struck at Malta by an apparent deterioration in his physique: he was still nimble and erect but there was the beginning of paunchiness. His features had coarsened under the punishing pace of events he was trying to control. He did most of the talking during parliamentary sessions, often showing imperious impatience with backbenchers demanding attention. But unlike Alexander II, Gorbachev stayed the course. Few Russian leaders since Peter the Great had so unequivocally assigned Russia the full responsibility for her condition; none had linked more firmly than Gorbachev the moral and political developments in the West and the rule of law with Western technological and material advancements. He was now openly asking for assistance from abroad—from America, Canada, Japan, and Western European nations—which merely stoked the fires of depression in the Soviet Union. The country had lost its confidence and its way. This is what the conservatives had been saying for nearly five years.

Gorbachev has put his faith in the inherent good sense of the people, and this will ultimately decide the fate of perestroika. The initial test of his faith in the popular will paid off. They seized their first real chance at election. In a nation starved of democratic traditions (not just since the Bolshevik revolution but throughout its history), huge numbers of people seized the opportunity that was offered to speak their minds and vote their grievances in the spring 1989 election for a new Soviet parliament.

The elections, at least in retrospect, created the illusion of an open political struggle while failing to meet the fundamental test of any democratic balloting—providing an opportunity for the people to change the way their country is run. For all the excitement of the campaign—the mass rallies supporting Boris Yeltsin and his spectacular victory in Moscow, the election of once-dissident historian Roy Medvedev—these were carefully managed elections. The winner was never in doubt. Nor were the people allowed a choice between competing political philosophies. Gorbachev's Communist Party members accounted for 90 percent of the candidates. A few widely publicized mishaps did not matter that much; the party's grip on the new parliament was never in doubt. Nor was Yeltsin a genuine threat to the system. After all, he was still a member of the Central Committee, and his agitation in behalf of the little man merely diverted the minds of people from revolutionary anti-Soviet politics.

Still, the election's outcome was the closest to a no-confidence vote the Communist Party has experienced since 1917. The weeks preceding the elections revealed a deep split over reforms. Ligachev came out openly against Gorbachev's plan to introduce private agriculture, saying, "It was not for this that we established Soviet power." Chebrikov, the former KGB chief, exhorted party officials a few months before his ouster from the Politburo in October 1989 to fight "the creation of legal and illegal structures standing in opposition to the party" and denounced independent organizations as posing "great harm to our mighty, positive social movement."[2]

The reformists countered with mass demonstrations in support of Yeltsin, demanding Ligachev's resignation. The conservatives sought to discredit Yeltsin a week before the election by leaking damaging material about his alleged deviations, and the party leadership, including Gorbachev, agreed to form a commission to investigate Yeltsin's views. The move rebounded on the conservatives, making Yeltsin a genuine national people's hero and making certain his overwhelming victory in the capital. Tens of thousands marched in support of Yeltsin, calling him "the son of the people" and shouting

"Hands off Yeltsin" and "Down with Ligachev." Politburo member Lev Zaikov, Yeltsin's successor as Moscow's party chief, was also attacked in public meetings.

What was more notable, however, was that the voters demonstrated that they no longer take Communist Party rule for granted. A number of regional party chiefs were disabused of their notion that they could fool the plebs by running unopposed. In many urban districts, the people crowded to the polling stations for the pleasure of drawing a fat pencil-stroke through the names of local leaders. From Karelia in the west to Khabarovsk in the east, top party officials were sent flying. There had been nothing like it since the people rejected the Bolsheviks in the only free elections in Russian history, held shortly after the 1917 October revolution. In Leningrad, the electorate rejected the entire top echelon, including the regional party chief, Yuri Solovyov, a nonvoting member of the Politburo; his deputy, the head of the regional council; the city party chief (he received 15 percent of the vote); and his deputy. In Kiev, the third-largest city, both the party leader and the mayor were rejected. Four other top Ukrainian regional party bosses also lost, although they ran unopposed. In Byelorussia, five senior officials were defeated. In the Siberian community of Kemerovo, the people rejected all Communist Party chiefs. In Lithuania, the party leader and his deputy, both approved by the grass-roots movement Sajudis, were elected; but most other officially approved candidates, including the republic's president and prime minister, were defeated. Sajudis won thirty-one of the thirty-four Lithuanian seats. The same percentages applied to the neighboring Latvia and Estonia.

This was something Gorbachev had wanted. He was anxious, as one of his top supporters put it, to have the voters "destroy the apparat." He wanted to weaken the Stalinist structure of the Communist Party and Soviet state. Only then could he move against his enemies, take decisive economic steps. The system was bankrupt and had to be completely revamped.

All this was taking place against the background of furious political struggles, which were becoming more heated as a result of the slow decline of the party's power and prestige. Party recruitment was dwindling. The conservatives were particularly strong in the countryside, where there was considerable opposition—and even greater indifference—to Gorbachev's plans to lease state-owned fields to farmers. He had to concede Ligachev's point. His advocacy of private initiative, he said, should not lead anyone to "the conclusion that the collective-farm system was ineffective."[3]

Until the 1990s, public opinion never played an important role in Russian politics. Gorbachev's own generation was the first to grapple seriously with this new concept, whose ultimate importance could not be predicted with any accuracy.

Indeed, his generation has been yearning for a new way of life, between past and present, between the security of a low-grade welfare state and the perceived anarchy of the Western market economies, between the Stalinist cog and the self-sufficient Westerner. The conflict between yearnings and possibilities was bound to remain the underlying social and political theme for the rest of this century and well into the next, irrespective of perestroika's fortunes. Which way would public opinion turn?

The whole enterprise is of a character poorly understood in the West, where perpetual changes are accepted as natural and inevitable and transformation is viewed as a process of growth. In Russia, such changes have always been effected by a benevolent autocrat and his retinue, who simply set the date for new procedures or administrative arrangements. Gorbachev understood this. Other tsar-reformers mistakenly thought they were bringing enlightenment to their people while in practice they were merely acquiring Western technology and grafting it by force onto a reluctant country. Genuine modernization and enlightenment require a change in the nature of government in Russia and a new social contract with the population. This is why Gorbachev wanted to carry out a revolution. And in a revolution one can expect cries of pain and resentment, since, as he put it, "One of the signs of a revolutionary period is a more or less pronounced discrepancy between the vital interest of society . . . and the immediate day-to-day interests of the people."

Gorbachev has been facing a classic Catch-22. What most people truly want they also fear the most. Soviet life offers security and satisfaction of the basic needs but few material advantages. People are prepared to follow Gorbachev enthusiastically only if his policies promise relief, not a rise in economic hardship. But Gorbachev has been asking for sacrifices now for a promise of later rewards. Perestroika introduced elements of risk, individual responsibility, initiative, sacrifice, hard work, cost accounting—all of which are alien to the system of values and attitudes inherent in a way of life based on the Stalinist system. He needs to show them that perestroika is working, but that proof has not been forthcoming, for it depends on a period of sustained growth in labor productivity, which, in turn, depends on incentives in the shape of visible benefits.

It is not surprising that many Soviet citizens as well as foreign observers have been inclined toward an apocalyptic view. How could it be otherwise? The centuries-long inheritance of absolutism and Stalinism still holds the spirit of the country in its grip.

His admirers see Gorbachev as the shining knight using every scrap of his energy and talent to save the Soviet Union from itself by breaking the pattern of Russian history and hurling it on a genuine path of modernization and growth—"our last chance." They fear his removal would plunge the country into an almost irreversible economic and moral decline.

His detractors, however, regard him as a dangerous heretic who has sullied the most cherished promise of an inevitable communist glory in the distant future by having earthbound accountants calculate that no such paradise is in store unless the country rolls up its sleeves and gets down to work, and that even then, under the best of circumstances, the old promise has been a fraud, a false dawn. By doing so, he has betrayed the Bolshevik ideals and exposed his country to foreign influences, and thus to foreign danger.

In the West, the crisis of communism is viewed as the onset of a "historic decline" of the Soviet Union. If that indeed is the case, it will take another twenty or thirty years to become fully clear.

This position is debatable at best, and it seems to ignore some basic facts of Russian history. The growth of Russian power since the time of Peter the Great has been almost uninterrupted, despite patches of adversity and retreat along the way. There is no firm evidence indicating that the current period of internal turmoil and foreign retrenchments is more than another period of adversity.

Indeed, one could argue that Gorbachev, deeply conscious of his country's weaknesses, has been pragmatic enough to de-escalate sharply his competition with the West for a generation or two and cultivate properly his own vast garden. Or, to put it differently, the whole purpose of perestroika has been to change the course of this competition and channel it into a more desirable and ultimately more profitable channel.

Nor is it reasonable to believe that Russia is incapable of reforms and changes—although it can be said with certainty that in Russia any such reforms and changes are bound to be slow and modest rather than quick and sweeping. One of the imponderables is to what extent Gorbachev, being a total politician, may have overdramatized the scope of the crisis to energize a lethargic nation or, more likely, to use the exaggerated picture as a weapon in his internal political combats.

The theology of communism has been altered during the Gorbachev years, probably irrevocably, and this has led to an ever graver crisis of the spirit in the Soviet Union, breeding unease, distrust, and contempt for the rulers, who are perceived as lacking a sense of direction. Yuri Bondarev articulated this streak of the Russian mind that finds it inconceivable—intolerable, even—that a people can be thrown into the tides of history without a functioning ideological compass. The Russians and the other peoples of the Soviet Union have been capable of suffering in silence, of making sacrifices, and of clinging to their ancient attitudes as long as they had something to believe in that was magnificent yet untested, pure yet unknown. They could find sustenance in the Orthodox Church and even in the sort of kindergarten Marxism that they were forced to absorb, because both held out the promise of Russia's salvation and future glory. It is hard for them to see such promises in perestroika.

Here is the paradox. The country is brimming with ideas and talent, it possesses a huge industrial base and enormous resources, yet it seems reluctant to organize all these things around perestroika. The degree to which Gorbachev will be able to change the thinking and attitudes and swing them behind his drive is the crucial issue. And this is risky. He cannot escape political arithmetic. By ceaselessly striking at the system and pressuring for changes, he has created opposition at all levels, thereby endangering his political survival. In spite of his victory over Ligachev and other conservatives, he has had to struggle to get each measure approved.

While focusing his attention on domestic affairs, Gorbachev has been buying time abroad. He has managed to regularize relations with the United States and China. He has advanced a more sophisticated approach to international affairs and created a climate in which he could encourage a reduction of the U.S. presence on Russia's flanks. He has shunned strategic responsibilities and engagements in the Third World, and instead sought to expand diplomatic and commercial relations. Moscow no longer pushes revolutions, or seeks to offer ideological inspiration to others; nor is it advancing itself as a model of economic development. In a curious way, Gorbachev's Russia seems to have stepped back from the traditional quest for supremacy. Unlike his predecessors, he has made concessions and sought a long-term strategic stalemate with the United States. The world has seemed poised on the threshold of a brave new era of economic growth and peace.

All these moves have been calculated. Gorbachev knew that the Kremlin's global position was weakened. He has been engaged in a rebuilding of Soviet society—and thus of Soviet power—and has been ready to pay the price to gain long-term goals. If successful, he expects a revival of Soviet power.

How realistic are such calculations? Is Gorbachev merely a realist seeking the maximum benefit for his country from an already untenable situation? Or has he been playing a deep and devious game to precipitate the breakup of Western unity? We can only speculate. There are indications that his need to see himself as master of events was directly related to his growing frustrations with the course of perestroika. He could not take the East European way toward political pluralism, nor was he willing to resort to the repressive Tiananmen approach of Deng Xiaoping. But glasnost and perestroika—his surrogates for democracy and the market—were not going to produce a communist system that is economically efficient and politically democratic. He wanted to make Soviet society more democratic, but internal pressures—the economic ruin, nationalist and secessionist agitation—were pushing him toward a personal dictatorship as the only way to restore authority and control. While a reassertion of a firm hand would be in line with the pattern followed by reformist tsars in Russian history, however, it would run counter to Gorbachev's deepest aspirations. Having reached this impasse, Gorbachev is using his imagination and energy on foreign policy—the only area where he can act decisively. It is essential to realize that he is, in fact, bringing sacrifices to the altar of perestroika. He may have been troubled by his own destiny—to preside over the disintegration of the empire he had inherited—but he probably found solace in the fact that he was divesting himself, in an orderly and dignified manner, of lands and peoples his predecessors had subdued by conquest and annexation.

By turning his back on Eastern Europe, he was bound to reap economic benefits while transferring political troubles to the West. The German reunification issue plunged the entire European system into turmoil. It was now only a question of time before the American military presence on the continent would be sharply curtailed. The shape of a united Western Europe after 1992 firmly linked to the United States became somewhat blurred as West Germany became mesmerized by the lure of a united Germany. Many Europeans feared a united Germany would dominate the continent. It also would become a powerful economic magnet for imoverished noncommunist governments in Eastern Europe. The East Europeans themselves would have to deal with the ancient animosities and tensions that led to two world wars in this century.

In the context of this stunning gamble, Gorbachev's New Thinking about European security suggested a diplomatic return to the pre-Cold War era. He expanded his "common European home" notion into the concept of Europe as a "commonwealth of sovereign democratic states," proposing a new Helsinki conference on European security and cooperation. He and Bush agreed that NATO and the Warsaw Pact should become instruments of political—instead of military—coordination. Communism was no longer a factor. He trusted Bush no more than Bush trusted him. But he needed the

American president's goodwill and was strong enough to restrain his style in order to allow Bush to shine at Malta. As far as the Soviet bloc was concerned, he said two days after the Malta summit, the East Europeans had moved decisively toward democracy, having crossed the "line beyond which there is no return the the past." The overriding impression was less of a calculated duplicity than of a high-risk move to save perestroika through a dramatic shift in the balance of power that would allow Moscow to retain its superpower status without the prohibitively high costs of responsibility for Eastern Europe. From the fall of 1989, the issue of German reunification would dominate European politics for a long time, easing pressures on Gorbachev's western flank and allowing him to play off one country against the other—or groups of countries against one another—thus retaining the capacity to influence the shape of any eventual alliances. It was decisive break not only with communist diplomacy but with that of the tsars as well, both of which, under different guises and armed with different sets of ideological arguments, were pursuing territorial aggrandizement. The Cold War was finally over.

The new climate has opened up possibilities for the West to engage a more flexible Kremlin leadership in efforts for building more durable relationships, especially in Europe. It will take time to find proper responses to the myriad opportunities.

The most striking opportunity of the Gorbachev era has been in the field of arms reductions. Indeed, perhaps one of his greatest achievements has been to revive the belief that East and West can curb the nuclear-arms race, a belief first articulated by John F. Kennedy in his 1963 American University speech (which quickly led to the first test-ban treaty). Another milestone achievement, at least in the context of his own country, has been Gorbachev's public recognition that human rights are an issue of universal importance.

Domestically, Russia has been changing, but not fast enough. Gorbachev faces difficulties yet to come, especially when the planned price reforms are implemented. By advancing such ambitious goals, he may have discounted Soviet society at large, its capacity—and even its desire—to assimilate his reforms.

What he wants to do is, in effect, to dismantle the world's largest welfare state. He wants to energize an ossified society. Millions of ordinary people have been genuinely baffled by his efforts. He has been trying to reason with them, and coax them. But a thousand years of despotism have conditioned the Russian psyche and taught people to respond mainly to force.

Gorbachev's Russia, at least theoretically, is a land of considerable promise. A whole class of intellectuals and professionals, the Soviet yuppies, are enthusiastic about the changes. They are indeed a middle class, but one that lacks any sense of corporate identity. Instead of forming a powerful interest group, they are fragmented, and participate in Gorbachev's reforms only to the extent that they benefit from them. They are the class from which Gorbachev himself comes. He was one of over 1.5 million lawyers and economists produced in Soviet universities since 1950. His daughter Irina, who graduated in 1980, was one of five million students in full-time higher education at the time; she became one of the country's 1.2 million physicians. For this emerging professional class, changes have been dramatic. There are new private restaurants with decent service and food, shops with neat striped awnings, Jane Fonda–type aerobics classes on television, open-air bazaars selling abstract and religious art. For the first time, Russians can hire a private attorney and purchase international publications such as the *Guardian,* the *International Herald Tribune, Le Monde,* and the *Financial Times,* as well as the West German fashion magazine *Burda* translated into Russian.

But this class is a tiny drop in the bucket of Soviet society. Outside the circle of government officials and intellectuals who wave the Gorbachev banner, we found varying degrees of ambivalence or hostility to his program. What forms the greatest challenge is the mass of workers and peasants standing outside the tides of historical debates, preoccupied instead with the shabby world of privations. Few among them have been impressed by the leader's elegant foreign-policy concepts or by perestroika itself. Their alienation seems total. "Although the majority live in bad economic conditions, they are not showing enthusiasm for changes," said a senior government economist.[4]

Managers too have been confused and perplexed by market instruments they suddenly had to master, or at least take into account. Nobody before has demanded that they learn the principles of financial self-sufficiency, thrift, better productivity, and other basic facts of capitalist life. The government and the people seem at cross-purposes. As one cynical observer put it, "While Gorbachev and company want to avert national economic disaster, the majority of people have only one concern—to avert personal disaster from another national con job."[5]

The people were, as economist Gennady Lizichkin put it, "afraid of the test of the market." It meant greater responsibility, higher productivity, and realistic prices. It also meant the "inevitability of substantial discrepancies in the level of productivity" and consequent social stratification.[6] The prospect of inequalities has brought the *uravnilovka* impulse back into play, and shop-floor Russian nationalists and demagogues have sought sustenance in the good old days, when things were clear-cut and orderly. Men like these, who are given to rough talk, have become overtly anti-Semitic, encouraging attacks on private shops and openly grumbling against the reformers. This in turn has hampered the spontaneous development of private cooperatives in production, marketing, and services. Envy has fueled bureaucratic interference and demands for heavy taxation of private enterprises. The new entrepreneurs are hated by their neighbors and harassed by the bureaucracy. The manager of Moscow's first cooperative café, on Kropotkinskaya Street, has been denounced with disturbing regularity in anonymous letters to the police. "Every month there is a new rumor that he has been arrested," a friend of his said. Contrary to what a Westerner would expect, most Russians are against the legislation allowing limited private enterprise. "These people are obviously only in it to get rich," a low-paid teacher said in a remark that was echoed in other quarters. "So what did we have the revolution for?"

A Moscow waiter who used to dream about having his own restaurant and becoming rich was cool toward perestroika. Why not open a cooperative café? we asked him. "Oh, no, that's not for me," he said, adding a mindless Russian parrot-cry: "I'm not a Jew."

Making money, in this deeply anti-Semitic nation, was something done by the Jews.

The problem with a Stalinist economic system is that, although the "majority of people live badly," their discontent is offset by the fact that everybody shares the same misery. A senior economist offered the following anecdote to illustrate this psychological point. The devil visits the torture room in hell, where there are three huge tubs in which sinners are boiled. The first tub is heavily guarded, the second has only a few guards around it, but nobody is watching the third tub. The chief devil demands an explanation from his subordinates. "Well," they explain, "we have to guard the first tub, because that is where the Armenians are; if one of them manages to sneak out, he is sure to pull the rest of them out with him. In the second tub are the Jews, who are divided into ideological factions: if one manages to jump out, he will pull a few of his friends out but not the others. And in the third tub are the Russians. We don't need any guards on them: if one of them tries to jump out, you can be sure the others will pull him back down again."

The problem is that perestroika has been dying. To bring it to life, Gorbachev started buying large quantities of Western food and consumer goods, promising to guarantee stable and ample food supplies by 1995. But to restructure agriculture and get the economy moving, Gorbachev has to create a new managerial class, which would get a grip on the cost of production and work out price reforms. It will take time to create such a managerial class. Price reforms, as China's experience could testify, are painful and politically dangerous. In the short run, however, he needs injections of consumer goods to pacify the population. Without clearly discernible changes for the better, Russians are most likely to drift, as time goes by, over to the hostile side of the fence. That is where the millions of alcoholics are, and the lazy, and the countless members of the older generation who still have Stalin in their hearts.

Here, on the hostile side of the fence, are ranged all the ordinary people who want no changes in a system that provides them with a living that may be pitiably third-class but is secure and undemanding. Their hostility to the leader bristled through a myriad of jokes about his crackdown on alcoholism and price-reform plans. After the government raised the price of sausage, a staple of the Russian diet, people vehemently complained, recalling the time when sausage had been cheaper, albeit unavailable. With higher-priced sausage in plentiful supply, they were hankering after the "good old days."

A ditty captured the popular mood. Roughly translated, it ran:

> *Sausage prices twice as high,*
> *Where's the vodka for us to buy?*
> *All we do is sit at home,*
> *Watching Gorby drone and drone.*

Though glasnost is important to intellectuals, workers will only respond to more practical and tangible improvements, which have not been in evidence. A joke illuminates the point. A man goes into a bar and asks for a pitcher of beer. The bartender tells him it costs a ruble. "A few months ago it was only fifty kopeks," the man says. The bartender replies, "Oh, but you have to pay for glasnost now—now you can say whatever you want here, so it's fifty kopeks for glasnost and fifty for beer." "Fine," says the man, "I like glasnost. Here's a ruble." But the bartender hands him fifty kopeks change. "What's this?" the man says. "You just said fifty kopeks for beer and fifty kopeks for glasnost." "That's right," says the bartender, "but we have no beer."

In the short run, the role of the silent majority is not crucial. There are more important groups—the party bureaucracy, the military, the KGB—that Gorbachev has to worry about. But in the long run, perestroika's fate will be decided in the nation's streets, factories, and farms. The outlook is uncertain. Most workers resist efforts to make a direct linkage between wages and productivity; they vehemently oppose price increases. Indeed, it is hard to find any ordinary Russian who favors plans for more rational pricing, which is the central aspect of Gorbachev's economic reforms. They could hardly be expected to: most prices have been artificial, and exceptionally low. The introduction of wage cuts for low productivity has already led to widespread disenchantment.

And yet, in a dim way, most people have grasped the inevitability of Gorbachev's policies. Many people in the elite have become aware of the outside world; many understand the tension between Stalin's society of obedient functionaries and inert workers and Gorbachev's vision of a society that would free native skills and entrepreneurship and generate more productive spontaneity. Many believe that eventually the latter will prevail. But they are frightened by the prospect. They have become aware that they must make the plunge if they are to avoid decline and decay. But even those who understand this still look to the state for protection and direction, as Russians have done for centuries. The country reminds him, Lizichkin said, of "a person afflicted by gangrene but afraid of amputation."[7]

Gorbachev himself was accused by Boris Yeltsin of being afraid to perform the surgery. The populist politician argued in his autobiography, published in 1990, that Gorbachev had come to relish the trappings of power, that he was out of touch with popular sentiments and aspirations, and that he seemed to have lost the capacity to listen to opposing views, which he tended to drown by his endless "monologues."

"I do believe that perestroika would not have ground to a halt, even with the tactical mistakes that have been made, if only Gorbachev had been able to get rid of his inhibitions over the question of the leadership's perquisites, if he himself had renounced all those completely useless, but pleasant, customary privileges." Instead, Yeltsin charged, the Soviet president had built for himself a new home in the Lenin Hills overlooking Moscow and a new dacha outside the capital; he had also restyled his Black Sea dacha at Pitsunda and constructed an "ultra-modern" summer home at Thorosin, in the Crimea.

"And then, to cap it all, he announces with pathos at the Congress of People's Deputies that he has no personal dacha. Didn't he realise how hypocritical that sounded?" Technically, Gorbachev was right, he did not have a personal dacha. The dachas were owned by the state and Gorbachev had exclusive use of them. However, Yeltsin said, this technicality made little difference to the people, who had lost faith in Gorbachev's slogans and appeals. "I believe the fault lies in his basic cast of character. He likes to live well, in comfort and luxury. In this he is helped by his wife Raisa."[8]

•   •   •

If cynicism is pervasive, so is escapism, the old Russian story. Some people patiently endure the drudgery of life; some find solace in the spiritual world. There has been a marked revival of the Orthodox Church as well as a new interest in yoga, the Hare Krishna movement, and other Eastern religious philosophies. Many have lost faith in their country and retreated into their personal lives. They have lived through too many false hopes and new beginnings to believe any longer that the system can change or that it will affect them in a meaningful way.

Over the years, we frequently visited a friend whose intellect and zest for life made him seem like an unlikely victim of apathy. When we first met him he was full of hope. His country was about to open up, to join the rest of the world. This was during the détente of the Brezhnev years, and Tolya, a Communist Party member, was deputy chief of a national service industry. What, we used to wonder, had led him voluntarily to give up an influential post, with all its privileges, and take a modest job well below his qualifications? Occasionally he talked about it, saying that the life of limousines and other perks could not outweigh the frustration he felt with the system's inefficiencies and dishonesty. He took a huge pay cut but was able to carve out a small zone of personal freedom. He became an amateur silversmith and delighted in making jewelry for his friends; he also took up photography. In his late forties, he led a rich life within the walls of his apartment, where the glow of warm hospitality obscured its shabbiness. But it was sad for us to see him a resigned man just at a point when the things he had hoped for a decade ago were actually happening. There had been so many pronouncements, such a chasm between what was said and what was delivered, that all connections between them had become meaningless and it was almost impossible to re-establish them. When we spent an evening with him in the fall of 1988 he told us the latest news he had heard on the Russian service of the BBC, and launched into a long and intricate analysis of Gorbachev's program; he sounded like a man who would like it to succeed. But why, we asked, was he talking about it as a curious onlooker? "It's all too late for me," he said.

"Even if things improve, it won't affect me. It's like placing flowers on a grave."

People like Tolya are sitting on the fence. Are they merely cowards, as poet Yevgeny Yevtushenko sees them? ("We are killing perestroika with civil temerity, waiting by the sidelines to see which side wins.") Or are they ill prepared, ill educated, ill led? Are there enough reformers to provide energy and direction? If perestroika is dying, what is the alternative?

When we visited with Tolya in late February 1990, the country was in the depth of despair and hopelessness. He, also, has lost hope. He related the latest joke, which captured the apocalyptic mood of the capital: "Soviet society is now divided into three categories. First are the optimists, who believe in Gorbachev's rhetoric; second are the pessimists, who are studing English and hoping to emigrate; and third are the realists, who are taking AK47 Kalashnikov automatic rifle lessons to prepare for civil war."

Chapter 21

A WORLD
WITHOUT COMMUNISM

The seeds of revolution that Gorbachev allowed to germinate in Eastern Europe eventually began to bud in the Soviet Union in 1990, when he lived up to his early promise of being a reformist tsar. In one stroke, he abandoned the principal tenet of Lenin and Stalin, that of dictatorship, and reversed Russia's centuries-long heritage of autocratic rule. On February 5, 1990, Gorbachev asked the Central Committee of the Soviet Communist Party to give up the party's constitutionally guaranteed monopoly on power. He offered the country yet another new beginning. When the Central Committee, after bitter and frequently acrimonious debate, voted two days later to endorse his proposal, Russia seemed to be heading toward what Lenin once derided as "bourgeois democracy"—a system of competing political parties and meaningful elections. The Communist Party, Gorbachev said, would compete for political power "strictly within the framework of the democratic process."[1]

It was a climactic point of Gorbachev's rule, and marked the onset of the age of post-communism.

The party as Lenin had created it was effectively no more; this was the party that had led Russia for the past seventy-two years, making a mammoth effort to haul the country up to the level of the Western world, only to see it fall dismally behind. By prodding the party into action and stimulating the country with the vision of democratic socialism, which the Kremlin always had derided, Gorbachev was trying to salvage its future.

Now more than ever he needed peace at home and abroad to transform Russia. He had guaranteed peace abroad by abandoning the conquests made by his predecessors, by making concessions in the field of arms control, by deliberately transforming the imperial mindset of the country. His voice was instrumental in German re-unification. He sought to keep peace on his western borders by political and diplomatic means, using as his forum the Helsinki conference on European security and cooperation. He reached agreements with the Bush administration on sharp cuts in forces in Europe and major reductions in chemical and strategic arms. The world looked at Moscow with different eyes, acknowledging that Gorbachev's policies altered the international order as it had been known since 1945.

Peace at home, however, was threatened by unexpected forces unleashed by glasnost and perestroika. Gorbachev was no longer in control of a society that was increasingly developing a multiform life of its own. From the standpoint of his country's ethnic relations, Gorbachev had opened a Pandora's box; the forces he had released could not again be contained. The declaration of independence by the Lithuanian legislature on March 11, 1990, foreshadowed more troubles for his new federalism. The domestic situation was made even more difficult by the fact that after five years in office he could not hope for immediate economic results. He had come to realize that perestroika was doomed and that his great economic reforms would require a generation to take hold and mature. The only way out seemed to be a change in the political system so dramatic that it would prod the country to learn political skills, offering new generations an outlet for the idealism, enthusiasm, and initiative that had been bottled up by the conspiratorial Bolshevik system of government.

Gorbachev pinned his hopes on the creation of a French-style system of executive presidency overseeing a cabinet responsible to the legislature. But not everyone shared his optimistic belief that once he became a powerful president with his base of support outside the party he finally would be equipped for a showdown with the party bureaucracy. And some liberals worried that such a concentration of power in the hands of one man—a man they suspected of being, deep down, contemptuous of democracy and the West—would be a bad precedent.

An unsympathetic observer could go further and argue that as the Soviet Union entered the nineties in agony over ethnic turmoil and economic disasters, Gorbachev had been forced to yield to the inevitable. He had sown dragon's teeth and was reaping the crop. His grip on power was weakening. His ostensible triumph merely reflected his consummate skill at shaping his own image. He was able to prevail only because he was stronger than a system growing rapidly more feeble. In reality he was presiding over the collapse of socialism as a moral, political, and economic idea; he was also presiding over the disintegration of the Russian empire.

Nevertheless, his supporters were elated. The system established by Lenin and Stalin, and maintained by Brezhnev and Chernenko, was an extension of the tsarist empire and had little to do with socialism. Gorbachev was trying to create a new kind of "democratic socialism," but that meant jettisoning the most cherished Marxist-Leninist assumptions. "We want to become a normal democracy," said the eye surgeon Svyatoslav Fyodorov, a member of the Central Committee and a Gorbachev supporter.[2] Hence the real task was not to restore the vigor of the system created by Stalin—or even to amend it radically—but rather to replace it altogether. Gorbachev was the last tsar, who wanted to become Russia's first elected president.

No leader of Russia had ever gone that far. The Russia of the Romanovs as well as the Russia of the communist tsars was an empire run on the military model with power flowing from above, its legitimacy grounded in the unchallengeable ideological tenets of the mystical "divine right" of Russian Orthodoxy or the Marxist-Leninist conspiracy enshrined in Article 6 of the Soviet Constitution, which said that "the leading and guiding force of Soviet society and the nucleus of its political system, of all state organization and public organization, is the Communist Party." It was inconceivable for a chief of the Communist Party voluntarily to relinquish power, even when he genuinely wanted to change things. But Gorbachev created a new parliament with a portion of members chosen in the first partially free elections; it was a very long way from parliamentary government but was farther from the nakedly dictatorial rule of his predecessors. Yet early on Gorbachev came under fire from the liberals for not going far enough. Led by Andrei Sakharov and Boris Yeltsin, they were clamoring for the abolition of Article 6, which stood in the way of their dream of an elective assembly possessing genuine legislative powers. For nearly two centuries this dream had been shared by all Russian reformers, but they had been frustrated first by absolutism and then by proletarian dictatorship.

Before the Bolshevik revolution, the Romanov tsars had held the strong conviction that they were carrying out the will of God as His obedient adjutants on earth. This justified the assertion of absolute authority in the name of the Almighty even by a weak tsar such as Nicholas II, who possessed no natural authority at all. Not that various Romanovs did not toy with the idea of political reforms. Under Alexander I at the beginning of the nineteenth century, Michael Speransky proposed a set of changes that would create an institution to be known as the Duma—an elective legislature that would pass laws requiring confirmation by the tsar. However Nicholas I, who succeeded Alexander, thought the idea of a national legislature sacrilegious lèse-majesté. Alexander II, who followed Nicholas, had on several occasions in the latter part of the nineteenth century expressed interest in the idea but only if this would not lead to the collapse of authority and—in his view—the ruin of the empire. It was not until shortly before the 1905 Russian revolution, one century after Speransky advanced his draft reforms, that a Duma was created; but even then, Nicholas II did not attempt to dilute the supremacy of the court and the bureaucracy. A brief and chaotic democratic experiment after his abdication at the height of World War I precipitated the Bolshevik revolution of 1917. The subsequent Bolshevik tsars clung to the same principle, except that they asserted absolute authority not in the name of the Almighty but in the name of the Marxist myth.

When, shortly before his death, Andrei Sakharov proposed from the rostrum of the Kremlin Hall of Congresses that Article 6 be abolished, he was ruled out of order by Gorbachev himself. Less than two months later Gorbachev was to make the same proposal to the Central Committee. Gorbachev aides said privately that he had intended to do this in due course and that his disagreements with Sakharov involved timing, not substance. But radical critics contend that Gorbachev received two hard knocks that brought him and his program to a turning point and forced his hand. His historic move, whether deliberately planned or a swift response to an unforeseen opportunity, came after the turmoil in Lithuania and Azerbaijan that electrified the country and demanded immediate corrective action.

January 1990 was a month of grave crisis.

First came Lithuania.

On Thursday, January 11, as Gorbachev began a three-day personal mission to Lithuania to temper local demands for outright independence, a huge crowd of about 200,000 assembled outside Vilnius's main Roman Catholic cathedral to dramatize pro-independence sentiments. Gorbachev was conciliatory, saying that he respected the Lithuanians' opinions but urging them not to demand outright independence. "There is no absolute freedom," he said in a televised speech that evening, reminding the Lithuanian demonstrators that it was his own policy that had enlarged Lithuania's autonomy. "We have started out on this road. I am the one that chose to go ahead with it. My own fate is linked to that choice."

He spoke to the crowds in Vilnius, arguing that a small, independent Lithuania would be launching herself on perilous international waters, where survival was uncertain. He assailed the Lithuanians with questions: "Do you think that if tomorrow you suddenly found yourself independent you would solve all your problems? Where are you going to run to? Why run away?" It was the spectacular performance of a desperate man counting on his powers of persuasion, his logic and reason, to stem the tides of nationalist passions.

But Lithuanian nationalism was on the rise. The Lithuanians liked and respected Gorbachev and recognized that his presence in the Kremlin was the guarantee of their newly acquired autonomy. Yet their attitude was summed up by a pro-independence leader, Vyatautas Landsbergis, who said that while Gorbachev was "a man of reason," the Russians ultimately would have to "give back what was stolen"—the Lithuanian territory must be returned to the Lithuanians.

If three days of Gorbachev's nationally televised walkabouts and discussions in Lithuania did not demolish the myth of the unity of Soviet nations and nationalities, another, far more brutal outburst, this time of Shiite Moslems, did. Both events impinged severely on Gorbachev's personal authority, and the subsequent use of force in Azerbaijan and later in Tadzhikistan produced panic in the upper echelons of Kremlin power.

While Gorbachev was still in Lithuania, an Azerbaijani Popular Front rally in Baku on January 13 degenerated into an uncontrolled anti-Armenian pogrom that spread to other parts of the southern region that borders on Iran and Turkey. As the pogrom extended into the countryside the next day, armed Armenian nationalists countered by slaughtering Moslem villagers along the Armenian-Azerbaijani border. The situation got out of control, escalating into civil war. On January 15, small contingents of military and security troops went into the area to impose calm on the inflamed Nagorno-Karabakh territory, a largely Armenian enclave in western Azerbaijan. Meanwhile, Azeri nationalists took up the cry of independence. Crowds carrying pictures of the late Ayatollah Khomeini, Iran's Shiite leader, went on the rampage. Moslem militants seized mortars, helicopter gunships, and other weapons from local army depots and used them against Soviet troops. The situation was threatening enough to justify almost any expedient. A Central Committee meeting scheduled for January 22 had to be postponed until February 5.

Gorbachev met violence with violence. On January 20 he appeared on national television to explain the decision to send troops and tanks to Baku to impose order. The 17,000-strong force met strong popular resistance; the Moslem nationalists unfurled a huge poster in the center of Baku the next day that read GORBACHEV—THE BUTCHER OF AZERBAIJAN. More than two hundred died and another four hundred were wounded in two days of street fighting before the military imposed its rule.

It was the cumulative impact of a variety of misfortunes—the swift collapse of communist power in Eastern Europe, the palpable sense that economic reforms were failing, the crumbling of the empire, more unrest in Moslem Central Asia—that made Lithuania and Baku turning points. Economically, both proved enormously disruptive. They made the whole country tremble, especially since they were preceded by the disastrous miners' strike of the previous summer and an even more calamitous slowdown of railway workers throughout the fall. (The Soviet transportation system is utterly dependent on the railways, and the slowdown produced dislocations in the pits, on the docks, and in the steel mills.)

The psychological impact was devastating, not merely because people were disturbed by bloodshed on their television screens and frightened by the prospect of the collapse of a fragile multinational state. Most of the old certainties were evaporating. Laid bare for all to see was the impotence of an authoritarian state—a state that could build sophisticated weapons but was incapable of feeding its population. A deep sense of shame was symbolized by the opening in Moscow of a McDonald's restaurant, geared to serve about 15,000 persons a day. As in the times of Peter the Great, who brought Germans, Dutch, and other Europeans to build factories, Muscovites again were gawking at things brought from a foreign land—this time at shiny counters, molded plastic, and pristine glass. They were awed by McDonald's operational style and quality control. "I must admit," said the anchorman on the nationally televised Sunday program "Seven Days," "that I feel deeply ashamed. But what's to be done? We have to learn."

The rapid succession of disastrous news items generated a bitter nationalist reaction among ordinary Russians. Conservatives were now joined by Russian traditionalists against a reforming tsar whose progressive changes had polarized society; Gorbachev's attempt to create a moderate, progressive center foundered. The death of Andrei Sakharov deprived the radicals on the left of a major moral force, leaving Boris Yeltsin as their main rallying point. On the right, Yegor Ligachev again gained ground, this time as a standard-bearer of Russian nationalism as well as a party conservative.

The weeks before the February 5 showdown were times of great factional infighting. Ligachev, speaking in Tomsk, indirectly assailed his chief's position by saying, "Without ever having flown around the Statue of Liberty [a jab at Gorbachev who *had*], I believe that we are marching toward communism." In that same speech he asserted, "There is not, nor has there ever been anywhere in the world, a political formation as solid as the Communist Party of the Soviet Union."[3]

Several weeks later, the flagship of perestroika, the weekly *Moscow News,* responded with an unprecedented personal attack on Ligachev, accusing him of a wide range of sins, including the glorification of Stalin, lying, and clinging to outmoded doctrinal concepts. The editorial was accompanied by a photograph of Ligachev giving a Nazi-like salute.[4]

No longer was this a subdued and muffled conflict. The party was deeply split. So was the country. The conservatives openly blamed Gorbachev as the main source of all troubles. The Russian nationalists also joined in; but the grounds on which they based their opposition to his policies were different. As Alexander Bukhanov, editor of *Soviet Literature,* put it, "For the West, Gorbachev is the destroyer of the communist monster, but in so doing he's destroyed everything that we believed in, everything that kept us together. Gorbachev hasn't built anything new, he hasn't thrown us a life ring! The people, myself included, are on a sinking ship, on a plane that's falling, and that's what terrifies us."[5]

It is hard to realize that this great drama was precipitated by the party general secretary; it was as though the 1917–18 factional struggle between Bolsheviks and Mensheviks was being fought all over again; and Gorbachev's views resembled those held by the Menshevik leader Martov rather than those of Lenin, the Bolshevik leader. The Mensheviks had opposed Lenin's notion of the party as the "political vanguard" holding all threads of power in its hands. Days before the plenum, the *Ogonyok* editor Vitali Korotich, speaking in imperfect English to Dan Rather, articulated the reformists' sentiments: "Our society was never so polarized as now. Before, we were all together, we felt the differences are not so important. It was necessary to build together and to march toward the happy future. Now we understand that we will never be in a happy future together. And being divided we start to fight for two futures, one for them and one for us. To our people this society was quite good. It's the same as what is now in China. A clever wise government decides about everything from the type of my belt to the type of my spectacles and to the type of our economy. In this happy society people must think about nothing. They simply receive everything from the government. Another type is telling please let's finish with this way, administrative way is finished. Now we must start something else. Please let's be individuals, let's have market economy, let's have free enterprise, let's have free press, and in this way we will reach more [sic]."[6]

Suddenly, perestroika alone was no longer a viable rallying point. Neither the left nor the right was satisfied with the middle course perestroika represented. There were only two ways to go. Ligachev demanded a return to centralization. The liberals demanded a true multiparty democracy. It was an old Russian dilemma. For, in a sense, both left and right were asking the party leadership to make a choice of civilizations, a choice between Europe and Asia, between West and East, between Westernizers and latter-day Slavophiles.

The liberals thought Gorbachev lacked the radicalism required to force the issue; Gorbachev, said journalist Alexander Bovin, tends to resort to half measures; he was increasingly being controlled by history, rather than making it. Radical reformist deputy Sergei Stankevich saw the Soviet president as an ambivalent figure, a product of the system, but at the same time wholly alienated from it, "with one foot standing outside the system." Gorbachev is a "transitional figure," Stankevich argued, because if the process of reform continues, it will inevitably reach a point at which Gorbachev must relinquish his preeminent position to become just an ordinary participant in the new political process.[7]

The conservatives sought to capitalize on the apocalyptic fears of an impending catastrophe and on popular discontent by spreading rumors that Gorbachev's days were numbered. The tone of a January 24 press briefing at the Soviet Foreign Ministry was surreal. The spokesman, Gennady Gerasimov, responded gingerly to questions about whether Gorbachev was still in full command. Yes, he was, said Gerasimov, because "there are no alternative leaders, no alternative policies." Then he quoted George F. Kennan, the noted American Sovietologist, as saying that the Soviet president was safe "because there is no one around who wants his job."

After a ten-day absence from public view, a haggard and worried Gorbachev appeared on January 30 to meet the new East German premier, Hans Modrow. Again Gorbachev talked about foreign affairs. He voiced his opinion that the prospect of German reunification was not in doubt, adding that "it is necessary to act responsibly and not decide this important matter in the streets." But on the same day a well-planted leak had Gorbachev on the verge of resigning as general secretary of the Communist Party; the report reverberated throughout Moscow and the world, touching off a flurry of selling in Western stock markets.

The next day, the main attraction on the evening news program "Vremya" was Gorbachev, saying that he had no intention of resigning—doing so during a photo opportunity as he was greeting Brazil's president-elect, Fernando Collor de Mello. President Bush made a public-relations gesture to shore up Gorbachev's crumbling position. Bush phoned the Russian leader, ostensibly to discuss arms-control prospects and to give him a preview of the proposals for troop cuts in Europe that would come a day later in the American president's State of the Union address. Tass promptly reported the conversation, suggesting that the Soviet leader was in control.

On the eve of the February 5 plenum, the reformists mounted a huge rally outside the Kremlin wall. Yeltsin, their putative leader, called for a multiparty system, saying that this was the party's "last chance" to preserve its credibility. Crowds estimated at 200,000 took part in demonstrations, carrying signs containing a variety of slogans: MIKHAIL SERGEYEVICH, WHICH SIDE YOU ARE ON?; SEND THE DINOSAURS INTO RETIREMENT; SOLDIERS! DON'T SHOOT AT YOUR OWN PEOPLE.

The final showdown never came. Gorbachev's victory was in a sense devalued by the fraudulent unanimity. Central Committee members, with Yeltsin as the sole exception, voted to remove Article 6 from the constitution. As so often in Russian history, in a face-to-face confrontation, the boyars could not defy the tsar. Also, as in the past, the tsar shrank from such a dramatic gesture as cutting himself off entirely from the huge bureaucratic establishment—unable to resolve his dilemma: although the bureaucracy was the root of all evil, he could not execute his reforms without it.

Casting a shadow on what was conspicuously an epoch-making plenum was the fact that Article 6 was eliminated without substantive debate, without any real soul-searching, without the substitution of a new vision. Haunted by bloodshed in the streets of Baku and elsewhere, the leaders dismissed Article 6 and squabbled instead over who was responsible for it all. The panic could be felt. The debate over who had ordered army troops to put down pro-independence demonstrations in the Georgian capital of Tbilisi the previous spring provided the most dramatic exchanges at the plenum, according to a transcript of the proceedings published by *Pravda* on February 8. The fearful carnage had claimed the lives of twenty unarmed civilians within minutes of the army's moving in on April 9, 1989.

The reformists publicly pointed an accusing finger at Ligachev. Ligachev said that the decision was taken by the entire Politburo. Gorbachev remained silent, but his friend Shevardnadze took the floor to "restore the truth."

There was no formal Politburo meeting on the matter, he countered, just "a meeting at the airport" on April 7, 1989, when most Politburo members gathered to greet Gorbachev upon his return from his trip to Britain. Local Georgian officials had requested that troops be sent in to maintain order, and Shevardnadze said that their request "was approved." But, he stressed, Gorbachev had insisted that the Tbilisi unrest be resolved "by political means, through political dialogue."

In this charged and unpleasant atmosphere, Gorbachev, far from losing his head, took the high road and pressed on with his reforms. By the time Secretary of State James Baker III met him in Moscow two days later, he was in a visibly good humor.

What chance does Mikhail Gorbachev have of surviving in a multi-party system?

Looking at the fate of Communist parties in Eastern Europe, one finds it hard to fathom how Gorbachev might succeed where so many have failed. But he and his supporters find sustenance in the fact that the Soviet party, unlike those in Eastern Europe, is not identified with foreign domination; that historically it has been associated with rising living standards; above all, Gorbachev has forced it to recognize the need for a multiparty system, and therefore the Soviet Party can avoid the pitfalls of half-measures. But perhap's Gorbachev's greatest chance of longevity derives from the fact that none of the numerous and poorly organized opposition groups offers a realistic alternative to the vision he has introduced. And there was no turning back: splits in the Communist Party ran so deep that no longer could anyone talk about a monolithic Leninist organization.

Gorbachev has changed before the eyes of the nation and of the world. He has formalized his thinking by trial and error. He has laid before his people a plan for a form of constitutional government—not a Western democracy, but a more democratic type of rule compatible with Russian traditions. He has accepted many concepts advocated by a new faction within the party known as the Democratic Platform, which sees an ill-defined social democratic model as the path for retaining its preeminence in a competitive environment. Like Franklin Delano Roosevelt, who introduced socialist legislation to save capitalism in the 1930s, Gorbachev is introducing capitalist measures to save some force of socialism in the Soviet Union.

Gorbachev has sought to become a Soviet-style de Gaulle, getting himself elected president by the Congress of People's Deputies and freeing himself, in one stroke, from the traditional constraints on a

Soviet leader's power—the party, the bureaucracy, the armed forces. In that sense, he also preempted radical pressures for fully democratic presidential elections in the fall of 1989. He was deeply aware of the fact that coherent reform from above might not be possible, and that he would have to respond to changes and pressures forced from below.

Direct presidential authority would free Gorbachev from the need to secure prior approval for his actions in the event of crisis. But he did not want to risk the massive economic and sectarian unrest, and the intervention of those who were unreconciled to the changes of the Gorbachev era, that unprecedented direct presidential elections might generate. Moreover, democratic presidential elections could result in a victory for Yeltsin. And while Yeltsin performs a useful function as a radical benchmark against which Gorbachev's reforms can be measured, it is far from clear what his populist brand of leadership and his simplistic platform could do to meet the country's needs at this critical juncture. Despite charges against Gorbachev of "authoritarianism" and "Bonapartism," his record in office entitles him to ask for the necessary authority to enact a reform program that eventually should embody the creation of a market economy in the Soviet Union and the establishment of a new federation based on consent rather than coercion.

It is entirely possible that ultimately Gorbachev will be rejected by the nation in a free election, and that in that sense his rule constitutes a "transitional" period between authoritarianism and democracy. But rather than a defeat, this would be a triumph of Gorbachev's reform; he would set the example for a democratic future in the Soviet Union by accepting an orderly transition of power.

Gorbachev has sought power and has enjoyed wielding it, not as a narrow-minded apparatchik amassing power for his own sake, but with a larger purpose. He is a strong leader who defied the old Russian saying "The tsar wishes but the boyars will not allow." He has imposed his will on the boyars. He has offered the country a vision of an exciting new society, more just and more efficient, a society that would take its rightful place in the family of nations it fled in 1917. He pursued his vision creatively as a superb political tactician. If he were to be faulted it would be on one point: his boundless confidence and ambition to harness his country's potential has led him to ignore an essential aspect of politics—that human beings do not always react the way one believes they will when designing programs for them.

The decade of the 1990s will be a period of turmoil and crisis in the Soviet Union. If Gorbachev prevails, he will continue to change his country and the world profoundly; if he does not, he could lose power to another leader. But in either case, his personal imprint on the age will remain.

Afterword

DEATH OF PERESTROIKA

On February 7, 1990, he successfully pressed for the abolition of Article 6 of the Constitution, which guaranteed communist monopoly on power. Gorbachev finally opened the door to democracy in the Soviet Union, but his action could not have been more ill-timed. All indices and analyses showed that two overwhelming factors were bound to combine to kill his program. One was popular hostility to a market economy; the other the threat of the union's collapse.

Gorbachev's decision to abolish Article 6 is the most momentous political act of his reign to date, with the most far-reaching consequences. It was undoubtedly his finest hour, a sort of apotheosis. His critics argued later that, at that point, he had no intentions of living up to his unambiguously stated promise that the Communist Party would give up "any and all legal and political advantages" and that it would struggle for power "strictly within the framework of the democratic process." It was clear immediately that whatever Gorbachev's motives, the party barons would not take this emasculation lying down. But instead of responding with vehement protests, the entrenched conservatives took a passive role, knowing that Gorbachev's ultimate defeat would result from the country's internal turmoil—rampant inflation, dizzying unemployment, civil disorder, and the chaotic disintegration of the union. No wonder Gorbachev was exhausted; a heavy fatality lay over the year 1990, a year of sunken spirits for him and his entourage. No wonder he slowly changed during the course of that year. At a point when every shred of his talent and energy was needed for the mammoth task of dragging his country into the modern age, he was forced to squander them not only on shadowy struggles with the conservatives but also on the more intractable problem of self-determination in the republics.

Lithuania was the first new tremor in a series of nationalist earthquakes threatening to destroy Gorbachev's neat federalist ideas. He imposed an economic blockade on Lithuania to force its leaders to suspend their independence declaration. He tried to fend off the rise of Boris Yeltsin as a national figure. Yet Gorbachev's situation deteriorated steadily as he battled problems on all fronts.

While he was engaged in a war of nerves with Lithuania, other republics started moving in the direction of sovereignty and independence, disrupting his equilibrium. First Estonia and Latvia; then larger republics along Russia's southern borders; then Russia itself, the largest republic, accounting for more than eighty percent of the territory; eventually the Ukraine, the second largest in size and economic process. Moreover, Soviet Jews began an exodus to Israel of unprecedented proportions, depriving the country of entrepreneurial skills desperately needed in a market economy.

The Baltic nations marked off the year with an open revolt against Moscow, bringing forward long-suppressed anti-Russian sentiments, deep and endemic throughout non-Slav Soviet republics. The revival of militant nationalism threatened to destroy everything Gorbachev had worked for. He no longer seemed blessed with a magician's touch. The prospect of collapse preyed on his mind; indeed the word he began using in his speeches with great frequency was *razval* (which means breakdown, disintegration, collapse). He had misjudged his own strength; above all, he had misjudged his people.

Public security was endangered in many parts of the land by armed nationalist gangs operating against one another and against the police. Russian residents of non-Russian areas in the country came under increased pressure to resettle in Russia proper. A mass exodus of Russians from the predominantly Moslem Tajikistan came in the wake of ethnic riots in February 1990. In the ensuing five months, more than 23,000 ethnic Russians moved out of Tajikistan (12,000 of them from its capital, Dusnanbe). Anti-Russian pogroms in the

Tuvinska Autonomous Republic, an area of southern Siberia bordering on Mongolia, also led to mass resettlements.

A heavy blow came in May 1990 when the conservatives took charge of the newly established Russian Communist Party, naming the hard-line apparatchik Ivan Polozkov as its first secretary. All leading opponents of perestroika were elected to the party's central committee, and according to one of his closest friends, Gorbachev was profoundly disturbed by this resurgence of the conservative influence.

By mid-1990 discontent with his programs was almost complete. Gorbachev and his colleagues were jeered by throngs of spontaneous demonstrators who joined the annual May Day Parade in Red Square. Television cameras caught a startled Gorbachev, his demeanor changed, his lips curled, watching from the top of Lenin's Mausoleum as fist-shaking protesters chanted, "Resign," and "Shamo," and waved banners saying: SOCIALISM NO THANKS, DOWN WITH THE KGB, DOWN WITH THE RED FASCIST EMPIRE, DICTATOR-PRESIDENT WITHOUT ELECTION, SEVENTY-TWO YEARS ON THE ROAD TO NOWHERE, GORBACHEV RESIGN, POLITBURO RESIGN.

The Czar jeered by his people! His eyes blazing, he put on his glasses to read the slogans, then impatiently tapped his hand on the rhubarb-red granite wall before leading his colleagues from the mausoleum. Within days the Supreme Soviet passed a new law making public insults of the president and his office a punishable offense.

The loss of prestige and authority rankled Gorbachev. The populist politicians were gaining support, men such as the newly elected anti-communist mayors of Moscow and Leningrad, and most especially Boris Yeltsin. Gorbachev had become almost paranoid about Yeltsin's challenge. On the eve of Thatcher's visit in June 1990, he granted an interview to Jonathan Dimbleby of the BBC on the condition that Yeltsin's name not be mentioned. When Dimbleby ignored the stipulation (Yeltsin, after all, was already the second most significant political personality of the land) he was rebuked and told he would never interview Gorbachev again.

There was a personal animus between the two men. The more Gorbachev sought to block Yeltsin's emergence as a rival leader, the more popular Yeltsin became. And at the end of the 28th Party

Congress, in July, Yeltsin stole the show when he announced from the rostrum of the Kremlin Palace of Congresses that he was quitting the party. He was followed by the leading reformist politicians, including the mayor of Moscow, Gavriil Ropov, and Leningrad leader Anatoly Sobchak. An anti-communist coalition was formed.

The congress was probably the last event of its kind. The Leninist party was no more. The congress gave Gorbachev what he wanted by endorsing the shift of power from the Politburo to the newly created Presidential Council. A few years earlier this would have been a landmark event. Now it was a Pyrrhic victory: it didn't matter. The party was increasingly irrelevant. Psychologically, the congress underscored the overwhelming futility of the previous seven decades, the degradation of a system built on lies and coercion, the emptiness of convictions that echoed repeatedly in the same vast chamber and were transmitted to national radio and television audiences over the years.

In contrast to previous congresses—when everything was a sacred secret and any sign of disagreement was carefully muffled—the 28th Congress was played out in public. As waves of familiar speeches rolled by, there were echoes from the past: calls for discipline, platitudes about "the noble idea of socialism," demands to strengthen the party, allusions about who was stripping the Soviet Union of security.

On the eve of the congress, Yegor Ligachev announced that the conservatives would mount an open challenge to Gorbachev. In an interview with *Pravda,* he said: "Let's ask the people what road we should take in reconstructing our society—either the socialist or the capitalist. Let's hold a national referendum."

Ligachev was a candidate for the new post of deputy general secretary, but the congress gave the job to Gorbachev's candidate, Vladimir Ivashko, the former party chief of the Ukraine. By a margin of four to one, the 5,000-odd delegates also reelected Gorbachev as general secretary. (In the past, the general secretary and Politburo members were elected by three hundred top party apparatchiks who formed the Central Committee.)

The new Politburo was enlarged and given over to regional or minor political figures. While all other top officials relinquished their

Politburo seats, thus making their government positions and seats on the presidential council the only source of their power and authority, Gorbachev refused to resign his party leadership. This was, in retrospect, a telling move on his part. He has struggled against the party long and vigorously, but ultimately he would not relinquish such a politically powerful base.

The structural changes appeared, somehow, irrelevant to the Soviet people. What was significant, however, was that the death of ideology had opened the floodgates of nationalism, and the surest way for local communist elites to maintain power was to embrace nationalist causes and interests. Under Gorbachev's prodding, the congress had accepted his argument that "federalization" of the party would revitalize and strengthen the crumbling Bolshevik edifice. As a result, communist parties in the republics were given broad permission to adopt their own policies to suit local conditions.

But this amounted to tampering with deeper, darker currents of history, and exposing the complexities of the "nationalities problem" (as the presence of 170 different ethnic groups speaking more than 200 languages and dialects is referred to). If the events in multi-ethnic Yugoslavia can be used as a guide, clearly "federalization" sealed the disintegration of the Bolshevik party.

By September Prime Minister Ryzhkov warned that the party's federalization was impinging on the government's ability to do its job. "To be, or not to be, a united country, that is the question," was his prophetic declaration before the Supreme Soviet.

In this confusing transition period, the Slavophile voice of writer Alexander Solzhenitsyn entered the national debate. Sitting in his Vermont exile, Solzhenitsyn declared that this was no time for Hamlet. Instead he proposed an all-Slav state to replace the Soviet Union. The Slavic republics—Russia, Byelorussia, the Ukraine, and a large part of Kazakhstan—must "loudly and clearly declare" their separation from the non-Slav parts to form a Russian Union. The new state should take its lead from Russian history rather than from contemporary Western models. The basis of its political system should be the *zemstvo* of the nineteenth century—self-governing village and town councils. Solzhenitsyn rejected large-scale capitalism but accepted the principle of a multi-party democracy with some private ownership.

The sixteen-thousand-word article published in two Soviet newspapers was Solzhenitsyn's first direct address to his compatriots since he was deported in 1974. In it, he returned to his old themes. The Communists, he said, have poisoned the soul and psychology of Russia. Now "the knell has sounded for communism, but the concrete structure has not yet toppled, and we face a danger of being crushed by its wreckage instead of being liberated." The novelist touched on the latent strains of Russian chauvinism, the always present and ineradicable conviction of the innate superiority of the Russian consciousness.

Gorbachev rejected the Slavophiles' call. It was perhaps at this point that he entered into an unholy alliance with those forces deeply entrenched in Moscow's ministries—the security forces, the Communist Party establishment, and regional military commands, all of whom wanted him to abrogate more authority in order to save the union.

The outward calm and public detachment which Gorbachev maintained in the face of continuous setbacks was uncanny. He seemed to have no sense of what was going on in his land, no ability to recognize the new spirit of nationalism for what it was. The Lithuanians in his eyes were not nationalists; the women of Tbilisi still mourning their murdered sons and husbands were not patriots; they were merely unruly subjects too ignorant to recognize the benefits of his new federalism.

The central issue confronting the president was how to reconstitute the union. He did not understand what Yakovlev and Shevardnadze understood reluctantly—that to cede more power to the republics was the only way to head off larger independence movements. The exception were the Baltic states, which Yakovlev admitted were more forcibly incorporated, implying that they eventually might go independent.

But such distinctions were lost on Gorbachev, and by the end of 1990, both Yakovlen and Shevardnadze were not of the inner circle.

Gorbachev's personality acquired a tragic dimension. Nobody

knows what were the inner monologues that must have plagued his private moments. But Margaret Thatcher, who visited Moscow in June 1990 and who liked Gorbachev, provided an insight into a troubled man devoid of energy. "I don't know what I have to do to get some sleep," Gorbachev confided to her. "I cannot sleep at night. I would like to sleep in the afternoon. I almost fell asleep at the Warsaw Pact [meeting]."

The Soviet economy was prostrate, national morale at rock bottom, perestroika dead, and expedience, more than strategy or vision, seemed to be governing Gorbachev's actions. His vacillation on Stanislav Shatalin's "Five Hundred Days" plan, more than anything, revealed Gorbachev's powerlessness on economic issues. The plan, supported by Yeltsin, called for a radical capitalist market cure. Prime Minister Ryzhkov objected furiously because of the brutal credit squeeze the plan would impose on the defense industries, leading inevitably to widespread bankruptcies. The blow to the traditional political patronage system, and particularly the fear of a popular backlash, forced Gorbachev to ultimately side with the military-industrial complex. But only after detours and zigzagging. He decided on August 4 to cooperate with Boris Yeltsin on the new package of economic reforms.

Then at the end of August, he pulled back from the deal and embraced Ryzhkov's compromise of a more gradual plan. This was, at least, what he told Ryzhkov.

Indeed, on September 10 Anatoly Lukyanov announced that the prime minister would present Gorbachev's plan for economic reforms to the legislature the next day. But when Ryzhkov's speech on the morning of September 11 provoked an uproar and demands by deputies that Gorbachev publicly take a stand on the matter, the president pulled the rug from under Ryzhkov. As far as he was concerned, Gorbachev declared, he favored the Five Hundred Days program of Shatalin over Ryzhkov's program. ("When did you learn that the president favors the Shatalin plan?" Viacheslav Terekhov of the Interfax news agency asked Ryzhkov after the session. "The same time you did," replied Ryzhkov.)

The Five Hundred Days program was a public relations miracle.

Yeltsin held out hopes for a smooth transition from Marxist slogans to capitalist wealth in a short time, a major step towards the millennium.

Gorbachev eventually accepted a compromise version of 720 days. But he and most of those around him knew that such a shift was impossible. The country at large was against a market economy. As he confided to Thatcher, "We're not fully prepared to face the psychological requirements of the market."

More and more the people began to talk about alternatives to Gorbachev. Once again, a joke sums up the public attitudes toward the floundering leader: A chicken farmer goes to the village priest when ten of his chickens die one day. "Give them all aspirin," says the priest. The farmer complies, only to find twenty chickens dead the next morning. "Father, I have more trouble," he says to the priest. "Don't worry, my son! Give them all castor oil." No luck. The farmer finds thirty chickens dead the next morning. "Give them all penicillin," again advises the priest. The farmer goes to the priest the next day completely dejected. "Father, they are all dead!" "What a shame," says the priest. "I had so many more fine remedies to try."

The ominous prospect of famine was in the air, something which acquired substance when Moscow began dumping large quantities of gold and diamonds on world markets to pay for food imports. By the summer of 1990 the government had to ask the armed forces to help with gathering the harvest; Defense Minister Dmitri Yazov dispatched 45,000 military trucks into the fields. By fall, white-collar workers—intellectuals, doctors, professors, and party officials— were again wading through ankle-deep mud outside Moscow and other major cities trying to rescue a potato harvest that became a metaphor for the country's economic quagmire.

As the winter set in, strikes spread throughout the land. Many factories were at a standstill because of disruptions in transport, gas, water, and electricity. Shops were empty. No work was done. The conservative opposition, moved by selfishness or fear or both, abandoned passive resistance in favor of deliberate obstructionist tactics. They, in fact, had nothing to offer; nostalgia for a return to the old Soviet Union is not a policy.

With a tragedy looming over their heads, the brightest and most intelligent men and women of Russia were once again at the same crossroads their ancestors reached a hundred years ago, and again debated endlessly on which way to turn. But Supreme Soviet debates became peripheral to a country that seethed with anger and indignation. Statistics for 1990 revealed sharp declines in the country's industrial output, oil production, and productivity.

At the end of September, the legislature finally granted Gorbachev sweeping presidential powers to carry out the crash reform program—involving a draconian credit squeeze and an immediate start to mass privatization. But virtually nothing happened. Instead, a plethora of signs showed Gorbachev responding to relentless conservative pressures.

A mindless cry—"Too little too late"—has been coming from liberal critics and highly intelligent but frustrated reformers who accuse him of becoming more irresolute and wavering, long on talk and short on deed, no longer able to broker compromises with his distinctive blend of vision and pragmatism. (Even his own advisers said privately that he had become too willing to split the difference every time he was faced with a difficult choice.)

But that is the old Russian story. One could argue with equal cogency that, far from being too little and too late, Gorbachev's policies were too much, too soon. He had pushed too hard, and while the vague ideal of constitutional government was starting to take hold of "society," it was kept alive—as were so many magnificent schemes in Russia's past—by the sheer force of rhetoric. To close the mind to this possibility is to show inadequate appreciation of Russia's history and social development.

Also dead was the promise of the orderly transformation of an inefficient economic system into a modern, productive one. Which in turn meant that his notion of creating a "new civil society"— through a genuine devolution of power to local governments rather than through authoritarian intervention—would have to be shelved for the time being.

By the end of 1990 the right-wing backlash against perestroika became broader, especially as the ethnic violence and secessionist demands by rebellious republics led to a revival of Russian nationalism. The demise of perestroika was announced by Nikolai Ryzhkov in his last official statement on December 19, 1990. The country was out of control, he said. "Perestroika has wrecked many established structures, but nothing effective has been put in their place. There is neither a plan nor a market."

The spirit of an aggressive chauvinism was already emerging with all kinds of variations in all sorts of men who had only one thing in common: the desire to preserve the Soviet state. The breadth of the new alliance was revealed when Gorbachev was urged to resort to authoritarianism in an open letter signed by top military men, including General Mikhail Moiseyev, the chief of staff; by the Patriarch Alexis of the Russian Orthodox Church; by Boris Gidaspov, the new conservative community chief of Leningrad; by prominent Russian nationalist writers; and such liberals as Nikolai Gubenko, the minister of culture and former Taganyka theater actor.

Gorbachev was now sixty and clearly worn down with disillusionment. No longer was he able to restore the reformers' flagging spirits. The leader who already had done as much as any man in the twentieth century to change the course of history, who stopped the arms race and engineered the end of the Cold War, the first Kremlin leader to win the Nobel Peace Prize, the man who made a gigantic effort to democratize his own society—that man was being slowly abandoned by everybody, including his closest friends and supporters.

To admit perestroika's collapse publicly was tantamount to conceding defeat. In his opaque way, Gorbachev found it harder to tolerate expressions of skepticism among independent voices in his entourage. He did not want to be confronted with the prospects of failure. Yet in his speech ushering in the year 1991, he implicitly conceded defeat by never mentioning perestroika, glasnost, or other mandatory buzzwords of his era, talking instead of the need for "law and order." And the bloodstained streets of Baltic cities where Soviet troops moved in to savagely crush independence movements in January 1991 bore eloquent witness to the change.

It was a measure of the strength of the conservative backlash that Gorbachev was unable to keep on board his closest advisers and friends, including Alexander Yakovlev and Eduard Shevardnadze. Shevardnadze, aware of the drift into reaction, quit publicly on

December 20, and was replaced by the veteran career diplomat Alexander Bessmertnykh. It was a disaster. His oldest friend, in an emotional address from the Kremlin Palace rostrum, declared that he could "not reconcile myself to the events which are taking place in" the Soviet Union, adding:

> Dictatorship is coming. I state this with full responsibility. No one knows what kind of dictatorship it will be and what the regime will be like. I want to make the following statement. I am resigning. Let this be—and do not react and do not curse me—let this be my contribution, if you like, my protest against the onset of dictatorship.

Gorbachev was stung. "To go now is unforgivable," he said about Shevardnadze's action. "We are not talking about a dictatorship but about strong rule. And the two must not be confused. But if we act irresponsibly, and if we do not listen to the signals from society, there may come a time when society will look for an exit through any option."

The old "perestroika gang" was no more. Most went quietly. Political scientist Fyodor Burlatsky was nudged out of his circle of advisers in April 1990; Lev Zaikov was pushed aside a month later and was retired soon afterward. Gorbachev's trusted friends from Stavropol were also gone. Vsevolod Murakhuvsky, once the superminister for food and agriculture, was retired; Georgi Razumovsky, a confidant who, as the Politburo member in charge of personnel was one of the most powerful figures in the nation, was exiled to Shanghai as consul-general. Among those retired and shunted aside before the year's end were Interior Minister Vadim Bakatin, Prime Minister Nikolai Ryzhkov, Deputy Prime Minister Leonid Abalkin, the ideological chief Vadim Medvedev, Anatoly Dobrynin, and scores of others.

After the Bloody Sunday of January 13, 1991, in Vilnius, the flagship of perestroika, *Moscow News,* published a letter on its front page that revealed the dramatic scope of Gorbachev's isolation. Among the signatories of the letter which denounced the Gorbachev regime's "final hours" were virtually all top reformers in the country.

Only in the West was Gorbachev still seen as a vigorous leader, but these perceptions were based on Western media reports in which Gorbachev lived as an endlessly active, ever-dynamic, perpetually imperiled figure at the visual center of everything that was happening in his vast land. He was like the captain of a rudderless ship, standing on the bridge in his splendid uniform and talking to other ships by radio telephone, but unable to relay messages to his engine room.

His North American journey and his first visit to the Bush White House did little to enhance his standing at home. Indeed, while he was on his way to Ottawa, Boris Yeltsin was elected president of Russia, the largest of the Soviet Union's fifteen republics. Gorbachev was visibly shaken when he heard the news that his former protégé-turned-rival had acquired a powerful political base. Yeltsin promptly called for the transformation of the Soviet Union into a loose confederation.

"If he is indeed playing a political game," Gorbachev said in Ottawa, "then we may be in for a difficult time."

A few days later in Washington, Yeltsin stole the headlines by opening direct trade negotiations with Lithuania's President Vyatautas Landsbergis in defiance of Gorbachev's economic blockade of Lithuania. Subsequently, under Yeltsin's prodding, the Russian parliament voted to challenge central authorities by asserting that local Russian laws took precedence over Soviet laws.

Nor did George Bush help matters by rejecting tariff easements for Soviet imports, one of the things that would have allowed Gorbachev to claim success. Indeed, he left Washington empty-handed, despite widespread public adulation.

Gorbachev's frustrations came through in his meeting with U.S. Congressional leaders. He bitterly alluded to the fact that Bush had extended tariff easements to China despite the Tiananmen massacre a year earlier. His tone was pleading:

When we began perestroika we thought that we would be able just to add a certain dynamic to our society, to improve the state of research and development in the Soviet Union and through that we would be able to get a better Soviet Union. But we found out that the old economic system rejected any type of scientific and technological progress. . . .

First, we began by introducing certain new economic forms such as leasehold, cooperatives, and some others. We tried various approaches but they did not work. They did not work. Why?

Trying to inject those new elements and the new forms of economic life, we continued to retain the entire old superstructure of economic management. And we understood that, really, we were being very naïve because that system, that system which evolved over decades, was really a kind of vise, a kind of clamp on our entire national economy, and it made impossible any initiative, decision making at various levels, and therefore we had to try to dismantle that command system. And to dismantle that command system we needed political reform in order to really dismantle the command and bureaucratic system. . . .

Now that we have done that, we have to do more. We have dismantled the old system but we have not yet put in place an effective system, a new system.

Frustrated by the Americans, Gorbachev made a power gamble that was nothing short of breathtaking. In mid-July he invited Chancellor Helmut Kohl to Stavropol for an intimate one-on-one chat.

Kohl himself was unprepared for what was to come. So were all other Western allies. After two hours of conversations at the Mineralnyie Vody, Gorbachev made a stunning concession by agreeing to NATO membership for a new united Germany.

The price was German financial and technical aid. In a single stroke and for a relatively small sum—the total funds pledged amount to 21 billion deutsche marks—Gorbachev relinquished Joseph Stalin's World War Two conquest.

The quest for a Soviet-German alliance was a desperate attempt by Gorbachev to revive his economy. The pact specified a ceiling on the German military forces and pledged the withdrawal of Soviet troops from East Germany within three to four years.

"All practical problems for German unification have been cleared up," announced a jubilant Kohl.

Looking from the outside, Gorbachev's foreign gamble showed

cool brilliance, but it did not do him much good at home. Throughout the fall there were rumblings among the military that the German deal was unwise and precipitate. Questions of "Who lost Germany?" were publicly raised by deputies belonging to the ultra-conservative Soyuz bloc of about four hundred members of the Congress of People's Deputies.

The promise of German aid failed to make a dent in the disastrous economic situation. Henry Kissinger, who admired Gorbachev's flair for diplomacy, noted the fatal dichotomy. "There is almost no relationship between his distinctive and constructive efforts—almost everything he has done in the economic field is a disaster."

It was in the shadow of the Persian Gulf drama that Gorbachev's slide into reaction took place.

Saddam Hussein's invasion of Kuwait and the subsequent war turned Western attention away from the Soviet Union. Suddenly, Iraq's activities most clearly impinged on the immediate interests of the industrialized world—its access to oil. In particular, there was a new and pressing reason to fear for the safety of pro-Western Arab governments in the Persian Gulf area.

Gorbachev's foreign policy remained consistent with New Thinking. Despite the Soviet-Iraqi Treaty of Friendship and Cooperation, he sided with the Western powers and endorsed the Security Council's demand for an Iraqi withdrawal from Kuwait. Several military officers who were elected to the Congress of People's Deputies and who belonged to the Soyuz bloc openly assailed Gorbachev's support for UN Security Council demands.

In his domestic policy, Gorbachev began to rely more and more on the very three institutions he had sought to curb and modernize—the army, the party, and the KGB. He seemed almost blinded by the need for personal control. Could the empire, always held together by military force, afford democracy? He was determined not to go down in history as the man who lost his country.

In retrospect, and only in retrospect, it is clear that Gorbachev's great adventure began to unravel with the abolition of Article 6, and that most of his actions were shot through with uncertainties and contradictions, if not with plain equivocation. Very striking indeed among the contradictions was his attitude toward the Communist party. He had planned to resign as secretary general and move the locus of power to the presidency, yet he reneged at the last moment and retained the party post.

Alexander Yakovlev revealed later in a private conversation that principal pressures on Gorbachev to slowly abandon perestroika came from generals who commanded military districts and as such commanded real troops. Early in 1990, according to this account, the regional military commanders were alarmed by the prospects of the union's collapse and by shrinking military allocations flowing out of an empty federal treasury. Order had to be restored in a land where all signs pointed toward an economic and geographic collapse. Together with entrenched regional party barons and leaders of the armaments industry, the generals began to voice their demands through a handful of junior officers who had been elected to the Congress of People's Deputies. In Moscow, they found understanding and support from their new chief of general staff, General Mikhail Moiseyev, and senior officers around him.

The generals did not merely talk, they acted.

On November 14, Gorbachev's military adviser, Marshal Sergei Akhromeyev, hinted that the army would be used to maintain the country's territorial integrity.

The same day Gorbachev appointed a conservative figure, Leonid Kravchenko, as head of state radio and television.

Three days later, Lieutenant Colonel Viktor Alksnis, leader of the conservative Soyuz group in the parliament, threatened before this solemn assemblage to have a vote of no-confidence in Gorbachev "if there is no turnaround in December. ("You have exactly one month," the colonel told his commander in chief. "If you are not able to restore discipline [in the country] which we vigorously demand, you will have to go.") This was a prelude to his demand for the suspension of all political parties, the dissolution of all parliaments, and the declaration of a state of emergency.

On November 26, the Supreme Soviet endorsed Gorbachev's proposal to submit the government to direct presidential control.

Soon after, Gorbachev banned all business deals that could damage the central planning system. In practice, the move required that almost all contracts between republics be approved by the State Planning Commission in Moscow.

In a final act of authoritarianism and unknown to anyone, Gorbachev instructed Lukyanov to compose a decree establishing joint army-police units to maintain order in all major urban centers. Although signed on December 29, 1990, its existence was kept secret until the end of January, shortly before it went into effect February 1, 1991.

Asked who was responsible for the death of fourteen civilians in Vilnius on January 13, 1991, Gorbachev said, "The manner of defense was decided by the commanding officer. I learned [about it] only in the morning, the early morning when they got me up." The assault came, he added, after a group of "workers and intellectuals" asked the commanding officer for "protection."

The Supreme Soviet ranted, functioning demonstratively and uselessly in a vacuum. The people marched. One half million Muscovites demonstrated in the heart of Moscow on January 20 demanding his resignation. COMRADES, THIS IS YOUR END, said one poster. MR. GORBACHEV—ENOUGH EXECUTIONS AND KILLINGS, said another. The people cheered whenever the name Boris Yeltsin was mentioned. They booed and whistled at each mention of Gorbachev's name.

Our story seems to need another ending. Perhaps Gorbachev has not yet reached his own personal limits. Perhaps, just perhaps, this is a temporary cooling-off period. Perhaps perestroika can be revived.

The sad thing, however, is that Gorbachev's plans are disintegrating, evaporating into thin air, leaving only the wondrous memories of a purposeful, vigorous young leader with an exciting new vision for his society and for the world. The sudden uncertainty of purpose, which is the most visible distinguishing mark of Russia at the onset of the nineties, probably reflected Gorbachev's ambivalence. Is he still a true believer? Or a consummate cynic? Or is he turning toward political expediency as all his predecessors have done?

A few days before Shevardnadze's resignation, Gorbachev held a meeting with intellectuals in the Kremlin. Such sessions have become his way of shaping his own image and creating his own legend.

Perestroika, he said, was born on a beach by the Black Sea where he was strolling with Shevardnadze. "That's when Shevardnadze said that everything has become rotten," he continued. "We said we could not go on living the way we lived before." What is odd about this statement is not that Gorbachev was creating a new fairy tale (he never mentioned this scene in his book *Perestroika*). Rather, what is revealing is that he inadvertently talked of perestroika as a thing of the past. For once, according to those present at the meeting, it seemed as though he had lost heart.

Gorbachev has gained extraordinary power and used it to tame the institutions of old authority. Now these very institutions are keeping him in power. He could console himself with the fact that while he seems more dependent on them than ever, they are even more dependent on him to provide them with legitimacy, respectability, and credibility, to maintain an illusion of perestroika and glasnost. He could remain in a position of leadership for some years to come, although he will be presiding over a different edifice from the one he had envisaged.

It is an ambiguous and uncomfortable alliance. Andrei Sakharov suggested on the day he died that Gorbachev "is something of a paradox for me"—a cautious, decent man who might also be unprincipled and driven primarily by his own lust for power. Or is he perhaps simply the man from Stavropol who changed the world but who almost destroyed his own country—a defeated leader bravely soldiering on and desperately trying to salvage something of his grand aspirations.

He was squeezed to the breaking point by conflicting pressures and he compromised, bringing, for all practical purposes, the story of perestroika to a close. But did he lack courage? We can only venture an answer: Gorbachev is a most courageous—perhaps recklessly courageous—politician. The standards he set and the goals he established will guide his country for a long time. But he wanted to lift his nation beyond its capacities; he wanted to transform the national spirit and change the way it lived and worked. This undertaking, he said on one occasion, left him with a feeling of running a distance of three lifetimes in five years. He was resisted by men and women of the old order who were fearful of ideas, change, and the future. And that may be the oldest of all Russian stories.

Notes

Chapter 1

1. Y. Moshkov, *Zernovaya problema v godi sploshnoi kolektivizatsiyi,* Moscow University Press, 1966. The author says some kolkhozes were no longer "under the organizing influence of the party and the state."

2. Authors' interview with a senior official.

3. Gorbachev, conversations with three editors of the Italian Communist Party newspaper *L'Unità,* May 18, 1987.

4. Authors' separate interviews with Georgi Smirnov, director of the Institute of Marxism-Leninism and former special assistant to Gorbachev. Also authors' interview with Dr. Slava Fyodorov.

5. Robert Conquest, *The Harvest of Sorrow,* Hutchinson, 1987.

6. Authors' interviews conducted in Stavropol, June 1985.

7. Authors' conversation with a senior official who said Gorbachev, at a Politburo meeting devoted to the issue of veterans' benefits, mentioned that his older brother was killed in the battle of Kursk in 1943. Gorbachev, in conversations during his visit to Britain in December 1984, said that his father had died during the war and that he had been brought up mainly by his grandparents (cited by Martin Walker, *The Waking Giant,* New York, Pantheon Books, 1986, p. 2). Gorbachev's official biography states that his father fought in the war, but does not say when he died.

8. Gorbachev, speech to the Komsomol, June 1985.

9. *L'Unità,* May 18, 1987.

10. Gorbachev, speech to the Komsomol Congress, April 16, 1987.

11. *M. S. Gorbachev: An Intimate Portrait,* New York, Time, Inc., 1988, pp. 70–71.

12. *L'Unità,* April 9, 1985.

13. Authors' interview with Alexander Yakovlev, member of the Politburo and secretary of the Central Committee.

14. *L'Unità,* April 9, 1985.

15. Authors' interviews with two members of the class of '55 of the Moscow State University Law School.

16. Ibid.

17. *Sunday Times* (London), January 4, 1987.

18. Branson's interview with U.S. Ambassador Arthur Hartman, February 1987.

19. Gorbachev, speech to the Komsomol Congress, April 16, 1987.

20. Authors' interview with a high official.

21. Authors' interview with a member of the Council on Foreign Relations delegation.

22. Gorbachev, *Toward a Better World,* New York, Richardson and Steirman, 1987.

23. Gorbachev, interview on NBC, December 1, 1987.

24. *Gorbachev: An Intimate Portrait,* p. 210.

25. Private communication to authors.

26. Authors' interview with Fyodor Burlatsky.

27. Gorbachev, *Toward a Better World.*

28. Gorbachev, in meeting with French parliamentarians, October 3, 1985.

29. Authors' interview with a Soviet official.

30. Information supplied by Flora Lewis of *The New York Times.*

Chapter 2

1. Roy Medvedev, *Khrushchev,* Oxford, Basil Blackwell, 1982, p. 235.

2. Quoted by Zhores Medvedev in his *Gorbachev,* Oxford, Basil Blackwell, 1986.

3. Authors' interviews with two members of the class of '55 of the Moscow State University Law School.

4. Authors' conversation with Georgi Smirnov.

5. Gorbachev, speech in Kiev, June 27, 1985.

6. Gorbachev, speech, June 19, 1986, quoted by Serge Schmemann, *New York Times,* January 5, 1987.

7. Authors' interview with a senior Soviet official.

8. *Izvestia,* February 10, 1983.

9. Minutes of Proceedings and Evidence of the Standing Committee on External Affairs and National Defence, House of Commons, Ottawa, Issue No. 95, Tuesday, May 17, 1983.

10. Authors' conversation with Alexander Yakovlev.

Chapter 3

1. Gorbachev, speech to the Stakhanovites, Moscow, September 20, 1985.

2. Gorbachev, speech at Smolensk, June 25, 1984.

3. Gorbachev, *Creative Effort of the People: Materials of the All-Union Scientific and Practical Conference,* Novosti Press Agency, December 1984.

4. Yegor Ligachev on Moscow Television, July 1, 1988.

5. Authors' interview with a senior official.

Chapter 4

1. Doder's interview with Ambassador Andreas Meyer Landruth.

2. Authors' interview with Alexander Yakovlev.

3. Gorbachev, *Perestroika,* London, Collins, 1987, p. 30.

4. Ibid.

5. Gorbachev, speech to the Komsomol Congress, April 16, 1987.

6. Authors' interviews with Yakovlev, Smirnov, and other officials.

7. Gorbachev, speech at the Central Committee plenum, January 27, 1987.

8. Gorbachev, speech in Riga, Latvia, February 19, 1987.

9. Authors' interview with Alexander Yakovlev.

10. See, for example, Martin Walker, *The Waking Giant,* New York, Pantheon Books, 1986.

11. *Izvestia,* April 29, 1988.

12. Authors' interview with Alexander Yakovlev.

13. Branson's interview with Georgi Arbatov, March 1987.

14. Gorbachev, speech at the All-Union Scientific and Practical Conference, Moscow, December 10, 1984.

15. Gorbachev, press conference, Geneva, November 21, 1985.

16. Gorbachev, speech in Leningrad, May 17, 1985.

17. See James Sherr, *Soviet Power: The Continuing Challenge,* New York, St. Martin's Press, 1987.

18. Branson's interview with U.S. Ambassador Arthur Hartman, February 1987.

19. Authors' interview with Alexander Yakovlev.

20. Ibid.

21. A. I. Lukyanov, *Promoting Democracy,* Moscow, APN Publishers, 1987, pp. 15–22.

22. Gorbachev, *Perestroika,* p. 30.

23. Tatyana Zaslavskaya, speaking at a Chautauqua, N.Y., conference, August 1987.

24. Authors' interview with Abel Aganbegyan.

25. Authors' interview with Georgi Smirnov.

26. *Pravda,* April 26, 1985.

27. *Novoe Vremya,* February 1,

1985. The photograph showed Stalin, Roosevelt, and Churchill at the Yalta Conference.

Chapter 5

1. Authors' conversations with Sergei Zalygin.

2. Authors' conversations with historian Yuri Afanasiev.

3. Gorbachev, speech to Indian Parliament, November 27, 1986.

4. A. I. Lukyanov, *Promoting Democracy,* Moscow, APN Publishers, 1987, p. 4.

5. The rumor was confirmed to the authors by a member of the Finnish Parliament present at the reception.

Chapter 6

1. *Sunday Times,* London, March 29, 1987.

2. Authors' interview with Georgi Arbatov.

3. Authors' interview with Sergei Losev, director general of Tass.

4. Authors' conversation with a senior Gorbachev aide.

5. Gorbachev, press conference, Geneva, Switzerland, November 21, 1985.

6. Authors' interview with a senior official.

7. Gorbachev, speech to Supreme Soviet, November 27, 1985.

8. Quoted by Don Oberdorfer, Washington *Post,* November 6, 1985.

9. Gorbachev, speech to Indian Parliament, November 27, 1986, Delhi.

10. *Pravda,* November 26, 1985.

11. Sam Donaldson, *Hold On,*

Mr. President!, New York, Random House, 1987.

12. *Pravda,* January 28, 1987.

13. Athos Fava, press conference, Moscow, March 4, 1987.

14. Yegor Ligachev's speech at Nineteenth Party Conference, Moscow, July 1, 1988.

15. Ibid.

16. Authors' interview with a senior official.

17. Yeltsin, interview in *Moskovskaya Pravda,* May 19, 1987.

18. Gorbachev, *Perestroika,* London, Collins, pp. 96–97.

19. Gorbachev, speech to Central Committee plenum, January 27, 1987.

20. Ibid.

21. Ibid.

Chapter 7

1. Gorbachev, *Perestroika,* London, Collins, 1987, p. 235.

2. Authors' interview with Leonid Ilyin, Cologne, May 27, 1986.

3. Quoted in Ronald Hingley, *The Russian Mind,* London, The Bodley Head, 1977.

4. Gorbachev, speech in East Berlin, April 18, 1986.

5. *Sunday Times,* London, May 27, 1986.

6. Gorbachev, *Perestroika,* p. 235.

7. The Politburo's report on the Chernobyl crisis, *Pravda,* July 20, 1986.

8. Lyubov Kovalevska, in *Literaturnaya Ukraina,* March 1986.

9. Gorbachev, speech, April 8, 1986.

10. *Literaturnaya Gazeta,* November 12, 1986.

11. Ibid., January 12, 1987.

12. Ibid., October 1, 1986.

13. *Pravda,* June 17, 1986.

14. Ibid.

15. Ibid.

16. Authors' interview with Alexander Yakovlev.

Chapter 8

1. Gorbachev, speech, *Moscow News,* No. 30, 1987.

2. Authors' interview with Georgi Smirnov.

3. *Pravda,* February 13, 1986.

4. Authors' interview with Vitaly Korotich.

5. Authors' interview with Anatoly Rybakov.

6. Alexander Novacic, *Sovjetski Izazov,* Zagreb, Globus, 1988, pp. 196–97.

7. Ibid.

8. Authors' interview with Sergei Zalygin.

9. Gorbachev, interview in *Time,* August 28, 1985.

10. *Pravda,* July 8, 1986.

11. Gorbachev, speech at Vladivostok, July 28, 1986.

12. Gorbachev, *Perestroika,* London, Collins, 1987, p. 237.

13. Gorbachev, speech on Soviet television, October 14, 1986.

14. Authors' interview.

15. Gorbachev's press conference, Reykjavík, October 12, 1986.

16. Authors' conversation with a senior official.

Chapter 9

1. *Pravda,* October 15, 1987.

2. Authors' conversations with several Soviet officials.

3. Gorbachev, speech in Bucharest, May 26, 1987.

4. Authors' interview with editors.

5. *Sovyetskaya Rossiya,* November 30, 1986.

6. *Izvestia,* December 5, 1986, and other press articles.

7. *Sotsiologicheskie Isledovania,* January 1987, pp. 48–53.

8. Gorbachev, interview with Indian editors, November 21, 1986.

9. Gorbachev, interview in *L'Humanité,* February 4, 1986.

10. Authors' interview with Fyodor Burlatsky.

11. Authors' interview with a senior Soviet official.

12. Lev Navrozov, "Andrei Sakharov: A Forgiven Slave Aiding His Masters," *New York City Tribune,* February 16, 1987.

13. Gorbachev, speech to the Komsomol Congress, April 16, 1987.

14. Ibid.

15. Gorbachev, speech to party and government activists and economic managers of Estonia, Tallinn, February 21, 1987.

16. Gorbachev, speech in Riga, Latvia, February 19, 1987.

17. Ibid.

18. Authors' interviews in Moscow in the spring of 1987.

19. Gorbachev, speech to Trade Union Congress, February 25, 1987.

20. Tass, December 18, 1986.

21. Gennady Kolbin, press conferences at the Press Center of the Foreign Ministry, June 26, 1988.

22. Authors' interview with Anatoly Rybakov.

Chapter 10

1. Authors' interview with Fyodor Burlatsky.

2. The account of the Shcherbakovtsi is based on interviews with several participants as well as members of the Moscow Institute of Sociology who have studied the incident and its implications.

3. Authors' interviews with Boris Grushin (professor of sociology), Yegor Yakovlev, and others, including Pamyat members.

4. *Vechernaya Moskva,* June 15, 1987.

5. Authors' interviews with Sergei Grigoryants, the editor of *Glasnost,* and various participants.

6. *Nauka i Zhizn,* No. 5, 1986.

7. Authors' interview with a Central Committee member, January 30, 1987.

8. Ibid.

9. Gorbachev, speech at Central Committee plenum, January 27, 1987.

10. Gorbachev, speech to the Central Committee, January 28, 1987.

11. Gorbachev, speech in Riga, Latvia, February 19, 1987.

12. *Moscow News,* No. 7, February 1987.

13. Gorbachev, speech to Trade Union Congress, February 25, 1987.

14. *Novoe Vremya,* January 30, 1987.

15. Gorbachev, speech to writers, June 19, 1986, quoted in *New York Times,* January 5, 1987.

16. Ibid.

17. Gorbachev in Estonia, February 19, 1987.

18. Gorbachev, speech to Trade Union Congress, February 25, 1987.

19. Letter to *Moskovskaya Pravda,* March 13, 1987.

20. Ibid.

21. Gorbachev, speech to Soviet editors, Tass, February 13, 1987.

22. *Pravda,* March 25, 1987.

23. Authors' interview with a Gorbachev aide.

24. Authors' interview with Roy Medvedev.

Chapter 11

1. Gorbachev, talk with Soviet writers, June 19, 1987, quoted in the *New York Times*.

2. *Kommunist,* No. 9, 1986.

3. *Kommunist,* No. 6, 1987.

4. Gorbachev, speech to an international gathering, Moscow, February 16, 1987.

5. *Pravda,* June 19, 1986.

6. Ibid., June 29, 1986.

7. Gorbachev, *Perestroika,* London, Collins, 1987, p. 250.

8. Gorbachev, speech on Soviet television, October 22, 1986.

9. Sakharov, quoted in *Time,* March 16, 1987.

10. Gorbachev, *Perestroika,* p. 153.

11. Gorbachev, speech, February 16, 1987.

12. Ibid.

13. Gorbachev, *Perestroika,* p. 240.

14. Gorbachev, *Toward a Better World,* Moscow, APN Publishers, 1987, p. 7.

15. *Pravda,* September 17, 1987.

16. Gorbachev, speech in Prague, April 10, 1987.

17. Norman Stone, *The Sunday Times* (London), November 22, 1987.

18. Don Oberdorfer, "Glasnost: An Accident or a Rewrite of Marx?," *International Herald Tribune,* April 27, 1987.

19. Ibid.

20. *Literaturnaya Gazeta,* May 6, 1987.

21. Ibid.

22. Authors' interviews with several Soviet officials.

23. *Time,* March 16, 1987.

24. Alexander Yakovlev, speech to Academy of Sciences, April 17, 1987, quoted in *Vesnik Akademi Nauk SSSR,* No. 6.

25. Peter Tarnoff, "Gorbachev and Sakharov on a Symbolic Venture," *Newsday,* February 19, 1987.

26. Authors' interview with Ambassador Bassiouny.

27. Gorbachev, *Perestroika,* p. 194.

28. Ibid., p. 245.

29. Ibid.

Chapter 12

1. *China Daily,* Peking, August 9, 1986.

2. Gorbachev, *Perestroika,* London, Collins, 1987, p. 188.

3. Authors' interviews with Soviet officials.

4. Gorbachev, press conference in New Delhi, November 28, 1986.

5. Don Oberdorfer, "Quagmire," *International Herald Tribune,* April 18, 1988.

6. *Pravda,* November 25, 1987.

7. Gorbachev, interview with the Indonesian newspaper *Merdeka,* July 23, 1987.

8. *Pravda,* June 22, 1987.

9. William J. Eaton, "Soviets Show Signs of Distress over Afghan War," *International Herald Tribune,* November 6, 1987.

10. Gorbachev, speech in Prague, April 10, 1987.

11. Gorbachev, *Perestroika,* pp. 164–68.

12. Gorbachev, speech in Prague.

13. Authors' interview with a senior official.

14. *Krasnaya Zvezda,* May 22, 1987.

15. *Pravda,* September 17, 1987.

16. Authors' interviews with Soviet officials.

17. Warsaw Pact communiqué, published in *Pravda,* May 30, 1987.

18. *Pravda,* May 31, 1987.

19. Ibid.

20. Authors' interview.

Chapter 13

1. Gorbachev, speech at Central Committee plenum, June 25, 1987.

2. Authors' interviews with senior officials.

3. Authors' interview with Abel Aganbegyan.

4. Ibid.

5. Authors' interview with Abel Aganbegyan.

6. Authors' interview with Academician Nikolai Federenko, one of the reformist economists involved in the preparation of Gorbachev's reforms.

7. Authors' interview with economist Lev Logvinov.

8. Authors' interview with Abel Aganbegyan.

9. Ibid.

10. Nikolai Shmelyov in *Novy Mir,* June 1987.

11. Authors' interview with Nikolai Shmelyov.

12. Authors' interview with a senior official.

13. *Literaturnaya Gazeta,* May 9, 1987.

14. Authors' interview with Georgi Smirnov.

15. *Moscow News,* No. 1, 1987.

16. Authors' interview with Alexander Yakovlev.

17. Authors' interview with a senior Egyptian official.

18. Authors' interview with Andrei Zamoshkin.

19. Authors' interview with V. Grushin.

20. Information based on authors' conversations with several persons present at the meeting.

21. *Pravda,* July 18, 1987.

22. Yevtushenko, in *Time,* June 27, 1988.

23. Gorbachev, *Perestroika,* London, Collins, 1987, pp. 78–82.

24. Gorbachev, interview in *L'Unità,* May 18, 1987.

25. A. M. Migranian, in the journal *Voprosi Filozofiji,* No. 8, pp. 78–91.

26. Vladimir Shlapentokh, "Alexander II and Mikhail Gorbachev—Two Reformers in Historical Perspective." Unpublished manuscript, original in authors' possession.

Chapter 14

1. Authors' interview with Alexander Yakovlev.

2. *Sovyetskaya Kultura,* May 21, 1987.

3. Viktor Afanasiev, speech at meeting of Journalists' Union, March 17, 1987, *Pravda,* March 18, 1987.

4. See Richard Pipes, *Russia under the Old Regime,* New York, Macmillan, 1976, pp. 260–80.

5. *Literaturnaya Rossiya,* May 1987.

6. Gorbachev, speech at Kremlin dinner for Mrs. Thatcher, April 1987.

7. Gorbachev, speech to Komsomol Congress, April 16, 1987.

8. Gorbachev, speech in Romania, May 26, 1987.

9. Gorbachev, speech to cultural and media executives, *Pravda,* July 15, 1987.

10. Ibid.

11. Authors' conversation with Alexander Yakovlev.

12. Alexander Yakovlev, speech to Academy of Sciences, April 18, 1987.

13. *Moscow News,* February 10, 1987.

14. *Literaturnaya Gazeta,* March 25, 1987.

15. Authors' interviews with conference participants.

16. Ibid.

17. For the full text of the manifesto, see *Guardian,* London, September 12, 1987.

18. Authors' interview with a senior official.

19. *Pravda,* August 27, 1987.

20. Ibid.

21. *Pravda,* September 12, 1987.

22. Agence France Presse, dispatch from Moscow, September 29, 1987.

23. Anatoly Lukyanov, speech to conference of scholars, June 15–17, 1987.

24. A. I. Lukyanov, *Promoting Democracy,* Moscow, APN Publishers, 1987, p. 21.

25. Anatoly Lukyanov, press conference, Foreign Ministry Press Center, Moscow, July 2, 1988.

26. Gorbachev, speech given in Murmansk, reported on Moscow Radio, October 1, 1987.

27. *Pravda,* October 2, 1987.

28. *Izvestia,* October 22, 1987.

29. Yeltsin, interview on BBC, May 30, 1988.

30. Gorbachev, live televised press conference, Moscow, June 1, 1988.

31. *New York Times,* March 2, 1988.

32. Ibid., October 30, 1987.

33. Authors' information obtained from official sources.

34. Gorbachev, *Perestroika,* London, Collins, 1987, p. 65.

35. Yeltsin, interview on BBC.

36. Gorbachev, speech to Trade Union Congress, February 25, 1987.

37. Thom Shanker, Chicago *Tribune,* November 17, 1987.

38. *Pravda,* November 16, 1987.

39. Authors' conversations with Fyodor Burlatsky.

Chapter 15

1. Authors' conversation with a Gorbachev aide.

2. Gorbachev, *Perestroika,* London, Collins, 1987, p. 155.

3. Authors' interview with a Gorbachev aide.

4. Leonid Abalkin, lecturing at Kennan Institute for Advanced Russian Studies, Washington, D.C., March 14, 1988.

5. *Time,* June 27, 1988.

6. Antero Pietila, Baltimore *Sun,* January 24, 1988.

7. Yegor Ligachev, interview in *Le Monde,* December 4, 1987.

8. M. S. *Gorbachev: An Intimate Portrait,* New York, Time Inc., 1988.

9. Gorbachev, speech on Moscow Television, April 29, 1988.

10. Gorbachev, in his keynote address to the Twenty-seventh Communist Party Congress, Moscow, February 25, 1986.

11. *Molodoi Leninets,* No. 13, 1988, pp. 4–5.

12. Seweryn Bialer, *U.S. News & World Report,* July 18, 1988.

13. Fyodor Burlatsky, *Literaturnaya Gazeta,* June 15, 1988.

Chapter 16

1. Soltan Dzazarov, Novosti Press Agency, February 2, 1988.

2. Gorbachev, speech to scientists and intellectuals, *Pravda,* January 8, 1989.

3. Yuri Andreyev and Gavril

Popov, in *Sovyetskaya Kultura,* April 21, 1988.

4. Information supplied by a prominent American who visited Gorbachev with a U.S. delegation.

5. Information supplied by Professor Seweryn Bialer of Columbia University.

6. Authors' information from Soviet officials.

7. "Povorot Kotorovo Ne bilo," *Komsomolskaya Pravda,* April 21, 1988.

8. Ivan Laptiev, editor of *Izvestia,* press conference at Foreign Ministry Press Center, Moscow, June 23, 1988.

9. Robert G. Kaiser, "Red Intrigue: How Gorbachev Outfoxed His Kremlin Rivals," Washington *Post,* June 12, 1988.

10. Authors' interview with a ranking Yugoslav official.

11. Laptiev, press conference, June 23, 1988.

12. Michel Tatu, *Sovset,* April 22, 1988.

13. Authors' interview with a senior Kremlin official.

14. Ibid.

15. Authors' interview with Roy Medvedev and other historians.

16. Tass, April 15, 1988.

17. *Sovyetskaya Kultura,* April 30, 1988.

18. *Pravda,* June 6, 1988.

19. Tass, May 10, 1988.

20. *Komsomolskaya Pravda,* June 7, 1988.

21. Gorbachev, press conference at Foreign Ministry Press Center, May 23, 1988.

22. *Izvestia,* July 28, 1988.

23. *Pravda,* April 10, 1988.

24. Gorbachev, interview with Katharine Graham and editors of the Washington *Post* and *Newsweek,* Moscow, May 22, 1988.

25. Authors' interviews.

26. Tass, June 5, 1988.

Chapter 17

1. *Pravda,* June 30, 1988.

2. *Izvestia,* July 3, 1988.

3. "Vremya," Moscow Television, July 1, 1988.

4. Yeltsin, interview in *La Repubblica,* Rome, January 7, 1989.

5. Vasili O. Klyuchevsky was one of the most prominent Russian historians of the nineteenth century. His *History of Russia* is regarded as one of the best works on the subject. After the Bolshevik revolution, Klyuchevsky's works were published only in limited editions for the use of scholars, and were not circulated among students or the general population.

6. Authors' conversation with a Gorbachev aide.

7. Gorbachev, "On Progress in Implementing the Decisions of the Twenty-seventh Party Congress and the Tasks of Promoting Perestroika," delivered on national television, June 28, 1988.

8. Ibid.

9. Ibid.

10. Ibid.

Chapter 18

1. Reuters, September 15, 1988.

2. "Vremya," Moscow Television, September 13, 1988.

3. Fyodor Burlatsky, in *Literaturnaya Gazeta,* September 14, 1988.

4. *Ogonyok,* September, October 1988.

5. *Pravda,* September 25, 1988.

6. *Izvestia,* November 14, 1988.

Chapter 19

1. *New York Times,* December 9, 1988.

2. Eduard Shevardnadze, speech in Paris, January 8, 1989.

3. Stephen S. Rosenfeld, Washington *Post,* reprinted in *International Herald Tribune,* January 25, 1989.

4. Gorbachev, speech to the scientists and intellectuals, *Pravda,* January 8, 1989.

5. "Vremya," Moscow Television, October 12, 1988.

6. Authors' interview with a Soviet official.

7. Bill Keller, *New York Times,* October 29, 1988.

8. Quoted by Robert Evans in a January 25, 1989, Reuters dispatch from Moscow.

9. *Pravda,* November 5, 1988.

10. Authors' information.

11. Quoted by Bill Keller, *New York Times,* reprinted in *International Herald Tribune,* December 31, 1988. Also quoted by Esther B. Fein, *New York Times,* reprinted in *International Herald Tribune,* January 30, 1989.

12. Authors' interview with a Soviet official.

13. Authors' interview with a senior Chinese official.

14. Michael Dobbs, Washington *Post,* April 8, 1989.

15. Jeff Trimble, *U.S. News & World Report,* April 3, 1989.

16. Authors' conversation with Dr. Slava Fyodorov.

17. William G. Hyland, *East-West Relations: Gorbachev's Russia and American Foreign Policy,* edited by Seweryn Bialer and Michael Mandelbaum, Boulder, Colo., and London, Westview Press, 1988.

18. *Pravda,* October 12, 1988.

19. Washington *Post,* January 12, 1989. Also see Mark Frankland, "Liberal Gains in Hungary Survive on a Knife's Edge," *Observer,* January 22, 1989.

20. *Izvestia,* January 19, 1989.

21. "Vremya," Moscow Television, January 21, 1989.

22. Henry Kissinger, South China *Morning Post,* February 5, 1989.

23. Mortimer B. Zuckerman and Jeff Trimble, "Conversations with Andrei D. Sakharov," *U.S. News & World Report,* January 30, 1989.

24. Michael Dobbs, Washington *Post,* April 8, 1989.

25. Angus Roxburgh, *The Sunday Times* (London), August 7, 1988.

26. Igor Klyamkin, "Pochemuy trudno govorit pravdu," *Novy Mir,* No. 2, 1989.

27. "Democracy in Conflict: Search for Legal Solution of National Problems in the USSR, Round Table Discussion," *Twentieth Century and Peace,* No. 12, 1988.

28. Ibid.

Chapter 20

1. *Time,* December 18, 1989.

2. *Pravda,* February 14, 1989.

3. Gorbachev, speech to the Central Committee, March 15, 1989.

4. Authors' conversations with Abel Aganbegyan.

5. Quoted by George Feifer, "The New God Will Fail," *Harper's,* October 1988.

6. Authors' conversation with Gennady Lizichkin.

7. Ibid.

8. Boris Yeltsin, *Against the Grain: An Autobiography,* London, Jonathan Cape, 1990, excerpted by *The Sunday Times,* February 11, 1990.

Chapter 21

1. *Pravda,* February 6, 1990.

2. Authors' interview with Dr. Svyatoslav Fyodorov, Moscow, February 1990.

3. The text of Ligachev's speech was published in *Za Sovyetskuyu Nauku,* December 14, 1989.

4. *Moscow News,* February 4, 1990.

5. Interviewed by Dan Rather of CBS News, February 1, 1990.

6. Ibid.

7. Sergei Stankevich, "Fenomen Gorbacheva," *Pozicija,* January 1990, p. 1.

Index